The Shell Guide
to the
Birds
of Britain and Ireland

James Ferguson-Lees
Ian Willis
J.T.R. Sharrock

Michael Joseph

*To the memory of the late Bernard W. Tucker who began modern
field identification techniques; to Roger Tory Peterson
who started the concept of field guides; and to Bruce Campbell
who suggested this one.*

First published in Great Britain by
Michael Joseph Limited
44 Bedford Square, London WC1
1983

ISBN 0 7181 2219 4

This book was designed and produced by
George Rainbird Limited
40 Park Street, London W1Y 4DE

Editors: David Burnie
Duncan J. Brooks
Design: Rod Josey Associates
Cartographer: Richard Natkiel
Production: Elizabeth Winder
Indexer: Lorna Gradden

Text filmset by Oliver Burridge and Company Limited, Crawley, Sussex
Illustrations originated by Aragorn Colour Reproduction, London
and Bridge Graphics Limited, Hull
Printed and bound by Brepols s.a., Turnhout, Belgium

The Author

JAMES FERGUSON-LEES, who planned and wrote this book, is one of Britain's foremost ornithologists. He has studied birds throughout the world, and has first-hand experience of all but a few species covered in this book. For many years, he was executive editor of the monthly magazine *British Birds*. A past president of the British Trust for Ornithology, he was awarded its Bernard Tucker Medal for his work in connection with *The Atlas of Breeding Birds in Britain and Ireland* (1976), and is now chairman of the working group currently organising the forthcoming atlas of winter birds. He has been chairman of the education and conservation committees of the Royal Society for the Protection of Birds, and was for two years its deputy director for conservation. He is currently chairman of the Records Committee of the British Ornithologists' Union, which maintains the official list of British birds. He has been co-author, collaborator or editor of a number of books, including the revised editions of *A Field Guide to the Birds of Britain and Europe* (1965, 1974) and the first volume of *The Birds of the Western Palearctic* (1977).

The Artist

IAN WILLIS, who painted all the plates in this guide, began his career as a wildlife illustrator and writer in 1968. He has had extensive experience of birdwatching, not only in the British Isles, but also further afield. He has travelled widely to study birds and flowers throughout Europe, North Africa, the Middle East and Siberia. His illustrations have appeared in many books and articles, ranging from children's books to more specialist publications, including *Flight Identification of European Raptors* (1974), a comprehensive study of raptor plumages. This has subsequently become a standard reference work. He has also produced the colour plates of raptors for the second volume of *Birds of the Western Palearctic* (1980). Much of his field knowledge for his works on birds of prey was gained in 1966, when, with several colleagues, he undertook a six-month expedition to Turkey mainly to study the migrations of raptors and other soaring birds. He is also particularly interested in owls and Middle Eastern birds, and has illustrated *The Barn Owl* (1982) and *Owls of Europe* (1983) as well as the forthcoming guide *Birds of North Africa and the Middle East*.

The Map Consultant

Dr J. T. R. SHARROCK, who compiled all the maps, is managing editor of the monthly magazine *British Birds*, which has been published continuously since 1907. Formerly a botanist, he has since become an ornithologist of international standing. His strong interest in bird distributions is reflected by his holding the position of chairman of the European Ornithological Atlas Committee since its formation in 1971. During 1969–76 he was national organiser of the project which led to the publication in 1976 of *The Atlas of Breeding Birds in Britain and Ireland*. He has been author or co-author of a number of other books on the birds of Britain and Ireland.

Preface

The last forty years have produced an enormous increase in interest in birds and a corresponding proliferation of books about them. With the development of travel and the growth of international scientific cooperation, books on bird identification have tended to cover whole continents. Thus, most of the current field guides deal not just with Britain and Ireland, but with Europe as a whole, sometimes extending to adjacent parts of northwest Africa and southwest Asia. As a result, a large number of species have had to be described in a limited space, and in many cases only adult plumages have been illustrated. For people watching birds in Britain and Ireland this has meant looking through pages of often irrelevant pictures.

By contrast, this new field guide is confined to the species which have actually been recorded in Britain and Ireland and it aims to show as many of the main plumages as possible. Just over 500 species have now been seen here and, of these, 263 may be classed as the 'regulars' which make up the bulk of this book: many of them nest and the others appear every year in appreciable numbers, either as winter visitors or as passage migrants between their breeding areas to the north and winter quarters to the south. The remainder are 'vagrants', wanderers from other parts of Europe and Asia or even America and Africa: some of these have been recorded here only once or twice (although for every one seen it is likely that more have been missed), while others turn up every year in very small numbers. This book contains all vagrants noted up to the end of 1980, except 14 species which have not reappeared since 1930.

Acknowledgments

Planning, research, writing and painting have taken the best part of three years. Various people have given a great deal of help. Karen Goldie-Morrison, of Rainbird, put much work into setting up the project. Lars Svensson and D. I. M. Wallace read the whole text in proof and made many suggestions. Others who similarly read sections were D. J. Britton (waders), Dr Bruce Campbell (habitat spreads), P. J. Grant (gulls, terns), Peter Harrison (seabirds), J. H. Marchant (waders), J. R. Mather (divers, grebes, ducks, skuas), Dr I. C. T. Nisbet (American vagrants), M. A. Ogilvie (swans, geese, ducks) and R. F. Porter (diurnal birds of prey). P. J. Grant also produced the topographical charts on page 11 from his drawings in *British Birds* for June 1981; and J. H. Marchant and M. A. Ogilvie, as well as Peter Colston, Martin Robinson and Donald Watson, gave additional help with specific problems by looking at skins, providing references to publications or advising on certain plates. Invaluable references were also turned up by Dr I. H. J. Lyster of the Royal Scottish Museum. Dr D. W. Snow, I. C. J. Galbraith and the staff of the Ornithological Section of the British Museum (Natural History) at Tring gave permission and help over examining skins. Heather Angel's photographs are well up to her own remarkable standard.

James Ferguson-Lees and Ian Willis owe much to their wives, Karen and Diane, for encouragement and understanding; Karen Ferguson-Lees also typed the entire manuscript. But our greatest single debts are to Duncan J. Brooks who not only read all the proofs and commented on many of the plates, but earlier helped to revise and reduce about half of the text drafts to an acceptable length; and David A. Burnie, of Rainbird, who went to great pains to help, advise, encourage, comment and check. If this book serves to engender a wider understanding of the identification, sexing and ageing of birds, and their place in Britain and Ireland, we shall be well satisfied.   I.J.F-L., I.W., J.T.R.S.

Contents

The bird families appear in this book in a sequence as close as
practicable to the scientifically established taxonomic order. However,
there are a few places where the sequence has been altered slightly
to aid identification, allowing similar birds – for example the Swift and the
Swallow – to appear on the same page. The page numbers for the
bird families are in two columns; the first refers to **regulars**,
and the second (in italics) to **vagrants**.

How to use this book

REGULARS and VAGRANTS (see page 4) are
arranged in separate sections, each in the
same sequence of families. This sequence
and that of the species within the families,
as well as the scientific names, follows the
List of Recent Holarctic Bird Species by
Professor Dr K. H. Voous (1977), with
only minor modifications to suit the layout
of the plates. To identify a bird, the reader
should first consult the REGULARS section
and then, if necessary, refer to the
VAGRANTS. The treatment of regulars is
intentionally fuller, with usually only two
or three species on each plate to allow
more text and a wider range of illustrated
plumages. The less detailed treatment of
vagrants often excludes plumages not seen
in Britain and Ireland.

Text

Species texts are set out as follows:

Name Both English and scientific names
are given. Although the latter may seem
rather off-putting at first, they have the
advantages of precision and of showing
relationships: the family is a grouping of
related genera, and the genus (the first of
the two words in the individual Latinised
name) is a grouping of related species (the
second word being the name of the
species). Sometimes, within the text, other
names are used in conjunction with the
initials of the scientific name: these refer
to subspecies, or 'races', with distinctive
characters (note, however, that there is
often no sharp dividing line between races,
which tend to grade into one another).

Size Birds vary as much as any other
animals in size. The extremes of the main
range of length are given in centimetres,
with an approximate mean in inches.

Field characters The first sentence of the
text gives the general characters of the
species, concentrating on shape and only
the more obvious plumage features, such
as contrasting colours, white rumps and
pale wing-bars.

Behaviour The second sentence describes
flight, gait and other actions, as well as
flocking.

Plumages and moults Under separate
headings, attention is drawn to the
characters and differences of males and
females, winter and summer plumages,
and immature stages; for some species
these differences are very marked, for
others slight. Certain of the passerines (the
'song-birds', from larks to buntings) are
indistinguishable from the adult by their
first winter, while many larger birds, such
as Gannets, eagles and gulls, take several
years to acquire adult plumage. The terms
used are 'juvenile' for the first covering of
true feathers; '1st winter' for the plumage
following a moult in the first autumn and
'1st summer' for that worn when the bird
is approaching one year old (or '1st year'
for these two combined); and so on
through second winter and second summer
if different from the adult. All species
moult once a year, many twice (at least
partially), and a few three times; some
also change appearance, even quite
strikingly, by wearing away through
abrasion the often duller tips and edges of
feathers moulted in autumn, to reveal
brighter colours or clearer patterns by
spring. Moult from one stage to another
may take weeks or even months through
many (often blotchy) mixtures of two
plumages and, even if the plumages are
similar, there is usually a contrast between
new well-pigmented and old faded
feathers: these mixtures cannot really be
described or illustrated, but the duration
of moult is given as far as possible to show
when such intermediates may be expected.

Voice Brief descriptions or renderings are
attempted for songs and main calls. These
are often characteristic, and so important
in identification, but notoriously difficult
to express phonetically; most species also
have wider vocabularies than can be
covered in a line or two. They become
familiar through experience rather than
by what is written in field guides.

Habitat A crucial basis for identification is
knowing where to expect a species, and the

typical habitats are briefly summarised (but migrants may turn up in strange surroundings). Some idea of the birds likely to be found in particular habitats is also given under broad groupings on pages 12–41.

Nest For the species which breed in Britain and Ireland, brief details are noted of nest site, clutch size, season, and number of broods; if breeding is in colonies, this is also stated. The season shown is that during which the nest is usually occupied: for most birds this means by either eggs or nestlings, but the downy young of divers, grebes, swans, geese, ducks, grouse, partridges, pheasants, rails, crakes, moorhens, coots, waders, gulls and terns leave the nest soon after hatching, and in their cases the season covers eggs only.

Food The main foods are listed, but generally just in very broad categories.

Range For the regulars, this complements the maps with the months of arrival/ departure and the destinations of summer visitors, and the seasons and origins of winter visitors and passage migrants. For the vagrants, it gives the total of records to the end of 1980, as an indication of likelihood of further sightings, with a brief summary of the months and counties or regions of occurrence in Britain and Ireland; the continents where the species breeds (but not necessarily winters) are set out at the end. Throughout, where additional months appear in brackets without the emphasising 'esp', these are the extremes of the period concerned.

Comparisons Under the regulars, there are often cross-references, either in the body of the text or at the end, to similar species and related vagrants (especially those which might be confused with them).

Annotations

♂   male
♀   female
ad   adult
juv   juvenile
imm immature

Sexes are given only if distinguishable ('ad' indicates either).

An **oblique** is used between any two plumages that are indistinguishable, *eg*
ad/juv   either adult or juvenile
1st winter/ad either 1st winter or adult
ad/1st winter either adult *winter* or 1st winter

A **dash** indicates a transitional stage, *eg*
juv–1st winter between juvenile and 1st winter plumages

Maps

Each of the 263 species in the main section of birds classed as 'regulars' has a map designed to show both population sizes and distribution at a glance. The 'vagrants' do not have maps as they by definition, do not occur in predictable numbers or locations.

Population sizes

The figures at the top right-hand corner of each map relate to the numbers of each species estimated to be breeding (B), or present during winter (W), spring (S) or autumn (A), in Britain and Ireland as a whole. The numbers are expressed as simple orders of magnitude, and refer to individuals, not pairs:

0	=	usually none
1	=	1–10
2	=	11–100
3	=	101–1,000
4	=	1,001–10,000
5	=	10,001–100,000
6	=	100,001–1,000,000
7	=	1,000,001–10,000,000
8	=	over 10 million

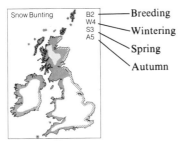

The order of magnitude is easily converted by thinking of it as the number of figures in the population size (or the number of zeros in the maximum). Thus, B5 shows a 5-figure breeding total (in the ten thousands) or at most 100,000; W6 indicates a 6-figure wintering total (in the hundred thousands) or at most 1,000,000. Although readers may find it helpful to refer to the above conversion table at first, the orders will quickly become familiar. This system has the advantages of ease of comparison and lack of spurious accuracy associated with definite figures.

It should be borne in mind that these orders of magnitude are for an 'average' year. The populations of some birds vary considerably from year to year, through such factors as hard winters, weather effects on migration, food supplies, and breeding success; the numbers of many species are highest in autumn through the summer's production of young. It should also be realised that 'B0' does not necessarily mean that a species is absent in summer: small numbers of some waders, for example, are often present then without breeding.

Distribution

Breeding areas are shown in blue, winter quarters are hatched, and regions where a species is found only on passage or wandering are stippled. The breeding distributions are based on the 1968–72 survey carried out by the British Trust for Ornithology and the Irish Wildbird Conservancy, as published in *The Atlas of Breeding Birds in Britain and Ireland* (1976), but updated to include major changes during 1973–80. For the sake of clarity (and also to conceal the precise localities of certain rare breeders), some small areas of distribution have been enlarged. As data for birds at sea are much less detailed than those for land species, the distributions of essentially marine species are shown in exaggerated coastal strips, indicating the shores from which these birds may often or sometimes be seen.

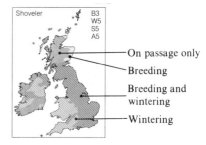

Bird topography

A knowledge of the superficial features of the body, or topography, is essential to describe birds fully and to understand identification, ageing and sexing. The diagrams below show all the main areas of the plumage and 'bare parts' (bill, eyes, legs) on a whole bird, a head and an underwing. In this book, however, the dictates of space and simplicity, coupled with the fact that the positions of the markings are usually clear on the facing plate, have made it more convenient often to adopt looser and more graphic terms with a human analogy such as 'face', 'spectacles', 'cheeks', 'moustaches', 'shoulders' and even 'armpits' and 'trousers', as well as 'arms' and 'hands' for the inner and outer parts of the wings; also, 'upperparts' (or 'above') and 'underparts' (or 'below') are used for the upper and under surfaces of the bird, and 'back' is sometimes loosely applied to the whole upper body. The 'speculum' (not illustrated) is the term for a patch of different colour found on the wings of certain ducks.

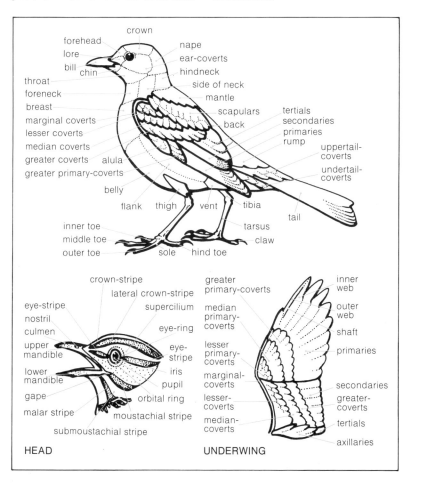

Towns, gardens and parks

Though our cities and bigger towns may
seem the dullest of habitats, more than 50
species regularly appear in towns, gardens
and urban parks and others occur on
passage or in hard weather. Among the
commonest are Feral Pigeons (descendants
of the coastal Rock Dove) and, of course,
Starlings and House Sparrows. Starlings
form vast noisy roosts in some cities in
winter; in contrast, on fine summer days
they glide gracefully high overhead
hawking insects. The real aerial insect-
feeders in summer, however, are the
Swifts and House Martins; both nest
under eaves in towns, the Swifts using

holes, and crevices in large buildings, and the House Martins building conspicuous mud cups. Swallows, on the other hand, penetrate only as far as the suburbs.

Gulls also hawk insects overhead and feed at town rubbish tips; they roost on urban reservoirs. Among other larger birds, Kestrels often nest in city centres, and Tawny Owls in gardens and parks. Ponds may hold Moorhens and Mallards (the latter often semi-domesticated) and larger lakes Coots and Tufted Ducks. Woodpigeons breed in town squares with trees, and Collared Doves have become a familiar suburban sight since the 1950s. Jackdaws, Rooks and, more locally, odd pairs of Carrion Crows nest in towns, while even Magpies and Jays appear in the suburbs and some central city parks.

But it is the small birds which the garden watcher sees most closely. Blackbirds, Song Thrushes, Robins, Wrens, Dunnocks, Chaffinches and Greenfinches are all common in urban gardens and parks. Blue Tits are the most numerous of the tits, and in winter they come to bird tables with Great and Coal Tits for nuts

and scraps: although only two or three Blue Tits may be seen at a time, a garden may well be visited by 30 or 40 in a day. Creepers on houses provide nesting places for Spotted Flycatchers, and for Pied Wagtails. A much more local city nester, the Black Redstart, usually first attracts attention over the traffic by its 'gravelly' song. Willow Warblers, Chiffchaffs, Whitethroats and Blackcaps wander through gardens on spring and autumn passage, while Blackcaps (and to a lesser extent Chiffchaffs) have now become regular in winter in small numbers. Other garden visitors include Bullfinches, Linnets, Redpolls and, in the latter part of the winter, Siskins. And almost anything may turn up: Long-tailed Tits or a Treecreeper; Redwings, Reed Buntings or even a Sparrowhawk in severe weather.

Fields and hedges

In 1950, the total length of field and roadside hedges in Britain was nearly four million kilometres. Today, although some parts of lowland Britain and Ireland are still a patchwork of arable and grass with these ancient dividing boundaries, sadly, many of these hedges have been grubbed out, to be replaced by wire fences or just larger fields. This drastically reduces the variety and numbers of birds.

In large fields Skylarks are often almost the only nesting birds, though Corn Buntings favour extensive arable and corn if there are wires from which to sing. Grey Partridges are widespread, although often outnumbered in lowland England by the introduced Red-legged; both usually need hedge-bottoms to nest in. Pheasants also feed in open fields, but mainly near woods. A gamebird which does breed in hay and corn is the Quail, a scarce summer visitor seldom seen and mainly heard at night. Another nocturnal caller, the Corncrake, is now confined largely to parts of Ireland and Scotland where the hay is cut later.

Lapwings nest early on ploughed land or short grass. Other waders that breed in fields include Oystercatchers in north Britain, Stone-curlews on flinty arable in the southeast, Ringed and even Little Ringed Plovers locally on stony patches in fallow and young crops, and Redshanks, Snipe or Curlews in water meadows, but none of these is typical of this habitat.

Many birds feed in fields, some taking seeds and shoots, others insects and worms. Woodpigeons, along with Stock Doves and Feral Pigeons, are familiar sights, as are flocks of Rooks and Jackdaws, and Carrion or Hooded Crows. Starlings are seen as parties of plain brown juveniles from June onwards and later in large flocks. In winter, too, come flocks of Lapwings and sometimes Golden Plovers, of gulls (especially Black-headed and Common), and of thrushes, finches and buntings. Locally, particularly in the north, Pink-footed and Greylag Geese feed on stubble and young crops. Other field birds in winter include Moorhens, Meadow Pipits and Pied Wagtails, while in summer Swifts and Swallows hunt insects over the grass.

But any real diversity depends on hedges, and the wider and taller the better. Many of the common birds of gardens

and wood-edges also breed in hedgerows, especially thrushes, Dunnocks and Chaffinches. Really thick hedges house Long-tailed Tits and, in southern Britain, Turtle Doves and Lesser Whitethroats, as well as Greenfinches, Bullfinches and Linnets. Those on banks or with dense bases attract Yellowhammers and Robins; if there are trees in them, Blackcaps, Redpolls, Goldfinches and, locally, Cirl Buntings enter the picture. Even Moorhens, Sedge Warblers and Reed Buntings will breed in hedges well away from water. Magpies build in high thorns, and Carrion Crows in large hedgerow trees (as do Buzzards in Wales), their old nests in turn providing sites for Kestrels, occasional Hobbies, and Stock Doves. The last also breed in cavities in mature hedgerow trees, as do Tawny, Little and even Barn Owls. Smaller holes make homes for Blue and Great Tits and Tree Sparrows (House Sparrows more usually building untidy domed structures in rank hedges). Green Woodpeckers often excavate their holes in timbered hedgerows and these may be taken over by Starlings or even Nuthatches.

In winter, Redwings, Fieldfares and other thrushes, and sometimes Waxwings, flock where berries are plentiful. Hedges are also important as connecting 'lanes' along which many birds, such as Great Spotted Woodpeckers, Jays, Treecreepers and tits, will travel from wood to wood.

Lowland broadleaved woods

Birds are often hard to see in woods and so it is important to learn their songs and calls. The largest areas of lowland broadleaved woods are in England and Wales, and here pedunculate oak, ash and beech are among the dominant trees. The richest woods are those where oaks are common, as these support huge numbers of invertebrates on which insect-eating birds feed.

The best time to see and hear woodland bird life is in late spring and early summer, when the annual chorus of bird song reaches its climax. Perhaps the most famous of woodland songsters is the Nightingale, a summer visitor to southern Britain: despite its name, it also sings by day and may be silent on cold nights;

it is hard to see in its dense thickets. Garden Warblers and Blackcaps, whose songs are often confused, are also found in these tangles, although the Blackcaps are confined more to the parts with taller trees, as are Chiffchaffs and Spotted Flycatchers. Willow Warblers, on the other hand, are heard in scrubby clearings and at wood edges, where there may also be the occasional pair of Whitethroats. Wood Warblers are found locally in lowlands, often in beech woods with little ground cover. Redstarts are dependent on old trees with cavities, while Tree Pipits use more open trees as song-posts and nest on the ground. Cuckoos are a typical spring sound of open woodland: only the male actually 'cuckoos'; the female, here laying her eggs in the nests of Dunnocks, Robins and Tree Pipits, gives a very different bubbling chuckle.

Among resident birds, Wrens, Robins,

Dunnocks, Blackbirds, Song and Mistle Thrushes, Great and Blue Tits, Chaffinches and Greenfinches account for most of the rest of the spring song. Redpolls are noisy in scrub areas, and Nuthatches call loudly in old trees. Distinctive too are Green and Great Spotted Woodpeckers. Unless their calls are known, Lesser Spotted Woodpeckers, Marsh and Willow Tits, Treecreepers, Tree Sparrows and Hawfinches are likely to be overlooked.

Lowland broadleaved woods have their share of larger birds as well. These may include Kestrels, Sparrowhawks and, very locally, Buzzards, Hobbies and a few Goshawks and Honey Buzzards, while Pheasants, Woodpigeons, owls and crows are well distributed throughout. But without doubt one of the most fascinating woodland birds is the Woodcock, with its squeak-and-croak call during its 'roding' or display flight at dusk.

From July to September, when song is all but over and many birds are moulting, the woods are much duller for the birdwatcher, and odd calls give just a tantalising hint of the species that are present. But the arrival of winter brings with it better conditions for watching birds as the last leaves fall. The resident birds are augmented by winter visitors, especially Bramblings in open beech woods and Siskins in birches and alders. Flocks of mixed tits, Goldcrests, Nuthatches and Treecreepers are then often to be seen as they flutter between the trees in search of food.

Upland broadleaved woods

Woods on the hillsides and valley slopes
of the west and north have a charm of
their own. Here sessile oaks are often
dominant, mixed with birch, alder, rowan
and holly. Small birds still include
the familiar Chaffinches, Robins, Wrens,
Dunnocks, Starlings and various thrushes
and tits, but fewer warblers. Coal Tits,
elsewhere associated more with conifers,

often outnumber the Blue and Great, and in Ireland, another conifer species, the Goldcrest, is one of the commonest birds of sessile oak woods. Nuthatches become scarce or absent except in Wales and southwest England, but Treecreepers are well distributed and Long-tailed Tits often nest in birch-forks.

The dominant summer visitors in more open parts are Willow Warblers. There are also Chiffchaffs, and the sessile oak woods of west Britain are a main haunt of Wood Warblers, which have recently also colonised similar places in one or two parts of eastern Ireland. Other warblers are scarce. There are no Nightingales, but at least visually their absence is compensated by the comparative abundance of Redstarts in old upland birch and oak woods. In west Britain, another delightful and characteristic bird of open oak woodland is the Pied Flycatcher, whose numbers are increased by the provision of nestboxes. Spotted

Flycatchers are also well distributed, as are Tree Pipits (in Britain only) where there is open ground.

Mature woods on steep hillsides in Wales are the special habitat of our now rather healthier remnant population of Red Kites: it is a marvellous sight to see one of these magnificent birds of prey circling over a valley. Other raptors of the scrub-woods are Sparrowhawks and, in west Britain, Buzzards, as well as Kestrels. Tawny Owls are common in broadleaved woods throughout Britain, but absent from Ireland where Long-eared Owls, normally linked with conifers, take over. Black Grouse are found in open upland birch, and Woodcocks anywhere with adequate cover. The only other larger birds of the upland broadleaved woods are Pheasants, Woodpigeons and some Stock Doves, Cuckoos, Green and Great Spotted Woodpeckers in Britain, and the inevitable members of the crow family, which here include some Ravens.

Coniferous woods and plantations

The only indigenous conifers are Scots pine, yew and juniper. Most conifer woods consist of about ten introduced species that have been extensively planted since the First World War. Obvious exceptions include the ancient yews of Kingley Vale in Sussex and the remnants of the Caledonian pine forest. Patches of indigenous conifers also occur in mixed woods.

The birds of conifers vary a great deal, depending particularly on geography and the age and spacing of the trees. In close plantations, when the trees are about 15 years old, they form a thick canopy, and this and the forestry practice of lopping off the lower branches and leaving them to lie destroys the undergrowth. They are then usually dull places for birds. Canopy-nesting Goldcrests, Chaffinches and perhaps Mistle Thrushes, together with Coal Tits that breed in mouse holes, are the main songsters. The spread of the Siskin, however, has been greatly aided by older plantations. The rest of the bird fauna consists largely of Wood-pigeons; Jays, Carrion or Hooded Crows and, more at the edge, Magpies; Tawny and especially Long-eared Owls; and Sparrowhawks as well as some Buzzards and, very locally, Goshawks. A few Blackbirds and Wrens persist in ground debris, while the provision of nestboxes adds Blue and Great Tits and, more patchily, Redstarts to the population. Crossbills may be quite widespread in

invasion years, feeding on the cones along with Great Spotted Woodpeckers. It is true that there are some colonies of Grey Herons and Rooks in plantations and that Kestrels, Hobbies and even Merlins will breed in old crow nests at the edges; also that in Scotland a few Capercaillies and Golden Eagles nest in such places, while in southeast England Stone-curlews have tried to adapt to wide fire-breaks. But, in general, older plantations have little interest for the birdwatcher.

It is a different story, however, when these areas are newly planted. In the first stages they provide homes for Nightjars and, in the north, for Black Grouse. As the trees develop in association with brambles, heather and other growth, the birds of low cover, such as Willow and Grasshopper Warblers, Whitethroats, Tree Pipits, Dunnocks, Wrens and

Yellowhammers, move in. Sometimes there are occasional pairs of Sedge Warblers and Reed Buntings which are normally associated with water. Locally, too, Hen and Montagu's Harriers, Short-eared Owls, Woodcocks and even Dartford Warblers nest among the young trees. When the trees are several years old, Blackbirds and Song Thrushes, Linnets, Greenfinches and Bullfinches, Garden Warblers and Lesser Whitethroats take over, followed later by Redpolls and Goldfinches, Blackcaps and Turtle Doves. By this stage, Tree Pipits are confined to edges and rides. Red-backed Shrikes used to nest in young conifers and some Firecrests do now in tall spruce or fir.

Caledonian forest

The remnants of the indigenous pine forests of the Scottish Highlands are among the most fascinating of woodland habitats. They are often much more open than artificially planted conifers, undergrown with heather, cowberry and bilberry as well as the ubiquitous bracken, and frequently mixed with scrubby birch, alder, rowan and juniper. This openness is shown by such birds of rough ground as Meadow Pipits and Whinchats.

Here there are not only Sparrowhawks, Kestrels and Buzzards, but also Golden Eagles and now a few Goshawks and Ospreys, as well as Peregrines where there are crags. Other predators include Tawny and Long-eared Owls; Ravens are often rather scarce away from cliffs, but there are Carrion and Hooded Crows and many intermediates between the two. Among other larger birds, this is one of the best areas to see Black Grouse displaying at their 'lek', a most exciting spectacle for the early riser who visits one of the traditional sites, often in rushy areas at the edge of pines and scrub, between March and May (and to a lesser extent in autumn). Another spectacular grouse is the huge Capercaillie,

reintroduced here in the 19th century, which holds sway in the hillside woods with its remarkable strutting display and 'cork-pulling' song. Woodcocks can be seen and heard on their 'roding' flights at dusk, but Nightjars have now all but disappeared from the Highlands.

The typical small birds of coniferous trees are common, including Goldcrests, Chaffinches, Greenfinches, Coal Tits and, because there are holes and crevices in the mature trees, other tits, Redstarts and Treecreepers. Holes are also provided by the spread of Great Spotted Woodpeckers up through the Highlands in the early part of this century. The scrub among the pines also holds Redpolls and provides song-

posts for Tree Pipits and Willow Warblers. Other warblers are rather scarce, but Wrens, Robins, Dunnocks and the commoner thrushes and finches are widespread.

But it is the specialities of these areas that the birdwatcher will particularly be looking for among the small birds. Above all, the Caledonian forest is the home of Britain's one endemic bird, the Scottish Crossbill, now regarded as a separate species distinct from both the widespread Crossbill of Europe (which breeds regularly elsewhere in Britain) and the Parrot Crossbill of Fenno-Scandia (which is a rare vagrant here): its beak is intermediate in size and, like the Parrot Crossbill, it is found in pines, and feeds almost exclusively on pine seeds, rather than spruce and larch. This is also the traditional breeding habitat of the Siskin, a finch which has now spread to conifers in other parts of Britain and Ireland over the last 150 years, and of the Crested Tit which, though widespread on the Continent, remains confined here to old pines with rank heather and decaying stumps. Finally, it is this region that some Scandinavian birds are colonising: a few Redwings, Fieldfares and possibly Bramblings breed here, as well as Wrynecks and now even Red-backed Shrikes – two species that have declined so disastrously in England.

Heaths and brecks

Heaths are flattish, sandy or gravelly areas overlying a layer of peat. Their soils are acidic, but usually much drier than moorland which they sometimes resemble. Extensive growths of heathers, gorse and broom, as well as scattered clumps of birches and pines, form a habitat that offers birds a good supply of food together with a certain amount of shelter. In the west and north, they are typically coastal, but in England they extend well inland. The Brecks are a comparable region of some thousand square kilometres in East Anglia. Also sandy and flat or undulating, they vary from calcareous grassland like that of downland to more acidic sands with cover similar to that on heaths. Depending on the vegetation, both heaths and brecks share many of the common scrub birds of lowland areas, but the larger heaths and breckland of southern and eastern England also hold certain species which are particularly characteristic.

Dartford Warblers in Britain are confined to the lowland heaths of the southernmost counties of England, notably Dorset and Hampshire, and are found typically in a mixture of heather and gorse. (These are our only truly resident warblers, apart from the newly colonising Cetti's Warblers of wetland tangles.) They share the habitat particularly with Stonechats, which otherwise have a much wider distribution in coastal scrub. Whinchats are also present, but prefer

grassier areas. These southern heathlands, like downland, hold a good proportion of our rarest breeding falcon, the Hobby, and here both it and the Kestrel use the old nests of Carrion Crows. Other raptors of wooded heaths include Buzzards and Sparrowhawks, while the occasional pair of the now rare Montagu's Harrier nests on gorse-clad areas. Two other predatory species, Rough-legged Buzzards and Great Grey Shrikes, are scarce winter visitors. Red-legged Partridges, which prefer drier habitats, outnumber the Grey. During this century the spreading Curlew has colonised some heaths, while the declining and very different Stone-curlew can be found in only the sandiest and most open parts. Another decreasing species, the Nightjar, is perhaps now most typical of dry heathland with scattered trees.

Curlews, Stone-curlews and Nightjars are also typical of the Brecks. Some marginal heathland birds, such as Lapwings and Wheatears, are commoner on the breckland grass. Two species which have declined drastically this century may be seen in these areas. The Woodlark, which used to breed in many parts of England and Wales, and also in Ireland, is now reduced to perhaps two hundred pairs, mainly in the extreme south and southwest of England and in the Brecks where it inhabits short grass with scattered trees. Similarly, the Red-backed Shrike once had a wide distribution in Britain but is now largely confined to dry heathland with thorn bushes and brambles in East Anglia. The open breckland also holds the remnants of a formerly much larger inland-nesting population of Ringed Plovers, while the pine woods of the Brecks and of the New Forest heathlands are the two well-established breeding areas of Crossbills.

Apart from these mainly scarce or local species, various other small birds can be found on heaths and brecks. Depending on the vegetation and the season, these include most of the common species of grasslands and scrub.

Downs and grasslands

Grasslands are found in both upland and lowland areas, and many of them overlap other broad habitat types, especially grass fields and grass moorlands. Calcareous grassland, however, is confined to the alkaline soils over limestone formations, particularly on the low undulating chalk hills of southern and eastern England from east Dorset to Yorkshire. This is the rolling 'downland' typified by the North and South Downs, Chilterns, Berkshire Downs and Salisbury Plain. Although these places are often naturally rich in plants and, for example, butterflies, they have a limited but interesting variety of birds. Sadly, the spread of cultivation and widespread use of herbicides and

fertilisers have done much damage to this special habitat.

Open downland in particular holds few nesting species, some of them the same as in large grass fields. Skylarks of course are everywhere. Meadow Pipits are scarcer and patchily distributed, as are Corn Buntings which need either wires or tall plants from which to sing. Lapwings are scattered over the flat and rolling grassland, but not on the steeper slopes. Grey Partridges nest in grass tufts, and Red-legged Partridges make their scrapes in some surprisingly open places; downland corn is also a favoured habitat of Quails. Stock Doves and Little Owls are two other birds of ordinary farmland that have adapted to the open downs: scattered pairs of both nest in rabbit burrows. Wheatears, which also breed in burrows, have never been as common here as on stony uplands, grass moors and rocky

islands; also, being adapted to life on short grass, they began to decrease with the decline in downland sheep grazing and, later, with the reduction in rabbits through myxomatosis, but some still persist. Apart from the brecks, this was at one time also the main habitat of Stone-curlews. Indeed, often it still is, but they need open ground, short turf and solitude: longer grass, increased cultivation and greater disturbance have reduced the total to perhaps a quarter of what it was.

The growth of low scrub, gorse and thorn enables many other birds typical of hedges, young conifer plantations and heaths to move in, including Dunnocks, Wrens, Blackbirds, Yellowhammers and Linnets; Whitethroats and Willow and Grasshopper Warblers; Stonechats or perhaps the odd pair of Whinchats; and, in taller cover, Chaffinches, Tree Pipits and Magpies. Nightjars nest on chalky patches among scrub in downland valleys. Sheltered southern slopes with thorn bushes and small trees are still favoured by Cirl Buntings and Woodlarks, both of which have greatly decreased, but Red-backed Shrikes have all but disappeared from this habitat. Clumps of trees provide nesting sites for Carrion Crows, and the Hobbies and Kestrels which use their old nests; a building may house Barn or Little Owls.

Many of the birds that feed in grass fields in winter may also be seen on the downs at other seasons, such as flocks of Lapwings, gulls, Rooks, Jackdaws and Starlings. Characteristic, too, are parties of Mistle Thrushes and Goldfinches. Migrant predators include Kestrels, Hen Harriers and, in less exposed parts, Short-eared Owls and sometimes also the odd Peregrine, Merlin or Montagu's Harrier.

Moors and mountains

The uplands of Scotland, and also of
north and southwest England, Wales and
various parts of Ireland, provide some of
our most spectacular scenery and birds.
Some species are associated with water,
such as the Greylag Geese, Teal and
Wigeon of moorland lochs and pools, and
the Dippers and Grey Wagtails of
mountain streams, but others are found
among the crags and the open heather. At
the top of the food chain are the predators:
Buzzards, Hen Harriers, Peregrines,
Merlins, Kestrels and Short-eared Owls,
and, in the Scottish Highlands, one of
Europe's strongest remaining stocks of
the magnificent Golden Eagle. Equally
typical are the grouse, although only the
widespread Red Grouse, with its
characteristic *gobak-gobak* call, is found
in Ireland. In Britain the Black Grouse is
restricted mainly to wooded moorland
edges and the Ptarmigan to the higher
slopes and hill tops of Scotland.

Uplands are also the breeding places of
a number of waders that we normally
associate with marshes and mudflats on
spring and autumn passage and in winter.
There are Curlews with their ringing cries
and bubbling songs, Snipe with their
constant chippering calls and drumming
displays, Golden Plovers and Dunlins
resplendent in summer plumage and, in
north Scotland, the elusive Greenshank.
There are also Lapwings and Redshanks,
usually on grass moors and bogs, and

Oystercatchers and Ringed Plovers, especially on grass and river shingle. In contrast, sparsely covered mountain tops are the home of another plover, the rare Dotterel, one of rather few species where the male does all the work of incubating the eggs and rearing the young. One more wader, the tittering Whimbrel, breeds on moorland in the Northern Isles, especially Shetland, sharing the habitat there with two other very local birds of Britain, the predatory and aggressive Great and Arctic Skuas. Various gulls breed locally on moors and moorland bogs, including Great and Lesser Black-backed, Herring, Common and Black-headed, although the last is mainly found near rushy pools which it sometimes shares with Common Terns. In north Scotland there are also colonies of Arctic Terns on dry moorland a kilometre or two from the sea.

Small birds are few in species, although some are very common in summer, especially Meadow Pipits (the main foster parents here for Cuckoos), Skylarks in the drier areas, and Wheatears among rocks and short turf. Stonechats need gorse or long heather, and Whinchats coarse growth in boggy places. Ring Ouzels are not uncommon on steep slopes with rocky outcrops, replacing Blackbirds and Song Thrushes which penetrate up valleys and to scrubby patches at moorland edges. Similarly, the Twite of moorland replaces the Linnet of scrub grassland. But the ubiquitous Wren will occupy a dry peat-face or any patch of rocks, and Pied Wagtails nest on crags. Rarer nesters include a few Snow Buntings on the barer mountain tops (joined by immigrants from Greenland and Scandinavia on the hills in autumn and winter) and, in the last decade, even fewer Lapland Buntings and Shore Larks.

In winter the moors become bleak and inhospitable with few birds.

Rivers and streams

Rivers and streams cut through a range of habitats and the birds associated with them to some extent reflect their surroundings. The shallow, fast-flowing, rocky streams and burns of the uplands are the special habitat of Dippers and Grey (as well as Pied) Wagtails; these also inhabit lower and slower reaches with weirs, mill-races and other artificial falls. Upland streams are the particular summer home, too, of Common Sandpipers. In contrast, lowland rivers and streams with suitable banks provide nest-sites for Kingfishers and Sand Martins, while open stretches hold many of our Mute Swans.

The bird life of rivers and streams includes a variety of waterfowl, waders, gulls and, in summer, smaller insect-eating species (although many of our commonest songsters, such as Wrens, Blackbirds and Chaffinches, often also nest in waterside tangles and trees). In particular, Grey Herons are commonly seen standing in river shallows, ready to strike at fish. Ducks, though much less numerous than on lakes and reservoirs, include Mallards everywhere. Teal nest by streams, Wigeon by moorland rivers. In the north, Goosanders breed near larger wooded rivers to a height of about 500m and Red-breasted Mergansers by both open and wooded rivers from around 300m down to the sea. Tufted Ducks and Pochards both nest by slow lowland rivers and small parties are sometimes seen on them in winter. Moorhens are widespread, but Coots are mostly seen on the slowest rivers with extensive reeds and really prefer the still waters of lakes and reservoirs. The Water Rail is a related and secretive bird of

thick waterside vegetation. Among waders, both Ringed and Little Ringed Plovers are sometimes found on upland river shingle, while Oystercatchers commonly nest there as well as on adjacent fields and moorland. Lapwings, Snipe, Curlews and Redshanks also breed in water meadows and other riverside areas, along with Black-tailed Godwits and Ruffs in East Anglia. Various other waders, such as Green and Common Sandpipers, occur by rivers on passage. Gulls, especially Black-headed and Herring, are opportunist feeders over any wetland areas. Common Terns also nest on upland river islets and shingle beds.

Many insects are found by rivers and Swifts, Swallows and House Martins, as well as Sand Martins, congregate there to feed on them, as they do over lakes and reservoirs. Reed and Sedge Warblers nest in stands of waterside vegetation, where they may often find themselves fostering Cuckoos. The rare and very local Marsh Warbler typically inhabits dry osiers with nettles or meadowsweet. Other summer birds of riverside water meadows include Yellow Wagtails and often the occasional pair of Whinchats, while Pied Wagtails and Reed Buntings may be seen there the year round. Streamside birches and alders often attract Redpolls and Siskins in winter, and riverside willows are favoured as nesting places by Little Owls and Redstarts.

Lakes, reservoirs and gravel pits

Natural and man-made stretches of fresh water vary greatly in size, from flooded gravel workings and the smaller lakes or reservoirs to the vast expanse of Lough Neagh, over 250 km² in area. The variety and numbers of birds on these fresh waters depends not only on size and location, but also on depth and, above all, on the quality of the water. The acid and often deep waters of upland Wales, north Britain and northern and extreme western parts of Ireland are oligotrophic, or nutritionally poor. They have little plant and invertebrate life, and therefore little shelter and food to offer to birds. In contrast, the alkaline and often shallow waters of the lowlands are eutrophic, or rich in nutrients, supporting a mass of plants ranging from algae to reeds and a profusion of invertebrate foods.

The breeding birds of oligotrophic lakes are very few in number. They are largely fish-eaters such as Red-throated and Black-throated Divers, Red-breasted Mergansers and Goosanders. Other waterfowl may roost there, and Common Gulls and Common Terns, for example, may nest at the edges, but sometimes the only birds to be seen are a pair of Common Sandpipers on a stony shore. In spring and autumn, the scene is enlivened by a few migrant waterfowl or waders pausing for a brief rest, but in winter these lakes are largely deserted.

At the other extreme, eutrophic lowland lakes with good stands of emergent vegetation at the edges are well stocked with nesting birds. There may be Great Crested and Little Grebes; sometimes a colony of Grey Herons in the trees; a variety of waterfowl, including Mute Swans, Canada Geese, Tufted Ducks,

Pochards, possibly Shovelers and Teal; many Coots and Moorhens, and perhaps Water Rails; Snipe and Redshanks close by if there are marshy areas; and Reed and Sedge Warblers, and Reed Buntings. Gulls, terns and waders may turn up on passage, even Little Gulls, Black Terns and Greenshanks, as well as Green and Common Sandpipers. In winter, such lakes and reservoirs can often provide a marvellous spectacle, with any of about a dozen dabbling-ducks, diving-ducks and sawbills – Wigeon, Teal, Pochards and Tufted Ducks, but also perhaps Gadwalls, Pintails, Shovelers, Goldeneyes, Smews and Goosanders – and rafts of Coots. There will also be grebes and gulls, perhaps Cormorants and Bewick's or Whooper Swans, possibly the odd diver.

Gravel pits also have many of the birds of eutrophic lakes, but, being open, silty, shallow and often in a wide variety of stages of flooding and plant growth, they have a character of their own. Little Ringed Plovers have spread over lowland Britain since the 1940s in this habitat, and some pits are favoured by colonies of Black-headed Gulls and Common Terns.

Marshes, fens and reedbeds

Marshes are wetlands where standing water covers just part of the surface. They tend to be eutrophic – rich in nutrients – and develop a thick growth of submerged plants and reeds, rushes, club-rushes and sweet-grass, making an attractive habitat for birds. Fens occur on peat where nutrients brought in by water from outside also promote rich vegetation.

Reeds and rushes may form narrow belts by rivers, at most 2–3 m wide and confined to sheltered corners, but in shallow lakes they are often extensive and in flooded marshes may cover many hectares. All these types of wetland hold much of interest to the birdwatcher, but the thickness of the vegetation often makes the more secretive species difficult to see.

Although it is not easy, nor desirable in the nesting season, to penetrate into reeds by wading or by boat, many of the characteristic birds can be seen feeding at the edges. Some marshes with extensive reedbeds and areas of open water, such as Minsmere (Suffolk), Stodmarsh (Kent)

and Leighton Moss (Lancashire), are reserves for several rare species, with hides from which to watch them. Conservation of such areas has had much to do with maintaining our tiny populations of Black-necked Grebes, Bitterns and Marsh Harriers, with the recovery of Bearded Tits from a handful in 1947 to about 400 pairs, with the return of Savi's Warblers since 1960 after an absence of 100 years, and with the colonisation of Cetti's Warblers since 1972.

Plenty of common birds breed in or around reedbeds. Great Crested and Little Grebes anchor their floating nests there. Gadwalls, Tufted Ducks and Pochards lay their eggs in grass or sedge tussocks. Water Rails may be heard 'sharming'. Coots and Moorhens are numerous. Among the smaller birds, the nests of Reed and Sedge Warblers attract Cuckoos. In autumn, reedbeds are roosting sites for Swallows and both martins, Yellow and Pied Wagtails, and Starlings, often in large numbers, and these in turn may draw falcons and Sparrowhawks looking for prey. In winter, Grey Herons (which sometimes nest in reeds), various ducks, Snipe and Kingfishers may be seen wading, swimming or fishing in the shallows, and many Wrens and Blue Tits make temporary homes there.

More open marshes, of which the winter-flooded Ouse Washes (on the borders of Cambridge and Norfolk) are a prize example, provide nesting places for other ducks of water meadows and muddy shallows, including Shovelers and a few Garganeys and Pintails. Among breeding waders are Snipe, Redshanks, Curlews, and now Black-tailed Godwits and a few Ruffs. Pheasants nest here in something like their original reedy habitats in Asia. Many waders arrive on passage, and large numbers of ducks and swans winter.

Estuaries and saltings

On sheltered coasts, where the action of waves is minimal, silts settle in the intertidal zone to form flats of mud mixed with sand. Vast numbers of marine invertebrates inhabit this area and at low tide provide an enormous food resource for waders and other shore birds. Over 30 of the estuaries and sheltered bays of Britain and Ireland, such as Morecambe Bay, the Wash, Solway, Ribble, Dee, Thames, Shannon/Fergus and North Bull, are of international importance as wintering grounds for waders and wildfowl, some holding hundreds of thousands of birds. The estuarine mudflats are often backed by saltmarshes, or saltings, a transitional zone between the sea and the land, where geese, seed-eating ducks and small numbers of waders that prefer the greater shelter of creeks are found.

For the birdwatcher, estuaries are at their best in winter. The commonest waders then are Dunlins, and, more locally, Knots, which roost and fly in huge dense packs. There are also large concentrations of Oystercatchers, Lapwings and Redshanks, slightly smaller numbers of Golden Plovers, Curlews and Bar-tailed Godwits, and a good scattering of Ringed and Grey Plovers, Turnstones, Snipe, Black-tailed Godwits and Sanderlings. Many other waders such as Greenshanks and Spotted Redshanks also occur on passage in autumn and spring.

The special goose of estuarine areas in winter is the Brent, which feeds particularly on eelgrass. Around half the world population of the dark-bellied form from arctic USSR winters in Britain, and the Greenland population of the pale-bellied race winters in Ireland. Barnacle Geese come in thousands to the salt-

marshes and adjacent pastures of the Solway and parts of Ireland and the Hebrides. Greylag and Pink-footed Geese feed inland and roost at night on estuarine flats and sandbanks, while many White-fronted Geese winter on lowland pastures and to a lesser extent on saltings. Mute and Whooper Swans also use estuaries, but Bewick's Swans show a preference for inland waters. Among ducks, large numbers of Wigeon, Pintails and Shelducks winter on estuaries. Mallards, Teal and Shovelers are rather scarcer, but some hundreds of Pochards and Goldeneyes are found in a few places, while there are concentrations of Scaups in the Firth of Forth and of Eiders in the Firth of Tay. Long-tailed Ducks and Common and Velvet Scoters are generally farther offshore, although they gather in a few, mainly northern estuaries. Red-breasted Mergansers and, especially on the Beauly Firth, Goosanders may also be seen.

Cormorants are often in estuaries, and there are always big concentrations of all the commoner gulls with the exception of the Kittiwake. Divers and grebes may sometimes be seen on the water, and occasional raptors, such as Peregrines and Merlins, winter here for the plentiful supply of prey available. The small birds of the saltings then are mainly Skylarks, pipits, wagtails, and Twites and other finches.

By summer, the bird life is relatively reduced. Shelducks, Mallards and Red-breasted Mergansers are often the only ducks. The main waders then are Oyster-catchers, Lapwings, Ringed Plovers and Redshanks, along with a few non-breeders of other species. Gulls and terns feed in estuaries and may be nesting nearby. Small birds include feeding pipits, wagtails and Starlings.

Sand, shingle and dunes

Compared with muddy and rocky coasts, sand and shingle are often rather barren for the birdwatcher. Beaches built up by the constant pounding of waves have a greatly restricted invertebrate fauna and so less food for birds; there is also little vegetation until marram and other grasses stabilise the dunes behind. Such beaches are found on many parts of our coastline. Some of the largest shingle areas are on the Kent and East Anglian coasts, as well as in Dorset, Wales, Cumbria and parts of Scotland. There are major dune complexes in Devon, in various sections of both the east and west coasts of Britain, and in east and south Ireland.

In summer, these habitats are essential to our five breeding species of terns – Common, Arctic, Roseate, Sandwich and Little – all of which are at risk from greatly increased human disturbance of what often used to be comparatively wild areas. The Little Tern, indeed, is almost restricted to coastal sand and shingle, and the Sandwich Tern largely to dunes and shingle, although it nests too on rocky and grassy islets like the Roseate. Herring and Lesser Black-backed Gulls also breed in these areas, notably on the dunes at Walney (Lancashire), and all the commoner gull species rest and roost on beaches. A few waders are characteristic nesters here, especially Oystercatchers, Ringed Plovers and, sometimes, Redshanks. Locally, Stone-curlews may occur on dunes and shingle, while stony islets in brackish lagoons hold many of the nests of our carefully nurtured population of Avocets. Mallards, Eiders and especially Shelducks nest in dune areas, as

well as, very locally, Pintails. A few Merlins breed in dunes. Grey and Red-legged Partridges, Stock Doves, Short-eared Owls and Nightjars are also marginal dune species. The small birds of marram-covered dunes are mainly Sky-larks, Meadow Pipits, Wheatears and Linnets.

Exposed sand and shingle beaches are generally poor for waders, but one species, the Sanderling, is adept at running along the tideline, so fast as to seem on wheels, darting to and fro with the advancing and retreating waves to snatch up sand-hoppers; a few non-breeders stay the summer, but most are passage and winter visitors. Apart from Oystercatchers and Ringed Plovers, various other waders will sometimes feed or rest on these beaches, often singly or in small parties, particularly Dunlins, Curlews, Grey Plovers, Bar-tailed Godwits and Turnstones.

In autumn, especially on the east and south coasts, the combination of onshore winds overnight and drizzle at dawn are ideal conditions for seeing falls of chats, thrushes, warblers, flycatchers and other migrants. Many of these quickly move inland to the nearest scrub, but often a Bluethroat or a Redstart, or any of a variety of warblers, will spend the day sheltering in the marram of the dunes.

High dunes are often good places from which to watch the passage movements of shearwaters, skuas, terns and auks along the sea. Sadly some of these birds, especially Guillemots, are all too often seen dead or dying after being fouled by oil and swept on to beaches. In winter, divers, grebes and sea-ducks swim off-shore. Otherwise, the main inhabitants of the open beaches then are gulls and scavenging crows and Starlings.

Rocky coasts and islands

Few sights are more spectacular for the birdwatcher than thousands of seabirds wheeling around their cliff colonies in a cacophony of sound. The cliffs and rocky islands of north and west Britain, and of many parts of Ireland, hold some of the largest seabird concentrations in Europe. Most numerous and conspicuous are the stiff-winged Fulmars, the gentle-looking but noisy Kittiwakes, and the tightly packed and vociferous Guillemots, from which the crevice-nesting Razorbills have to be picked out. Cormorants and Shags are also easily seen (but often confused by the beginner) and the clown-faced Puffins stand outside their burrows among the sea-thrift on the turf-clad slopes. Herring and Lesser Black-backed Gulls circle around the upper slopes, while each headland often holds the odd pair of the more solitary Great Black-backed Gulls.

Also rather solitary, a few Black Guillemots may be found near the foot of the cliff or on the sea close by, with their bold white shoulders and bright red gapes and legs: unlike many of the seabirds, they stay all the year round. Difficult to see because they enter and leave their underground burrows only at night, are Manx Shearwaters, Storm Petrels and, on a few north and west Scottish islands, Leach's Petrels. A visit to a colony after dark when the air is full of their screaming, cackling, churring, laughing and crooning calls is an experience to remember. But most impressive of all, because of their size and gleaming whiteness, their powerful flight and spectacular plunges, must be the Gannets: over 200,000 pairs, or three-quarters of the world population, nest in just 15 colonies around our coasts.

Several birds of prey also nest on sea-cliffs, notably Peregrines, Kestrels, Buzzards, and a few of our Golden Eagles in west Scotland; attempts are now being made on Rhum, in the Inner Hebrides, to reintroduce the White-tailed Eagle. The north and west coasts of Ireland and Scotland are the last bastions of the wild Rock Dove population, while Irish coasts are the main stronghold of the Chough. Ravens, Jackdaws and Carrion or Hooded Crows also nest on coastal crags. Closer to the water, Eiders make their downy nests among the rocks and swim sedately near the shore even in rough seas. The widespread Turnstone and the much more local Purple Sandpiper are two waders seen at their best on rocky coasts in autumn and winter; Common Sandpipers, Dunlins, Redshanks and Whimbrels feed there on passage; and Ringed Plovers often nest on rock slabs.

Although small birds are usually few around rocky shores, the ubiquitous Wren manages to make a home for itself in all but the barest cliffs, sharing the habitat with Rock Pipits and Pied Wagtails. Starlings and, more locally, Swifts and House Martins also breed on cliffs, while a few pairs of Black Redstarts annually nest there in southeast England. Wheatears are common on rocky islands, and Stonechats where there is gorse at the cliff-top. Autumn winds and drizzle can bring big falls of migrants; then thrushes and warblers may be seen looking for food in scrubby patches of vegetation.

DIVERS (Gaviidae)

Red-throated Diver *Gavia stellata* 53–59 cm (*c*22 in). Smallest diver, with slender uptilted bill, small head, thinnish neck. Flies with fast beats of long thin wings, usually low but also high, with sagging neck, trailing legs, white underwings as all divers; swims low, turns on side when preening, dives often; takes off easily; awkward on land, heaving jerkily with feet. *Ad summer* Dull red throat looks black at distance; head and sides of neck grey, hindneck striped; upperparts uniform slate-brown. *Ad winter* White of lores defined above by dark grey cap; white extends round eyes; largely white neck looks very thin; upperparts with small white spots (mantle paler than wing coverts). *Juv* As ad winter, but browner above, with fewer, larger, less white spots (mantle often darker than coverts); forehead darker, sides of neck speckled; bill paler grey; moults in Dec–Jul. VOICE Flight-cackle *kwuk-kwuk-kwuk* when nesting; mewing wail, barking croak; song harsh throaty cooing, rising and falling, often in duet. HABITAT Breeds at lochs, moor pools; winters mainly off coasts. NEST On islets or loch-sides, or built up in shallows, 2 eggs, mid May–mid Jul; 1 brood. FOOD Fish, also frogs, invertebrates. RANGE Breeding areas Apr–Sep; coastal Sep–May, inc many from N Europe, also Greenland.

Black-throated Diver *Gavia arctica* 56–69 cm (*c*24½ in). Bulkier than Red-throated, with straight bill, heavier head; smaller than Great Northern, with more slender bill, thinner neck, often sloping forehead. Wing-beats shallower, slower than Red-throated; rises from water less easily. *Ad summer* Black throat bordered by stripes; grey head and hindneck; upperparts black with 4 sets of squarish white spots; bill black. *Ad winter* Darker than other divers; forehead and upperparts uniform black-brown, crown and hindneck paler; often bold white patch on rear flanks; bill grey. *Juv* As ad winter, but upperparts browner with much pale scaling; bill blue-

Black-throated Diver

juv

ad winter

ad summer

Red-throated Diver

juv

ad winter

ad summer

white; moults to look as ad winter Jan–
Jun. VOICE Usually silent in flight; song
loud rhythmic wailing *tlooeet-to-tlooeet-
to-tlooeet . . .*; also short wails, croaks.
HABITAT Breeds at freshwater lochs; win-
ters off coasts. NEST On islets, 2 eggs,
May–Jun; 1 brood. FOOD As Red-throated.
RANGE Breeding areas Apr–Sep; coastal
Sep–May, inc many from N Europe.

Great Northern Diver *Gavia immer* 69–81
cm (*c*29½ in). Bulky, with deep heavy bill,
steep forehead and thick neck; usually
looks much bigger than Black-throated.
Powerful wing-beats slow and shallow;
takes off laboriously. *Ad summer* Glossy
black head and neck, striped part-collars;
upperparts black with white spots, large
and square on scapulars; bill black. *Ad
winter* Crown/hindneck darker than
mantle and pale-edged scapulars; pale eye-
rings; jagged division of dark/light on
neck-sides; bill grey with dark culmen. *Juv*
As ad winter, but paler above and very
distinctly scaled; throat and sides of neck
speckled brown; bill blue-white, but

culmen dark; moults throughout 1st year.
VOICE Moaning calls from autumn flocks.
HABITAT Winters mainly off coasts. RANGE
Winter visitor from
Iceland/?Green-
land, Oct–May
(mid Aug–Jun); has
bred NBr, at least in
1970.

COMPARE White-
billed Diver (250),
also swimming
Cormorant (54).

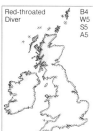
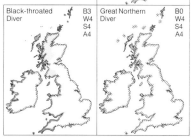

Great Northern Diver

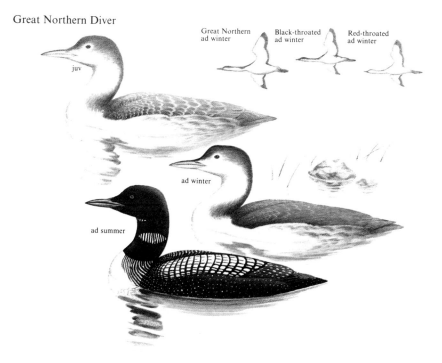

GREBES (Podicipedidae)

Red-necked Grebe *Podiceps grisegena*
40–46 cm (*c*17 in). Stocky, with thick neck
and bulbous head, black and yellow bill;
crown down to eyes always dark; well-
defined cheeks and throat. Flight as Great
Crested, but shape less attenuated, no
white along scapulars; more secretive in
summer, usually close to cover; walks
more easily. *Ad summer* Bill black with
bright yellow base; black cap down to
brown eyes, short double crest; pale grey
cheeks and throat outlined in white;
foreneck and upper breast chestnut, flanks
mottled grey. *Ad winter* Bill greyer, with
dull yellow base; crown and upperparts
paler grey-brown, cheeks and throat white
but for grey patch just under eyes; front
and sides of neck greyish, upper breast
and flanks mottled grey. *Juv* Bill paler with
more yellow, eyes yellow; resembles ad
summer, with paler chestnut-buff
foreneck, but crown and upperparts
browner, sides of head striped blackish,
and flanks mottled paler grey-brown.

1st winter After moult in Sep–Jan, as ad
winter, but bill stays paler and eyes yellow.
VOICE Generally silent except when
breeding. HABITAT Breeds on smaller
waters with more cover than Great
Crested; winters mainly along coasts and
estuaries, rarely on lakes and reservoirs.
FOOD Insects, also small fish, molluscs,
crustaceans, worms, tadpoles. RANGE
Winter visitor from Baltic region, Oct–
Mar (Aug–Apr); since 1974 single ads
or pairs have summered, even displayed
or built nest, mainly in NBr.

Great Crested Grebe *Podiceps cristatus*
45–51 cm (*c*19 in). Large, with long-slender
neck, pinkish dagger-like bill; face and
supercilia white. Flies little, extended
neck and feet hanging lower than humped
back, showing white on forewings, secondaries and scapulars; like all grebes,
rises awkwardly, pattering along surface;
swims with body low and neck erect, or
rests with neck sunk into shoulders and
bill often buried in neck-feathers; dives
expertly; usually not shy; seldom on land,

Red-necked Grebe

juv

ad winter

ad winter

ad summer

waddling awkwardly or flopping along on breast; like all grebes, covers eggs if leaving nest, later carries chicks on back; often loosely gregarious in winter. *Ad summer* Black crown extending to double crest, chestnut and black tippets erected in complex head-waggling and other displays; white face and supercilia divided by black line from bill to red eyes; rufous tinge to sides of neck and flanks. *Ad winter* Crown grey-brown, crest smaller, no tippets, less rufous on neck and flanks; head, neck and underparts otherwise boldly white, but for dark line down hindneck, black in front of eyes, and chestnut and blackish marks on rear cheeks. *Juv* Head and neck with broken stripes of black-brown and rufous; upperparts browner, bill paler, eyes orange. *1st winter* After moult in Jul–Jan, as ad winter, but almost no crest, sides of head whiter without chestnut and blackish marks. VOICE When breeding, harsh or guttural croaks, growls, snarls, also mooing; quiet *kek* and *gung*; song barking *rah-rah-rah*; young pipe persistently.

HABITAT Breeds on lakes, reservoirs and gravel pits, locally also rivers, among reeds, sedges; winters on reservoirs, estuaries, coasts. NEST Sometimes loosely colonial; soggy heap floating among reeds or weeping branches, or built up from bottom, 3–5 eggs, Apr–Jul (Feb–Aug); 1–2 broods. FOOD Fish, also insects, crustaceans, molluscs, tadpoles, frogs. RANGE Leaves smaller lakes Aug–Feb; many along coasts Sep–Apr, inc some from Low Countries/Denmark.

COMPARE Smaller grebes (46, 250).

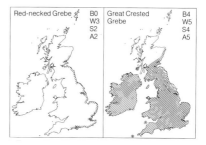

Red-necked Grebe	B0 W3 S2 A2	Great Crested Grebe	B4 W5 S4 A5

Great Crested Grebe

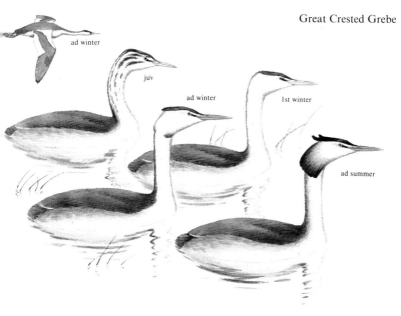

ad winter

juv

ad winter

1st winter

ad summer

Slavonian Grebe *Podiceps auritus* 31–36 cm (*c*13 in). Small and snaky-headed, with stubby bill, flat crown, and often erect neck (*cf* Black-necked). Flies readily, showing white secondaries and forewing-wedge; not shy; often dives with forward jump; usually seen in ones and twos. *Ad summer* Head and tippets black, with golden 'horns' back from eyes; neck, upper breast and flanks chestnut. *Ad winter* Black cap (grey spot before each eye), demarcated at eye-level from white of cheeks which almost meets across nape; thin blackish hindneck. *Juv* Until moult in Oct–Jan, blacks browner, border between cap and more mottled cheeks ill-defined, flanks whiter. VOICE When nesting, nasal descending *yaaarr*; trills in duet like Little Grebe. HABITAT Breeds on lochs with sedges, mare's-tails, reeds; winters in bays, estuaries, also lakes, reservoirs. NEST Soggy floating heap anchored to vegetation, 4–5 eggs, mid May–Jul; 1–2 broods. FOOD Insects, fish, also some crustaceans, molluscs, worms. RANGE Breeding lochs Mar–Sep; winter visitor Nov–Feb (Sep–May), esp from Iceland/Scandinavia.

Black-necked Grebe *Podiceps nigricollis* 28–33 cm (*c*12 in). Small, with thin uptilted bill, high rounded crown, and often curved neck (*cf* Slavonian). Flies little (white only on rear wings, reaching inner primaries); shy, likes cover; often skims insects off surface, usually dives without jump; gregarious in winter. *Ad summer* Head, neck and upper breast black, with golden fan behind eyes; flanks chestnut, mottled black. *Ad winter* Like Slavonian (*cf* juv), but duller cap (no grey spot) diffusely down to cheeks, dark hindneck broader. *Juv* Until moult in Aug–Dec, upperparts browner, cheeks duskier, sides of upper neck tinged buff, dusky collar above breast, flanks paler. VOICE When breeding, soft fluty *poo-ee*, harsh chatter. HABITAT Breeds on shallow lakes and meres with reeds or sedges; winters on estuaries, reservoirs, lakes. NEST Often colonial; small soggy floating heap in vegetation, 3–5 eggs, Mar–early Jul; 1–2

Slavonian Grebe

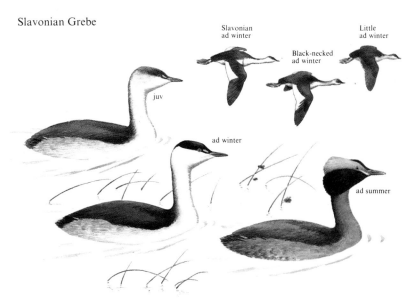

Slavonian
ad winter

Little
ad winter

Black-necked
ad winter

juv

ad winter

ad summer

broods. FOOD As Slavonian, but few fish.
RANGE Breeding areas Apr–Sep; passage/
winter visitor from Continent, Aug–May.

Little Grebe *Tachybaptus ruficollis* 25–29
cm (*c*10½ in). Dumpy, with blunt fluffy
brown-grey stern (can look whitish), and
short bill and neck. Flies readily (plain
wings), often dives on touch-down; swims
buoyantly; shy when nesting; perches,
walks, even runs, more easily than other
grebes; gregarious in winter. *Ad summer*
Bright yellow-green gape-patch; mainly
blackish but for chestnut panel on cheeks
and foreneck, rufous patches at sides of
rump, brown flanks. *Ad winter* Bill more
yellowish at base, but bright gape lost;
dull brown above, sandy-buff below with
greyer flanks and stern. *Juv* Stripy head;
darker above than ad winter, deeper buff
below with browner-grey flanks; much as
ad after moult in Sep–Dec. VOICE Main
breeding call high whinnying trill, often
in duet; sharp *wit wit* in alarm. HABITAT
Breeds on ponds, lakes, reservoirs, rivers,
marshes, with reeds, sedges, submerged

bushes; winters on lakes, reservoirs,
estuaries. NEST Soggy floating heap in
cover or anchored in open, 4–6 eggs,
Apr–mid Aug (late
Feb–early Sep); 2–3
broods. FOOD As
Slavonian; less fish,
more molluscs.
RANGE Disperses to
open waters Aug–
Apr; some from
Continent. COMPARE
Pied-billed Grebe
(250).

Slavonian Grebe — B2 W4 S4 A4

Black-necked Grebe — B2 W4 S4 A4

Little Grebe — B5 W5 S5 A5

Black-necked Grebe

ad winter

juv

ad summer

Little Grebe

juv

ad summer

ad winter

GANNETS (Sulidae)

Gannet *Sula bassana* 86–96 cm (*c*36 in). Largest indigenous seabird, with long narrow wings; spear-bill (often pointing down), long body and pointed tail give distinctive 'cigar-shape'; ad mainly white with black wing-tips, imms range from blackish to pied. Flight powerful: deep beats mixed with glides on angled wings and, in stronger winds, banks and soars like shearwater, esp Cory's (50), for which imms sometimes mistaken at long range; characteristically plunges for food, wings folded back, from heights of 5–40 m; swims with head and tail up, sometimes immersing head and diving from surface; take-off laboured, flapping over water; waddles awkwardly on land; often singly at sea. *Ad* Shining white, but for creamy-yellow head and neck, black wing-tips; bill blue-white with dark lines; feet grey-black, with yellow-green lines on ♂, blue-green on ♀. *Juv* At distance, looks black with paler breast and belly, whitish V above tail: mainly black-brown speckled with white, but lower breast and belly whiter, mottled dark, most of underwings silvery-grey; bill and legs dark. *Imm* Much variation in timing, but over *c*4 years turns increasingly white: first to whiten are lower underbody and axillaries; next, head and neck, also losing dark breast-band in 2nd autumn; then upper mantle and, by 3rd autumn, upperbody, smaller wing-coverts; last dark areas are some secondaries and tail-centre. VOICE Noisy at colonies, esp barking *urrah*, groans, croaks, and yapping of young; otherwise silent unless several feeding together. HABITAT Essentially marine, breeding on rocky stacks, islands and cliffs. NEST Colonial; on cliff-ledges, island slopes, 1 egg, Apr–Sep. FOOD Fish, offal. RANGE Nesting areas Jan–Oct; some inshore all year, but others disperse, esp in 1st year, south to W Africa. COMPARE Larger shearwaters (50).

PETRELS, SHEARWATERS (Procellariidae)

Fulmar *Fulmarus glacialis* 44–50 cm (*c*18½ in). Rather gull-like petrel with stout tube-nosed bill, dumpy bull-necked body and long, centrally set, narrow wings; usually white with grey back and upperwings (but light patch on inner primaries), paler rump and tail, dark eyes emphasised by blackish patch in front, and yellow bill with green to blue-grey base. Flight powerful, with glides, neat turns and banking on stiff wings, mixed with more frequent and persistent flapping than shearwaters; often follows trawlers; swims buoyantly, but seldom dives; take-off awkward, pattering along surface; unlike shearwaters, diurnal at colonies, wheeling about cliffs, often close to people, and making several dummy runs before settling; on land shuffles on tarsi, but can stand; when alarmed, ads and young both spurt oil; abundant, gregarious. *Ad/juv* Head, neck and underparts usually white or tinged yellow, with contrasting grey upperparts (browner when worn) and dusky edges to underwings; some have pale grey crown, hindneck and often also belly; fewer show darker grey crown and pale grey breast (but almost uniform dark grey 'Blue Fulmars' mainly vagrants from Arctic.) VOICE At nest, chuckling or cackling, as well as thin whine when regurgitating food for young and squeaky growl when about to spurt oil; soft croon in flight, and feeding flocks grunt and cackle. HABITAT Oceanic, but breeds on cliffs, locally on dunes, scree, ruins, even crags several km inland. NEST Colonial; on ledges or in recesses, 1 egg, mid May–mid Sep; 1 brood. FOOD Crustaceans, cephalopods, fish, offal. RANGE Some stay inshore all year, even visiting nesting cliffs; others disperse as far as Greenland. COMPARE Larger shearwaters (50).

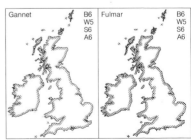

Gannet B6 W5 S6 A6 Fulmar B6 W5 S6 A6

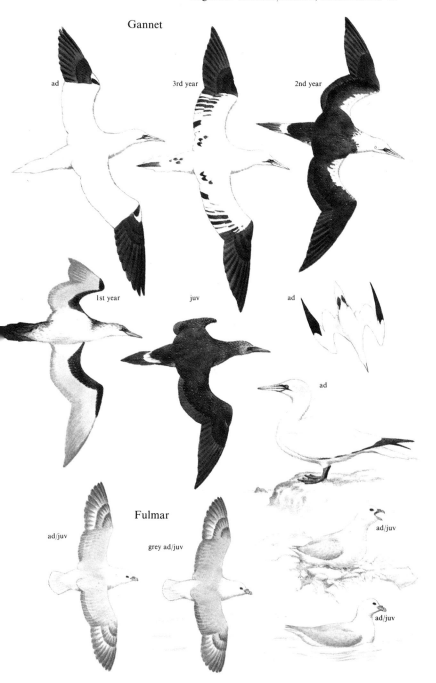

Gannet

ad

3rd year

2nd year

1st year

juv

ad

ad

Fulmar

ad/juv

grey ad/juv

ad/juv

ad/juv

SHEARWATERS (Procellariidae)

Cory's Shearwater *Calonectris diomedea* 43–48 cm (*c*18 in). Heavy and big-headed, with thick pale bill, and long, comparatively broad wings; brown above, white below, with distinctive greyish hood (*cf* Great Shearwater). Flight not unlike Fulmar (48) but glides and banks on more bowed wings; in light winds, alternates glides with several deep, slow, loose flaps; in rough weather, soars as Gannet (48) or towers; may swim in rafts; feeds at surface or plunges. *Ad/juv* Bill yellow; head and hindneck grey-brown merging into white of throat, no pale collar; rest of upperbody brown with, in new plumage, distinct grey feather-fringes and whitish-tipped tail-coverts sometimes forming pale horseshoe (*cf* Great); wings and tail dark brown; underparts all white, but for grey-brown or dark wing-border, faint grey mottling on lower flanks. VOICE Silent at sea. HABITAT Oceanic, occasional inshore. FOOD Fish, cephalopods, crustaceans, offal from fishing boats. RANGE Scarce visitor from Mediterranean/Cent Atlantic, Jul–Sep (Apr–Nov); sometimes in numbers (17,000 + in 1980 was exceptional and 10 times previous total).

Great Shearwater *Puffinus gravis* 42–49 cm (*c*18 in). Narrow-headed with slender dark bill and moderately long wings; brown above, with well-defined dark cap, and white below, boldly marked with dark brown on underwings (*cf* Cory's Shearwater). Flight more like Manx Shearwater (52) than Cory's, gliding and banking mixed with rapid beats of straight, stiff wings; gregarious and often swimming in large rafts; feeds both at surface and by plunging. *Ad/juv* Bill blackish; cap black-brown, contrasting with white of throat and pale greyish collar; upperbody brown to grey-brown with distinct light feather-fringes and white-tipped tail-coverts usually forming pale horseshoe; wings darker than back, and primaries and tail dark brown; underwings white, boldly blotched and streaked dark brown and with darker wing-border than Cory's; underbody white, but grey-brown patch on

belly (often obscure), smaller patches at chest-sides, and brown-spotted flanks and undertail-coverts. VOICE Sometimes raucous squawks from feeding flocks. HABITAT Oceanic. FOOD Fish, cephalopods, offal from fishing boats. RANGE Annual visitor from S Atlantic, Jul–Oct (Mar–Nov), rare winter.

Sooty Shearwater *Puffinus griseus* 39–44 cm (*c*16½ in). Heavy-bodied but with thin head and long slender bill; narrow wings appear set far back; all dark but for pale strip along underwings (*cf* dark Balearic Shearwater, 50, which is smaller, slimmer, shorter-winged). Flight usually direct and powerful, more 'mechanical' than Manx (52), with more backswept wing-beats; swims readily; feeds at surface by plunging; usually singly or in small parties. *Ad/juv* Wholly sooty-brown above, but for paler tinge to scapulars and wing-coverts in some lights; greyer-brown below, not quite so dark, offset by whitish chin, greyer flight-feathers and esp pale wing-coverts which catch the sun at long range in banking flight; bill blackish. VOICE Silent at sea. HABITAT Oceanic, sometimes inshore. FOOD Cephalopods, crustaceans, fish. RANGE Annual visitor from S oceans, Aug–Sep (Jul–Oct), rare rest of year.

COMPARE Fulmar and imm Gannet (48), Manx Shearwater (52), Little Shearwater (252).

Cory's Shearwater B0 W0 S1 A3

Great Shearwater B0 W0 S0 A4

Sooty Shearwater B0 W0 S2 A5

Cory's Shearwater

ad/juv

ad/juv

ad/juv

Great Shearwater

ad/juv

ad/juv

ad/juv

Sooty Shearwater

ad/juv

ad/juv

ad/juv

Manx Shearwater *Puffinus puffinus* 30–38 cm (*c*14 in). Medium-sized shearwater (but smaller runts occur), with a smallish head, long thin bill; black and white (but note that Balearic race all browner). Banks on stiff wings, now looking black, now white, with periodic rapid beats; often in flocks, at distance like lines of wheeling black or white crosses; swims readily and feeds also by hovering, with paddling feet, or plunging; shuffles awkwardly on land. *Ad/juv (P.p. puffinus)* Black above, extending down under eyes; white below but for dark wing-borders, mottling on sides of neck, breast, flanks and axillaries. *Balearic Shearwater (P.p. mauretanicus)* Dark brown above; tinged grey-brown below, sometimes entirely, but often centre of body and underwings whitish; looks all-dark in poor light (*cf* Sooty Shearwater, 50). VOICE Silent at sea; raucous caws, weird croons and screams at night at colonies. HABITAT Breeds on turf-topped islands, headlands, also scree-slopes; otherwise oceanic. NEST Colonial; in burrows, 1 egg, May–Sep; 1 brood. FOOD Fish, also cephalopods, crustaceans, offal. RANGE Breeding areas Feb–Oct, otherwise at sea ranging to S America; Balearic Shearwater scarce visitor, Jun–Oct (Mar–Jan), off Channel coast and rarer north to Scotland. COMPARE Other shearwaters (50, 252).

STORM-PETRELS (Hydrobatidae)

Storm Petrel *Hydrobates pelagicus* 14–16 cm (*c*6 in). Small, shortish-winged; feet do not project beyond squarish tail; black with white rump, band on underwings. Bat-like fluttering and short glides; patters on surface, wings raised; follows ships, to and fro across wake; sometimes settles on sea; flutters on land, or shuffles on tarsi. *Ad/juv* Sooty, but for white rump curving down to lower flanks, variable whitish band on underwings and, in new plumage, thin whitish line on upperwings (broader on juv). VOICE Silent at sea; *turr-chik*, *wik-wik-wik* and *pee-pee-pee* at night at colonies; sustained purring on nest ends in hiccup. HABITAT Breeds on rocky or turfy islands and headlands; otherwise

oceanic. NEST Colonial; under boulders, in rock-crevices, stone walls or burrows. 1 egg, Jun–mid Oct; 1 brood. FOOD Plankton, tiny fish, offal scraps. RANGE Breeding areas Apr–Oct; rarely storm-driven inshore or inland in autumn or spring; otherwise at sea, ranging south to S Africa.

Leach's Petrel *Oceanodroma leucorhoa* 19–22 cm (*c*8 in). Larger, more attenuated than Storm Petrel, with longer wings and forked tail; also browner, with less defined rump, pale bar on upperwings only. Flight buoyant, bounding with sudden direction changes, now gliding and banking, now hovering, now flapping with deep beats; glides with wings arched in flattened M; patters on surface, wings slightly raised; seldom follows ships. *Ad/juv* Dark brown, but for white rump bisected by faint grey strip, pale bar on upperwings. VOICE Usually silent at sea; chatters and screeches at night at colonies; churrs on nest, interspersed with indrawn *whee* or chatter. HABITAT Breeds on turfy islands; otherwise oceanic. NEST Colonial; in burrows or under boulders, 1 egg, Jun–mid Oct; 1 brood. FOOD As Storm Petrel. RANGE Breeding areas Apr–Nov; rarely storm-driven in-shore in numbers in autumn; otherwise at sea, ranging south to S Africa.

COMPARE Vagrant petrels (252).

Manx Shearwater

B6
W1
S7
A7

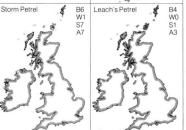

Storm Petrel

B6
W1
S7
A7

Leach's Petrel

B4
W0
S1
A3

Manx Shearwater

puffinus ad/juv

puffinus ad/juv

puffinus ad/juv

mauretanicus ad/juv

mauretanicus ad/juv

mauretanicus ad/juv

Storm Petrel

ad/juv

ad/juv

underwing
variations

Leach's Petrel

ad/juv

ad/juv

CORMORANTS (Phalacrocoracidae)

Shag *Phalacrocorax aristotelis* 72–80 cm
(*c*30 in). Smaller, slighter than Cormorant,
with slender bill, steeper forehead and
thinner neck; ad all dark and imms also
more uniformly brown on underparts, with
less bare facial skin than Cormorant.
Flight and behaviour as Cormorant, but
wing-beats faster, glides more, flies high
less often; dives with more marked
forward spring; mainly on or near rocks.
Ad summer Glossy green-black; upcurved
crest in spring; mantle, scapulars and
wing-coverts purplish and scaled black;
bill black with elongated yellow gape-
patch, eyes green. *Ad winter* Duller, less
glossy, with paler, mottled throat; no
crest, less gape-patch. *Juv* Brown above
with only faint gloss, mantle and scapulars
scaled darker; buff-tipped wing-coverts
tend to form pale wing-patches (*cf* juv
Cormorant); underparts buff-brown, typically more uniform than Cormorant (esp
breast), but chin white; bill pink-brown
eyes yellow-white. *1st year* Slow moult to
glossier upperparts scaled with black as
ad, black-brown throat and foreneck with
paler speckling, and darker brown underparts. *2nd year* As ad winter above, but
dark brown below, only speckled, glossy
green down to breast. VOICE At nest, main
sound throat-clicking; ♂ also grunts, ♀
hisses. HABITAT Rocky coasts, islands.
NEST Colonial; on rock ledges, often in
sea-caves, or under boulders, 3 eggs, mid
Mar–Aug; 1 brood. FOOD Fish, some
crustaceans. RANGE Disperses Sep–Mar;
some, esp 1st year, cross to coasts between
Norway and Biscay, few reach SBr from
NW France; prolonged onshore winds
cause food shortages and so movements to
flat coasts or inland (esp imms).

Cormorant *Phalacrocorax carbo* 84–98 cm
(*c*36 in). Long-necked with heavy bill
(but thin as Shag on some juvs); dark,
but ad has white on face (also on thighs
in summer) and imms often whitish below;
face always shows obvious bare yellow
skin. Flight goose-like, with neck
extended in kink, but primaries separated

Shag

ad summer

2nd year

ad winter

ad winter

juv

1st year

on downstroke of measured beats; sometimes glides; usually low over water, but often at some height, when flocks may be in echelon; swims low in water, resembling diver (42), but bill more raised, neck more erect; dives from surface, swims underwater; take-off laboured, with much flapping; rests on rocks, banks, posts or trees, often with wings hanging open; on land, waddles awkwardly. *Ad summer* Head and body glossy blue-black, but for white cheeks, throat and thigh-patch; scapulars and wing-coverts bronze, scaled black; bill grey and yellow, eyes green; in spring, long white feathers on crown and upper neck, often few and soon wearing off, but sometimes over most of head like Continental race (*P.c. sinensis*). *Ad winter* Less glossy, white of cheeks and throat mottled brown, no white on thighs. *Juv* Mainly dark brown above, flecked blue-black; bronzy wing-coverts also look dark (*cf* juv Shag); variable below from sooty with light spots to, more usually, white on central throat, breast and belly; bill mainly yellow, eyes grey-brown. *1st year*

As juv, but glossier above, often whiter below. *2nd year* As ad winter, but less glossy, variously mottled whitish below. VOICE When nesting, variety of guttural croaks. HABITAT Breeds mainly on seacliffs, rocky islets, locally by fresh water (esp Ir); winters on all coasts, estuaries, tidal rivers, large lakes, reservoirs. NEST Colonial; on cliffs or rocks, or usually dead trees by fresh water, 3-4 eggs, end Mar-Aug; 1 brood. FOOD Fish. RANGE Disperses to all coasts Sep-Mar, locally inland, some south to Iberia; some immigrants from Low Countries/Denmark.

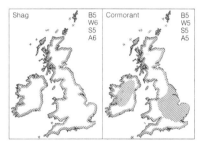

| Shag | B5 W6 S5 A6 | Cormorant | B5 W5 S5 A5 |

Cormorant

carbo ad winter

2nd year

carbo ad summer

sinensis ad summer

carbo ad winter

juv light

juv dark

1st year

BITTERNS, HERONS (Ardeidae)

Bittern *Botaurus stellaris* 70–80 cm (*c*30 in). Stocky, thick-necked; buff, but more rufous on flight-feathers, all marked with black. Flight owl-like; very skulking and usually crepuscular; walks deliberately with lowered head and hunched shoulders, or clambers in reeds; if alarmed, stretches neck, points bill up, and sways with the reeds, eyes swivelled forward. *Ad* Golden-brown and buff, mottled, barred and striped with blackish and brown; black crown and moustaches; bill yellowish, legs green. *Juv* Paler, with browner crown, moustaches and breast-stripes; as ad after moult in Jul–Nov. VOICE Harsh *kau-kau* in flight; ♂ foghorn-like boom *upwoomp* in spring audible for 2–5 km. HABITAT Large reedbeds; reedy patches by lakes or rivers in winter. NEST In old reeds, 4–6 eggs, Apr–Jul; 1 brood. FOOD Fish, frogs, insects. RANGE Some winter dispersal and immigration from Continent, Nov–Feb (Aug–Apr). COMPARE American Bittern, imm Night Heron (254).

Grey Heron *Ardea cinerea* 90–100 cm (*c*37 in). Tall, with heavy bill, long neck and legs; grey and white marked with black. Flight slow, with deep flaps of bowed wings, neck retracted in bulge and legs extended; walks deliberately, often stands motionless in or near water, with neck erect or hunched; not shy. *Ad* Blue-grey upperbody, contrasting white head and neck to belly, with black crest and markings; yellow bill and brown legs turn orange or red in spring. *Juv* More compact; generally dark grey (some mainly brownish), inc top of head, with little white on face, foreneck and underbody, and lacking clear black marks; bill browner, legs dark grey. *1st year* After moult in Sep–Feb, bluer-grey above (inc forehead and crown), whiter cheeks and underbody, some black on foreneck, slight crest. *2nd–3rd year* Variable: more as ad, but duller, greyer, with mainly grey forehead and crown; black crest and markings, pale neck and bill/leg colours assumed gradually. VOICE Harsh *frarnk* in flight; much noise and bill-snapping at

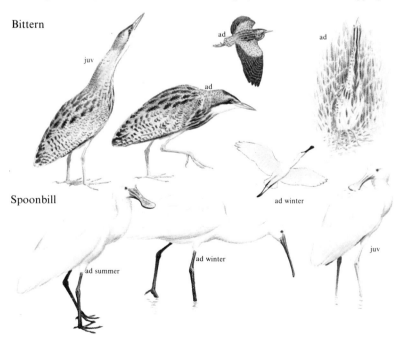

Bittern

juv

ad

ad

ad

Spoonbill

ad winter

ad summer

ad winter

juv

nest. HABITAT Rivers, lakes, marshes, estuaries; nests may be far from water. NEST Colonial; in trees, locally in bushes, reeds, long heather or on cliff-ledges or rocks, 3–5 eggs, Feb–Aug; 1–2 broods. FOOD Fish, frogs, voles, insects. RANGE Much post-breeding dispersal, also immigration from Norway/Low Countries, Aug–Apr. COMPARE Brown juv with Purple Heron (256); albinos stockier than Great White Egret (256), with less snaky neck.

IBISES, SPOONBILLS (Threskiornithidae)

Spoonbill *Platalea leucorodia* 80–90 cm (*c*34 in). White, heron-like, with un-mistakable spatulate bill, long neck and legs. Flies slowly, also glides, with sagging neck and trailing legs; sweeps bill-tip from side to side in shallows. *Ad summer* White with loose crest, yellowish gorget; yellow-tipped blackish bill, bare yellow throat, black legs. *Ad winter* No crest or gorget. *Juv* As ad winter, but black tips to primaries; pink bill, throat and legs. *1st year* Bill mainly yellow with blackish base;

legs olive-grey, then slate; but no crest or gorget, some black on wing-tips. VOICE Silent. HABITAT Marshes, estuaries. FOOD Insects, fish, crustaceans, molluscs. RANGE Scarce visitor from Netherlands, all months, esp May–Jul in E Anglia, Sep–Mar elsewhere; bred in Br to *c*1650. COMPARE Egrets (256), swans (58).

Bittern		B2 W3 S3 A3

Grey Heron		B5 W5 S5 A5

Spoonbill		B0 W1 S2 A2

Grey Heron

imm

ad

ad spring

brown juv

grey juv

ad

SWANS, GEESE, DUCKS (Anatidae)

Mute Swan *Cygnus olor* 145–160 cm (*c*60 in). Very large, with rounded head, curved neck, longish tail, wings often arched; orange bill has black base and knob. Loud rhythmic throbbing of slow powerful wing-beats; swims with bill slanted downwards; immerses head and neck to feed, or up-ends; waddles clumsily on land; takes off with laboured flaps, pattering feet; often gregarious; not shy. *Ad* All white, some stained rusty on head or belly by ferrous water; bill pink to red-orange, with black knob (larger on ♂ in spring), basal triangle and edges; legs black (pink or grey on 'Polish' variety). *Juv* Unevenly dingy grey-brown and whitish ('Polish' all white); bill grey with black base, no knob. *1st year* Slowly whitens, but juv wings and tail kept until Jun–Aug; bill turns pink, then dull orange, grows knob. *2nd winter* Until Jan or later, some show brown spots and shaft-streaks on head, wings, rump. VOICE Snorts and hisses near nest. HABITAT Any fresh or salt water from rivers and lakes to marshes, estuaries, bays; also fields nearby. NEST By water on banks, islets, marshes, or among reeds, 2–9 eggs, end Mar–Jun; 1 brood. FOOD Water-plants; also grazes on land. RANGE Resident, but much local movement.

Bewick's Swan *Cygnus columbianus* 116–128 cm (*c*48 in). Resembles Whooper Swan, but smaller, stockier, with shorter and thicker neck, more rounded head, slightly concave culmen and truncated yellow base to bill. Flight more goose-like, with faster beats; swims and walks easily with neck less stiffly erect; equally gregarious; less shy. *Ad* All white, but some stained rusty (*cf* Mute); bill black with yellow base rounded, jagged or squared at front behind nostrils. *Juv* Slightly paler and greyer above than Whooper, with browner head; bill darker pink towards tip. *1st–2nd winter* Changes as Whooper, but body whitens more quickly. VOICE Repeated honking, sharper, more abrupt than Whooper, more baying in chorus; herds produce musical babble.

Mute Swan

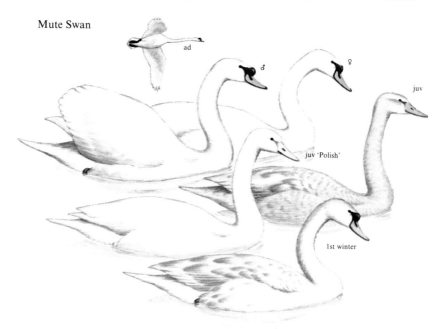

ad

♂

♀

juv

juv 'Polish'

1st winter

HABITAT Floods and lakes, adjacent fields. FOOD As Whooper; digs for roots. RANGE Winter visitor from N Russia/NW Siberia, Nov–Mar.

Whooper Swan *Cygnus cygnus* 145–160 cm (*c*60 in). Size of Mute Swan, but distinguished by long flat profile of head and stiffly erect neck; wings not arched, tail short; bill black with pointed yellow base. Wings make only swishing noise in flight; swims with neck straight, bill horizontal; feeds as Mute, but forages more on land, walking easily with neck straight or kinked back; highly gregarious; wary. *Ad* All white, but often stained rusty (*cf* Mute); bill black with yellow base extending in wedge usually to below or beyond nostrils. *Juv* Brown-grey and whitish; bill dirty pink with dark tip. *1st year* Body whitens somewhat in Jan–Mar; bill turns black at tip, whiter and then yellowish at base, developing ad pattern. *2nd winter* Usually some brown feathers on head or wings, dark shaft-streaks on scapulars. VOICE Loud *whoop-whoop*,

trumpet-like in flock. HABITAT Winters on bays, estuaries, floods, large lakes, adjacent fields. NEST On loch banks or islets, marsh hummocks, 3–5 eggs, mid May–Jun; 1 brood. FOOD Waterplants, also grass, grain, potatoes. RANGE Winter visitor from Iceland/ ?N Eurasia, Oct– Apr; few summer in NBr/Ir.

Mute Swan · B5 W5 S5 A5

Bewick's Swan · B0 W4 S4 A4

Whooper Swan · B1 W4 S4 A4

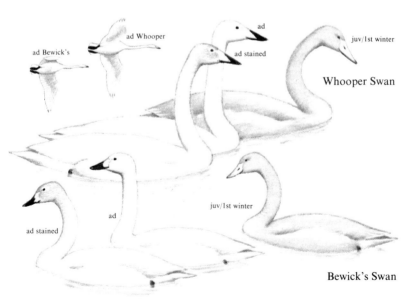

ad Whooper

ad Bewick's

ad

ad stained

juv/1st winter

Whooper Swan

ad stained

ad

juv/1st winter

Bewick's Swan

Bean Goose *Anser fabalis* 71–89 cm (28–35 in). Larger, taller, longer-necked than Pink-footed, slimmer than Greylag; brown with dark head/neck, longish black and orange bill, orange legs; in flight, all dark (forewings hardly paler) with long head, thin neck. Actions much as Greylag; often among other geese; shyer than Pink-footed, feeds more slowly, seldom on stubble. *Ad W race (A.f. fabalis)* Head and neck dark brown, blacker on forehead, but some show white by base of bill (*cf* White-fronted, 62); otherwise, dull brown above with bold pale bars, and buff-brown below with obscurely banded darker flanks and belly; bill orange with black nail, variable black at base. *Juv/1st winter* Duller with less clear pattern on back/flanks, grey-orange on bill/legs; as ad with moult in Oct–Apr. *Ad W tundra race (A.f. rossicus)* Smaller, bill and neck shorter, forehead steeper; bill black with narrow orange band. VOICE Not noisy: *ung-unk* or *ow-ow*, lower and more braying than Pink-footed. HABITAT Winters in wet pastures. FOOD Grass, grain, crops. RANGE Scarce winter visitor from N Europe, end Dec–Mar (Oct–Apr).

Pink-footed Goose *Anser brachyrhynchus* 61–76 cm (24–30 in). Compact, with round head and short neck; pinkish-brown with dark head/neck, short blackish and pink bill, and pink legs; forewings ash-grey in flight. Flight faster than Greylag, and more buoyant and tumbling; walks/feeds much more quickly; often large flocks. *Ad* Head and upper neck dark brown, but some show white by base of bill (*cf* White-fronted, 62); otherwise, pinkish-grey above with pale bars, and pinkish-brown below with obscurely banded darker flanks and belly; bill pink with black nail, variable blackish at base, legs pink. *Juv/1st winter* Darker, browner, with less clear pattern on back; as ad with moult in Oct–Feb. VOICE High yelp *wink-wink*, cackling *ang-ang-ank*. HABITAT Winters on stubble, pastures, crops, locally saltmarshes, roosting on lakes, estuaries, sand-banks. FOOD Grass, grain, cereals, potatoes. RANGE Winter visitor from esp Iceland/Greenland, mid Sep–May.

Greylag Goose *Anser anser* 76–89 cm (30–35 in). Bulky, with big head and thick neck; all brown-grey with triangular orange bill, orange eye-rings and pink legs; forewings bold blue-grey in flight. Flight direct, strong, fast, with glides; flocks in Vs or lines, at times plunging or banking; takes off with short run, or flapping and pattering on water; planes down to land, braking with wings turned forward and tail spread, dropping with rotary flutter; swims well; slow rolling walk; wary. *Ad W race (A.a. anser)* Head to breast buff-grey with indented lines on neck-sides; brown-grey above with pale bars, flanks and belly grey with blackish marks; bill orange with pink tinge behind white tip. *Juv/1st winter* Pattern on back and flanks less clear, no belly marks, legs dull pink; as ad in course of moult in Sep–Jan. *Ad E race (A.a. rubrirostris)* Slightly larger, paler; longer bill all pink but for white nail. VOICE Like farmyard goose: main flight-call loud, deep, sonorous, cackling *aahng-ung-ung*. HABITAT Boggy moorland lochs, heathery coastal islets in NBr (also feral on lakes, gravel pits); winters as Pink-footed, but more on flooded grassland. NEST Among heather or rushes near water, 4–6 eggs, mid Apr–May; 1 brood. FOOD Green plants in summer; grass, grain and roots in winter. RANGE Most breeders sedentary; winter visitor from esp Iceland, mid Oct–mid Apr; E race vagrant.

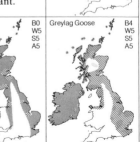

| Bean Goose | B0 W2 S0 A0 |

| Pink-footed Goose | B0 W5 S5 A5 |

| Greylag Goose | B4 W5 S5 A5 |

Bean Goose

fabalis ad *rossicus* ad *fabalis* ad

fabalis ad

juv

Pink-footed Goose

juv ad ad ad

Greylag Goose

anser ad

juv *anser* ad *rubirostris* ad

White-fronted Goose *Anser albifrons* 65-76 cm (26-30 in). Smaller/slimmer than Greylag (60), with squarer head, deep chest, longish pink or yellow bill, orange legs; grey-brown, ad with white face and black-barred belly; in flight, mainly dark (no contrasting forewings) and not unlike Bean Goose (60) when patterns of face and belly not visible, although head and neck shorter, wings longer/narrower. Actions as Greylag, but wing-beats faster, more agile when taking off or in flight, able to rise or turn more sharply than other grey geese; often large flocks, tending to bunch rather than straggle in lines. *Ad Eurasian race (A.a. albifrons)* White around base of bill (rarely extending to forecrown), bordered blackish; otherwise, grey-brown above with pale bars on back (less contrasting than on Bean); buff-brown chest in contrast to darker grey-brown flanks and belly with variable bold black bars or patches; bill pink, but tinged yellow behind white nail. *Juv/1st winter* Forehead blackish, no black bars below; browner and more mottled, with indistinct pale bars on back, and duller bill and legs, not unlike Greylag; as ad in course of moult in Nov-Mar. *Ad Greenland race (A.a. flavirostris)* Slightly larger and darker, more olive-brown than Eurasian race, with less white on forehead, less contrasting chest, usually more black patches below; bill longer, heavier, orange-yellow. *Juv/1st winter* Darker than juv Eurasian race, more olive-brown above; bill dull orange-yellow. VOICE Musical *kow-yow* very dog-like in flock, also loud buzzing and, in flight, high laughing *lyo-lyok*. HABITAT Wet grassland, saltmarshes, peat bogs and fields, roosting on estuaries, floods. FOOD Grasses, clover, grain, winter wheat, potatoes. RANGE Winter visitor from arctic Russia/Greenland: Eurasian race mainly Dec-mid Mar, esp England/Wales; Greenland race mainly mid Oct-Apr, esp Ir, also W Scotland/W Wales. COMPARE Lesser White-fronted Goose (258).

Snow Goose *Anser caerulescens* 64-79 cm (25-31 in). Medium to large, with stout bill, oval head; either all white with

black wing-tips, or mainly blue-grey with white head. Actions as Greylag (60); agile on ground and in air; often with other geese. *Ad Lesser race (A.c. caerulescens)* Either all white except black primaries, blue-grey primary coverts and often orange-stained head; or ('Blue Goose') dusky blue-grey above and grey-brown below, with white head/upper neck, bold white-edged blackish elongated scapulars and tertials, and white undertail-coverts, axillaries and often belly; intermediates between these phases vary, but often much white below; bill always red with black cutting edges/white tip, legs red-pink. *Ad Greater race (A.c. atlanticus)* As white Lesser, but larger, stockier, with longer and heavier bill, thicker neck, longer legs. *Juv/1st winter (except blue Lesser)* Mainly grey-brown above, with paler grey-white forehead, cheeks and underparts; dark line through eyes, mottled back and coverts, patterned scapulars, black primaries; bill and legs dark grey; as ad in course of moult in Oct-Mar. *Juv/1st winter (blue Lesser)* Much as ad but head and neck slate-brown; browner above, with shorter and less contrasted scapulars and tertials, and paler below; head mottled white *c*Nov-Feb. VOICE Harsh abrupt *kaah*. HABITAT Marshes, wet grassland, stubble, roosting on water. FOOD Grasses, winter wheat, water-plants, grain. RANGE Scarce migrant from arctic America/NW Greenland, mainly Oct-Mar, esp Ir/NBr, but position confused by escapes from captivity (wild birds often with Greenland White-fronted). NOTE **Ross's Goose** *A. rossii* sometimes escapes too: similar to white Snow, but smaller with rounder head, no black on tiny bill.

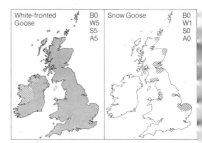

White-fronted Goose

albifrons ad

albifrons juv

flavirostris juv

albifrons ad
light barring

flavirostris ad

albifrons ad
heavy barring

Snow Goose

caerulescens ad
white

caerulescens ad
white

atlanticus ad

caerulescens ad
'Blue Goose'

caerulescens ad
'Blue Goose'

caerulescens juv
white

caerulescens juv
'Blue Goose'

Canada Goose *Branta canadensis* 55–110 cm, but most in Br/Ir *c*90–100 cm (*c*36–40 in). Usually big and long-necked; grey-brown with black head/neck, whitish chest and white 'throat-strap'. Actions much as Greylag (60); dips head and up-ends; not shy. *Ad* Head/neck glossy black; buff-white tips on upperparts and flanks form bars. *Juv/1st winter* Head/neck duller brown-black, throat-strap tinged brown till early autumn, bars on upperparts/flanks less even; as ad in course of moult from autumn on. *Vagrant races* Probably *B.c. hutchinsii* (small, pale) and *B.c. parvipes* (medium, pale) and perhaps *B.c. minima* (small, dark) and *B.c. interior* (large, darkish): size, colour and proportions of bill, neck and legs vary between *c*10 N American races. VOICE Trumpeting flight-call *wah-onk* rises on 2nd syllable. HABITAT Lakes, gravel pits, rivers, marshes, farmland nearby; also certain estuaries. NEST On lake islets or marsh hummocks, 5–7 eggs, end Mar–May; 1 brood. FOOD Grass, water-plants, clover, cereals, grain. RANGE Introduced in 17th century; some moult-migration and local dispersal; small vagrants from N America with Greenland White-fronted or Barnacle Geese in Ir and W Scotland most winters.

Barnacle Goose *Branta leucopsis* 58–69 cm (23–27 in). Usually larger than Brent, with longer neck and small bill; black, grey and white, with creamy face and black crown, neck and breast; wings show grey in flight. Actions as other geese, but in general less wary; more terrestrial than Brent. *Ad* Face white or creamy, black from bill to or through eyes; crown to breast black, upperparts black to blue-grey with broad white-edged black bars, flanks delicately barred greyish-white. *Juv/1st winter* Face tinged grey, blacks browner, wings duller with buff bars, flanks pale grey-brown; more as ad in course of moult in *c*Oct–Mar, but wings with buff bars till 2nd autumn. VOICE Shrill fast barks like yapping dog; muffled growls when feeding. HABITAT Winters on coastal machair, pastures, marshes. FOOD Grass, clover, rush or sedge seeds. RANGE Winter

visitor from NE Greenland/Spitsbergen (few USSR), end Sep–mid May.

Brent Goose *Branta bernicla* 56–61 cm 22–24 in). Small, stocky, with short neck and legs, longish wings; dark, with black head to breast, whitish neck-patches, white stern accentuated by tiny black tail. Fast wing-beats; flocks fly in undulating lines; swims on sea, stern high, also up-ends; walks daintily; seldom with other geese. *Ad Dark-bellied race (B.b. bernicla)* Ragged white neck-patches; little contrast between black of head to breast and grey-black upperparts or slate-grey underbody, but whitish barring on flanks. *Ad Pale-bellied race (B.b. hrota)* Underbody much paler, upperparts browner. *Ad E Siberian/NW American race (B.b. nigricans)* Broader white neck-patches almost join; very dark with more contrasted whitish flanks. *Juv/1st winter* Head to breast browner, no contrast on flanks, no neck-patches at first, but pale lines on wings; 2 main races often similar below, but still distinct above; as ads with moult in Oct–Feb, but lines on wings till 2nd autumn. VOICE Guttural *krrook*, clamour in flocks. HABITAT Mudflats and sea, locally on adjacent grass/cereals. FOOD Eelgrass, green algae, salt-marsh plants. RANGE Winter visitor: Dark-bellied from USSR, esp Nov–Mar, E/SBr; Pale-bellied from Greenland/Spitsbergen, esp Oct–Apr, Ir and NE England; *nigricans* vagrant.

Canada Goose

ad

parvipes ad

ad

juv

hutchinsii ad

minima ad

minima ad

Barnacle Goose

ad

ad

ad

juv

Brent Goose

bernicla
1st winter

bernicla ad

bernicla ad .

hrota juv

nigricans ad

hrota ad

Egyptian Goose *Alopochen aegyptiacus*
66–72 cm (*c*27 in). Stout, heavy-billed,
long-legged sheldgoose; mainly rusty or
olive-grey above, with paler head and
underparts, chestnut 'goggles', collar and
breast-patch, and bold white forewings
above and below in flight. Flight fast and
goose-like on broad wings; stands upright
and spends much time on land, also
perching on trees, but swims readily, stern
high, and even dives; usually in pairs or
family parties; often somewhat wary. *Ad*
Proportions of red-brown and grey vary:
darkest (esp in fresh plumage) show much
chestnut at base of bill, round eyes, down
hindneck, on collar and in patch on breast,
with mantle and scapulars rusty-brown;
palest (esp in worn plumage) have less or
almost no chestnut on head, narrower
collar and smaller or no breast-patch, and
brown to olive-grey mantle and scapulars;
rump and tail black; white wing-coverts
(partly hidden at rest) contrast with black
primaries and metallic-green or purple
secondaries in flight; bill largely pink, legs
pink to purplish-pink. *Juv/1st winter* Like
dull ad without chestnut on head, neck
and breast; wing-patches mainly pale
grey-brown; bill and legs yellowish-grey;
as ad with moult in Aug–Dec. VOICE Often
silent; breeding ♂ loud hoarse wheezing
or chuffing; ♀ cackles harshly; both hiss.
HABITAT Lakes, pools and adjacent
pastures, parks and wet open woodland.
NEST In thick cover or in holes in ground
or in trees, 8–9 eggs, late Mar–early May;
1 brood. FOOD Grass, plant leaves. RANGE
Introduced from Africa in 18th century.
COMPARE Ruddy Shelduck in flight (258).

Shelduck *Tadorna tadorna* 58–64 cm (*c*24
in). Long-headed, rather goose-like duck;
mainly white with bold contrasting areas
of black, dark green and chestnut. Flight
slower and steadier than typical ducks,
parties tend to form Vs or lines; walks and
runs easily; spends much time on mud or
sand, but swims well, though ads rarely
dive; usually in pairs or parties. *Ad ♂*
White with greenish-black head, chestnut
body-band, black outer scapulars,
primaries and tail-end, green-glossed

Egyptian Goose

ad

juv

grey ad

juv

red-brown ad

secondaries, chestnut tertials and blackish belly-stripe; bill pink-red, becoming bright red with prominent knob in spring, legs reddish-pink. *Ad* ♀ As ♂, but head duller with, when worn, some white round bill; chestnut belt paler and narrower; scapulars duller and belly-stripe narrower; bill duller pink with black tip and no knob. ♂ *eclipse* (variably in late Jun–early Dec) At extreme, head dull brown-black with hoary white face; chestnut on mantle paler, mottled blackish and white; underparts with only traces of chestnut and black; when flightless (for c1 month in Jul–mid Oct), looks still whiter without black flight-feathers. ♀ *eclipse* As ♂ eclipse, but head paler, face much whiter, and underparts white but for some tawny at sides of breast. *Juv* Crown, hindneck and upperparts dark grey-brown, contrasting with white face, spectacles and underparts; tail sooty-brown; forewings pale grey and all but outermost flight-feathers tipped white; bill and legs pinkish-white. *1st winter* Much as ads by Dec, but duller with more

broken patterns (esp ♀s), and juv wings retained till at least spring. VOICE Noisy in spring and summer: ♂ various melodious whistling calls; ♀ loud laughing *ak-ak-ak* and longer growling *aark-aark*. HABITAT Sandy shores, muddy estuaries, locally inland waters. NEST In rabbit burrows, other holes, thick cover, 8–10 eggs, May–Jun; 1 brood (many join into crèches). FOOD Mainly molluscs, crustaceans, insects. RANGE Many make moult-migration to NW Germany (also *eg* Somerset, Wash, Forth) for cJul–Nov, then return; some winter immigrants from esp Scandinavia.

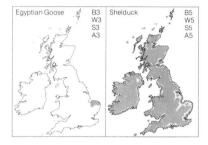

Egyptian Goose | B3 W3 S3 A3 | Shelduck | B5 W5 S5 A5

Shelduck

juv

juv

♂

♂ eclipse

1st winter

♂

♀ eclipse

♀

Ruddy Duck *Oxyura jamaicensis* 36–43 cm
($c15\frac{1}{2}$ in). Dumpy stifftail-duck, with
broad and slightly upcurved blue or grey
bill, contrasted 2-tone head, short neck,
short rounded wings; longish tail often
held upright; summer ♂ black, white and
chestnut; other plumages dark brown, off-
white and barred. Swims buoyantly, dives
or just sinks; gregarious; in courtship,
stretches up neck and tail, erects ear-tufts,
fans tail, shakes or rolls head, puffs up
neck and breast, slaps chest with bill;
seldom leaves water, and walks
awkwardly; flight rapid and whirring. ♂
summer Bright blue bill, glossy black cap,
white cheeks, and mainly rich chestnut
body with bold white undertail-coverts;
tail and wings brown with white central
underwings. ♀ *summer* Similar pattern,
but bill blue-grey, cap dark brown, cheeks
off-white divided by indistinct dark line,
upperparts brown tinged rufous, underparts barred buff and brown; more white
on underwings. ♂ *winter* Eclipse lasts
*c*Aug–Mar; resembles ♀, but cap dull
black, cheeks still white, back often mixed
with chestnut. ♀ *winter* Back browner,
more barred, no rufous; cheeks greyer,
with ill-defined line. *Juv* As ♀, but duller,
greyer, scaled on breast and more clearly
barred on back, flanks, also undertail; as
♀ from moult in Aug–Oct. VOICE Courting
♂ low belch, grunt and non-vocal rattling
and slapping with bill; ♀ high squeak, hiss
and distinct bill-rattle. HABITAT Lakes,
gravel pits, with reedy edges; open
reservoirs in winter. NEST Platform in
emergent reeds, rushes, 6–10 eggs, mid
Apr–Sep; 1 brood. FOOD Insect larvae,
seeds of water plants. RANGE Introduced
from N America, breeding ferally since
1960; sedentary but for local seasonal
movements. NOTE Eurasian **White-headed
Duck** *O. leucocephala* does escape, could
occur wild: recognised by swollen bill-
base, no white under tail; ♂ mainly white
head, greyer back; ♀ stronger cheek-line.

Mandarin *Aix galericulata* 41–47 cm (*c*17
in). Large-headed perching-duck with
thick neck, longish tail and yellowish legs;
♂ flamboyant with multicoloured crest,

Ruddy Duck

♂ summer   ♀ summer   ♂ summer   ♀ summer

♂ displaying   ♂ summer   ♀ summer

♂ winter   ♀ winter   juv

orange side-whiskers and wing-sails; ♀ crested grey head, white spectacles and cream-spotted below; in flight, primaries white-edged, secondaries white-tipped and speculum green. Flight fast, agile among trees; swims high on water, tail often raised, but seldom dives; in courtship, ♂ erects crest and sails, spreads whiskers, stretches neck up, shakes or jerks head, or flicks bill; walks easily, perches on branches; gregarious in autumn to winter. *Ad ♂* Bill red; exotic shape and plumage dominated by metallic sheens, cinnamon, orange-chestnut, white, black. *Ad ♀* Bill brown to pink; head mainly greyish, with white spectacles, white beside bill to throat; olive-brown above, breast/flanks greyer with oval creamy spots. *♂ eclipse* (*c*May–Sep) Becomes much more as ♀, but bill dull red, spectacles less clear, no white beside bill, breast/flanks streaked buff. *♀ eclipse* As ♂ eclipse, but bill browner, head paler grey, crest shorter, upperbody duller. *Juv* As ♀ eclipse but more uniform above with indistinct head-markings, and streaked/spotted sepia below. VOICE Often silent: courting ♂ whistles; ♀ loud sharp Coot-like *kek*, repeated plaintive *ak*. HABITAT Pools, lakes, slow rivers, edged by broadleaved woods. NEST In tree-holes, or rarely on ground in cover, 9–12 eggs, mid Apr–mid Jun; 1 brood. FOOD Acorns, chestnuts, beechmast, seeds, insects, snails. RANGE Introduced from E Asia, breeding ferally since *c*1930s; sedentary. NOTE Similar American **Wood Duck** *A. sponsa* often at large in Br: ♂ darker-headed, lacks sails and whiskers; ♀ whiter round eyes and on throat, darker and glossier above, bill-base U-shaped (not straight).

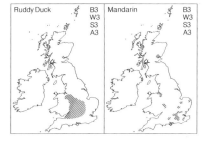

| Ruddy Duck | B3 W3 S3 A3 | Mandarin | B3 W3 S3 A3 |

Mandarin

Wigeon *Anas penelope* 43–48 cm (*c*18 in).
Short-necked dabbling-duck with small
bill, steep forehead, pointed tail, narrow
wings: ♂ has chestnut and cream head,
mainly grey body, and white forewings; ♀
variably rufous or greyer, but bold white
belly as ♂. Flight fast; often swims with
neck retracted, up-ends infrequently;
walks easily, feeds much on land; highly
gregarious. *Ad* ♂ Head chestnut with
creamy-yellow forehead and crown; body
grey with pinkish breast, white band of
wing-coverts showing along sides, and
white strip in front of black stern; in flight,
white forewings and belly. *Ad* ♀ Variably
rufous or greyer, and broadly or narrowly
barred paler on brown upperparts, but
head always pink-brown spotted with
black, breast more or less tinged pink,
flanks cinnamon; in flight, white belly,
blackish speculum edged with white, grey-
brown forewings. ♂ *eclipse* (Jun–Oct) As
ad ♀, with similar variations, but crown and
mantle darker, head, breast and flanks
more rufous; white forewings still show.
♀ *eclipse* (Jul–Nov) As ad ♀, but head and
neck more spotted, and mantle, breast and
flanks darker with fewer bars. *Juv* ♂
Resembles ♀ eclipse, including colour
variations, but upperparts blacker, belly
sometimes mottled; forewings paler,
greyer and often some white. *Juv* ♀ As juv
♂, but head paler yellow-brown, mantle
more uniform, forewings more as ad ♀.
1st winter As ads with moult in Oct–Apr,
but juv wings kept at least in part to 2nd
autumn. VOICE ♂ loud whistle *whee-oo*; ♀
rhythmic purring growl. HABITAT Breeds
by lochs, pools and rivers in moorland,
marshes and wooded country with
adjacent cover; winters along muddy
coasts and on fresh water. NEST In thick
cover, 7–9 eggs, May–Jun; 1 brood. FOOD
Many water-plants, grasses; eelgrass on
coast in winter. RANGE Breeders move only
short distances; huge immigration from
Iceland/N Europe/W Siberia, Sep–Mar.
COMPARE American Wigeon (258).

Gadwall *Anas strepera* 48–54 cm (*c*20 in).
Rather uniformly-coloured dabbling-
duck with abrupt forehead, white

Wigeon

1st winter ♂

♀

♂

♂ eclipse

barred rufous ♀

♂

plain grey ♀

juv ♂

speculum and belly; ♂ greyish with black stern; ♀ greyer than ♀ Mallard (72) with smaller, orange-sided bill. Flight fast, pointed wings similar to Wigeon; floats high in water; in pairs or small parties. *Ad* ♂ Head and neck grey-brown peppered with black, darker at rear; otherwise dark grey, including tail and primaries, but for black stern, black crescents on breast and buff on scapulars; in flight black and white speculum, chestnut wing-coverts, white belly. *Ad* ♀ Head browner than ♂, spotting coarser; like other ♀ *Anas* but greyer with grey-brown tail; bill has well-defined orange-yellow sides, legs orange-yellow; in flight, white speculum as ♂ (sometimes much reduced), chestnut on coverts (sometimes absent), white belly. ♂ *eclipse* (Jun–Aug) Much as ad ♀, including bill, but darker and less patterned above, more streaked on head, sometimes black spots on belly; wings still as ad ♂. ♀ *eclipse* (Jun–Sep) As ad ♀, but darker above, more spotted on head, dusky spots on belly. *Juv* Like ad ♀, but more blackish above, underparts strongly marked with brown; ♂ with more black and chestnut on wings than ♀. *1st winter* In Aug–Nov becomes as eclipse ♂♀, then ads, but juv wings and some juv plumage often retained to Mar or later. VOICE ♂ croaks and whistles; ♀ quacks and chatters. HABITAT Breeds by lakes and pools with extensive reeds; winters also on more open lakes, even estuaries. NEST In thick cover, 8–12 eggs, late Apr–end Jun; 1 brood. FOOD Water-plants. RANGE Most English birds introduced, sedentary; many Scottish winter in Ir; immigration from Iceland/N Europe, Aug–Apr.

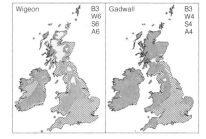

| Wigeon | B3 W6 S6 A6 | Gadwall | B3 W4 S4 A4 |

Gadwall

♂

♀

♂

♀

juv ♂

1st year ♂

♂ eclipse

Teal *Anas crecca* 34–38 cm (*c*14 in). Compact dabbling-duck with oval head, short neck, narrow pointed wings, told by small size alone from all regulars except scarce summer Garganey (74); ♂ chestnut and green head often simply looks darker than body, white line above wings and creamy stern-patches show best; ♀ dark, mottled, with obscure face-pattern, dark forewings, clear speculum, light patch at tail-sides (*cf* Garganey). Flight fast, swerving, wader-like, often low; shoots up from water; swims daintily, rarely dives; walks clumsily; often highly gregarious. *Ad ♂ Eurasian race (A.c. crecca)* White horizontal scapular line; in flight, green and black speculum with broad buff-white bar in front and faint whitish line behind. *Ad ♀* Some darker above, others paler or more barred; breast mottled, breast-sides with dark crescents, flanks streaked; bill dark or olive-grey, edges yellowish dotted with black; speculum as ♂ but bars thin, white. *♂ eclipse* (*c*Jun–Oct) Like ad ♀, but breast more spotted, breast-sides and flanks with wavy bars, wings as ad ♂; bill blackish, edges plain yellow to olive. *♀ eclipse* (*c*Jul–Nov) As ♂ eclipse, but breast-sides/flanks streaked, wings and bill as ad ♀. *Juv ♂* Much as ♂ eclipse, including wings, but spotted lower breast and belly; bill mainly pinkish; much as ad after moult Aug–Nov. *Juv ♀* As juv ♂, but wings as ad ♀, pinkish bill dotted on lower sides. *♂ American race = Green-winged Teal (A.c.carolinensis)* Vertical white crescent on breast-sides, no scapular line, less cream outline to green eye-curves. VOICE ♂ high, far-carrying, bell-like whistle *preep* or *krit* and quiet piping notes; ♀ as Mallard. HABITAT Breeds near moorland pools and burns, also marshes, reedy lakes; many winter on reservoirs, also estuaries. NEST In thick cover, 8–11 eggs, mid Apr–early Jun; 1 brood. FOOD Aquatic seeds, plants, invertebrates. RANGE Often resident, but some go south as far as Iberia; huge immigration from Iceland/N Europe, Sep–Apr; American race vagrant (total 160: Oct–Jun, wide-scattered). COMPARE Blue-winged and Baikal Teals (260).

Teal

Mallard *Anas platyrhynchos* 55-62 cm (*c*23 in). Very common bulky dabbling-duck with longish bill, head and neck; ♂ metallic green head, white neck-ring; ♀ mottled brown. Flight fast, with shallow beats; rises easily from water; walks well, body level; swims high with tail raised, up-ends, rarely dives; gregarious. *Ad* ♂ Pattern unmistakable; note curled black central feathers on white tail; legs orange-red, bill yellow to olive; forewings greyish in flight, purple-blue speculum edged black and white. *Ad* ♀ Buff variably patterned blackish; plain throat/foreneck, whitish tail; legs as ♂, bill dark with greenish to dull orange sides; forewings browner than ♂, speculum narrower. ♂ *eclipse* (*c*Jun–Sep) As ad ♀ but darker, more uniform above, paler greyer face, brown-centred white tail, breast often tinged chestnut, wings as ad ♂; bill dull olive-yellow. ♀ *eclipse* (*c*Jul–Oct) Little change: more uniform above, crown darker. *Juv* ♂ Like ♂ eclipse, but underparts narrowly streaked, tail grey-brown marked with buff; bill red-brown slowly darkening, legs yellowish; much as ad after moult *c*Aug–Feb. *Juv* ♀ As juv ♂, but back more marked buff above, wings as ad ♀; bill paler, often dotted along edge. VOICE ♂ weak nasal *raib*, also whistles, grunts; ♀ quacks, including laughing decrescendo series. HABITAT Any fresh or salt water; also fields. NEST In ground cover or tree-holes, may be 2 km from water, 9–12 eggs, Mar–mid Jul; 1 brood. FOOD Seeds, plants, invertebrates. RANGE Resident; also passage/winter visitor from N Europe, Sep–Apr, esp EBr. COMPARE Black Duck (258).

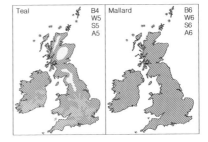

| Teal | B4 W5 S5 A5 | Mallard | B6 W6 S6 A6 |

Mallard

Pintail *Anas acuta* 53–59 cm (*c*22 in) +
< 10 cm elongated tail of ♂. Slender
dabbling-duck with longish bill and neck,
and pointed tail; ♂ grey with chocolate
head and white neck; ♀ paler and greyer
than other *Anas*, with conspicuous eyes
and grey bill. Flight fast with rapid beats,
often in lines or Vs; floats high (neck
often straight and tail raised), up-ends;
walks gracefully; gregarious. *Ad* ♂ White
underparts with stripe extending up side
of chocolate head; back and flanks grey,
with black and cream scapulars; long
black central tail-feathers; stern black and
cream; in flight, bronze-green speculum
shows less than buff line in front and white
behind. *Ad* ♀ Pale, greyish; crescents on
flanks, bill blue-grey; in flight, obscure
speculum bordered with white at rear,
pointed tail mainly brown, underwings
darker than whitish belly. ♂ *eclipse* (Jul–
Sep) As ad ♀, but crown blacker, upperparts greyer and more uniform, flanks less
boldly marked, tail blacker and more
pointed, wings as ad ♂. ♀ *eclipse* (Aug–
Nov) As ad ♀ but paler above, upperparts

more narrowly marked, belly often more
spotted. *Juv* ♂ As ad ♀ but darker, back
and flanks browner barred with white,
belly heavily marked; wings as ad ♂, but
borders to speculum narrower. *Juv* ♀ As
juv ♂, but mantle unbarred, wings as ad
♀ with narrower border to speculum. *1st
winter* During Sep–Nov becomes like
eclipse ♂♀, then ads, but juv wings kept
and some juv plumage on upperparts and
belly. VOICE ♂ low whistle and long nasal
whee, ♀ quacks and growls, but both
usually silent in flight. HABITAT Breeds by
moorland pools, lochs with drier shores,
also in marshes in E Anglia; winters on
estuaries and fenland floods. NEST In short
cover, 7–9 eggs, late Apr–Jun; 1 brood.
FOOD Water-plants, invertebrates. RANGE
Some breeding sites irregular; many immigrants from Iceland/N Europe, Sep–Apr.

Garganey *Anas querquedula* 37–41 cm (*c*15
in). Small dabbling-duck with flattish
crown and slender neck; ♂ brown with
white supercilia, greyish flanks, drooping
scapulars, blue-grey forewings; ♀ like

Pintail

♂

♀

♂

♀

juv ♀

♂ eclipse

juv ♂

pale ♀ Teal (72), but more contrasted head, no pale patch at tail-sides. Flight fast and direct; swims low, dabbles but seldom up-ends; walks very awkwardly; in pairs or small parties, unobtrusive. *Ad ♂* Rich brown head with white curve from eyes to nape; upperparts black-brown mottled paler, with long scapulars striped with blue-grey, black and white; breast pink-brown with blackish markings, undertail white spotted with brown; flanks greyish in flight, forewings blue-grey, underwings white with dark leading edges, and sharp division between breast and white belly. *Ad ♀* Like ♀ Teal, but white throat, pale patch by base of bill and clearer supercilia contrasting with blackish eyestripes and line below eyes; speculum greyer with more white at front and esp rear; underwings as ♂. *♂ eclipse* (Jun–Feb) As ad ♀, but crown darker, sides of head more streaked, upperparts with narrower grey and buff feather-edges; wings as ad ♂. *♀ eclipse* (Jul–Feb) As ♂ eclipse but back-feathers all edged with buff, wings as ad ♀. *Juv ♂* As ad ♀, but

back-feathers edged with grey not buff; all underparts marked brown; wings as ad ♂ but forewings duller, speculum narrower. *Juv ♀* As juv ♂, but feather-edges buff and wings as ad ♀, though speculum dark grey, white borders narrower. *1st winter* Becomes like ads in winter quarters. VOICE ♂ dry crackling rattle, both settled and in flight; ♀ short quack. HABITAT Reedy meres, fens, water meadows. NEST In coarse grass, 8–11 eggs, end Apr–Jun; 1 brood. FOOD Inverte-brates, water-plants. RANGE Summer visitor, Mar–Sep, wintering in Africa.

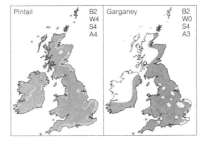

Garganey

Shoveler *Anas clypeata* 47–53 cm (*c*20 in).
Heavy-looking dabbling-duck with huge
spatulate bill, flattened head and small
pointed wings set far back in flight; ♂
white, chestnut and black with blue forewings (*cf* Garganey, 74); ♀ mottled brown
with mainly dark belly, greyer forewings.
Flight much as Wigeon (70), often on
wing in spring; rises easily with wing-
rattle; swims with front end low, dabbling
bill in water or mud, also up-ends; pairs or
small parties often swim in circles head to
tail; pumps head up and down in threat;
walks awkwardly; not shy. *Ad ♂* Green-
black head and chestnut underbody show
against white breast, scapulars and rump-
sides, black back and stern; blue forewings
and green speculum divided by white bar.
Ad ♀ Mottled brown with whitish tail and
orange legs as ♀ Mallard (72), but pink-
tinged feather-edges; wings much duller
than ♂; bill grey-brown edged with
orange-yellow, eyes brown to yellow.
♂ eclipse (*c*Jun–Aug) Resembles ad ♀,
but much darker and more uniform
above, crown black, breast and flanks

richer pink-buff, undertail-coverts clearly
barred, forewings still blue as ad ♂; bill
yellow-brown, eyes rich orange-yellow.
♂ supplementary (*c*Sep–Nov) With further
moult, head black mottled with white (at
peak forming crescent on forecheeks),
breast and scapulars white with black
crescents and bars, flanks chestnut heavily
marked with black. *♀ eclipse* (*c*Jul–Oct)
Darker, less pink than ad ♀; head not as
dark as ♂ eclipse, upperparts with broader
pale fringes, breast/flanks dark brown
edged buff. *Juv* As ♀ eclipse, but crown
blacker, cheeks and underparts grey-
brown or buff with finer markings, tail
brown barred with buff; ♂ forewings grey-
blue, ♀ faintly grey. *1st winter* During
Aug–Apr, becomes as eclipse, then
supplementary (♂) and finally ads. VOICE
♂ hoarse *took-took*; ♀ quacks. HABITAT
Reedy meres with mud and weeds, marshy
pools; open shallow lakes in winter. NEST
In grass, rushes or heather, near water,
8–11 eggs, mid Apr–Jun; 1 brood. FOOD
Small crustaceans, molluscs, insects, and
seeds, water-plants. RANGE Most breeders

Shoveler

emigrate to Mediterranean area; winter visitors from NE Europe/Iceland, Oct–Apr. COMPARE Blue-winged Teal (260).

Red-crested Pochard *Netta rufina* 53–59 cm (*c*22 in). Plump diving-duck, with big round head and longish neck; ♂ red bill, golden-chestnut head, black, white and brown body; ♀ brown with clear-cut pale cheeks and throat (*cf* ♀ Common Scoter, 86). Flight strong with rapid wing-beats, but rises awkwardly, pattering on surface; swims high on water, often up-ends; walks smoothly; wary. *Ad* ♂ Red bill, eyes and legs; bushy golden crown, chestnut head, glossy black neck and underparts, white flank-patches; in flight broad white band on hindwings, white shoulder-line, white underwings. *Ad* ♀ Pale greyish cheeks/throat contrast with dark cap/hindneck; pale brown above and grey-brown below with some barring; eyes brown (redder in spring), bill dark with pink edges and band near tip, legs pink; wing-band tinged grey, underwings white as ♂. ♂ *eclipse* (May–Oct) As ad ♀, but darker above.

mottled whitish on breast, with bushier head; bill, eyes, legs and wings as ad ♂. ♀ *eclipse* (Jun–Oct) As ad ♀, but darker, much white mottling on breast/belly. *Juv* As ad ♀, but greyer above, mottled cheeks, yellow-brown eyes, and duller bill. *1st winter* ♂ After moult Aug–Nov, much as ad, but belly duller and mottled, bill paler, eyes duller. VOICE Migrants quiet. HABITAT Reed-fringed lakes, brackish lagoons; reservoirs on passage. FOOD Water-plants, seeds. RANGE Scarce visitor from Continent, most Sep–Mar, but status confused by escapes which have also nested in SBr.

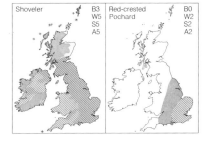

swimming high on water | Shoveler | B3 W5 S5 A5 | Red-crested Pochard | B0 W2 S2 A2

Red-crested Pochard

Pochard *Aythya ferina* 44–48 cm (*c*18 in). Stocky diving-duck with longish bill and forehead, high crown, and sloping back; ♂ chestnut, black and pale grey; ♀ rather yellow-brown with hoary face and greyish back; in flight, broad grey wing-stripe. Flight strong but looks heavy, rapid beats produce slight whistling sound; floats low with tail on surface; dives for food, often with jump, and occasionally up-ends; patters along surface to take off; often stands or sits on shore and walks quite easily; in scattered flocks. *Ad* ♂ Chestnut head, black breast and stern, pale grey back and flanks; eyes red, bill pale grey in middle, dark at ends. *Ad* ♀ Head and forebody yellow-brown with darker crown, hoary pattern round bill, cheeks and throat, often streak behind eyes, and whitish markings on breast; mantle, scapulars and flanks vermiculated grey-brown; eyes brown but reddish in spring, bill as ♂ but darker. ♂ *eclipse* (Jun–Sep) Like ad ♂, but head duller brown with dark crown, throat/neck mottled; breast blackish, speckled paler; back browner-grey. ♀ *eclipse* (Mar–Oct) As ad ♀, but back and scapulars more uniform and darker greyish-brown, flanks yellower-brown. *Juv* As ad ♀, but head and neck duller and greyer without pale streak behind eyes, upperparts also greyer (speckled white on ♂), breast and flanks dark grey variably marked with yellow-buff. *1st winter* ♂ starts to become like ad Sep–Dec, but variable amount of juv feathers remain, esp on underparts, at least until spring; ♀ retains more juv feathers throughout winter. VOICE Mostly silent, but ♂ soft wheeze in courtship, ♀ growl in flight. HABITAT Breeds by lakes and slow rivers with reeds; winters on open fresh water and estuaries. NEST In thick cover, 8–11 eggs, late Apr–early Jul; 1 brood. FOOD Water-plants, invetebrates. RANGE Disperses in winter, some emigrate; also many passage/winter visitors from N/Cent Europe, Sep–Apr.

Ferruginous Duck *Aythya nyroca* 39–43 cm (*c*16 in). Dainty diving-duck with high crown and white under tail; ♂ mainly

Pochard

♀   ♂   ♂ eclipse

♀   ♂

juv ♂   ♀ eclipse

chestnut with white eyes, ♀ duller and browner; in flight, broad white wing-stripe, white underwings and belly. Flight less heavy than other diving-ducks; floats buoyantly with tail more raised; takes off more easily; often skulks. *Ad ♂* Head, neck, breast and flanks rich chestnut, purplish on crown and hindneck, paler below esp towards rear flanks; collar and upperparts black or blackish; white under tail and belly; eyes white, bill grey, paler near black nail and on sides. *Ad ♀* Rather like ♂, but head and underparts browner and paler, some white mottling on throat, upperparts browner, often speckled with yellow-brown; in worn plumage, face paler, upperparts with more obvious buff edges; eyes brown, base and top of bill blacker. *♂ eclipse* (Jun–Sep) As ad ♂, but head and neck duller, crown and hindneck blacker, breast and flanks barred paler. *♀ eclipse* (Apr–Sep) As ad ♀, but head paler and browner, throat and foreneck more mottled grey-brown. *Juv* As ad ♀, but head and neck paler (yellower on sides, greyer

on hindneck, more buff on throat) under-parts more mottled with buff, undertail with dark marks; eyes grey-brown, bill grey-black with paler base. *1st winter* Variable: some much like ad by end Nov, others still with much juv plumage in Mar; ♂ eyes pale grey, ♀ brown. VOICE Migrants silent. HABITAT Shallow fresh water with much vegetation. FOOD Water-plants, invertebrates. RANGE Scarce visitor from E/S Europe, mainly Sep–Apr, but pattern obscured by frequent escapes. NOTE *Aythya* hybrids, esp ♀s of Pochard × Ferruginous Duck, can be very similar.

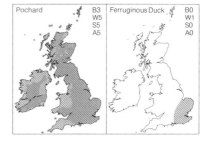

| Pochard | ♂ | B3 W5 S5 A5 | Ferruginous Duck | ♂ | B0 W1 S0 A0 |

Ferruginous Duck

Tufted Duck *Aythya fuligula* 41–45 cm (*c*17 in). Round-headed diving-duck with distinctive drooping crest and short neck; ♂ black with white sides; ♀ mainly dark brown with paler flanks; bold white wing-bar and white underwings in flight. Flight and actions as Pochard (78), but rises more easily; swims with tail on surface, dives with leap; comes ashore readily; in scattered parties or flocks. *Ad* ♂ White flanks and belly contrast with purple-glossed head and otherwise black body; eyes yellow, bill grey-blue (usually white line behind broad black tip). *Ad* ♀ Shorter crest than ♂; mostly dark brown, mantle and breast with cinnamon feather-tips, and often whitish speckling on scapulars; flanks variably mottled whitish, belly white; grey-brown mixed with white under tail, but sometimes all white (*cf* Ferruginous); often white by bill-base ('Scaup-faced'), but usually less than ♀ Scaup and less well defined; eyes as ♂, bill darker grey. ♂ *eclipse* (Jun–Sep) Like ad ♂, but crest tatty, mantle/breast duller and speckled white, flanks grey-brown barred with blackish; may show whitish by bill. ♀ *eclipse* (Mar–Sep) As ad ♀, but browner above, no more than white spot at bill-base; flanks yellower without white markings. *Juv* Generally greyer with buff feather-edges, buff at base of bill, and dark-blotched whitish undertail. *1st winter* Head turns dark brown Aug–Nov, ♂ blacker, ♀ often with some white at base of upper-bill; becomes much like ad by Apr, sometimes by Dec. VOICE ♂ mostly silent, but low whistle in courtship; ♀ growling *kurr-kurr*. HABITAT Lakes and slow rivers with reedy shores, often with islets; winters on more open waters, occasionally sheltered estuaries. NEST Usually in thick cover near water, 8–11 eggs, mid May–Jul; 1 brood. FOOD Invertebrates, water-plants. RANGE Resident, but moves from NBr to Ir; passage/winter visitor from Iceland/N Europe, Sep–Apr. COMPARE Ring-necked Duck (260).

Scaup *Aythya marila* 46–51 cm (*c*19 in). Broad-bodied diving-duck with large bill and crestless head higher at front and

Tufted Duck

♀ 'Scaup-face'

♀ eclipse

1st winter ♂

♂ eclipse

♂

♀

♂

juv

more sloping at back than Tufted; ♂
black at both ends, pale in middle; ♀
like ♀ Tufted but broad white face-band in
winter, whitish patch on ear-coverts in
summer; in flight, wing-bar and underwings as Tufted. Flight and actions as
Pochard (78), but seldom seen on land;
often in large but scattered flocks. *Ad* ♂
Back pale grey, head green-glossed; eyes
yellow, bill blue-grey with narrow black
nail. *Ad* ♀ Head dark brown with white
face, sometimes little whitish on hind-
cheeks; forebody paler with buff fringes;
back with grey tinge; flanks pale yellow-
brown and white; belly white, undertail
grey-brown and white; eyes yellow, bill
dark grey, darkest along ridge. ♂ *eclipse*
(Jun–Aug) Black areas duller than ad ♂,
with some whitish around bill, on hind-
cheeks and on breast; flanks marked
grey-brown. ♀ *eclipse* (Mar–Sep) As ad ♀,
but more uniform and yellower; less white
around bill and, except in fresh plumage,
increasingly clear whitish patch on hind-
cheeks. *Juv* Greyer than ad ♀, with white
often only on chin; belly mottled. *1st*

winter ♂ Starts to become like ad in Aug–
Oct, but plumage often still mixed in
Apr. *1st winter* ♀ Becomes like ♀ eclipse
by spring, but underparts as juv. VOICE
♂ mostly silent; ♀ growling *karr-karr*.
HABITAT Breeds by moorland lakes, pools,
rivers; winters along coasts, esp bays and
estuaries, and visits adjacent fresh water.
NEST As Tufted Duck, 8–11 eggs, May–
Jun; 1 brood. FOOD Invertebrates (esp
molluscs), water-plants. RANGE Passage/
winter from Iceland/N Europe, Oct–Mar;
few summer; nests sporadically NBr.

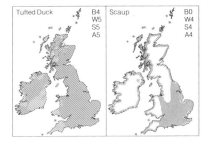

| Tufted Duck | B4 W5 S5 A5 | Scaup | B0 W4 S4 A4 |

Scaup

Eider *Somateria mollissima* 55–61 cm (*c*23 in). Bulky, short-necked, long-bodied sea-duck with long slope of bill and fore-head, eyes set far back, and diagnostic feathering to below nostrils; ♂ only duck with white upperparts and breast, black flanks and belly; ♀ cinnamon-buff mottled and barred with blackish. Flight strong and direct, often low over water in single file, but looks heavy on short, broad wings; take-off laboured; usually swims with head retracted and dives well, or dips head in shallows, occasionally up-ending; walks rather upright with slow rolling gait; regularly rests on rocks and sand-banks, esp in spring and autumn; often in scattered groups or large flocks; not shy. *Ad* ♂ Mainly white except for black crown, flanks, belly, stern and all but front of wings; green patches on rear head, pink-tinged breast, white circles at sides of rump. *Ad* ♀ Head and neck cinnamon-brown, streaked on crown and otherwise spotted black, with indistinct pale buff stripe from lores to behind eyes; rest of body barred cinnamon-buff and blackish,

becoming darker through wear; in flight, 2 white wing-bars border blackish (or sometimes purple-tinged) secondaries. ♂ *eclipse* (Jul–Nov) Flanks, belly and stern remain black to sooty-brown, and wing-coverts and back (but not mantle) white; other white areas become largely black-brown variably mottled with buff, much darker than ♀, and darkest on head but for often conspicuous mottled whitish stripe through eyes corresponding to ♀'s; mantle, scapulars and breast often show white feather-bases and some white feathers. ♀ *eclipse* (Aug–Mar) As ad ♀, but much darker; head sooty-brown with eye-stripes often more conspicuous; upperparts, breast and flanks with narrower pale bars, and rest of underparts dark brown almost unbarred. *Juv* As ad ♀, but upperparts almost uniform dull black on ♂, very dark brown on ♀, and underparts boldly marked with dense, narrow bars of buff and whitish; mottled whitish streak through eyes; cheeks and throat paler buff streaked with dark brown; usually no white wing-bars. *1st*

Eider

year ♂ Very variable, but from Sep/Oct to spring head first grows blacker (but for more contrasted white eye-stripes), and then white feathers, often with blackish tips or mottling, develop on chest, sides (esp left) of breast, and mantle and lower scapulars, later particularly on head with mixture of green and black; but lower back, rest of underparts and wings remain as juv. *2nd year* ♂ From following Jul assumes eclipse as ad ♂ except for juv wings; then becomes like ad ♂, but white of head, neck, mantle and, to lesser extent, of foreneck, breast and patches at sides of rump mottled blackish and buff (this later often decreasing through abrasion), and forewings suffused sooty-brown. *1st year* ♀ As ad ♀ eclipse, but during Nov–Apr crown, nape and upperparts become still darker, cheeks and sides of neck still more heavily streaked blackish; wings as juv, usually without white bars. VOICE Very vocal, esp in spring and autumn flocks: ♂ various low but loud crooning, dove-like moans, as *coo-oh-wah* with 2nd syllable emphasised; ♀ repeated guttural *gok-gok-*

gok-gok ('like distant fishing vessel'). HABITAT Essentially marine, breeding on offshore islands, rocky coasts and by sand-flats and saltings, but also estuaries and sea lochs and, locally, several km inland by freshwater lakes and rivers; in winter often well out to sea, but also inshore, esp over mussel-beds and reefs. NEST Sometimes colonial; hollow lined with abundant down, in short turf or marram, or well-hidden in heather, bracken or rocks, 4–6 eggs, late Apr–end Jul; 1 brood. FOOD Largely molluscs, esp mussels; also many crabs, starfish, other invertebrates. RANGE Mainly sedentary or locally dispersive, but non-breeders wander south; some immigration from Netherlands, also Denmark, in winter. COMPARE King Eider, Steller's Eider (260).

Eider

	B5
	W5
	S5
	A5

♂

♀

♀ eclipse

♂ eclipse

♂

♀

Long-tailed Duck *Clangula hyemalis* 41–45 cm (*c* 17 in) + 13 cm tail-streamers of ♂. Elegant sea-duck with short upturned bill, steep forehead, small head and triangular wings; only extensively white duck with all-dark wings; ♂ otherwise black-brown and white in summer, largely white with dark patches at other times; ♀ mainly dark brown above and white below. Flight distinctive, rapid and usually low in straggling lines or flocks, swinging from side to side showing alternate dark and white, with downcurved wings hardly brought above body on upstroke but coming unusually low on backward-flicking downstroke; swims buoyantly, long tail of ♂ often trailing on surface but raised to 45° or more when alert, and dives frequently, throwing head back and plunging forward with tail spread and wings often partly opened; lands breast first, without glide; seldom on land; often in restless flocks. Moults very complex, autumn + winter plumages corresponding to main plumage of other ducks. ♂ *autumn* (Sep–Nov) As ♂ winter, but head and neck white except for mottled grey-brown patch on lower cheeks and upper neck. ♂ *winter* (Nov–Apr) Head and neck white apart from pale grey area round eyes and blackish/chestnut patch below; white body and pale grey flanks contrast with black-brown breast-band joining in Y on back; wings uniform blackish above, but for chestnut secondaries, and mainly grey below; bill pink or orange-yellow with blue-grey nail and black base. ♂ *summer* (May–Jun) Head, neck and chest blackish-brown but for grey and white face-patch; mantle/scapulars black with chestnut and buff edges. ♂ *eclipse* (Jul–Sep) Much as ♂ summer, but duller and darker, no tail-streamers; new scapulars shorter, brown, narrowly edged buff; flanks browner. ♀ *autumn* (Nov–Dec/Feb) As ♀ winter but head/neck as ♀ eclipse. ♀ *winter* (Dec–Apr, although some remain as autumn) Head blackish but for grey-brown throat and central foreneck, buff sides of head with white round and back from eyes, and white lower neck; mantle, scapulars and wing-coverts dark brown with warm

Long-tailed Duck

♀ autumn

♀ winter

♂ eclipse

♂ winter

♂ summer

♂ autumn

brown edges, secondaries duller than ♂; underparts white but for brownish breast-band, flanks sometimes greyish; bill dark grey. ♀ *summer* (May–Jul/Aug) Head sooty-black but for mottled grey throat, dark grey sides of head in front of eyes, white round eyes to nape, and white neck-sides; upperparts as winter, but darker with narrower grey or buff feather-edges; underparts as winter, flanks sometimes greyer. ♀ *eclipse* (Aug–Nov) Head and neck white but for mottled blackish crown (sometimes also forehead) and cheek-patch, grey tinge to throat; otherwise as summer, but upperparts mottled brown, upper breast and flanks grey-brown. *Juv* Head mainly grey, darker on throat and hindneck, but for mottled blackish from forehead to nape and patch on rear and sides of neck, and white streak from eyes to nape; upperparts almost uniform dark grey-brown, with paler-edged scapulars; underparts whitish, with brown-grey across breast and paler on flanks. *1st winter* ♂ During Sep–Dec many develop new feathers as ♂ autumn then as

♂ winter on head, neck, upperparts and flanks, but very variable; some assume much white on head and neck, grey and white scapulars and occasionally tail-streamers, others stay on to spring; pink on bill from Oct. *1st summer* ♂ From Apr–May more like ♂ summer, but no dark breast-band; much as ad from Aug. *1st year* ♀ Much as ♀ autumn, or winter, then summer, but head-pattern less defined, mantle/scapulars edged with grey, under-parts as juv. *2nd winter* ♀ As ♀ winter, but scapulars with broad white edges. VOICE ♂ noisy on sea and in flight, esp loud yodel *a-ahulee*; ♀ low quacks. HABITAT Essential marine; rare inland. FOOD Molluscs, crustaceans. RANGE Passage/winter visitor from parts uncertain of N Eurasia/Greenland; has nested NBr.

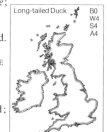

Long-tailed Duck

| B0 |
| W4 |
| S4 |
| A4 |

♀ winter

♂ winter

juv

1st winter ♂

♀ eclipse

1st summer ♂

♀ summer

1st winter ♀

Common Scoter *Melanitta nigra* 46–51 cm
(*c*19 in). Squat sea-duck with deep-based
bill, short neck, longish pointed tail and
blackish legs; ♂ all black but for yellow on
bill, ♀ brown with pale cheeks; in flight,
undersides of primaries show paler. Flight
strong with rapid whistling beats, usually
low over sea in snaking lines or ragged
bunches; swims buoyantly with tail often
raised and dives for food; postures include
stretching neck and raising tail, shaking
head, fanning and raising tail vertically;
seldom on land or even on sand-banks
unless nesting or oiled and sick; walks
upright and awkwardly; highly gregarious,
♂s often predominating in NBr (gathering
here earlier also) and ♀s/imms farther
south; shy. *Ad* ♂ Body all glossy black;
knobbed bill with orange-yellow ridge-
patch. *♂ eclipse* (*c*Apr–Nov) Only slightly
duller, with mixture of old/new feathers.
Ad ♀ Defined buff-white cheeks/ throat
contrast with blackish crown, mainly dark
brown body; fading and wear cause pale
barring on body, greyish belly; small-
knobbed bill green-black but often yellow

line on ridge. *Juv* As ♀, but greyer-brown
above and paler below; crown brown,
breast and belly white; knobless bill olive
with yellow-pink by nostrils. *1st year* ♂
With moult from Nov, esp Apr–May,
mottled black on head, upperparts, flanks,
later breast and under tail; as ad ♂ by
*c*Jun–Jul, but duller black with some
brown; orange-yellow first shows on bill
from *c*Jan. *♂ American/E Asian race (M.n.
americana)* Whole bill-base and flatter
knob yellow. VOICE Whistling, piping: ♂
high-pitched, plaintive; ♀ hoarse or
grating. HABITAT Nests by open moorland
lochs, in Ir on large loughs with wooded
islets; winters along sheltered coasts, but
odd migrants well inland. NEST In cover
near loch or on islet, 6–8 eggs, end May–
mid Jul; 1 brood. FOOD Mussels, cockles,
also crustaceans, fish eggs, worms, larvae,
seeds. RANGE Summer visitor to nesting
places, Apr–Sep; winter visitors from
Iceland/N Europe, esp Sep–Apr, but non-
breeders offshore all year; *americana*
vagrant (2 records). COMPARE ♀s of Ruddy
Duck (68), Red-crested Pochard (76).

Common Scoter

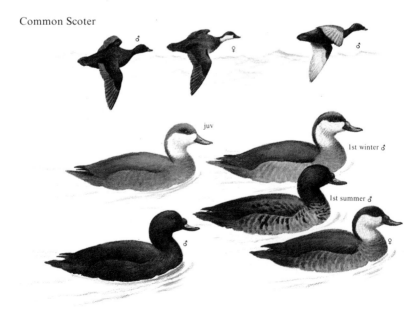

Velvet Scoter *Melanitta fusca* 53–59 cm (*c*22 in). Heavy-headed sea-duck with long swollen bill, thick neck, short pointed tail, white wing-patches and reddish legs; ♂ black with white eye-patches, ♀ brown with (usually) 2 pale head-patches; in flight, white secondaries (*cf* Goldeneye, 88; Merganser, 90). Actions as Common Scoter, but swims less buoyantly, red legs show less when diving; rises from water less easily, rests more on sand-banks; swims in smaller parties, often in line; tamer. *Ad* ♂ Glossy black, white crescent by whitish eyes; bill with swollen black base, orange-yellow sides, redder nail. ♂ *eclipse* (Apr–Nov) Only slightly duller, with some browner feathers. *Ad* ♀ Dark brown in new plumage *c*Nov–Jan; with wear, some grey-buff barring above, much white mottling on belly, and 2 whitish patches on sides of head prominent till Oct. *Juv* As ♀, but greyer-brown above, paler and more barred below, with larger patches on head; juv ♂ darker mantle and contrasting grey-edged scapulars, juv ♀ more uniform above and whiter belly; legs greyish-pink

to yellowish. *1st year* ♂ During moult beginning Nov–Jan, head blackens by *c*Mar, then scapulars, breast, flanks; but body still mottled brown in 1st summer and no white crescent by eyes; bill-sides paler from *c*Jan, yellow by spring. *1st winter* ♀ Head darker than body, no pale patches until worn. VOICE Rather silent: odd pipes or croaks from flocks. HABITAT Winters along open coasts and estuaries. FOOD Mussels, cockles, crabs, shrimps, starfish, worms. RANGE Winter visitor from N Europe, Oct–May; few all year. COMPARE Surf Scoter (262), esp ♀s.

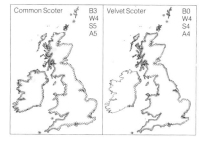

| Common Scoter ♂ ♀ | B3 W4 S5 A5 | Velvet Scoter ♂ ♀ | B0 W4 S4 A4 |

Velvet Scoter

♂
♀ (fresh plumage)

juv ♂

early 1st winter ♂

late 1st winter ♂

♀ (worn plumage)

♂

Goldeneye *Bucephala clangula* 40–48 cm
(16–19 in). Stocky sea-duck with short bill
and neck, high-peaked head and humped
back; ♂ boldly pied, with white blob
behind bill; smaller ♀ mottled grey, with
chocolate head, whitish collar and wing-
patches (showing at rest). Flight fast, often
low, with rapid beats making singing
sound (ad ♂ loudest); swims buoyantly,
often on rough water with head held
forward or sunk in shoulders (hiding
collar and exaggerating humpback); dives
tirelessly, sometimes several in unison;
rises more directly from surface than
diving-ducks; seldom on land, but walks
easily, upright; restless, shy; singly or
in parties, also big flocks. *Ad* ♂ Mainly
black above and white below, but for
green-glossed head, greyer tail, and white
loral blob, scapular bands and square
wing-patches; eyes yellow. *Ad* ♀ Chestnut
head, white and greyish collar, blackish
upperparts mottled with grey, greyish
chest to flanks, white belly, broken white
wing-patches; eyes yellow-white, bill
yellow near tip. ♂ *eclipse* (Jul–Oct) As ad

♀, but larger, head darker with blackish
lores, collar grey-brown, mantle and
flanks browner, wings as ad ♂. ♀ *eclipse*
(Jun–Nov) As ♂ eclipse, but head duller
with no blackish, wings as ad ♀. *Juv* As ♀
eclipse, but head greyer-brown, upperparts
and chest mainly brown; ♂ slightly larger,
usually with bigger whitish patch on wing-
coverts, yellower eyes. *1st year* With
variable moults in *c*Sep–Nov/Mar, head
becomes redder-brown (♂ some black
tinge), chest greyer-brown; by spring,
some as ads but for juv wings, but often
still many juv feathers and ♀ generally
greyer fore-collar. VOICE Usually silent
except in display, when ♂ loud *zeee-zeee*
and soft rattle. HABITAT Coasts, estuaries,
reservoirs, large rivers; breeds on wooded
lakes and rivers. NEST In tree-holes or
special nestboxes, 8–11 eggs, mid May–
Jun; 1 brood. FOOD Molluscs, crustaceans,
insects. RANGE Passage/winter visitor from
N Europe, Oct–Apr; since 1970, small but
increasing numbers breeding NBr. NOTE
Barrow's Goldeneye *B. islandica*, of Ice-
land/N America, seen rarely Br, believed

Goldeneye

to be escapes: ♂ has oval, purplish head and white crescent (not blob), less white on scapulars; ♀ has richer chestnut head, ragged nape, more yellow on stubbier bill.

Smew *Mergus albellus* 36–43 cm (14–17 in). Compact sawbill-duck with small bill, steep forehead, slight crest, but more elongated with stiff straight neck in flight; ♂ looks mainly white on water, but pied in flight; smaller ♀ greyish with contrasting chestnut cap and white cheeks. Flight very fast and agile, taking off and swerving like Teal (72), groups in diagonals and Vs (not usually bunched); floats high, dives constantly; walks very upright; usually shy; singly or in small parties. *Ad ♂* White with black patches and lines, greyer stern; in flight, black back/wings with bold white pattern. *Ad ♀* Cap chestnut, lores blackish, mantle blackish-grey; white areas on wings smaller than ♂. *♂ eclipse* (mid Jun–Oct/Nov) As ad ♀, but larger, cap more orange-brown, no black on lores, mantle blackish with grey fringes, wings as ad ♂. *♀ eclipse* Head as ♂ eclipse; otherwise

much as ad ♀, but browner above. *Juv* As ♀ eclipse, but cap paler orange-buff, mantle still browner, median coverts more grey-brown than white; ♂ already larger. *1st winter ♂* With moults in *c*Sep–Mar, first more as ♂ eclipse, but still juv wings; by *c*Dec–Jan, cap and scapulars mixed with white, lores blackish, breast-sides with faint blackish lines. *1st winter ♀* Much as ♀ eclipse but for juv wings, then lores blacken. VOICE Usually silent in winter. HABITAT Reservoirs, lakes, also estuaries. FOOD Fish, also invertebrates. RANGE Winter visitor from N Europe, Nov–Apr.

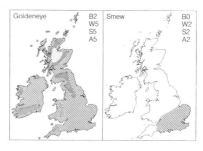

Smew

late 1st winter ♂

Red-breasted Merganser *Mergus serrator*
♂ 56–61 cm (*c*23 in), ♀ 51–56 cm (*c*21 in).
Slender, rakish sawbill-duck with long
thin bill, thin neck and wispy double crest;
♂ dark-looking with bottle-green head,
tortoiseshell breast, grey flanks; ♀ has
brown cap/crest, dark mask, indistinct
whitish throat and rufous head/neck
shading into brown-grey upperparts; very
elongated cigar-shape in flight, with thin
neck held stiffly level, white on inner wings
with 1–2 black bands. Flight fast with
strong beats, often low over water but
sometimes quite high; take-off laboured;
less buoyant than other sawbills, often
swimming with to-and-fro head-motion;
dives constantly, or may just submerge
head; walks easily; usually in small parties,
also flocks. *Ad* ♂ Red bill, green-black
head, white lower neck, black-spotted
red-buff breast; otherwise black, white and
grey, boldly marked at breast-sides; inner
wings mostly white with black leading
edge and 2 bars. *Ad* ♀ Brown-red bill,
brown head with rufous cheeks and neck-
sides shading into ill-defined whitish

throat, mottled brown-grey upperparts,
greyer flanks; variable black by or around
eyes, white streak on lores; white on inner
wings confined to patch on rear half with
black bar across. ♂ *eclipse* (Jun–Nov) As
♀ eclipse, but mantle/scapulars blacker,
bill redder, wings as ad ♂. ♀ *eclipse* (Jul–
Dec) As ad ♀, but no black by eyes or
white on lores, crest shorter. *Juv* As ♀
eclipse, but crest still shorter, sides of head
more buff, mantle/scapulars greyer, bill
duller red-brown; ♂ already larger. *1st
winter* With moults in *c*Nov–Mar, ♂s
variously assume ad plumage, some
completely by spring but for juv wings;
♀s much as ad ♀, but usually no black by
eyes. VOICE In courtship, ♂ rattling purr,
♀ harsh *krrrr* or softer croak. HABITAT
Breeds on islets in sea-lochs, or by open or
forested lakes and rivers; winters mainly
along sheltered coasts/estuaries. NEST In
ground cover or holes, 8–10 eggs, May–
mid Jul; 1 brood. FOOD Fish, also invertebrates. RANGE Mainly resident, moving to
coasts in winter; also winter visitor from
Iceland/Scandinavia, Sep–May.

**Red-breasted
Merganser**

♂

♀

♂ eclipse

♂

♀

Goosander *Mergus merganser* ♂ 63–69 cm (*c*26 in), ♀ 57–62 cm (*c*23½ in). Larger and bulkier than Red-breasted Merganser, with compact shaggy nape; ♂ also much whiter; ♀ cleaner blue-grey above with sharply demarcated richer rufous head, white throat and whitish-grey lower neck; in flight, more white on inner wings (esp ♂) at most only part-broken by dark bar. Actions as Merganser; more wing-noise (humming whistle) in flight; floats higher. *Ad* ♂ Mainly white, tinged with pink or cream below, but for green-black head, black back, blackish outer wings, grey stern; bill bright red. *Ad* ♀ Mainly grey to blue-grey, but for crested rufous head, white throat and belly, blackish outer wings, white secondaries; bill dull red. ♂ *eclipse* (Jun–Nov) As ♀ eclipse, but mantle/scapulars blacker, flanks whiter, wings as ad ♂. ♀ *eclipse* As ad ♀, but crest shorter, crown browner, head paler, usually light streak from bill to eyes. *Juv* As ♀ eclipse, but bill yellow-brown, crest much shorter and thinner, head more grey-buff, white throat less defined (*cf*

Merganser), upperparts browner; ♂ already larger. *1st winter* ♂ Moults in same way as 1st winter ♂ Merganser. VOICE In courtship, ♂ twanging, croaking and bell-like notes, ♀ harsh *karrr* and cackle. HABITAT Large lochs and rivers, esp in wooded areas; winters also on open lakes, reservoirs, sometimes estuaries. NEST In hollow trees, holes in rocks or banks, also among heather, 8–11 eggs, Apr–mid Jun; 1 brood. FOOD Fish. RANGE Resident; also winter visitor from N Europe, Oct–Apr.

COMPARE Hooded Merganser (262).

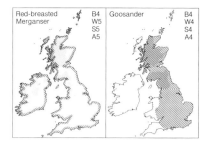

Red-breasted Merganser — B4 W5 S5 A5 · Goosander — B4 W4 S4 A4

Goosander

♂

♀

♂ eclipse

juv

♂

♀

KITES, HARRIERS, HAWKS, BUZZARDS,
EAGLES (Accipitridae)

Honey Buzzard *Pernis apivorus* 50–58 cm
(20–23 in). Slimmer than similar-sized
Buzzard (100), with slender bill, comparatively small Cuckoo-like head protruding
on thin neck; more pointed wings look
pinched in at body, and tail is usually at
least as long as width of wing, looking thin
when closed and slightly rounded at
corners; ad usually grey-brown above (but
some darker brown), and very variably
scallop-barred or mainly dark brown or
white below, with buzzard-like dark
carpal patches, but diagnostic pattern of
barring on flight-feathers and tail, latter
having broad band at tip and 2 narrower
bands at base; juv even more variable,
with less distinct barring, inc 4 tail-bands.
Flight strong with soft, deep, flexible
beats, often maintained for longer periods
than other raptors; glides with wings
angled and slightly arched (carpal joints
pressed forward, long 'hands' pointing
back slightly below level) and tail twisted
as rudder; soars with wings flat or just
upcurved and edges almost parallel at
right-angles to body; in courtship flights,
pair soars and undulates, ♂ dives and
swoops up or, most characteristically,
rises steeply, stalls, raises wings vertically
above back several times and quivers them,
then dives and repeats performance;
walks easily, even runs, on ground with
neck extended and body horizontal, and
uses feet for digging, but usually locates
wasp nests from tree perch or in flight; shy
and secretive; solitary, but flocks on
migration abroad. *Ad* Typically grey-
brown above with 3 bands on tail and
corresponding bands on trailing edge of
wings, bases of primaries and tips of
greater coverts, but usually ♂ greyer on
crown and head-sides, ♀ more brownish,
and some individuals rather darker on
upperparts; below, main bands on flight-
feathers and tail always clear, otherwise
typically whitish with variable dark
barring on body and wing-coverts and
distinct carpal patches, but dark birds
have more or less uniformly dark brown

Honey Buzzard

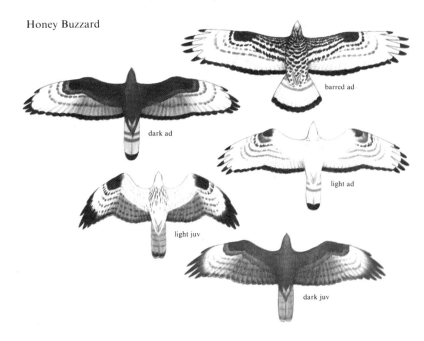

barred ad

dark ad

light ad

light juv

dark juv

underbody/wing-coverts and flight-feathers varying from whitish to dark grey on secondaries, pale birds have largely cream or white underbody/inner wing-coverts, and others are intermediate; cere dark blue-grey, eyes orange to red (♂) or yellow (♀). *Juv/1st winter* Typically dark brown above but for obscurely barred pale patch on primaries, thin whitish lines along tips of greater coverts and flight-feathers, whitish U on uppertail-coverts, and usually 4 indistinct blackish bars and whitish tip to tail, but pale birds also have white head with dark eye-patches, dark-mottled whitish forewings; typically dark rufous to blackish-brown below with dark grey tail and secondaries but whitish patch at base of primaries and often pale band along greater coverts, 4 indistinct tail-bars, 3-4 obscure bars and more extensive dark tips on wings (though no broad band like ad on trailing edge); pale birds have whitish underbody/coverts, often with brown streaks (not bars); cere yellow, eyes brown. *1st summer* With moult from early in year, becomes increasingly like ad, but

worn and faded juv flight-feathers retained till *c*Jun–Aug. VOICE Much less noisy than Buzzard: main call piercing whistled *pew-ee-ew* or *pee-a*. HABITAT Old broadleaved woods, esp beech, but also mixed and coniferous; migrants often over open country. NEST High in trees, often on foundations of old Crow or Buzzard nests, 2 eggs, Jun–early Sep; 1 brood. FOOD Larvae, pupae, adults and honeycombs of wasps and bumble-bees, as well as ant pupae, mainly dug up with feet; also other insects and some voles, lizards, frogs, worms, eggs and young birds, even berries.

RANGE Very scarce and local summer visitor, May–Sep, wintering in Africa: also scarce passage-migrant, probably from S Scandinavia, Apr–Nov, mainly May–Jun, Sep–Oct, very rare as far west as Ir.

Honey Buzzard   B1
W0
S2
A2

ad

dark juv

light juv

ad at wasp nest

Red Kite *Milvus milvus* 58–64 cm (*c*24 in).
Buzzard-sized, but slimmer, rakish, with
much longer, deeply forked tail (notched
even when spread) and long broadish
wings set well forward; very rufous with
pale head, black-cornered tail, blackish
flight-feathers and broad buff diagonal
across inner wings above, and large white
patch at base of primaries below. Flight
graceful, with slow deep flaps and up-and-
down body-movement; when gliding/
soaring, wings held forward, slightly
arched and kinked, and, like tail, constantly flexed and twisted independently;
in courtship, pair circles high on crossing
paths; takes prey on ground, where hops
awkwardly; perches on trees; shy; solitary.
Ad Mainly rufous-chestnut, browner
above, with whitish head, all streaked
blackish; tail bright rufous with black
corners; white patch beneath primaries
often not reaching rear of wing. *Juv* Head
less whitish, tail browner; above, wing-
diagonal broader/paler, also whitish line
along greater coverts, pale rufous tail-
coverts; below, clearly streaked buff-white,
with whitish patch on primaries almost to
rear edge. *1st year* Much as ad after moult
in *c*Oct–May, but wings/tail as juv. VOICE
Shrill mewing *weeoo*, rapidly repeated
weee-wee-wee. HABITAT Steep valleys with
mature woods, open ground. NEST High
in broadleaved trees, 2–3 eggs, Apr–mid
Jul; 1 brood. FOOD Small mammals, birds,
carrion. RANGE Widespread in Br to late
18th century, now rare; mainly sedentary,
but some wander end Jul–Apr; vagrants
from Continent, mostly Mar–Apr.
COMPARE Black Kite (264).

Marsh Harrier *Circus aeruginosus* 48–56
cm (19–22 in). Bulkiest, broadest-winged
of the harriers, which are rather slim,
elongated, ground-nesting hawks with long
wings, tails and legs, that hunt low over
reeds, heather or corn, gliding and soaring
with wings in shallow V. ♂ has dark back,
upperwing-coverts and underbody
contrasting with grey central wings and
tail; ♀/juv mainly dark but for variably
creamy head and (♀) buff shoulders and
breast. Flies with several heavy flaps, then

Red Kite

a glide, usually low over reeds or water, but soars high; in courtship flight, ♂ dives with wings half-closed, shoots up again, loops-the-loop, or falls spinning; ♂ passes food to ♀ in air, ♀ turning on back with claws out; takes all prey on ground or water; perches low on posts, bushes, and often settles on ground, walking heavily; solitary, but ♂ sometimes polygamous. *Ad* ♂ Streaky head, dark brown back and coverts (sometimes creamy shoulders), grey mid-wings and side-barred tail, black wing-tips, rarely whitish rump; below, streaky rufous body, pale grey tail, and variably whitish underwings with coverts rufous-buff to creamy-white and more or less dark trailing edges (old ♂s palest). *Ad* ♀ Mainly chocolate-brown, but creamy head with dark eye-band, creamy-buff shoulders and breast-patch, and pale-based primaries below; tail tinged rufous, or variably grey on older ♀s. *Juv* As ad ♀, but largely lacks pale shoulders and breast, and sometimes all-dark but for slightly lighter tail and often paler-based primaries below. *Imm* ♂ By 1st summer develops

streaked crown; by 2nd winter greyish mid-wings with black tips, brown-grey tail with some brown side-barring and broad band near end; in 2nd summer more streaked below. VOICE ♂ shrill *kee-oo* in courtship flight. HABITAT Extensive reed-beds, adjacent open country. NEST On or near ground or in shallows in reeds, 4–5 eggs, May–early Aug; 1 brood. FOOD Small mammals, birds, eggs, nestlings, carrion. RANGE Rare summer visitor, Apr–Sep, wintering south to Africa; scarce passage migrant from Continent, esp Sep–Nov, Mar–May; odd ones all year.

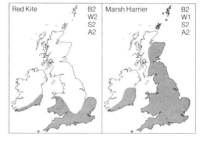

Red Kite — B2 W2 S2 A2 / Marsh Harrier — B2 W1 S2 A2

Marsh Harrier

♂

♀

♀

♂

all-dark juv

♂

♀

juv

Hen Harrier *Circus cyaneus* 43–51 cm (17–20 in). Intermediate in bulk between Marsh (94) and Montagu's; ♂ grey and white, but for black wing-tips and dark trailing edges, with white rump; brown, white-rumped 'ring-tail' ♀/juv separated from ♀ Montagu's by head-pattern. Flight as Marsh Harrier, but wing-beats faster, glides usually shorter and sometimes on flat or bowed wings, though normally glides and always soars with wings in shallow V; ♂ courtship flights include steep dives, upward swoops, rolls, somersaults; similar food-pass; walks easily. *Ad ♂* Grey above, but for white rump, black wing-tips, faint dark trailing edges (more obvious from below); mainly white below, with well-defined grey throat/chest. *Ad ♀* Streaky owl-like head with barely darker crescent on rear cheeks separated by indistinct pale collar from ruff of dark streaks; otherwise dark brown above with white rump, dark-streaked buff below with broad bars on flight-feathers and tail. *Juv* Very like ad ♀, but underparts and wider fringes to upperwing-coverts more

rufous, secondaries and cheeks usually (sometimes much) darker. *1st summer/ 2nd winter ♂* With moult in *c*May–Oct, gradually more as ad ♂, but browner-grey above and some rufous marks below. VOICE When breeding, ♂ dry cackling *chuk-uk-uk*, ♀ sharper higher *kek-ek-ek*; also whistled squealing *whit-tew* (esp ♀). HABITAT Moors, young conifer plantations; winter/passage also over downs, fields, dunes. NEST On ground in heather, rushes, conifers, 4–6 eggs, May–early Aug; 1 brood. FOOD Small birds, rodents. RANGE Mainly sedentary, but some emigrate; passage/winter visitor from Continent, mostly ring-tails, mainly Sep–Apr.

Montagu's Harrier *Circus pygargus* 39–46 cm (15½–18 in). Slimmer, with narrower wings, than Hen Harrier; ♂ looks dirtier, being darker grey, with black bar on upperwings, dark lines on underwings, rufous streaks on flanks, usually grey rump; ♀ separated from 'ring-tail' Hen Harrier by head-pattern, usually smaller white rump, but juv also unstreaked rufous

Hen Harrier

below. Actions as Hen Harrier, though wing-beats more leisurely and buoyant, glides more wavering with wings always in V, often deeper V when soaring. *Ad ♂* Grey above, but for black wing-tips and mid-wing bar, slight barring on outer tail, but rump sometimes whitish; white below, with dark grey throat/breast, rufous streaks on flanks/wing-coverts, 1–2 black bars and thin greyish trailing edge on secondaries, pale grey tail lightly barred. *Ad ♀* Dark crescent on rear cheeks (*cf* dark-cheeked juv Hen Harriers), white around eyes divided by faint dark streak, no pale collar; otherwise much as ♀ Hen Harrier. *Juv* Much as ad ♀, but mostly plain rufous below, with dark secondaries, and darker above, usually with pale nape-spot and thin pale line along greater coverts. *1st summer ♂* Brown-grey above with browner head, broad rufous streaks on grey-brown throat/chest and buff-white underbody, worn juv flight-feathers and outer tail. *2nd summer ♂* Much as ad ♂, but browner above (esp head), white marks on nape, less extensive grey below. *Melanistic form*

♂ all sooty-grey above and blackish below with paler tail; ♀ all dark chocolate but for banded tail (no white rump); both show whitish patch at base of primaries below. VOICE When breeding, staccato *yek-ek-ek* (♀ shriller), thin plaintive *psee-ee*. HABITAT Young conifer plantations, heaths, moors, dunes, reeds, corn. NEST On ground in dense cover, 4–5 eggs, mid May–late Aug; 1 brood. FOOD Small birds, rodents. RANGE Rare summer visitor, May–Sep, wintering in Africa; some passage Apr–May, Aug–Oct. COMPARE Pallid Harrier (264).

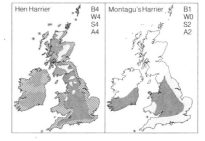

Montagu's Harrier

Goshawk *Accipiter gentilis* 48–58 cm (19–23 in), ♂ much smaller than ♀. Like large ♀ Sparrowhawk (♂ not much bigger, but ♀ Buzzard-sized), with more protruding head, deeper chest, longer wings and wider-based, rounder-ended tail; grey-brown above, closely barred brown on white below, with paler-banded tail than Sparrowhawk, dark ear-coverts forming hood, and whiter supercilia and undertail-coverts (esp ♀); browner juv streaked and often orange-tinged below. Flight as Sparrowhawk, but stronger, heavier, with slower beats; glides on flat wings with tips somewhat pointed and trailing edges S-curved; often soars, with rounded wings held slightly forward and tail usually well spread (*cf* Sparrowhawk); courtship flights include soaring with white under-tail-coverts spread, interspersed with slow harrier-like beats, also plummeting dives and switchback of plunges and upward swoops; hunts by weaving with speed and agility among trees, or watching from perch, then dashes and glides at quarry; will chase birds into thick cover or from branch to branch; solitary. *Ad* ♂ Grey-brown above, with blackish crown above whitish supercilia and nape; tail grey-brown with *c*4 narrow dark bars and broader band behind thin white tip; whitish below, closely barred dark brown on body and underwings and banded on flight-feathers and greyish tail; eyes red-orange. *Ad* ♀ Browner above, with clearer white supercilia and undertail. *Juv* Brown above, tinged rufous or buff by pale fringes, with bolder tail-bands; whitish to rufous below with dark drop-like streaks, stronger-barred flight-feathers; eyes green-grey, turning yellow; much as ad from 2nd year. VOICE Shrill chattering *gek-gek-gek*, short plaintive scream *hee-aa*. HABITAT Lowland or upland woods, plantations. NEST In trees, 3–4 eggs, May–Jul; 1 brood. FOOD Birds, mammals. RANGE ?. Feral, nesting more since 1960s; wanderers may include Continental immigrants; 6 records of American race.

Sparrowhawk *Accipiter nisus* 28–38 cm (11–15 in), ♂ much smaller than ♀.

Goshawk

juv ♀

♀

♂

juv ♂

♀

Smallish, fierce-looking, with long square-ended tail, shortish broad wings usually looking much blunter than Kestrel or Merlin (104); grey (♂) or brown above with banded tail; whitish below, barred rufous-orange (♂) or brown, but for white undertail-coverts. Flight dashing burst of rapid beats, then short glide; soars with wings flat and slightly forward, tail often closed or only briefly fanned (*cf* Goshawk); courtship flights include soaring mixed with slow harrier-like wing-beats and shallow undulations; and ♂ also dives at perched ♀ or chases her through trees; hunts mainly by surprise, waiting on hidden perch, weaving through trees, or flying low along hedge and then flicking over to other side, also chases prey into thick cover; solitary. *Ad ♂* Slate-grey to paler blue-grey above with rufous cheeks; tail with 3-4 narrow dark brown bars and broader band behind thin white tip; whitish below, narrowly barred orange-red on body and underwings (often looking all-orange) and banded dark on flight-feathers and greyish tail; eyes yellow.

Ad ♀ Dark brown or grey-brown above, with whitish supercilia; barred brown below or rufous on flanks. *Juv* Brown above, tinged rufous by pale fringes; whitish to buff below with brown bars (more rufous and broken on breast of ♂); eyes green-grey, turning yellow; much as ads in 2nd year after moult in May–Aug. VOICE Shrill *kek-kek-kek*, plaintive *wee-oo*. HABITAT Woods (esp coniferous or mixed), farmland, also upland scrub, suburbs. NEST In trees, 5–6 eggs, May–Jul; 1 brood. FOOD Small birds. RANGE Sedentary; also passage/winter from Continent, Sep–Apr.

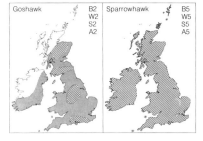

Sparrowhawk

Buzzard *Buteo buteo* 50–56 cm (20–22 in). Medium-sized and compact, with broad head and short neck (not projecting like Honey Buzzard, 92, or Golden Eagle, 102), fairly broad wings, and short tail (only $c\frac{3}{4}$ width of wing-base) rounded when spread but showing clear corners; varies from largely dark brown to mainly creamy-white, but in Br/Ir mostly dark with pale crescent on lower breast; lacks distinct tail-bands and wing-barring of Honey Buzzard and complete white tail-base of Rough-legged. Flight strong but slow, heavy-looking, with stiff, rather laboured and not very deep beats, mixed with easy glides; glides with wings flat or just upcurved, carpal joints pressed forward and trailing tips quite pointed; soars with whole wings raised and pressed forward, tips upcurved, and tail broadly fanned; sometimes hovers; in courtship, soars in circles, plunges and swoops up; perches prominently on trees, bushes, rocks, posts, telegraph poles; drops on to prey on ground, walks awkwardly; usually solitary, although sometimes several in air together. *Ad* Typically dark brown above, often with paler area at base of outer primaries (but may be mottled, streaked, blotched or largely creamy-white on head, body, wing-coverts and even extreme base of tail, *cf* Rough-legged Buzzard); typically dark brown below, often paler on throat, normally pale U on breast and pale bar on median coverts, always lighter flight-feathers with well-defined dark trailing edge and obscurely barred greyer tail with brown subterminal band (but sometimes much white below or showing distinct blackish carpal patches and dark flanks or belly, *cf* Rough-legged Buzzard). *Juv* Below, dark rear wing-edge and tail-band narrower, more obscure; as ad after 1st summer moult. VOICE Loud, drawn-out, plaintive, ringing *pee-yow*. HABITAT Moors, scrub, woods, cliffs, locally wooded heaths, farmland. NEST In trees or cliffs, 2–4 eggs, Apr–Jul; 1 brood. FOOD Rabbits, voles, also carrion, young birds, frogs, worms, insects. RANGE Mainly sedentary; some winter in Aug–Apr, irregular passage in Aug–Nov, Mar–Apr.

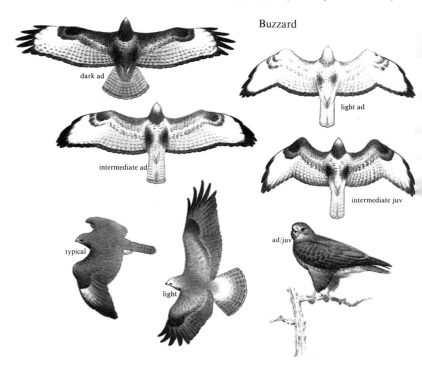

Buzzard

dark ad

light ad

intermediate ad

intermediate juv

typical

ad/juv

light

Rough-legged Buzzard *Buteo lagopus*
50–61 cm (20–24 in). Smaller head than
Buzzard, longer narrower wings, longer
tail (at least equalling width of wing-
base), feathered legs; tail white-based
with broad blackish subterminal band and
1–4 narrower bars on distal half (ad) or
just broader paler subterminal band (juv);
pale head and grey to whitish patch on
primaries above, esp juv (*cf* juv Golden
Eagle, 102, also with white-based tail),
and usually obvious dark carpal and belly
patches below. Actions as Buzzard, but
slower, more flexible beats; glides with
'arms' raised, 'hands' level. *Ad* Dark
above but for dark-streaked whitish head,
variable pale area on primaries, whitish
leading edge to wings, blackish-banded
white tail; below, throat/chest and wing-
coverts vary from mainly dark brown to
white more or less streaked brown, with
dark carpal patches, whitish U on breast
extending down to divide blackish patches
on sides of belly, whitish flight-feathers
with blackish tips and trailing edge and
variable dark barring on secondaries, tail-
pattern as from above. *Juv/1st winter*
Usually paler above, esp on head and
wing-coverts, with more distinct whitish
patch at base of primaries, but less white
at tail-base and paler broader subterminal
band; also paler below, sometimes largely
white but for blackish wing-tips, carpal
patches and usually all-dark belly, with
tail-end hardly contrasting. VOICE Thin
mournful mewing; migrants mostly silent.
HABITAT Open marshes, moors, hills,
heaths, dunes. FOOD Rabbits, voles, some
birds. RANGE Usually scarce winter visitor
from Scandinavia, Oct–Apr (Sep–May).

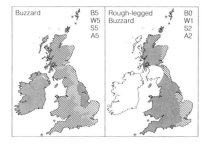

Buzzard — B5 W5 S5 A5 Rough-legged Buzzard — B0 W1 S2 A2

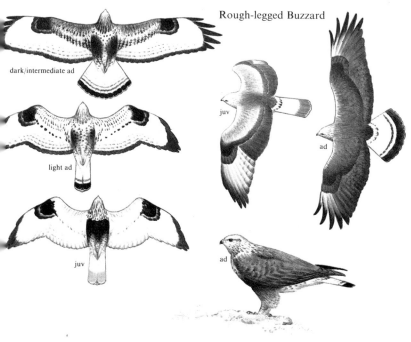

Rough-legged Buzzard

dark/intermediate ad

light ad

juv

juv

ad

ad

Golden Eagle *Aquila chrysaetos* 76–90 cm (30–35 in). Large, with protruding head, long wings bulging at secondaries but narrower by body, rounded tail as long as width of wing-base, feathered legs; often confused with much smaller Buzzard or Rough-legged Buzzard (100), but proportions of head, wings and tail quite different; ad mainly dark with golden head and often wing-coverts, imms with conspicuous white centre of wings and base of tail. Flight powerful with deep leisurely beats, long glides; soars with wings in shallow V and held slightly forward, primaries upcurved, tail spread; wings less raised when gliding; courtship flights include plunging and swooping up, rolling over; hunts fairly low, dropping on prey with half-closed wings; perches on crags, trees; solitary, but families together through autumn. *Ad* Dark brown to blackish (wearing much paler) with golden to buff crown/nape, often obvious grey to yellowish oblong on upperwing-coverts, and paler grey-brown flight-feathers and tail shading to broad blackish tips. *Juv* Mainly blackish-brown, with rather paler crown/nape and 'trousers', often some whitish mottling (white feather-bases) on body, but esp bold white bases to flight-feathers (usually forming patch only on inner primaries above, but band along much of wing below) and whitish basal $\frac{1}{2}$–$\frac{2}{3}$ of tail. *1st–4th year* After slow moult in 1st summer, crown/nape dull tawny, body much as ad; but variable amount of white shows on wings and esp tail until at least well into 3rd summer. VOICE Usually silent; mewing *wee-o* (not unlike Buzzard), shrill yelping bark. HABITAT Hills, mountains, moorland crags; locally pine forests, sea-cliffs. NEST On cliffs or in trees, 2 eggs, mid Mar–Jul; 1 brood. FOOD Mammals, birds, carrion. RANGE Sedentary; formerly bred Ir, also NIr 1953–60. COMPARE White-tailed (264).

OSPREYS (Pandionidae)

Osprey *Pandion haliaetus* 51–59 cm (20–23 in). Moderate-sized raptor habitually near water, with smallish but well-

Golden Eagle

juv

ad

juv

ad

ad

protruding and slightly crested head, long and narrow-ended angled wings, shortish tail; dark above, but much white on head and underparts, setting off blackish eye-bands, carpal patches and greater coverts, with narrowly barred tail and flight-feathers, pale-based black-tipped primaries. Flight powerful with shallow, flexible beats; soars and esp glides with wings bowed or kinked like large gull; courtship flights include plunges, upward swoops, and pauses on rapidly beating wings with slanted body; hunts by flapping and gliding *c*10–30 m over water, hovering at intervals with dangled legs, then diving down (feet forward at last moment), partly or wholly submerging but for upheld wings, but also dives from perch or plucks from surface; carries fish head first, usually with one foot behind the other; shakes wet off after rising and, having fed, often trails feet in water to clean them; perches on bare trees, posts, rocks; solitary. *Ad* Dark brown above, contrasting whitish rear-crown and nape; rusty-brown breast-band. *Juv* Paler above

through creamy feather-tips, crown/nape more streaked, breast-band less clear; much as ad through wear by 1st summer (when mostly stays in winter quarters). VOICE Shrill repeated whistling or yelping *cheep* or *chewk*, esp when breeding. HABITAT Lakes, large rivers, coasts. NEST Near tops of conifers with dead branches, 3 eggs, mid Apr–Jul; 1 brood. FOOD Fish averaging *c*300 g. RANGE Ceased to nest 1917–54, now scarce summer visitor, Apr–Sep, wintering in Africa north to Mediterranean; also on passage from Scandinavia, Apr–May, Aug–Oct.

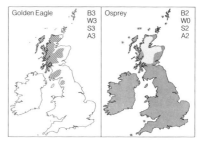

| Golden Eagle | | B3 W3 S3 A3 | Osprey | | B2 W0 S2 A2 |

Osprey

FALCONS (Falconidae)

Kestrel *Falco tinnunculus* 33–36 cm (*c*13½ in). Longish tail and long pointed wings; ♂ with blue-grey head and much of tail, black-spotted chestnut back; ♀/juv rufous above with blackish bars. Flight with fast shallow beats, occasional glides and twists; hunts by hovering head to wind, hanging almost motionless or with rapid shallow wing-beats, tail fanned, body sloping, then drops steeply to ground; also catches feeding or perched birds by sudden dashes; soars with wings and tail spread (*cf* Sparrowhawk, 98); perches on trees, poles, power lines, buildings, rocks; solitary. *Ad* ♂ Crown/hindneck blue-grey, mantle/wing-coverts black-spotted chestnut, wing-ends blackish, tail blue-grey with black band and white tip; buffish below, spotted black on breast, flanks and under-wings, faintly barred on flight-feathers. *Ad* ♀ Dark-barred rufous above (rump and often tail greyer) with blackish wing-ends, broader band behind white tail-tip; creamy-buff below, more streaked than ♂,

boldly spotted on underwings, barred on flight-feathers and tail; cere yellow. *Juv* As ad ♀, but more chestnut rump, and broader and paler streaks below, cere greenish; more like ads after body moult in Aug–Apr, but 2nd winter ♂ still with rufous crown, varying amount of grey and bars on tail, not fully ad until 3rd year. VOICE Shrill *kee-kee-kee*. HABITAT Open woods, farmland, parks, towns, cliffs, moors, marshes; often hovers over verges of motorways. NEST On ledge or in hole, esp cliff, old building, old Crow nest, hollow tree, or on ground, 4–6 eggs, Apr–mid Jul; 1 brood. FOOD Small mammals, birds, insects. RANGE Mainly sedentary, some move south to N Iberia; immigrants from Continent, Aug–May, esp in EBr.

Merlin *Falco columbarius* 27–32 cm (*c*10½–12½ in), ♂ thrush-sized, ♀ larger. Shortish tail and broad-based pointed wings; ♂ slate-blue above, ♀/juv dark brown with barred tail, all variously dark-streaked below, but moustaches obscure. Flight dashing and direct with fast win-

Kestrel

nowing beats, short glides, often low over ground (*cf* Sparrowhawk, 98); circles high over nesting area, but soars little, seldom hovers; hunts with shallow beats and undulating action through briefly closing wings, but when chasing prey follows every twist and turn; perches on rocks, hummocks, walls, fences, less on trees; solitary. *Ad ♂* Slate-blue above, palest on rump/tail but for broad black tip, with darker crown and wing-ends, rufous nape, rufous or greyish cheeks, obscure moustaches; buffish to rusty below with extensive blackish streaks, rufous-marked underwings, dark-barred flight-feathers, black-ended whitish tail. *Ad ♀* Largely dark brown above with cream-barred tail, whitish nape, streaky cheeks, greyer back/ rump and rusty fringes on mantle/scapulars; whitish to creamy below with heavy brown streaks, dark-barred flight-feathers and tail; cere yellow. *Juv* Very like ad ♀, though darker above, browner-white below with darker brown streaks, cere bluish to greenish; ♀s larger than ♂s, with darker cheeks, wider streaks; as ads from

1st summer/2nd winter after moults in Feb–Nov. VOICE Fast shrill chattering *kik-ik-ik* or *kee-kee-kee* near nest. HABITAT Moors, fells, bogs, rough ground above cliffs, coastal dunes; winters more widely in open country, marshes. NEST Scrape on ground, or sometimes in old Crow nests on cliffs or in trees, 3–5 eggs, May–Jul; 1 brood. FOOD Mainly small birds. RANGE Upland birds winter lower or go south, few to Iberia; passage/winter from Iceland/?N Europe, Aug–May.

COMPARE Other falcons (106, 264, 266).

| Kestrel | | B6 W6 S6 A6 | Merlin | | B4 W4 S4 A4 |

Merlin

Hobby *Falco subbuteo* 30–36 cm (12–14 in), ♂ rather smaller than ♀. Smallish slender falcon with shortish tail and scythe-like wings (♀ broader-based), like huge Swift (184); dark slate above, heavily streaked below, with pointed black moustaches, cream throat and cheeks, rufous thighs and undertail (buff on juv). Flight dashing, with rapid stiff winnowing beats, short glides; soars with wings flat and tail spread, seldom hovers; courtship flights include spectacular plunging, spinning, rolling over, looping-the-loop; stoops on or outflies birds, but hawks insects (held in foot and eaten in flight) with slower flatter wing-beats and leisurely soaring; ♂ passes food to ♀ in air; perches mainly in trees; usually solitary. *Ad* Dark slate above, browner in worn plumage (esp ♀), with slightly paler tail, obscure buff-white nape-band; bold blackish moustaches against cream throat and neck-sides; cream to buff below streaked blackish, with rufous thighs/tail-coverts, dark-spotted wing-coverts, narrowly barred flight-feathers and tail, darker wing-tips; cere yellow. *Juv* Blacker above with buff feather-edges, more heavily streaked below, with buff thighs/tail-coverts, cere grey-blue or greenish; as ad from 1st summer/2nd winter after moult in Mar–Sep. VOICE Clear plaintive *kew-kew-kew*, esp near nest with young. HABITAT Heaths/downs with pine clumps, farmland with old hedgerow trees, also wood-edges. NEST In old crow nests in trees, 3 eggs, Jun–Aug; 1 brood. FOOD Small birds (*eg* larks, martins, even Swifts), large insects. RANGE Summer visitor, late Apr–Sep, wintering in Africa; some on passage from Continent, Apr–Jun, Aug–Oct.

Peregrine *Falco peregrinus* 38–48 cm (15–19 in), ♂ smaller than ♀. Largish, compact, robust falcon with slightly tapered tail and pointed, broad-based wings; blue-slate above with paler rump, barred tail, broad moustaches, and mainly barred below, but juv dark brown above, streaked below. Flight powerful with stiff shallow winnowing beats, short or long glides, faster and with deeper beats when

Hobby

hunting; soars on more or less level wings, hangs on updraughts, but rarely hovers; courtship flights include spectacular plunging and shooting up, rolling over, figures-of-eight, talon-grappling; usually stoops on prey from height, very fast (*c*150–250 km/h) with wings nearly closed; ♂ passes food to ♀ in air; perches hunched on cliffs, rocks, also buildings, fences, trees; solitary. *Ad* ♂ Blue-slate above, faintly barred blackish, with darker wing-ends, banded blackish and grey tail; blackish head and rounded moustaches against white throat and cheek-patches; cream to pink-buff below, flecked on chest and otherwise barred black, with paler flight-feathers and tail; legs and cere yellow. *Ad* ♀ Darker above, nape sometimes buffish; often more heavily barred below, larger drop-like markings on chest. *Juv* Dark brown above with pale feather-edges, creamy forehead, buff nape, narrower moustaches, and cream to rufous-buff below with brown streaks (not bars), heavier on ♀; legs and cere blue-grey to greenish; as ads from 1st summer/2nd winter after moult in Mar–Dec. VOICE Harsh staccato chattering *kak-kak-kak*, shrill whining *kee-errk*, creaking *wee-chew*, esp near nest. HABITAT Moorland, mountain and coastal cliffs, locally crags in wooded areas; juvs/immigrants winter also in open country, estuaries, marshes. NEST On cliff ledges, 3–4 eggs, Apr–Jul; 1 brood. FOOD Largely birds (pigeons, seabirds, grouse). RANGE Sedentary, but juvs disperse; also autumn/winter immigrants from Fenno-Scandia.

COMPARE Other falcons (104, 264, 266).

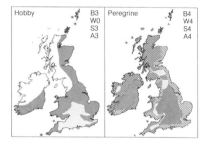

Hobby | B3 W0 S3 A3
Peregrine | B4 W4 S4 A4

Peregrine

ad

juv

juv

♀

♂

ad

GROUSE (Tetraonidae)

Red Grouse *Lagopus lagopus* 33–39 cm
(13–15½ in). Endemic Br/Ir race of N
Eurasian Willow Grouse, common sight
and sound of moors; plump, stout-billed,
with small head, short rounded wings and
tail, white-feathered legs; usually rufous
or buff, barred black, looking all-dark at
distance, with blackish wings (variably
white on under-coverts) and tail (hidden
at rest by long coverts), but much variation: some predominantly blackish or red
(esp ♂s), or more spotted or barred
whitish-buff (esp ♀s), while white marks
of winter on belly/flanks may form patches
(*cf* Ptarmigan). Flight fast, strong, with
rapid beats and long glides on bowed
wings after whirring take-off with noisy
cackling, usually low over heather, often
rocking from side to side; walks with roll,
or runs, with rounded back; may settle in
trees and ♂ will perch up on posts; shy,
but often crouches until approached
closely; gathers in family parties in
autumn, then small flocks (often mainly
♀s/imm ♂s). *♂ summer* With moult in
*c*Apr–Jun, rufous to tawny heavily barred
black; red combs prominent. *♂ winter*
With continuing moult in *c*Jul–Nov,
darker rufous and chestnut more finely
barred, variably tipped white on belly/
flanks. *Ad ♀* Changes as ♂ (though
summer moult in *c*Mar–May), but
smaller, paler and more contrastingly
barred and spotted: in winter more like
summer ♂ (but tipped white below), in
summer much yellower; combs less
prominent. *Juv* Like small ♀ (winter above,
summer below), but buffs duller, barring
browner underneath, no combs; as ads
after moult in *c*Jul–Nov. VOICE Rapid
cackling *ko-ko-ko* . . .; crowing *raa ka-
ka-ka . . . gobak-gobak-bak-bak-bak*. . . .
HABITAT Drier heather moors, also peat-
bogs, nearby stubble. NEST In heather,
rushes, 5–9 eggs, Apr–Jun; 1 brood. FOOD
Heather, also berries, insects. RANGE
Sedentary; introduced Shetland, SWBr.

Ptarmigan *Lagopus mutus* 33–36 cm (*c*13½
in). Mountain grouse, slighter than Red,

Red Grouse

with daintier bill, shorter legs and narrower wings; grey, brown or buff, finely barred, with white wings and underbody, becoming all-white in winter but for black tail (obvious only in flight). Actions as Red Grouse, but flies spectacularly up and down steep slopes; walks agilely over rocks; often crouches, or ♂ may perch boldly; inquisitive but shy. *♂ summer* With moult May–Jun, dark grey-brown, barred and speckled blackish, buff and white, but white wings, underbody and feathered legs; combs red. *♂ autumn* With continuing moult in Jul–Sep, dark areas paler buff-grey with fine black barring; combs yellow-red, smaller. *♂ winter* After further moult in *c*Sep–Dec, more or less white but for black lores, black-sided tail; usually some coloured feathers. *Ad ♀* Changes as ♂ (though moults faster, in May, Sep): in summer more sharply barred golden-buff and blackish, much less white below; by autumn as ♂ but yellower-grey, still some bold-barred golden feathers, and in winter rarely black on lores; combs smaller, orange-red when

breeding. *Juv* Like small autumn ♀, but wings and tail as upperparts (not white or black), no combs. *1st autumn* As autumn ads, but still many non-white juv wing-coverts, mottled primaries; as winter ad after moult in *c*Sep–Dec, but often some primaries still mottled. VOICE ♂ hoarse crackling and ♀ higher yapping *kuk-uk-uk, aar-orr-kakarr*; song *er-ook-ka-ka-ka-ka . . . kwa-kwa-kwa*, belching then cackling, softer at end. HABITAT Stony mountains, esp above 700 m. NEST On ground, 4–9 eggs, mid May–mid Aug; 1 brood. FOOD Shoots, leaves, berries. RANGE Sedentary.

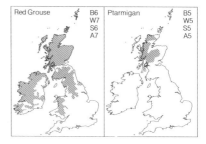

Red Grouse		B6 W7 S6 A7	Ptarmigan		B5 W5 S5 A5

Ptarmigan

♂ winter

♂ autumn

♂ summer

♀ summer

Black Grouse *Tetrao tetrix* ♂ 51–56 cm
(*c*21 in), ♀ 40–44 cm (*c*16½ in). Longer-
necked than Red Grouse (108), with tail
lyre-shaped (♂) or slightly forked (♀);
♂ glossy black with white wing-bar, undertail and underwings; ♀ mainly black-
barred rufous, with 2 narrow whitish
wing-bars, white on underwings. Flight as
Red Grouse, but sometimes much higher
with long glides over open moors and
valleys; tilts between trees like Capercaillie; walks sedately or runs; perches
on trees, walls, usually roosts on ground;
shy; often gregarious, sexes may segregate;
♂s display communally at regular leks (*cf*
Ruff, 134) with spread tail, drooped wings,
distended combs. *Ad* ♂ Mostly glossy
blue-black with contrasted white areas
and red combs (largest in spring), but in
Jun–Jul head and throat marked with
white and nape/neck (sometimes crown/
mantle) also barred rufous. *Ad* ♀ Mainly
rufous, barred glossy black above and
brown-black below; grey-white tips to
scapulars, belly, all tail-coverts. *Juv* Like
small dull ♀, often more buff and less
rufous (esp juv ♀) with duller, narrower
bars; buff-white shaft-streaks on scapulars
and wing-coverts. *1st year* ♂ Much as ad
♂ after moult in *c*Jul–Nov, but less glossy,
with various dark rufous bars or mottling
above and white marks on throat/breast,
tail less curved, small combs hidden.
VOICE At lek, ♂ hissing *chew-oosh* and
bubbling dove-like song ('rookooing'); ♀
loud barking *chuk-chuk* from perch, *kok-
ok* in flight. HABITAT Birch scrub, young
conifers, wood- and moor-edges, rushy
pastures. NEST In ground cover, 6–11 eggs,
May-Jul; 1 brood. FOOD Buds, shoots,
leaves, catkins, berries. RANGE Sedentary.

Capercaillie *Tetrao urogallus* ♂ 82–90 cm
(*c*34 in), ♀ 58–64 cm (*c*24 in). Very large
with heavy bill, longish neck, broad wings,
rounded tail; turkey-shaped ♂ dark with
yellow bill, white shoulder-patches/inner
underwings; ♀ mainly orange-buff boldly
barred blackish, but nearly plain rufous
chest, white on dark-mottled belly/flanks
and underwings. Flight powerful, tilting
from side to side among trees, sometimes

Black Grouse

♂ displaying

♂ Jun-Jul

♂

♀

sustained and high; noisy flapping on take-off; walks sedately, but can run fast, esp ♀; much in trees, esp roosting and in winter, perching even on tops; shy, sometimes in parties, ad ♂s usually solitary; ♂ displays on tree, rock or ground, with neck and fanned tail erect, wings drooped, throat-feathers stuck out or whole neck bristled in ripples. *Ad ♂* Blue-slate with brown mantle and wings, green-glossed breast, white shoulder-patches, whitish markings on tail-coverts, tail and belly, red skin by eyes. *Ad ♀* Pale buff to orange-brown, boldly barred blackish, but orange-chestnut breast-patch, much white on flanks and belly; tail barred rufous and dark brown; pale red skin by eyes. *Juv ♂* Like small ad ♀, but greyer above and on throat, still with dark bars; wing-coverts with buff-white shaft-streaks; breast rufous mottled dark brown, flanks rufous-buff, belly buff-white; tail barred/speckled whitish, buff, dark brown; no red by eyes. *Juv ♀* As juv ♂, but more rufous and bolder-marked above, throat black-spotted buff, flanks/belly barred dark

brown. *1st year ♂* As ad ♂ after moult in *c*Jun–Sep, but smaller with shorter bill and tail, duller head and breast. VOICE ♂ raucous retching or croaking, and 'song' of accelerating clicks, then pop like bottle cork, ending with rhythmic wheezing gurgle; ♀ soft whining bray, harsh cackling *kok-ok*, loud crooning. HABITAT Coniferous or mixed woods, esp pines on hillsides. NEST In ground cover, esp by trees, 5–11 eggs, end Apr–Jun; 1 brood. FOOD Plants, berries; conifer needles in winter. RANGE Extinct by 18th century, reintroduced in 19th; sedentary.

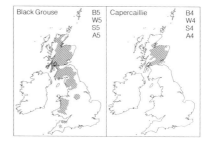

Black Grouse		B5	Capercaillie		B4
		W5			W4
		S5			S4
		A5			A4

Capercaillie

♀

♂

juv ♂

♀

♂ displaying

PARTRIDGES, PHEASANTS (Phasianidae)

Red-legged Partridge *Alectoris rufa* 33–36 cm (*c*13½ in). Larger, more upright than Grey Partridge, but with similar rufous tail; plain olive-brown to chestnut above, bold white supercilia and throat, black necklace, heavily barred 4-tone flanks, red bill and legs (but see juv). Actions similar; more often in open, tends to run rather than fly; coveys taking wing often scatter; often perches on fences, walls. *Ad* Supercilia and throat white, complete black necklace; flanks barred blue-grey, whitish, black, chestnut; belly orange-buff. *Juv* Faint supercilia and throat buff-white, sparse mottling instead of necklace, slight whitish and brown barring on orange-buff flanks, pale speckling and dark bars or blotches on mantle and esp scapulars/ coverts; bill brown, legs pinkish; as ad after moult in Aug–Nov. VOICE Harsh *chuk chuk chukuk chukar*; song *kok-chak- chak* with rhythm of steam-engine. HABITAT Farmland, brecks, heaths, dunes, coastal shingle. NEST In ground cover, 10–16 eggs, end Apr–mid Jul; 2 clutches (1 incubated by ♂). FOOD Much as Grey Partridge. RANGE Introduced from SW Europe since *c*1770; sedentary.

Grey Partridge *Perdix perdix* 29–32 cm (*c*12 in). Rotund, chicken-like, with short rufous tail, rounded wings; pale-streaked above, with orange face, grey neck/breast, chestnut-barred flanks, variable inverted chestnut U on breast ('*montana*' variety has much more rufous below). Flight fast, whirring, low, with glides on bowed wings; neck stretched up when running for cover; crouches blob-like in large fields; rarely perches; shy; as other gamebirds, small young fly at only 2–3 weeks; autumn/ winter coveys tend to keep together when flushed. *Ad* ♂ Face orange-chestnut; grey breast, greyish forecrown, neck, mantle (greyest *c*Apr–Jul); bold chestnut horse-shoe; legs flesh-grey. *Ad* ♀ Face paler, neck/upperparts browner, breast buff-grey, horseshoe reduced to blotches or absent, lesser/median coverts barred; after moult in Mar–May, neck/chest with buff spots, breast/flanks barred also

pale and blackish. *Juv* Head/upperparts dark brown streaked pale, breast/flanks buff-brown streaked whiter, throat whitish, legs yellow; as ads after moult Aug–Jan. VOICE Slowing cackle *krikrikri- kri-kri kri*; song hoarse *kirrr-ik kirrr-ik* like rusty lock. HABITAT Farmland with hedges; also moors, dunes. NEST In thick cover, 9–20 eggs, mid Apr–mid Jul; 1 brood. FOOD Seeds, leaves, roots; some insects. RANGE Sedentary.

Quail *Coturnix coturnix* 17–18.5 cm (*c*7 in). Heard far more than seen; smallest game-bird, like part-grown juv partridge but longer thinner wings, more pointed brown tail; buff-barred blackish above with pale streaks, crown-stripe and supercilia, and sandy to rufous below, with black-edged pale streaks and blackish barring on flanks. Very secretive, flying only if nearly trodden on. *Ad* ♂ Variable blackish central throat-stripe and 2 bands curving up to cheeks. *Ad* ♀ No central stripe, 2 bands broken into spots, brown moustaches; breast-sides spotted blackish. *Juv* As ♀, but narrower streaks above, smaller breast-spots; as ads after moult in Aug–Oct. VOICE Double croak; song liquid *kwic-we-wic* by day or night, ventriloquial. HABITAT Corn, long grass. NEST In crops, 7–12 eggs, end May–mid Aug; 1–2 broods. FOOD Seeds, insects. RANGE Summer visitor, May–Oct, wintering in Africa/S Europe.

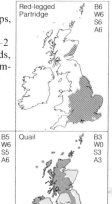

Red-legged Partridge	B6 W6 S6 A6
Grey Partridge	B5 W6 S5 A6
Quail	B3 W0 S3 A3

Red-legged Partridge

Grey Partridge

Quail

Pheasant *Phasianus colchicus* ♂ 75–90 cm (30–35 in), ♀ 52–64 cm (20–25 in). Typical ♂ has green-black head, red facial skin, coppery body and barred tail, buff wing-coverts; ♀ brown and buff, with some chestnut, all marked black. Flight strong, direct, with rapid beats and long glides after whirring take-off and fast climb, usually to no great height; walks slowly or runs with long tail level or raised; roosts in trees; wary; small flocks in winter, sexes may segregate. *Ad* ♂ Mixture of several races, esp SW Asian *colchicus* (bronze-black crown, no collar, mainly coppery but wing-coverts and narrow-barred tail more buff) and E Asian *torquatus* (olive crown, white eyebrows and collar, mainly yellow-buff but coppery breast, greyish wing-coverts and rump, broad-barred tail); may be paler, more chestnut or greener above, or have white wing-coverts; melanistic form mainly glossy green above and glossy purple below. *Ad* ♀ Buff to pink-buff and brown, chestnut on mantle and chest, with dark marks; may be more rufous, or sandier. *Juv* Like small short-tailed ♀ but duller, usually paler, more spotted on head, more streaked buff above; much as ads by Sep–Nov. VOICE ♂ crowing *korrk-kok* and *kutuk . . . kutuk*; ♀ husky *kia kia* and purr. HABITAT Woods, fields, marshes, upland scrub. NEST In ground cover, 8–15 eggs, Apr–Jul; 1 brood. FOOD Seeds, berries, shoots, invertebrates. RANGE Introduced from Asia since 11th century; sedentary.

Golden Pheasant *Chrysolophus pictus* ♂ 89–109 cm (35–43 in), ♀ 61–71 cm (24–28 in). Smaller and slimmer than Pheasant, even longer tail; ♂ mainly yellow and red; ♀ buff, barred and speckled black, but more rufous tail, and yellowish bill, legs and facial skin (*cf* Lady Amherst's). High steps, springy jumps; flies little except to tree roost, wing-beats less noisy. *Ad* ♂ Barred 'cape', buff tail laced with black. *Ad* ♀ Crown cinnamon-barred black, otherwise buff and cinnamon marked with black, esp breast/flanks broadly barred. *Juv* As small short-tailed ♀ but markings fainter, esp on chest/flanks. *1st year* ♂ Partly as ad ♀ by Oct–Nov, but

much of head orange-yellow, rump/tail-coverts red. VOICE ♂ harsh crowing *chak* or *cha-chak*. HABITAT Dense conifers, mixed woods. NEST In ground cover, 5–12 eggs, Apr–May; 1 brood. FOOD As Pheasant. RANGE Introduced from SE Asia since end 19th century; sedentary.

Lady Amherst's Pheasant *Chrysolophus amherstiae* 115–150 cm (45–59 in), ♀ 58–68 cm (23–27 in). Bulkier than Golden, ♂ tail much longer, ♀ shorter; ♂ green-black and white, with some red and yellow; ♀ paler buff than ♀ Golden, with bolder barring, less marked throat and belly, and blue-grey bill, legs and facial skin. May interbreed with Golden. *Ad* ♂ Black-scaled white 'cape', black-barred white and buff tail. *Ad* ♀ Forehead rufous, crown cinnamon-barred black; otherwise pale buff and cinnamon with clear black bars. *Juv* As small short-tailed ♀ but no rufous on forehead or black on crown, all barring duller. *1st year* ♂ Partly as ad ♂ after moult by Oct–Nov, with cape and tail shorter, head duller black, mantle and wings more as ♀, lower back and rump rufous-chestnut, long tail-coverts tipped orange-red, much whitish-buff below. VOICE ♂ sibilant crowing *ssu-ik-ik-ik*. HABITAT Woods with rhododendrons, brambles. NEST In ground cover, 6–11 eggs, Apr–May; 1 brood. FOOD As Pheasant. RANGE Introduced from SE Asia since *c*1900; sedentary.

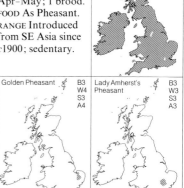

Pheasant · B6 W7 S6 A7

Golden Pheasant · B3 W4 S3 A4

Lady Amherst's Pheasant · B3 W3 S3 A3

Pheasant

melanistic ♀

colchicus ♂

♀

melanistic ♂

♀

torquatus ♂

Golden Pheasant

♂

♀

Lady Amherst's Pheasant

♂

♀

RAILS, GALLINULES, COOTS (Rallidae)

Water Rail *Rallus aquaticus* 27-29 cm
(*c*11 in). Like small Moorhen (118) with
long reddish bill; streaky brown above,
grey or buff below with boldly barred
flanks, whitish undertail marked buff and
black. Crepuscular, secretive; flutters
on short rounded wings with longish legs
dangling; swims short distances with jerky
Moorhen-like actions, but heard far more
than seen. *Ad* Chin white, face to breast
dark blue-grey, black flanks barred white;
legs pink-brown, sometimes greenish. *Juv*
Bill less red; throat whitish and face and
underparts buff, all mottled brown; flank-
barring dark brown and buff. *1st winter*
During Jul-Dec becomes more like ad, but
larger whitish chin, browner face, some
dark barring on brown-grey throat/breast.
VOICE 'Sharming' of grunts and squeals;
song measured hammering *kipp kipp kipp*.
HABITAT Dense reeds, sedges, osiers, in
lakes, rivers and fens; in winter also
reedy ditches, watercress beds. NEST In
reeds, sedges or grass tussocks, 6-11 eggs,
Apr-Jul; 2 broods. FOOD Mostly invertebrates, plants. RANGE Mainly sedentary;
winter visitor from Continent/Iceland,
Sep-early May (many in hard weather).

Spotted Crake *Porzana porzana* 22-24 cm
(*c*9 in). Smaller than Water Rail and with
shorter bill, tail and legs; upperparts and
less grey breast speckled with white, flanks
barred with brown, undertail buff, narrow
white line along outer primary. *♂ summer*
Lores blackish; spotting on rear of blue-
grey supercilia/throat, more over slate-
brown breast; bill yellow with red base
and olive tip, legs pale green. *♀ summer*
Supercilia and throat more spotted with
white than *♂*. *Ad winter* Head and breast
browner with more white spotting, lores
duller; *♀* usually browner than *♂*. *Juv* As *♀*
winter, but breast more brown-buff with
few spots; bill dark with yellowish base.
VOICE *♂* Explosive whistling *hwet . . . hwet
. . . hwet* ('whiplash'); mainly at dusk and
in night. HABITAT Fens, bogs and thickly
overgrown lake-sides; passage-migrants
also in open marshes, ditches. NEST In
dense vegetation or in tussocks in shallow

water, 8-12 eggs, mid May-end Jul; 1-2
broods. FOOD Invertebrates, plants. RANGE
Breeding scattered and seldom proved,
but probably now annual, esp NBr; also
passage-migrant, Mar-May, Oct-Nov;
occasional in winter, most European birds
moving to Africa. COMPARE Sora, Little
and Baillon's Crakes (268).

Corncrake *Crex crex* 25-28 cm (*c*10½ in).
Terrestrial rail, like slender gamebird;
mainly yellow-buff, streaked above, with
chestnut wings and flank-bars. Crepuscular, often only heard; in some areas
seen flying low, walking in open or even
perching on walls; usually walks with
head and tail down. *♂ summer* Upperparts
yellow-buff variably tinged grey, with
black feather-centres; grey-blue supercilia
and grey tinge to throat-sides and breast.
♀ summer As *♂*, but with less grey. *Ad
winter* After rapid moult in Aug-Sep,
purer yellow-buff above, with narrower,
grey supercilia, less grey elsewhere; *♀* often
has only tinge of grey on supercilia, none
on breast. *Juv* As ad winter, but without
grey; flanks redder, less barred. VOICE *♂*
repeated, loud, rasping *krrx-krrx*. HABITAT
Mowing grass, rank clover, boggy
pastures, nettle-patches. NEST In hay,
nettles, 8-12 eggs,
mid May-Jul; 1-2
broods. FOOD
Invertebrates, plants.
RANGE Summer
visitor, mid Apr-
Sep, wintering in
Africa; on passage
mid Apr-May, Aug-
Oct; formerly
nested in most of Br.

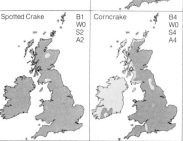

Water Rail

ad

juv

1st winter

ad

Spotted Crake

ad

♀ winter

juv

♂ summer

Corncrake

ad

♀ winter

♂ summer

juv

Moorhen *Gallinula chloropus* 31–35 cm (*c*13 in). Stocky waterbird with chicken-like bill and long toes; mainly blackish and slaty, but for white stripe along flanks, white-sided undertail, and coloured bill and legs. Low and brief flight looks laboured with legs dangling or trailing behind tail; swims buoyantly, jerking head and often tail, and patters along surface before taking off; rarely dives but can stay submerged in cover with only beak up; walks jauntily, with head up and tail horizontal or cocked and nervously flirted, but runs for cover with head down and wings flapping; perches or clambers in bushes; not usually gregarious; rather wary. *Ad* Blackish-brown above and slaty below, with ragged white streak along flanks, bold white undertail divided by black; red frontal shield and yellow-tipped bill, and red-gartered, yellow-green legs. *Juv* Pattern as ad, with similar undertail, but head and underparts much browner, with whitish throat and belly, buffish flank-stripe; green-brown bill, dull green legs. *1st winter* During Aug–Jan head and neck become more like ad, but still tinged brown and with whitish throat; underparts slaty but variably tipped buffish, flank-stripe thinner. *1st summer* From Apr, like ad but head and underparts brownish-slate. VOICE Deep, throaty *curruc* of alarm; short, high squawk *kik*, stammering *kikikikikik-kik-kik-kik*. HABITAT Almost any fresh water with emergent or adjacent cover, from urban ponds and woodland streams to lakes, rivers and marshes; also pastures and hedges some distance away. NEST In reeds, waterlogged branches, tussocks, also under brambles or in hedges or trees, 5–11 eggs, mainly mid Mar–mid Aug; 2–3 broods. FOOD Water-plants, grass, seeds, insects, worms, molluscs. RANGE Mainly sedentary; but joined by winter visitors from Low Countries/S Scandinavia, Sep–Apr. COMPARE Imm with imm American Purple Gallinule (268).

Coot *Fulica atra* 36–40 cm (*c*15 in). Rotund and thickset bird of open water, slaty-black, with glossy head and white frontal shield and bill, and long, lobed toes. Flight usually low, with large feet trailing like long tail; swims high, with neck hunched, back rounded, small head moving back and forward, and dives often but briefly; patters along to take off; splashes down breast first with feet lowered; walks easily, but usually stays near water; sometimes roosts in bushes; quarrelsome, but highly gregarious in winter, often with ducks. *Ad* Jet-black head with white frontal shield and bill; otherwise slate-black, greyer below, with variably clear whitish-tipped secondaries in flight; legs mainly green-grey. *Juv* Brownish-black above and brown-grey below, but much white on face, neck, breast and belly; bill and small frontal shield greyish. *1st year* During Aug–Dec becomes more like ad, but tinged with brown all over and often a few white feathers on throat and neck. VOICE Loud, piping squawk *kowk* or higher *tewk*; various shrill, metallic, clipped or explosive notes, and measured tapping sounds. HABITAT Lakes, reservoirs and slow rivers with extensive reeds and sedges, and on adjacent water-meadows, also tidal waters in Ir; in winter on any large water body including bare reservoirs and estuaries. NEST Built up from bottom in reeds, sometimes in open, or in tussocks, 4–8 eggs, late Mar–end Jul; 2–3 broods. FOOD Mainly water-plants, grass and seeds, also insects, molluscs, leeches, tadpoles, fish, eggs, young birds. RANGE Mainly sedentary, but gathering on larger waters in winter with many winter visitors from Low Countries/E Europe, Oct–Apr. NOTE **American Coot** *F. americana*, recorded in Cork in 1981, has white under tail, dusky band on bill, slight reddish bump at top of smaller white shield.

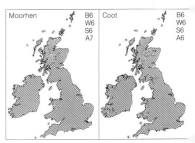

Moorhen

Coot

OYSTERCATCHERS (Haematopodidae)

Oystercatcher *Haematopus ostralegus*
41–45 cm (*c*17 in). Bulky pied wader with
stout orange-red bill, white wing-band.
Flight strong with shallow beats; walks
sedately, runs fast; perches on fences
near nest; gregarious. *Ad summer* Glossy
black; bill/eye-rings orange-red, bill-
tip often yellower, legs pink, eyes red. *Ad
winter* Duller black; white throat-band;
bill orange, tip duskier; legs duller. *Juv*
Throat-band indistinct, upperparts
brownish with buff feather-edges; bill
more pointed, darker; legs greyish, eyes
brown, no eye-rings. *1st year* After moult
Aug–Dec, as ad but browner
above; bill orange with brownish tip, legs
dark grey, eyes become redder, eye-rings
yellowish; half-collar not lost until 2nd
summer or older. VOICE Loud, shrill *peek*
or *peek-kapeek*; in song, notes accelerate
into trill. HABITAT Open shores; in NBr
nests on river shingle, grass near lochs.
NEST Scrape on shingle, sand, grass, crops,
3 eggs, Apr–Jul; 1 brood. FOOD Bivalve
molluscs; worms inland. RANGE Inland
only in summer; some emigrate as far as
Iberia; also passage/winter visitor from
Iceland/NW Europe, Jul–May.

STILTS, AVOCETS (Recurvirostridae)

Avocet *Recurvirostra avosetta* 41–45 cm
(*c*17 in). Elegant white-and-black wader
with long upturned bill, blue-grey legs.
Flight fairly fast with legs projecting;
walks gracefully with neck curved, often
bobbing head when alert; feeds in shallows
with side-to-side sweeps of bill, but in
deeper water dips head or even up-ends;
often in parties or small flocks. *Ad* Marked
with black or brown-black; some ♀s have
whitish mottling on forehead in winter;
♂ eyes redder-brown. *Juv* Cap brown with
some buff flecks; other markings dark
brown mottled with pale buff, extending
to mantle; white tail-coverts and tail
tipped with pale brown. *1st winter* As ad,
but cap browner with white mottling at
front; wings as juv through 1st summer.
VOICE Liquid melodious *kleep* or *kloo-it*.
HABITAT Breeds in shallow brackish
lagoons, also by estuaries; winters on
estuaries and mud-flats. NEST Scrape by
water, 3–4 eggs, mid Apr–early Jul;
1 brood. FOOD Insects, crustaceans, worms.
RANGE Summer visitor, Apr–Sep, but most
winterers of Br stock; also on passage
from Continent, end Mar–Jun, Jul–Sep;
recolonised in 1940s after century gap.

STONE-CURLEWS (Burhinidae)

Stone-curlew *Burhinus oedicnemus* 38–43
cm (*c*16 in). Ungainly-looking terrestrial
wader, mainly brownish, with staring
yellow eyes, yellow bill-base and legs and,
in flight, 2 black-edged white wing-bars.
Shy, active evening and night; slow wing-
beats, glides, but high and erratic at
dusk; walks with short steps, or runs
furtively, hunched up, pausing at intervals;
lies flat if alarmed; sociable. *Ad* Buff to
grey-brown streaked blackish, belly and
underwings white, undertail cinnamon;
usually only wing-bar on greater coverts
visible at rest. *Juv* Paler with narrower
streaks; bar on lesser coverts less clear,
on greater coverts thinner. VOICE Wailing
coor-ee, shriller than Curlew (140);
wild clamours during night. HABITAT Open
stony, chalky or sandy country; increasingly, arable land
and forestry rides.
NEST Scrape on bare
ground, 2 eggs, Apr–
Jul; 2 broods. FOOD
Insects, worms,
young birds. RANGE
Summer visitor,
Mar–Oct, wintering
in W/S Europe to
Africa.

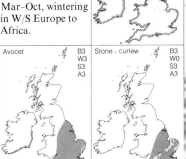

| Oystercatcher | B5 W5 S5 A5 |

| Avocet | B3 W3 S3 A3 | Stone–curlew | B3 W0 S3 A3 |

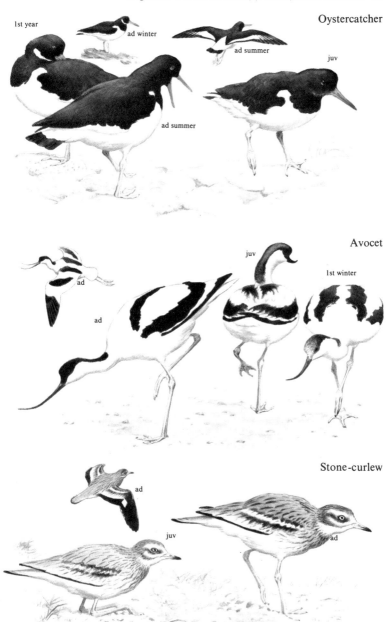

Oystercatcher

1st year

ad winter

ad summer

juv

ad summer

Avocet

juv

1st winter

ad

ad

Stone-curlew

ad

juv

ad

PLOVERS (Charadriidae)

Little Ringed Plover *Charadrius dubius* 14–16 cm (*c*6 in). Slighter than Ringed Plover, more 'tapered' rear, less rounded underbody; bill thinner, largely black; yellow eye-rings; longer dull pink or yellowish legs; black bands often narrower, white line above mask (ad); no real wing-bar. Actions as Ringed, but less gregarious. *Ad summer* Mask/breast-band black, ♀ often browner-black (esp behind eyes); bold eye-rings yellow. *Ad winter* Moults in Jul–Nov; mask/breast-band browner. *Juv* Whole cap brown, but pale buff forehead; eye-rings duller; upperparts scaled buff; breast-band brown, often incomplete. *1st winter* As ad winter, but (esp ♀) head-pattern less clear and brown breast-band narrower in centre; still some coverts with worn buff edges, eye-rings duller. VOICE High *pee-u*; grating *cree-a cree-a* in display flight. HABITAT Gravel pits, shingle by rivers and reservoirs, silt tips. NEST Scrape on ground, 4 eggs, Apr–Jul; 1–2 broods. FOOD Insects, also tiny molluscs. RANGE First nested in 1938 and now summer visitor, end Mar–Oct, wintering in Africa.

Ringed Plover *Charadrius hiaticula* 18–20 cm (*c*7½ in). Plump, with stubby bill and shortish legs showing orange to yellowish; white and black collars, pied head-pattern; broad white wing-bar and white-sided tail clear in flight. Flight fast, often low, with deliberate beats, gliding to land, then running with raised wings; runs like clockwork, pauses abruptly with head up, tilts body to pick up food; bobs head if uneasy; often in parties. *Ad summer* Mask/breast-band black (♂) or browner (♀); bill-base and legs orange, thin eye-rings orange (♂) or yellow-grey (♀). *Ad winter* From *c*Aug, mask/breast-band brownish (esp ♀), blacker again from *c*Jan; bill-base, eye-rings and legs duller (esp ♀). *Juv* Head-marks brown, but whitish forehead and stripe behind eyes (*cf* Little Ringed); breast-band brown, usually incomplete; upperparts scaled buff; bill blackish, legs dull yellowish. *1st winter* As ♀ winter from moult Aug–Jan, but some coverts with worn buff edges; less colour on bill. VOICE Soft *poo-i*, more piping *queep*; trilling *kwitaleeyu* in display flight. HABITAT Shingle or sand by sea, locally inland; winters esp on mud-flats. NEST Scrape on ground, 3–4 eggs, Apr–Jul; 2–3 broods. FOOD Many invertebrates. RANGE Mainly resident; also passage/winter visitor from Scandinavia/Iceland/Greenland, Aug–May. COMPARE Semipalmated (274).

Kentish Plover *Charadrius alexandrinus* 15–17 cm (*c*6¼ in). Smaller, slighter and paler than Ringed; bill and longer legs blackish; patch at each side of breast; white forehead extends into supercilia; wing-bar thinner, white tail-sides wider. Actions as Ringed; runs very fast as if on wheels. ♂ *summer* Breast-patches and head-marks black, crown rufous. ♀ *summer* Crown, mask and breast-patches all tawny-brown. *Ad winter* As ♀ summer after moult Jul–Sep, but browner; ♂ has broader white supercilia and collar, may start to show some black from Nov–Dec. *Juv* Paler, with buff supercilia, mottled breast-patches, scaled upperparts. *1st winter* As ♀ winter but some coverts with worn buff edges; ♂ starts to show black like ad. VOICE Soft *wit-wit-wit*, rolling *chirrirrip*. HABITAT Mud, sand, shingle. FOOD Mainly insects. RANGE Scarce migrant, end Mar–May, Aug–Oct; few bred SEBr to 1956, 1 pair EBr in 1979. COMPARE Greater Sand Plover (274).

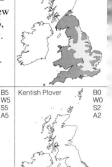

Little Ringed Plover	B3
	W0
	S3
	A4

Ringed Plover	B5
	W5
	S5
	A5

Kentish Plover	B0
	W0
	S2
	A2

Little Ringed Plover

ad winter

ad

♂ summer

juv

1st winter

Ringed Plover

ad

juv

♂ summer

♀ winter

Kentish Plover

juv

♂ summer

♂ winter

♂ summer

♀ summer

Golden Plover *Pluvialis apricaria* 27–29 cm (*c*11 in). Fairly large plover, with rather slender black bill, rounded head and green-grey or grey legs; upperparts speckled gold and black, underparts blackish in summer, whitish in winter; in flight, 'arm-pits' white, underwings whitish, wing-bar usually indistinct, no pale rump or visible tail-marks (*cf* Grey Plover). Flight fast with rapid beats; runs, pauses and tilts body like other plovers (*cf* Ringed Plover, 122); in breeding season often stands upright on moorland hummock; highly gregarious in winter. ♂ *summer S race (P.a. apricaria)* Breast and belly dusky, face dusky, indistinct whitish or yellowish border to underparts. ♀ *summer* Duller below, belly flecked with brown and whitish. ♂ *summer N race (P.a. altifrons)* Black face (to above bill) and underparts broadly bordered with white. ♀ *summer* More like S ♂, with black above bill indistinct, face dusky-brown flecked with yellow, white border much less distinct and more broken. *Ad winter* Underparts whitish, flecked gold on face

and breast; moult starts Jun–Jul, completed by Oct–Nov; summer plumage assumed Feb–May, often by mid March. *Juv* Like ad winter, but gold speckling paler, duller and more distinctly spotted; belly and flanks washed pale brown. *1st winter* Largely like ad from Sep–Nov, but more spotted scapulars and speckled flanks and belly often visible to Dec–Jan. *1st summer* Wing-coverts worn and greyish; summer plumage attained late (May), often incomplete. VOICE Liquid whistle *tlui*; in alarm when breeding, melancholy *tlee* or *tlee-oo*; in display-flight, mournful *tirr-pee-oo*. HABITAT Breeds on moors, bogs, upland pastures; winters on upland and lowland arable, pastures, much less on shores and mud-flats. NEST Scrape in heather or grass, often on bog hummocks, 3–4 eggs, Apr–Jun; 1 brood. FOOD Insects, worms, plants. RANGE Mainly resident, but breeding grounds deserted Sep–Feb, some cross Channel; many passage/winter visitors from Iceland/Fenno-Scandia, Aug–May; breeders mostly S type, late passage

Golden Plover

ad/1st winter

ad winter

juv

altifrons
♂ summer

apricaria
♀ summer

apricaria
♂ summer

includes N birds and few nest NBr.
COMPARE Lesser Golden Plover (274).

Grey Plover *Pluvialis squatarola* 28–31
cm (*c*11½ in). Stouter than Golden Plover
with thicker bill, larger eyes and longer
blackish-grey legs; in summer, speckled
with silver and grey above, all black
below but boldly bordered with white on
head, breast-sides and vent; in winter,
more uniform brownish-grey above and
whiter below than Golden, but juv shows
yellowish spotting above and streaks on
breast; in flight, easily distinguished by
black 'arm-pits', stronger wing-bar and
white rump. Behaviour much as Golden
Plover, but has more hunched, almost
dejected look at rest; wades much more
freely; usually in small parties, scattering
to feed. ♂ *summer* Face and underparts
black, rear belly and undertail white.
♀ *summer* Browner-black with whitish
mottling, undertail more barred brown.
Ad winter Brown-grey with whitish fringes
above, largely white below, but some
black often retained, at least to Oct–Dec;

moults to summer in Feb–May. *Juv* Grey-
brown above, spotted pale yellow and
cream, not unlike Golden; streaked buff-
brown on breast and flanks. *1st winter*
Upperparts more spotted than ad, median
coverts as juv until yellow wears away,
underparts largely white; juv plumage
moulted Sep–Jan. *1st summer* Much as ad
winter, little or no breeding plumage;
primaries moulted in May–Aug. VOICE
Plaintive whistle *tlee-oo-ee*. HABITAT Mud-
flats, sand beaches. RANGE Passage/winter
visitor from arctic USSR, end Jul–May;
some (esp 1st year) stay through summer.

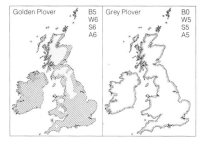

| Golden Plover | B5 W6 S6 A6 | Grey Plover | B0 W5 S5 A5 |

Grey Plover

ad/1st winter

ad/1st winter

juv

1st winter

♀ summer

ad winter

♂ summer

Dotterel *Charadrius morinellus* 20–23 cm (*c*8½ in). Fat-bodied small-billed plover with upright stance, whitish supercilia and breast-line, dull yellow legs; shows grey, chestnut and black in summer, but much duller in winter; in flight, no real wing-bar but pale leading edge to primaries and white fringe to short tail. Runs, pauses and tilts like other plovers; in small parties on migration, and on breeding grounds ♀s group while ♂s incubate; can be remarkably tame. *Ad summer* Blackish crown and grey and brown upperparts contrast with broad white supercilia forming V on nape, and whitish throat; grey-brown upper breast separated from chestnut below by white line; belly black, vent/undertail white; ♂ usually duller than ♀, with streakier crown, less bold supercilia, browner back and chest, less black on belly. *Ad winter* Upperparts paler, throat streaked, breast browner, supercilia and breast-line dull whitish, belly white; moult in Jul–Nov finished in wintering areas; spring moult, Mar–Jun, finished on breeding grounds.

Juv Resembles ad winter, but upperparts darker brown with broader sandy-buff fringes, breast-line indistinct and breast brown-buff and streaked. *1st winter* Moults in Sep–Dec, then paler, more like ad winter, but retains juv wing-coverts. *1st summer* As ad summer, but some juv inner median coverts and very worn primaries. VOICE Soft *peep-peep* in flight, *titi-ri* in alarm. HABITAT Breeds on mountains at 800–1300 m among short cover and bare stony stretches; on passage in open upland country and often traditional sites on lowland fields, heaths, coastal marshes. NEST Scrape in sparse vegetation, 3 eggs, late May–mid/late Jul; 1 brood. FOOD Mainly flies, beetles and spiders. RANGE Summer visitor, May–Aug, wintering in N Africa; on passage (some from N Eurasia), Apr–May, Sep–Oct.

Lapwing *Vanellus vanellus* 29–32 cm (*c*12 in). Large plover with distinctive wispy crest; looks black-and-white at distance, but upperparts mainly green; in flight, boldly pied, with broad rounded wings

Dotterel

ad summer

juv

ad winter

♀ summer

dull ♂ summer

(but ♀'s less so than ♂'s). Flight often tumbling and erratic; distinctive flopping wing-beats; actions much as other plovers (*cf* Ringed Plover, 122), but does not run so fast or raise wings; outside breeding season, usually in large, loose parties that fly in straggling formations. *♂ summer* Face, throat and breast black; sides and back of head white with black markings; upperparts mainly glossed bronzy-green, undertail cinnamon; tail white with black band, flight-feathers black with whitish tips to outer primaries, underwing-coverts white. *♀ summer* As ♂, but crest shorter, black face and throat mixed with white, upperparts less glossy. *Ad winter* As ♂/♀ summer, but face less black (♂ more than ♀ in front of and below eyes), throat and foreneck white, some buff fringes above; moults in Aug–Nov and partially in Feb–May. *Juv* As ad winter, but crest very short; duller green above and paler with cream fringes, breast-band browner. *1st winter* After moult in Jul–Dec, difficult to distinguish from ads, but crest shorter (esp ♀), wing-coverts duller and some with buff

edges until these wear off. VOICE In flight shrill, nasal *pee-vit*; song *perr-yu-weet weet-weet . . . perr-yu-weet*, last part coinciding with headlong plunge. HABITAT Open country from sea-level to 1000 m; uplands largely deserted after breeding, when flocks common on farmland and flat coasts. NEST Scrape in open, 3–4 eggs, mid Mar–early Jul; 1 brood. FOOD Invertebrates, some seeds, grasses. RANGE Some sedentary, others winter south to N Africa; also passage/winter visitor from N/E Europe, Jun–May, with strong onward movements in cold weather.

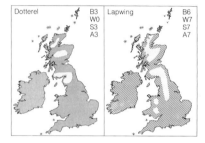

Dotterel		B3	Lapwing		B6
		W0			W7
		S3			S7
		A3			A7

Lapwing

ad summer

♀ winter

1st winter

♂ winter

♀ summer

♂ summer

juv

TYPICAL WADERS (Scolopacidae)

Sanderling *Calidris alba* 19–22 cm (*c*8 in). Just larger than Dunlin (132) and plumper, with shortish straight black bill, black legs, no hind toes, more 'bicycling' gait; in summer mainly rufous above, in winter pale grey and white with blackish 'shoulders'; bold white wing-bar in flight. Dashes to and fro by waves on sandy shores, legs moving so fast as to seem like wheels, bill darting from side to side; also feeds more sedately at pool edges; gregarious. *Ad summer* Head/breast rufous spotted with black, demarcated from white belly; otherwise black above fringed with rufous (♂) or greyish (♀), but wing-coverts grey edged paler. *Ad winter* After moult in Jul–Nov, white but for pale grey crown, back and white-fringed coverts, and blackish leading wing-edge. *Juv* Crown streaked blackish; chequered above with cream and white spots on blackish; breast washed buff. *1st winter* Much as ad after moult in Sep–Dec, but worn brownish juv coverts/tertials with traces of spots. VOICE High liquid *tyik-tyik*, twittering in flock. HABITAT Esp sandy shores, also mud-flats; scarce inland. FOOD As Dunlin. RANGE Passage/winter visitor from High Arctic, mid Jul–early Jun (esp Oct–Mar).

Little Stint *Calidris minuta* 14–15.5 cm (*c*5¾ in). Tiny, portly, with short fine bill, black legs; in summer dark-mottled rufous above, in winter grey-brown and white, but juv has bright chestnut fringes and whitish lines on blackish back. More active than Dunlin (132); flight faster, picks from surface, wades infrequently; usually tame. *Ad summer* Blackish above with bright rufous fringes; white below but for brown-speckled rufous chest. *Ad winter* After moult Aug–Dec, grey-brown above with pale-fringed coverts, greyish breast-sides (or gorget). *Juv* Black-brown above with bright chestnut and whitish fringes, latter forming clear Vs on back; nape usually greyish; buff chest-band mottled darker at sides; much as ad winter after moult Sep–Dec but for browner coverts, inner medians with rufous tips.

VOICE High *tit* or lower twitter; song soft flat trill. HABITAT/FOOD Much as Dunlin. RANGE On passage from NE Europe/Siberia, late Jul–mid Oct, scarce Apr–May, wintering in Africa (few north to Br). COMPARE American stints (276).

Temminck's Stint *Calidris temminckii* 13.5–15 cm (*c*5½ in). Much plainer and greyer and more attenuated than Little Stint, with usually complete grey breast-band, green-brown to yellowish legs and, in flight shorter wing-bar and white (not grey) sides to often fanned tail. Flight more erratic and fluttering, often towers when flushed. *Ad summer* Grey-brown above marked blackish and dull rufous; breast grey-brown with dusky streaks. *Ad winter* After moult in Jul–Nov, plain dark grey-brown above (but for white-fringed coverts) and on breast (or only sides). *Juv* Brown-grey above with fine dark crescents and scaled buff; breast buff-grey with contrasting white throat-patch; much as ad after moult in Aug–Dec, but worn brown juv inner medians tipped with whitish-buff. VOICE Short high trill; song ethereal trill, rising and falling. HABITAT Muddy patches, often with cover, in marshes, lakes, estuarine creeks. NEST Scrape in short grass, 4 eggs, Jun–Jul; 1 brood. FOOD Mostly insects. RANGE Scarce passage-migrant from N Europe, May–mid Jun, end Jul–Oct, wintering Africa; has nested NBr since 1969.

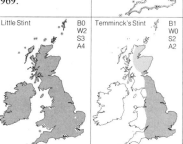

Sanderling B0 W5 S5 A5

Little Stint B0 W2 S3 A4

Temminck's Stint B1 W0 S2 A2

Sanderling

ad winter

ad winter

♀ summer

♂ summer

juv

Little Stint

juv

ad summer

ad winter

juv

Temminck's Stint

ad summer

juv

ad summer

ad summer

ad winter

Knot *Calidris canutus* 24–27 cm (*c*10 in). Much bigger than Dunlin (132), rounded, with shorter bill, neck and legs; mainly chestnut in summer, and grey and white in winter, with greenish legs; in flight shows thin white wing-bar, and all-pale rump. Actions as Dunlin but slower, more deliberate; flight stronger, often in huge dense flocks that carpet mudflats and fly in even tighter ever-changing formations. ♂ *summer* Blackish above with chestnut fringes, coverts grey edged white; rich rufous head (crown streaked blackish) and underparts. ♀ *summer* Fringes above much greyer; underparts mixed with white, belly whiter. *Ad winter* After moult Jul–Oct, mainly grey above with thin white fringes, whitish below with some streaks on greyer breast. *Juv* Browner-grey above with clear dark and creamy scaling; strongly tinged pink-buff below. *1st winter* Much as ad after moult Sep–Dec, but for browner juv coverts with some scaling. VOICE Low hoarse *knut*, twittering in flock; higher, more whistled *kwit-it*, esp in spring. HABITAT Mud/sand of estuaries; scarce inland. FOOD As Dunlin. RANGE Passage/winter visitor from High Arctic, end Jul–May; few non-breeders summer.

Pectoral Sandpiper *Calidris melanotos* 17–21 cm (*c*7½ in). Size variable; elegant, with short bill just decurved, small head, longish neck often upstretched, yellow-brown legs; dark above, usually 2 pale lines at sides of mantle; well-streaked breast ends sharply against white belly; in flight, faint wing-bar, dark-centred rump/tail. Flight sluggish; feeds slowly; stands still in grass like snipe. *Ad summer* Blackish above with chestnut and buff fringes forming pale lines on mantle, but coverts grey-brown with paler edges. *Ad winter* After moult in Aug–Oct, greyer-brown above with less contrasting, less rufous fringes. *Juv* Much as ad summer above, but brighter fringes and clearer whitish lines on scapulars, buff-fringed coverts; breast buff with finer streaking; as ad winter after moult in Sep–Dec, but darker juv inner medians with buff fringes. VOICE Loud reedy *krreet*. HABITAT Marshy places, wet meadows with short grass and pools. FOOD Insects, crustaceans. RANGE Visitor from N America, Aug–Oct (few Apr–Jul, also Nov): 25–50+ per year. COMPARE Sharp-tailed Sandpiper (278).

Purple Sandpiper *Calidris maritima* 20–22 cm (*c*8¼ in). Larger than Dunlin (132) and much stockier, almost portly, with slightly decurved bill, short legs; distinctively sooty (purple gloss on back) with some paler fringes (rufous in summer) but for whitish throat, white marks on breast, mainly white flanks and belly, weak wing-bar with white patch near body, and dull yellow legs and bill-base. Flight low, direct; found on rocky shores, where swims readily; tame; often with Turnstones. *Ad summer* Wide rufous and whitish fringes above; blackish streaks and spots on throat, breast, flanks. *Ad winter* After moult in Aug–Nov, mainly slate-grey and blackish; whitish fringes on inner coverts, white throat and belly, white mottling on lower breast and brown-streaked flanks. *Juv* Narrow chestnut, buff and whitish fringes above; like ad winter below but breast spotted. *1st winter* As ad winter after moult Sep–Dec, but for broad whitish fringes to juv median coverts and chestnut-tipped inners. VOICE Low *weet-wit*; often silent. HABITAT Rocky coasts, also groynes. FOOD Molluscs, crustaceans. RANGE Passage/winter visitor from N Europe/Arctic, end Jul–May (esp Oct–Apr); few summer; nested NBr 1978–80.

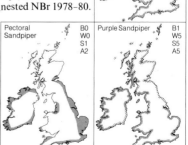

Knot	B0
	W7
	S6
	A7

Pectoral Sandpiper	B0
	W0
	S1
	A2

Purple Sandpiper	B1
	W5
	S5
	A5

Knot

ad winter

ad winter

♀ summer

juv

♂ summer

Pectoral Sandpiper

ad summer

juv

ad winter

Purple Sandpiper

ad winter

juv

ad winter

ad summer

Curlew Sandpiper *Calidris ferruginea*
18–20 cm (*c*7½ in). Elegant and rather
upright, with longish legs, neck and thin
evenly curved bill; much chestnut-red in
summer, grey-brown and whitish in
winter, with white rump. Actions much as
Dunlin but wades more deeply; not shy;
usually singly or small parties. *Ad summer*
Dark brown above with broad chestnut-
red fringes, wing-coverts as winter; rump
slightly obscured by blackish bars; rich
chestnut-red below (♀ paler), variously
marked with brown and whitish (esp ♀),
and whitish around bill. *Ad winter* After
moult in Jul–Dec, brown-grey above with
dark streaks, but whitish fringes to coverts,
whitish supercilia; white below with thin
grey-brown streaks on chest. *Juv* Dusky
above with brownish coverts, all scaled
with broad pale buff fringes (some tinged
with chestnut); clean buff-white below,
barely streaked just on chest; as ad winter
after moult in Sep–Dec but for buff-edged
inner median and lesser coverts. VOICE Soft
whistling or twittering *chirrip* or *chirririp*.
HABITAT On passage much as Dunlin.

FOOD As Dunlin. RANGE Passage-migrant
from Siberia, mid Jul–mid Oct, also end
Apr–early Jun, wintering in Africa; much
commoner in some years; rare in winter.
COMPARE White-rumped Sandpiper (276).

Dunlin *Calidris alpina* 16.5–19 cm (*c*7 in).
Commonest shore-wader, rather hunched,
with shortish black legs, variably longish
bill slightly decurved at tip; in summer
black belly, in winter grey-brown above
and white below with streaked breast; in
flight, white wing-bar and rump-sides.
Flight fast, flocks wheeling in unison,
tilting to appear dark or white, and
changing shape from balls to lines or
towers; glides to land, then briefly holds
wings up, like many waders; usually walks
delicately with rounded back, head
lowered to peck at and probe mud or sand;
often wades or swims in shallows; stands
on one leg, facing into wind, bill buried in
feathers; small parties quite tame, large
flocks much less so; flocks feed close
together; mixes with other waders. *Ad
summer S race (C.a. schinzii)* Blackish

Curlew Sandpiper

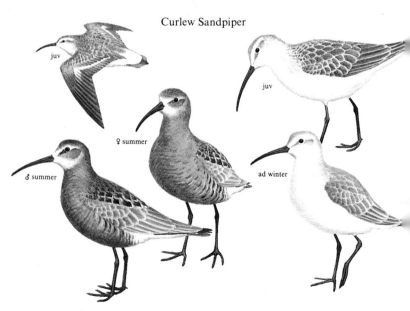

above with cinnamon and whitish fringes, wing-coverts as winter; nape of ♂ greyish contrasting with cap and mantle; breast buff-white with blackish streaks, small blackish belly-patch mixed with white. *N race (C.a. alpina)* As S race, but fringes on upperparts richer chestnut; grey nape of ♂ more contrasted; breast whiter, belly-patch larger and blacker. *NE Greenland race (C.a. arctica)* Paler above with buff and greyish fringes; faint breast-streaks, small belly-patch. *Ad winter* Brown-grey above, coverts greyer with whitish fringes, and white below with grey-brown breast-streaks; races indistinguishable, though those with short straight bills probably S ♂s and those with long curved bills probably N ♀s. *Juv* Blackish above with buff-white and chestnut fringes, but coverts browner with buff or chestnut fringes; as ad winter below, but blackish spots on flanks. *1st winter* As ad after moult in Aug–Nov, but brown inner median coverts with buff or chestnut fringes. VOICE Short, shrill, rasping *tree*, breeders also *wot-wot* and *kwoi-kwoi* when

uneasy; song rich purring trill in flight or on ground. HABITAT Mud-flats, salt-marshes, sand or shingle coasts, also inland marshes, lake-edges; breeds on hummocky grass moors with peaty pools, lowland mosses, grassy saltmarshes. NEST In tussocks, 4 eggs, May–early Jul; 1 brood. FOOD Worms, small molluscs, crustaceans, insects. RANGE S race breeds Apr–Aug, some crossing Channel to winter; both races abundant passage/winter visitors from SE Greenland/Iceland/N Europe, mid Jul–May, also some *arctica* from NE Greenland.

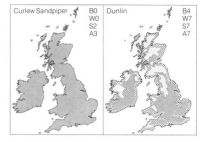

Dunlin

ad winter

ad winter

juv

alpina ad summer

arctica ad summer

schinzii ad summer

Ruff *Philomachus pugnax* ♂ 27–31 cm
(*c*11½ in), ♀ 22–25 cm (*c*9¼ in). Lumpy
wader, very variable in size, with small
head, longish neck and short, slightly
downcurved, mainly dark bill; legs range
from orange-red through yellow to green-
brown and grey; ♂ in summer has remarkable coloured head-tufts and ruff, which
give thick-necked appearance in flight;
other plumages less distinctive, but upperparts more or less scaly-looking, breast
plain buff (juv), greyish (ad winter) or
marked with sepia (♀ summer); in flight,
narrow white bar on rather long paddle-
shaped wings and obvious oval white
patch at sides of dark rump to tail. Flight
flicking, with erratic beats, sometimes
gliding; stands quite upright, but walks
deliberately with body rather horizontal,
searching in grass, probing in mud or
wading in shallows; often small flocks on
passage, also in ones and twos; many
autumn migrants in Br/Ir are juvs. ♂
summer During *c*Apr–Jul, head-tufts and
huge ruff in different combinations of
black, purple, chestnut, buff and white,

barred or plain; same colours extend to
much of upperparts, while sides of breast
and flanks sometimes correspond to ruff
but usually glossy purplish-black flecked
with white; contrasting white belly and
undertail-coverts; forecrown and lores
become bare, warty, and brown, yellow
or red. ♂ *moulting* Head-tufts and ruff
grown (Apr) and lost (Jun–Jul) rapidly:
without them, blackish above, variably
scaled and marked white, grey or rufous,
and lightly to heavily mottled blackish on
breast and flanks, contrasted with white
throat, foreneck and belly. ♀ *(Reeve)*
summer No tufts or ruff; head and hindneck variably streaked black; back black
or variably rufous, scaled with pale edges;
coverts grey-brown with paler tips; throat
white spotted dusky, breast and flanks
barred or mottled dark brown and scaled
with white, belly white. *Ad winter* More
uniform grey-brown above with some
scaly effect, esp on wing-coverts; sometimes white collar or pale head; white or
whitish below, with breast, sides of neck
and flanks greyish; legs and bill-base, as

Ruff

♂ summer

♂s DISPLAYING AT LEK

in summer, orange-red or pinkish, sometimes yellowish; sexes alike, but ♂s usually obviously larger. *Juv* Bold scaly pattern above of blackish-brown edged with warm buff; throat, foreneck, breast and flanks distinctively almost uniform buff; bill-base paler brown, legs yellow-brown or greenish, sometimes greyish; ♂ already larger than ♀. *1st winter* As ad winter after moult Aug–Oct, but still some juv feathers above; legs become browner or greener, and some have pink or orange tinge. *1st summer* Moults later than ads, usually retaining more winter feathers in spring; otherwise as ads but inner median coverts still often buff-fringed, primaries often very worn; ♂'s ruff usually smaller. VOICE Usually silent; occasionally low *chuk-uk* in flight. DISPLAY ♂s gather at special arenas, or leks, often on slight rise; each has small court, where scuttles about with head and neck horizontal, head-tufts raised, and wings spread, fluttering; periodically crouches with bill touching ground, ruff and tail spread, and shivers feathers; interspersed are short circular

flights and mainly mock fights; ♀s visit ♂s at leks for mating. HABITAT In Br breeds in grassy meadows after winter floods; passage/winter on marshes, sewage farms, mud edges of lakes and reservoirs, less often on side-creeks of estuaries. NEST Usually within *c*400 m of lek; hidden in sedges or grass, 4 eggs, May–mid Jun; 1 brood. FOOD Mainly insects, also worms, molluscs, crustaceans, seeds. RANGE Rare breeder, formerly much more widespread but ceased to nest regularly after 1871 (sporadically to 1922), then recolonised 1963; passage from Low Countries/ Scandinavia, end Mar–early Jun and, esp, mid Jul–Oct; winters in Mediterranean/Africa (where many stay over 1st summer), but some now regularly in Br/Ir. COMPARE Juv with Buff-breasted Sandpiper (278).

Jack Snipe *Lymnocryptes minimus* 18–20 cm (*c*7½ in). Small snipe with obviously short bill and silent escape flight – slower, more direct than Snipe (no real zigzag or towering), usually for short distance so that distinctive lack of white on more wedge-shaped tail hard to see. Often stays hidden until almost trodden on; not gregarious. *Ad/juv* Crown blackish in centre; upperparts glossed with purple and green, with brighter pale buff stripes than Snipe; neck and breast streaked rather than spotted with blackish, and flanks indistinctly mottled, not barred. VOICE Usually silent when flushed, sometimes a low, weak note. HABITAT Marshes, usually in thick, low cover. FOOD Insects, molluscs, worms, seeds. RANGE Passage/winter visitor from N Europe, Sep–May.

Snipe *Gallinago gallinago* 25–28 cm (*c*10½ in). Medium-sized with very long bill (6–7.5 cm), richly patterned in black, brown and rufous with cream stripes on head and back; white line along rear of secondaries and some white on edges of tail visible in flight. When flushed, usually calls and flies in low zigzag, then towers up and makes off with rapid beats, bill pointing down and body still tilting from side to side; often simply crouches and sometimes travels only short distance before landing, but flight seldom as weak and direct as Jack Snipe; largely crepuscular; often in small parties; secretive, seldom allows close approach. *Ad* Head striped, with buff down centre of crown; buff stripes down sides of mantle and scapulars; neck and breast buff with lines of dark brown spots and V-marks; flanks buffish barred dark brown; belly white. *Juv* Difficult to distinguish: buff stripes on back usually narrower and paler, sometimes almost white; light tips to wing-coverts lack ad's central blackish line. *Melanistic 'Sabine's Snipe'* (chiefly in Ir) Black and dark rufous above without buff stripes; neck, breast and flanks dull reddish-buff marked with sepia; belly sooty-brown. VOICE In flight, hoarse *scaap*; song quick, hollow *chip-per* constantly repeated; in display-dives, spread outer tail-feathers produce throbbing *vuvuvuvuvu* (drumming). HABITAT Marshes, water-meadows. NEST In tussocks, 4 eggs, mainly Apr–Jul; 1 brood. FOOD Worms, insects, seeds. RANGE Mainly resident, some move to France; also passage/winter visitor from N Europe, Aug–Apr. COMPARE Great Snipe (278).

Woodcock *Scolopax rusticola* 32–36 cm (*c*13½ in). Heavy wader of open woodland; marbled red-brown with broad dark bars on back of head, finely barred below; shows rufous tail when flushed; in flight, ponderous with rather rounded wings, bill pointing down. Mainly nocturnal. When flushed, rises with swishing wings, dodging among tree-trunks; flight fast and straight or slow and wavering, but in roding display at dawn and dusk rather owl-like; walks with bill inclined down, tail sometimes cocked; solitary and shy. *Juv* Very like ad, but forehead more spotted, black bars on hindcrown duller and separated by narrower buff lines, barring on underparts narrower and paler. VOICE Generally silent except when roding: deep, grunting *kwar kwar* followed by thin, high-pitched *tsiwick*. HABITAT Woodland with ground cover, open rides and wet areas; also more open country. NEST Scrape under bracken, brambles, or tree, 4 eggs, early Mar–mid Jul; 1 brood. FOOD Worms, insect larvae. RANGE Mainly sedentary, few winter south to Iberia; also passage/winter visitor from Continent, mid Oct–Apr.

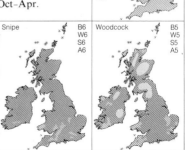

Jack Snipe   B0 W5 S5 A5

Snipe   B6 W6 S6 A6

Woodcock   B5 W5 S5 A5

Jack Snipe

ad/juv

ad/juv

Snipe

ad

melanistic ad

drumming

juv

ad

Woodcock

roding

ad

juv

ad on nest

Black-tailed Godwit *Limosa limosa* 38–43 cm (*c*16 in). Large upstanding wader with long, almost straight bill (7.5–12.5 cm) and long legs trailing beyond black-banded white tail in flight; bold white wing-band; at rest, visible tibia half as long again as Bar-tailed; in summer, head and breast chestnut, flanks variably barred; in winter grey above and white below. Flight quite fast with rapid beats; walks rather gracefully, neck often at least partly upstretched; probes deeply in mud or sweeps bill in shallows, wading up to belly and even submerging head; gregarious. ♂ *summer Continental race (L.l. limosa)* Head and breast cinnamon-chestnut which seldom extends past breast, upper-parts marked dark-brown and red-buff, but wing-coverts grey-brown with whitish fringes. ♂ *summer Icelandic race (L.l. islandica)* Redder-chestnut clearly more extensive on breast/flanks; bill often obviously shorter. ♀ *summer* Races as ♂, but usually duller: crown browner, rest of head paler or brownish, upperparts with less red-buff; underparts paler with less

extensive chestnut, brownish-speckled and with fewer bars. *Ad winter* After moult in Jun–Oct, rather uniform grey-brown above with white edgings to wing-coverts; underparts white, face, neck, breast and flanks brownish. *Juv* More like ad summer than winter, with rufous tinge to neck and breast and pale pink-chestnut fringes on dark brown upperparts, but also red-buff edges to wing-coverts. *1st winter* After moult in Aug–Nov, as ad winter but some worn and faded buff-fringed wing-coverts remain. VOICE Loud clear *weeka-weeka-weeka* in flight; noisy when nesting, *krru-wit-tew* song in display-flight. HABITAT Breeds in water-meadows and adjacent crops, rough pastures, marshes and, in NBr, rushy bogs; winters on saltmarshes, sheltered estuaries. NEST Scrape in lush waterside vegetation, 4 eggs, mid Apr–mid Jun; 1 brood. FOOD Worms, molluscs, insects, seeds. RANGE Ceased to breed early 19th century, regular again since 1952, in nesting areas Mar–Jul; also passage/winter visitor from Iceland (esp Ir, N/WBr) and Continent

Black-tailed Godwit

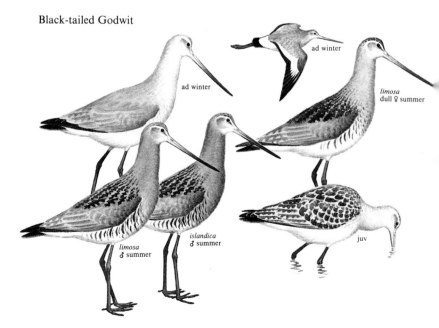

ad winter

ad winter

limosa dull ♀ summer

islandica ♂ summer

limosa ♂ summer

juv

(esp SE/SBr), Jul–May; some non-breeders summer on coasts.

Bar-tailed Godwit *Limosa lapponica* 36–40 cm (*c*15 in). Less upstanding than Black-tailed, with more upturned bill about same length as Icelandic race (7–11 cm); shorter legs (with shorter visible tibia at rest) barely extend beyond barred tail in flight, when also shows whitish rump-triangle; no clear wing-bar; in summer, ♂ has whole underparts red-chestnut, ♀ much duller and browner; in winter, paler and less uniform than Black-tailed. Flight and behaviour as Black-tailed, but wing-action less loose; looks stockier and less graceful on ground, walks faster. ♂ *summer* Head, neck and all underparts red-chestnut, streaked dark brown on crown and nape, lightly marked on flanks and undertail; upperparts resemble Black-tailed. ♀ *summer* Much duller and browner than ♂, sometimes only little summer plumage: throat, breast and flanks at best pale pink-chestnut marked with brown; upperparts paler; bill usually longer. *Ad*

winter After moult in Jul–Nov, obviously more streaked above than winter Black-tailed, also with more pale fringes; more white below, with faint streaks at sides of breast. *Juv* More brown and buff, and more streaked, than juv Black-tailed. *1st winter* After moult in Sep–Feb, as ad winter but some buff-fringed coverts remain. *1st summer* Often little summer plumage attained. VOICE Flight-call quick, low *kirrik kirrik*. HABITAT Mud-flats, sandy shores. FOOD Worms, molluscs. RANGE Passage/winter visitor, from NE Europe, Jul–May; few stay summer.

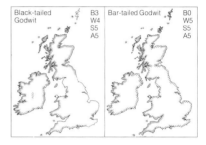

Black-tailed Godwit — B3 W4 S5 A5

Bar-tailed Godwit — B0 W5 S5 A5

Bar-tailed Godwit

ad winter

juv

ad winter

♂ summer

♀ summer

Whimbrel *Numenius phaeopus* 39–43 cm (*c*16 in). Like small Curlew, with shorter bill (7.5–10 cm) kinked down near tip, striped crown, and whiter throat; darker above, wings more uniform in flight; Wing-beats faster; generally less wary. *Ad Eurasian race (N.p. phaeopus)* Whitish rump; upperparts indistinctly marked buff. *Juv* Dark scapulars and wing-coverts clearly notched and spotted buff. *1st winter* Some faded spotting retained to at least No. *N American race (N.p. hudsonicus)* No white rump; browner underwing. VOICE Tittering whistle *ti-ti-ti-ti-ti-ti-ti*; song repeated *teeeu* followed by very Curlew-like bubbling. HABITAT Breeds on boggy moorland; on passage, mud-flats, rocky shores, adjacent fields. NEST Scrape on low hummocks, 4 eggs, mid May–early Jul; 1 brood. FOOD Inland, insects, berries, molluscs; on coast, crabs, molluscs. RANGE Summer visitor, May–Aug, wintering mainly in Africa; on passage, also from Iceland/N Europe, mid Apr–mid Jun, Jul–Oct; American race vagrant (2: May, Oct, Shetland/Kerry.)

Curlew *Numenius arquata* 51–61 cm (*c*22 in). Very large, streaky brown, with long and evenly curved bill (♂ 9.5–14 cm, ♀ 14–18.5 cm); whitish triangular rump. Flight often leisurely, rather gull-like; walks sedately; probes in mud or pricks from surface; often in large flocks which fly high in lines and bunches but scatter to feed; usually extremely wary. *Ad* Scapulars and coverts with indistinct pale markings. *Juv* Upperparts warm brown (not grey-brown like ad) with broad buff edges, and scapulars and dark-centred wing-coverts edged and notched buff; bill obviously shorter at first. *1st winter* As ad, but to at least Jan–Feb retains many juv scapulars and inner median coverts which become worn and heavily notched. VOICE Ringing *coour-lee*; alarm fast *kvi-kvi-kvi*; song of slow, then accelerating, liquid notes and bubbling trill, in display-flight shoots up, hangs poised, planes down on bowed wings. HABITAT Breeds on moors, upland pastures, locally lowland heaths, water-meadows, mixed farmland, dunes; winters mainly on mud-flats and adjacent

grassland. NEST Scrape on moss hummocks or in tussocks, 4 eggs, mid Apr–end Jun; 1 brood. FOOD Inland, insects, worms, plant material; on coast, worms, molluscs, crabs. RANGE On nesting grounds Mar–Aug, then moves to coasts, some to France and Iberia; also passage/winter visitor from N Europe, Jul–May.

Turnstone *Arenaria interpres* 22–24 cm (*c*9 in). Portly, with stubby bill, orange legs; pied plumage, chestnut back in summer; unmistakable pattern in flight. Tosses aside weeds and stones with bill. *♂ summer* White head and underparts, streaked on crown and patterned with black on face and breast; mantle and scapulars black-brown and orange-chestnut. *♀ summer* Duller, with streaked head, buffish on nape; mantle and breast-pattern duller. *Ad winter* After moult in Jul–Oct, head, upperparts and breast blackish with some greyish fringes. *Juv* Browner than ad winter, upperparts scaled buff; legs duller than ad. *1st winter* After moult in Aug–Nov, as ad winter, but may show buff fringes on medians/scapulars. *1st summer* After moult in Mar–Jun, some ♂s resemble ad ♀ summer, others and ♀s assume little summer plumage. VOICE Staccato *tukatuk*.
HABITAT Rocky/ stony coasts, also sands, mud-flats. FOOD Invertebrates, carrion. RANGE Passage/winter visitor from N Europe/NE America, end Jul–May; some in summer.

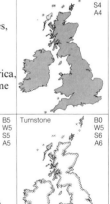

Whimbrel | B3 W1 S4 A4

Curlew | B5 W5 S5 A5

Turnstone | B0 W5 S6 A6

Whimbrel

hudsonicus
ad/juv

phaeopus
ad/juv

juv

ad

Curlew

ad

juv

ad

Turnstone

♀ summer

♂ summer

ad winter

ad winter

juv

Spotted Redshank *Tringa erythropus* 29–32 cm (*c*12 in). Larger and more elegant than Redshank, with longer legs and longer finer bill; black, or grey and white (or mottled in moult), with long white patch on back and rump above barred tail (*cf* dowitchers, 278). Actions as Redshank; less noisy; wades in deeper water, often swims. *Ad summer* After moult Mar–May, mainly black, spotted above with white; ♀ has pale fringes on crown and underparts, more white under tail; bill-base dull red, legs dark brown-red. *Ad winter* With moult *c*Aug–Nov, mainly grey above, broadly fringed white on browner scapulars/wing-coverts; white supercilia; white below, grey wash on chest/flanks; legs orange-red. *Juv* Dark brown above spotted white, white below barred brown; much as ad winter by *c*Nov. VOICE Loud clear *tchu-it*. HABITAT/FOOD As Redshank. RANGE On passage between Fenno-Scandia and SW Europe/Africa, Jul–Oct, also Apr–Jun; increasingly in winter.

Redshank *Tringa totanus* 26–30 cm (*c*11 in). Red legs, longish straight red-based bill; brown or grey-brown and white with triangular white rump and white inner rear wings in flight. Nervous, noisy; flight fast, erratic, tilting, with jerky shallow beats; bobs if suspicious, stretching neck up and jerking tail down; when nesting, perches on posts, trees; gregarious. *Ad summer* After moult in Feb–Apr, brown above with some darker streaks and bars; white below, variably mottled/barred dark brown; legs orange-red. *Ad winter* With moult in Jul–Jan, more uniform grey-brown above; more white round eyes, finely streaked greyish throat/breast, less barred flanks. *Juv* Brown above with buff fringes; buff breast lightly streaked; legs orange-yellow. *1st winter* As ad after moult in Aug–Jan but for buff tips to inner median coverts. VOICE Musical whistle *tlu* or down-slurred *tlu-leu-leu*, taking wing with excited babble; alarm incessant *tewk*; song *teu* or *taweeo* increasing in speed. HABITAT Estuaries, saltings, marshes, muddy reservoirs; breeds in wet meadows, rushy fields, grassy moors. NEST In tussocks, 4 eggs, mid Apr–mid Jun;

1 brood. FOOD Crustaceans, molluscs, worms, insects. RANGE Resident, but moves to coasts in winter, some cross Channel; also passage/winter visitor from Iceland/N Europe, Jul–May.

Greenshank *Tringa nebularia* 29–32 cm (*c*12 in). Taller, lankier than Redshank, with longer and stouter slightly upturned bill, longer legs green (very rarely yellow); in flight, white wedge up back, and dark wings longer, narrower and more pointed than Redshank. Flight stronger, usually straighter; feeds by picking, probing, sweeping, and lunging; singly or parties. *Ad summer* After moult in Feb–May, blotched grey and black above, with head and breast heavily streaked/spotted blackish. *Ad winter* Pale greyish above, fringed white and sepia; wings darker; face whitish, neck and breast grey finely streaked. *Juv* Dark brown above, greyer on scapulars, with broad buff fringes; breast sparsely streaked. *1st winter* As ad with moult in Aug–Mar, but for some coverts buff-fringed and wearing to plain brown. VOICE Loud ringing *teu-teu-teu*, excited *chip*; song whistled *teu-i* repeated. HABITAT As Redshank; breeds on bare moors, open pine forest. NEST Open scrape, 4 eggs, May–mid Jun; 1 brood. FOOD As Redshank, also fish. RANGE Nesting areas Apr–Jul; passage/winter as Spotted Redshank. COMPARE Marsh Sandpiper, Greater Yellowlegs (280).

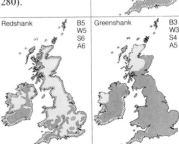

Spotted Redshank	B0
	W3
	S4
	A4

Redshank	B5
	W5
	S6
	A6

Greenshank	B3
	W3
	S4
	A5

Spotted Redshank

ad summer

ad winter

ad winter

juv

Redshank

juv

ad winter

ad summer

ad winter

ad winter

Greenshank

ad winter

juv

ad summer

ad winter

Green Sandpiper *Tringa ochropus* 22–24 cm (*c*9 in). Larger, stouter than Wood Sandpiper, with shorter legs, broader wings; dark olive-brown upperparts and breast-streaks, and dark underwings, give all-black look in flight, but for white belly, rump and banded tail. Shy, solitary; escape-flight similar to Snipe (136), zigzagging low, then towering with twisting jerky action; bobs head and tail, but not constantly teetering like Common Sandpiper. *Ad summer* By May, whitish spots above (nearly worn away by Aug), streaked head. *Ad winter* With moult *c*Aug–Nov, more uniform above with fewer indistinct buffish spots. *Juv* Paler olive-brown with copious deep buff spots, especially on tertials; much as ad by *c*Oct. VOICE Ringing *weet tweet weet-weet*; more rippling *tu-loo-ee*. HABITAT Mud gullies by lakes, rivers, marshes. FOOD As Common Sandpiper. RANGE On passage between NE Europe and Mediterranean/Africa, Jun–Nov, Mar–May; also winter; has bred NBr. COMPARE Solitary Sandpiper (280).

Wood Sandpiper *Tringa glareola* 19–21 cm (*c*8 in). Slender, with shorter bill, longer (usually pale) legs, thinner wings than Green Sandpiper; browner and more spotted, with streakier head, clearer supercilia, but less contrasting whitish rump, more barred tail, pale underwings. Escape-flight fast, erratic, with jerky shallow beats, often rising high, but not zigzagging or towering; less secretive; gregarious; noisy. *Ad summer* By Apr, dark brown above, barred and chequered buff and white; breast whitish, streaked and spotted dark brown. *Ad winter* With moult Jul–Oct, more uniform, less obviously spotted; breast grey-brown obscurely streaked. *Juv* Warmer brown above, copiously spotted rich buff; breast grey-brown, mottled paler; much as ad by *c*Oct. VOICE Shrill *chiff-iff-iff*; song *deedl-eedl-eedl*. HABITAT Marshes; breeds near lochs. NEST Scrape in grass or heather, 4 eggs, end May–early Jul; 1 brood. FOOD As Common Sandpiper. RANGE On passage between NE Europe and Africa, Jul–mid Oct, also Apr–May; has bred NBr since 1959. COMPARE Lesser Yellowlegs (280).

Common Sandpiper *Actitis hypoleucos* 18.5–20.5 cm (*c*7¾ in). Compact, with shortish pale-based bill and short grey-green legs (rarely yellowish), but rear body rather elongated and constantly wagging or 'teetering'; olive-brown and white, with white wedge behind rounded brown breast-sides; in flight, brown rump and white tail-sides, wing-bar and rear edge to secondaries. Flight particularly distinctive with wings stiffly flicked and bowed in brief glides, low over water; circles rapidly in courtship flight; singly or small parties. *Ad summer* After moult in Feb–May, bronzy-brown above with fine dark marks; grey-olive chest-sides well-streaked. *Ad winter* With moult in Jul–Oct, more uniform olive-brown above, wing-coverts obscurely barred (*cf* juv); chest-sides thinly streaked. *Juv* Brown above, barred darker and tipped buffish, coverts and tertial-edges barred sepia and buff; chest-sides mottled; much as ad by *c*Nov. VOICE Shrill *tsee-wee-wee*; song fast *titirri-tirri-tit* in flight or on ground. HABITAT Lakes, reservoirs, marsh runnels, estuaries; breeds by rocky streams, rivers, lakes. NEST Scrape esp on banks near water, 4 eggs, May–mid Jul; 1 brood. FOOD Insects, also molluscs, crustaceans, worms. RANGE Summer visitor Apr–Aug, wintering mainly in Africa; on passage (inc from Fenno-Scandia), end Mar–May, Jul–mid Oct; few winter. COMPARE Spotted Sandpiper (280).

Green Sandpiper

B0
W3
S4
A4

Wood Sandpiper

B1
W0
S3
A4

Common Sandpiper

B5
W2
S6
A6

ad summer

ad/juv   ad/juv

Green Sandpiper

ad winter   juv

ad summer

ad/juv   ad/juv

Wood Sandpiper

ad winter   juv

juv

ad/juv

Common Sandpiper

ad winter   ad summer

Red-necked Phalarope *Phalaropus lobatus*
17–19 cm (*c*7 in). Dainty, habitually
swimming wader with black, needle-like
bill, slate-grey legs; in summer, mainly
dark slate to brown above and white below
with orange on neck (♂ all duller than ♀);
in winter, grey and white with dark eye-
patches (*cf* Sanderling, 128); bold white
wing-bar and white sides to rump in
flight. Full flight fast but often flits
erratically over pools; runs quickly,
darting about, but much more often seen
swimming with Moorhen-like head-
bobbing, pecking from side to side, often
spinning round like top, even dipping head
or up-ending; floats buoyantly with neck
erect, back sloping down, tail level or
depressed; usually in ones and twos; very
tame. ♀ *summer* Slate-grey above, with
golden-buff lines on back; throat white,
and neck-patches orange-red mixing into
grey chest-band. ♂ *summer* Much duller
with brownish upperparts (mantle with
more buff streaking), ill-defined whitish
throat, less extensive orange on neck. *Ad
winter* After moult in Jul–Jan, sometimes
by Oct, pale blue-grey above, streaked
with white, and white face and underparts, but for darker wings, blackish
eye-patches and blue-grey breast-sides.
Juv Much darker than ad winter with
more extensive black-brown cap, upperparts dark brown with golden-buff lines;
lower throat, breast-sides and flanks all
suffused with pink-buff; legs blue-grey
to yellowish-pink, esp on toe-lobes. *1st
winter* More like ad winter, with some
grey above, but cap usually larger and
browner, upper mantle mottled black-
brown. *1st summer* Some assume summer
plumage, others remain in worn 1st
winter. VOICE Low *tyit*; *tchirrek* in alarm.
HABITAT Boggy edges of shallow pools,
waterlogged peat-cuttings, with bogbean,
sedges, and yellow iris; on passage mainly
at sea, rare inland. NEST In tussocks, 4 eggs,
Jun–mid Jul (♂ incubates); 1 brood. FOOD
Small insects, molluscs, crustaceans.
RANGE Rare summer visitor, May–Aug,
and scarce passage-migrant from Iceland/
Fenno-Scandia, Apr–Jun, mid Jul–Oct,
wintering at sea on tropics.

Red-necked Phalarope

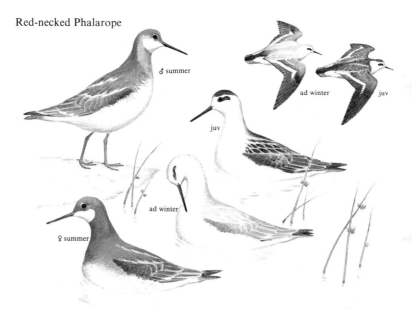

♂ summer

ad winter

juv

juv

ad winter

♀ summer

Grey Phalarope *Phalaropus fulicarius*
19–21 cm (*c*8 in). Little larger/stockier
than Red-necked, with stouter broader
bill (often yellowish base), heavier head,
thicker neck, longer tail, shorter legs
(often yellowish toe-lobes); in summer,
chestnut-red below, with bold white sides
of head; in winter, as Red-necked but
upperparts more uniform and paler above,
wing-bar less contrasting. Swims with
back more level and tail higher than Red-
necked, giving more boat-shape, bill often
held more down-pointed; looks like tiny
gull on sea; often singly, sometimes in
flocks. ♀ *summer* Black-brown cap, white
cheeks, rich chestnut underparts; bill
yellow with black tip. ♂ *summer* Browner
cap and mantle streaked buff, cheeks
dingier, underparts duller, often some
white on belly; bill black with yellow base.
Ad winter After moult in Aug–Dec, much
as Red-necked, though paler grey, more
uniform and less streaked with whitish
above; bill black-brown, often yellowish
at base. *Juv* Black-brown above, streaked
with buff; white below, washed pink-buff
on face to chest; bill blackish, base
browner. *1st winter* More like ad winter,
but cap/mantle mixed grey and brown, and
with blackish juv wing-coverts and
tertials. *1st summer* Perhaps assumes only
partial summer plumage. VOICE Shrill
twit, higher-pitched than Red-necked.
HABITAT On passage at sea, rare inland.
FOOD Mostly invertebrates. RANGE
On passage between Iceland/Arctic and
seas off W Africa, late Sep–Nov (occasionally in hundreds); rare other months.

COMPARE Wilson's Phalarope (272).

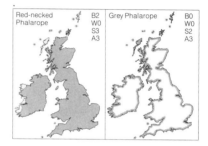

Red-necked Phalarope	B2 W0 S3 A3	Grey Phalarope	B0 W0 S2 A3

Grey Phalarope

juv

ad winter

1st winter

♂ summer

♀ summer

ad winter

SKUAS (Stercorariidae)

Great Skua *Stercorarius skua* 56–61 cm
(*c*23 in). Big, stocky, with relatively
shorter, broader and less pointed wings
than other skuas, similar to large immature gull but for stout hook-tipped bill and
short tail with slightly projecting central
feathers; dark brown above, greyer-brown
to rufous below, streaked and mottled
rufous and buff, with bold white flash
across bases of primaries. Flight somewhat like large gull, often heavy, almost
laboured, but fast, dashing, hawk-like in
pursuit of birds; like other skuas, chases
terns and gulls in air, following every twist
and buffeting them until they are forced
down or drop/disgorge food, which it
snatches up, usually in flight; even tackles
Gannets, sometimes seizing wing or tail;
when nest is threatened by man or other
predator, makes awesome attacks, either
swooping from height or sailing in low,
shooting up at last moment and sometimes striking with foot; hovers to pick
up food from surface and will dive in;
settles on water more than other skuas
and, when nesting, habitually bathes in
lochs and pools; waddles on ground and
often stands on mounds on breeding
areas; raises wings in courtship, threat and
greeting; does not usually allow close
approach; often solitary when not nesting.
Ad summer Dark brown above with
obscure rufous streaks, much bolder
yellowish streaks on sides and back of
neck; grey-brown below, mottled rufous,
also streaked rufous and buff on darker
throat and on flanks; wing-flashes extensive. *Ad winter* After moult in *c*Jul–Feb,
lacks yellowish streaks around head.
Juv/1st year Darker and more uniform,
more blackish on head and upperparts
without yellowish streaks; wing-flashes
smaller. *2nd summer* More as ad, but still
somewhat darker and more uniform above
with thinner neck streaks, less marked
rufous all over. VOICE When nesting, loud
ha-ha-ha and gruff *kak-ak-ak*, or combined in attacking intruder. HABITAT
Breeds on moors near sea; otherwise
mostly pelagic. NEST Loosely colonial; on
ground, 2 eggs, mid May–mid Jul; 1

brood. FOOD Fish, birds, eggs, offal.
RANGE Summer visitor, end Mar–Sep,
wintering mainly in Atlantic west of
Europe, imms farther south; on passage
(inc some from Iceland) Mar–Apr, Aug–
Oct, esp off WIr; rare in winter and inland.

Pomarine Skua *Stercorarius pomarinus*
43–53 cm (*c*20 in). Smaller than Great
Skua, but larger, more thick-set and
stouter-billed than Arctic (150) with
similar slender and pointed wings angled
at carpal joint; central tail-feathers of ad
rounded and twisted, looking thick-ended
from side, and projecting 5–10 cm (unless
broken), but of juv straight and only
0.5–2 cm; light (most common) and dark
phases, with intermediates, much as
Arctic but 5–6 primaries white-shafted
with more white at bases. Flight heavier.
Light ad summer Contrasting dark rear
belly; often (esp ♀s) dark-barred chest and
flanks, white in tail-coverts. *Light ad
winter* With moult in Aug–Mar, cap and
upper back scaled pale, sides/back of neck
barred; underparts and tail-coverts
always as summer; tail 3–6 cm. *Juv* Varies
from all-dark to (usually) having underparts and esp all tail-coverts barred buff/
dark, underwing-coverts barred white/
blackish, upperparts scaled; rarely,
whitish dark-capped head, mostly whitish
underparts. *1st winter–4th summer* Gradually as ad; underwing barring lost last
(light birds). VOICE Migrants silent.
HABITAT Offshore and pelagic, also
coastal; occasionally on moors, inland
waters (mostly juvs). FOOD At sea, fish,
offal. RANGE Passage-migrant from arctic
Russia, Apr–early Dec (esp Aug–Nov),
wintering in tropical seas; rare in winter.

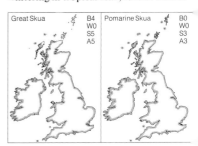

Great Skua		B4	Pomarine Skua		B0
		W0			W0
		S5			S3
		A5			A3

Great Skua

ad summer

ad summer

Pomarine Skua

light ad summer

dark ad summer

light 1st summer

light juv

light ad winter

Arctic Skua *Stercorarius parasiticus*
38–48 cm (*c*18 in). Medium-sized, with
rakish shape, narrow pointed wings;
central tail-feathers of ad tapering and
pointed, projecting 6–10 cm, but of juv
blunter and only 1–2 cm; plumage varies
greatly from almost uniform dark brown
all over to dark above with light whitish
cheeks, hindneck and underparts but for
grey-brown breast-sides or pectoral band,
while imms variously barred; 3–4 primaries white-shafted, variable whitish bases
esp from below. Flight buoyant, graceful,
interspersed with glides, or dashing,
falcon-like when harrying terns and gulls
like Great Skua (148); will attack intruders
at nest or distract by fluttering on ground;
reluctant to settle on water; usually alone.
Dark ad All dark brown, usually more
greyish below, with blacker cap and, in
summer, yellowish streaks on cheeks/
neck. *Light ad summer* Cheeks/collar
typically yellow-white, underbody white
with grey-brown breast-sides, flanks,
undertail-coverts and often chest-band,
but many intermediate. *Light ad winter*
With moult in Aug–Dec, buff cheeks/neck
marked dark brown; chest to undertail-
coverts whitish barred black, belly mostly
white; scaled whitish above, uppertail-
coverts marked white. *Juv/1st winter* Very
variable: black above or variably barred
buff to white, head black to streaked
brown/buff; underparts including wing-
coverts all-dark, variably mottled, or
barred dark/white. *1st summer* (spent in
tropics) Much as juv after moult in Nov–
Mar (Jun), but crown darker, hindneck
streaked dark/yellowish; less barred
above, upperwing-coverts uniform. *2nd
year* Like ad winter but underwing-coverts
more as juv; some breeding plumage on
head/mantle in summer. *3rd–4th summer*
As ad, but light birds have some white
marks on mantle and all tail-coverts,
underbody with dark bars, underwing-
coverts as 2nd year. VOICE Miaowing
kay-yow, high pitched *took-took*; dry
tik-a-tik-tik when attacking intruder.
HABITAT/NEST As Great Skua, but locally
nests farther from sea; wanders inland
more (esp juvs). FOOD Fish, esp from gulls/
terns; also small mammals, birds, eggs,
insects, berries. RANGE Summer visitor,
end Apr–Sep, winters mainly in S Atlantic;
on passage inc some from N Europe/
Iceland, Apr–Nov; rare winter.

Long-tailed Skua *Stercorarius longicaudus*
38–56 cm (*c*21 in). Smaller, slimmer, with
finer bill than Arctic Skua; central tail-
feathers of ad flexible and tapering to long
point, projecting 13–25 cm (unless broken)
but of juv bluntly pointed and only
1.5–3 cm; ad summer pattern similar to
light Arctic, but almost grey above and on
underwings, with neater blacker cap,
yellower cheeks, white chest and dusky
rear belly (white in Greenland race
pallescens), while juv colder grey-brown
variably barred pale; only 2 primaries
white-shafted, little or no white at bases.
Flight more buoyant and tern-like; chases
terns/gulls less; swims more. *Ad winter*
With moult in Oct–Feb, face whitish,
mantle fringed pale, uppertail-coverts
boldly barred; white below but for dark
chest-band, barred flanks/undertail;
underwing stays uniform. *Juv* Ranges
from mainly grey-brown with faint pale
mottling/scaling, but pale patch on nape/
rear cheeks, to, more usually, neatly
barred upperparts and flanks, with dark
cap and largely whitish face/neck/breast/
central belly, but underwing- and all tail-
coverts usually boldly barred (*cf* Arctic).
1st year/2nd winter With moult in Oct–
Jun, as ad winter but underwings barred.
2nd summer Still many imm feathers.
VOICE Migrants silent. HABITAT As
Pomarine (148). FOOD Mainly fish at sea,
catching most itself. RANGE Scarce
passage-migrant from N Europe/? Greenland, May–Nov, wintering in S Atlantic.

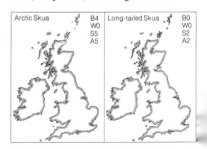

| Arctic Skua | B4 W0 S5 A5 | Long-tailed Skua | B0 W0 S2 A2 |

Arctic Skua

light ad
summer

dark ad
summer

light
juv/1st winter

light ad
winter

intermediate ad
summer

Long-tailed Skua

ad summer

juv/1st winter

ad winter

2nd/3rd year

GULLS (Laridae)

Mediterranean Gull *Larus melanocephalus* 37–40 cm (*c*15¼ in). Intermediate in size between Black-headed (154) and Common Gull (156), but stockier, chunky-headed, with heavy droop-tipped bill, longer legs; ad has blackish patch back from eyes, or black head in summer, and pale grey and white wings; 1st year head much as ad, but wings like more contrasted 1st year Common Gull with narrower tail-band. Flight heavier than either, with stiffer beats of less angled wings; struts, often hunched; mixes (even breeds) with Black-headed. *Ad* Only black streak at front of white wing-tips; in *c*Feb–Oct, head black with white eye-crescents, bill rich red (sometimes dark-banded/yellow-tipped), legs bright red; in *c*Aug–Mar, head white with variable blackish patch back from white-crescented eyes, bill/legs orange-red to blackish (bill often yellowish at tip). *Juv* Much brown on head, breast-sides and scaly mantle, with narrow white eye-crescents; wings with bands of brown, pale grey and black; tail white, black band near tip; bill/legs blackish. *1st winter* After moult in *c*Jul–Oct, head and mantle as ad winter; wings and tail still juv, but faded; bill-base brown, pink or yellowish, legs blackish or green-grey to orange-red. *1st summer* After moult in Feb–Apr, head variably black; wings and tail very faded, but some new grey inner coverts; bill/legs as 1st winter or red. *2nd year* Much as ad winter/summer after moults in Jun–Oct and Feb–Apr, but variable black marks on outer 3–6 primaries, summer hood sometimes white-flecked. VOICE Mellow *kee-ow*. HABITAT Coastal lagoons, marshes, estuaries, rare inland. FOOD Fish, invertebrates. RANGE Scarce, all months: most Jul–Nov, Mar–May; 6 nests 1968–80.

Little Gull *Larus minutus* 27–29 cm (*c*11 in). Smallest gull, dainty, with rather rounded wings, more pointed on imm; ad has blackish eye/ear-marks and grey crown, or black head in summer, no black on upperwings but dark underwings; 1st year blackish cap, tail-band and bold W

Mediterranean Gull

ad winter

1st winter

juv

juv

2nd winter

ad summer

1st summer

across wings (*cf* Kittiwake, 162), white underwings; juv also blackish crown and mantle. Flight buoyant, tern-like; picks from surface. *Ad* Blackish underwings, white trailing edges above and below; in *c*Feb–Oct, whole head black, bill dark reddish, legs scarlet; in *c*Aug–Apr, head white with grey crown/nape and blackish eye/ear-marks, bill blackish, legs dull red. *Juv* Head white, with blackish eye/ear-marks, crown, nape, breast-sides and mantle; wings with broad blackish W from outer primaries across inner wings and rump, and faint bar on secondaries, underwings white; tail sometimes slightly notched, white with black band near tip, wider in middle; bill blackish, legs reddish-flesh. *1st winter* After moult in *c*Jul–Nov, much as juv with blackish crown and W, but nape, breast-sides and mantle grey. *1st summer* After moult in Feb–May, head with variable grey, brown or black hood, and whitish hindneck and often breast-sides; wings and tail as juv, but blackish bands faded to pale brown and often some (even all) new white tail-feathers; legs dull

red. *2nd year* Much as ad winter/summer after moults in Jun–Oct and Feb–May, but variable blackish marks on outer 2–6 primaries; underwings grey or blackish, but smaller coverts paler; summer hood often white-flecked (rarely not developed), legs dull red. VOICE Low *kek-ek-ek* or higher *ka-ka-ka*. HABITAT Coasts, estuaries, inland lakes. FOOD As Mediterranean Gull, but many insects. RANGE Visitor all months: most Mar–May and esp Jul–Oct; 2 unsuccessful nests 1975–78. COMPARE Other dark-headed (154, 282) and W-winged gulls (162, 284).

Mediterranean Gull B1 W2 S2 A2

Little Gull B0 W2 S4 A4

Little Gull

2nd winter

juv

ad summer

ad winter

1st winter

juv

ad summer

1st summer

Sabine's Gull *Larus sabini* 32–34 cm (*c*13 in). Shape of small Kittiwake (162), with forked tail (not always apparent), and 3-coloured wing-pattern of white, black and grey (confusable with 1st year Kittiwake at long range); ad blackish nape and eye-marks, or grey hood and black collar in summer; juv has much grey-brown on head and breast-sides, scaled mantle and wing-coverts, tail-band. Flight buoyant, almost tern-like, feeding from surface; also runs on mud. *Ad* Grey mantle and inner wings, white tips and 'mirrors' on black primaries; underwings white with narrow black tips to primaries, faint bar on greater coverts; in *c*Mar–Oct, whole head grey with black collar; in *c*Sep–Mar, white with blackish eye-crescents and dark grey nape sometimes extending to cheeks, lower neck and rear crown; bill black with yellow tip, legs dark grey. *Juv* Grey-brown upper head and breast-sides, but white on face and around eyes; wings much as ad, but coverts, mantle and scapulars browner and scaled dark and whitish, only small white primary-tips, clearer dusky bar on

underwings; tail white with black band near tip, emphasising fork; bill black, legs pinkish-grey. *1st winter* After moult in Nov–Dec, head and grey mantle as ad winter; wings and tail still juv, but blacks faded, some new grey wing-coverts. *1st summer* Much as ad summer after complete moult in Feb–Apr, but partial grey hood on upper head only (often with blackish half-collar), small white primary-tips, sometimes some black on tail; less or no yellow on bill, legs pinkish-grey. VOICE Harsh, tern-like. HABITAT Mainly offshore, wind-blown to coasts and lagoons. FOOD Invertebrates and fish. RANGE On passage from Arctic, Aug–Nov, rare Dec–Jul, wintering in S Atlantic.

Black-headed Gull *Larus ridibundus* 35–38 cm (*c*14½ in). Most widespread small gull, with slim build, rounded head and tail, thin bill and narrow pointed wings, clearly smaller and slighter than Common Gull (156); outer wings always with dusky area below and white leading edge, both bolder on ad; ad has blackish eye/ear-

Sabine's Gull

ad winter

1st winter

juv

1st summer

ad summer

juv

marks on white head, or brown forehead and white eye-rings in summer; 1st year shows brown carpal bar, blackish secondaries, tail-band; juv has much ginger above. Flight buoyant with fast beats; glides and soars, also hawks for insects; follows plough; swims, walks easily; perches anywhere; often tame; gregarious. *Ad* Black primary-tips; in *c*Mar–Oct, chocolate hood but white hindneck and eye-rings, bill and legs dark red; in *c*Aug–Mar, head white with blackish eye/ear-marks and 1–2 dusky bands running up from these, bill-base/legs dull red. *Juv* Much ginger on head, mantle and breast-sides; wings grey with brown carpal bar and white-tipped blackish trailing edge, and white panel on outer part; tail with black band near tip; bill-base and legs dull flesh-yellow. *1st winter* After moult in *c*Jul–Sep, head and body as ad winter; wings and tail juv, but dark areas faded and white tips worn. *1st summer* After moult Feb–Apr, variable brown hood (often flecked white); wings and tail juv, but very worn/faded; bill-

base/legs orange; usually as ad after moult in *c*Aug–Oct. VOICE Harsh angry *kwarr*, short *kuk*; noisy when nesting. HABITAT Breeds in gravel pits to moorland bogs, or coastal marshes and dunes; ubiquitous in winter, roosting on estuaries, lakes, and ranging far over surrounding fields and towns. NEST Colonial; in tussocks, or on flat ground, also in bushes over water, 2–3 eggs, mid Apr–Jul; 1 brood. FOOD Invertebrates, seeds, scraps. RANGE Resident, but much winter dispersal, a few moving south to Iberia; passage/winter visitor from Continent/Iceland, Aug–Apr.

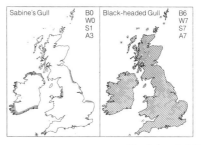

| Sabine's Gull | B0 W0 S1 A3 | Black-headed Gull | B6 W7 S7 A7 |

Black-headed Gull

ad winter

ad winter

1st winter

juv

1st summer

ad summer

juv

Common Gull *Larus canus* 38–43 cm (*c*16
in). Larger and wings less pointed than
Black-headed (154), the other widespread
smallish gull; ad pattern more as Herring
but much smaller with slenderer yellow-
green bill/legs, rounded head, thinner
wings projecting more beyond tail at rest,
daintier walk and easier flight; ad blue-
grey and white, but for black outer
primaries with white tips and bold
'mirrors'; 1st year has dense brownish
streaking on crown, cheeks and breast-
sides, brown carpal bar, blackish flight-
feathers (but greyish inner primaries) and
well-defined tail-band, black-tipped bill;
juv also has scaly brown mantle. Actions
much as other gulls, but drops molluscs as
Herring Gull; flight buoyant, walks
easily; favours fields and sheltered waters,
rather than cliffs and sea. *Ad* Blue-grey
mantle and wings, bold white trailing
edges and tertial-crescents, white tips to
black primaries and large 'mirrors' on 2
outermost, legs greenish-yellow; in *c*Aug–
Mar, head white with dark streaks/eye-
marks and white eye-crescents, breast-
sides and flanks often with odd dark
streaks, bill yellowish with darker base
and faint band near tip; in *c*Mar–Oct,
head and underparts white, bill yellow-
green, red rings round brown eyes. *Juv*
Crown, cheeks, lower nape, breast and
flanks much more densely streaked/
mottled than ad winter; mantle scaly buff;
wings with bands of brown, grey-brown
and blackish (less contrasted than imm
Mediterranean Gull, 150, and underwings
more dark-marked) and greyish showing
on inner primaries between blackish
outer wings and secondaries; tail white
with clear blackish band near tip; bill
blackish with usually paler base, legs
flesh. *1st year* With moults in *c*Jul–Sep and
Feb–Apr, mantle blue-grey, head and
body progressively whiter and less
streaked; wings and tail still as juv, but
increasingly faded to pale brown and
whitish; bill clearly black-tipped, legs
sometimes tinged with yellow. *2nd year*
With corresponding moults, becomes
more as ad with mainly blue-grey wings
and white tail, but black on outer wings
extends to carpal joint, white tips and

'mirrors' smaller; head and flanks more
streaked until summer; dark-tipped bill
and legs grey-green to yellowish. VOICE
Shrill *kee-ya*, trumpeting *hieeya*, higher
and weaker than Herring Gull. HABITAT
Breeds by lochs and on moors, shingle;
winters on coasts, reservoirs, farmland.
NEST On ground, 2–3 eggs, May–Jun;
1 brood. FOOD Mainly worms, insects,
molluscs, fish. RANGE Resident, but much
dispersal south; passage/winter visitor
from Scandinavia/Baltic, Aug–Apr.
COMPARE Ring-billed Gull (282).

Herring Gull *Larus argentatus* 53–59 cm
(*c*22 in). Heavily built, with relatively short
broad wings; ad all grey and white but for
black outer primaries with white tips and
'mirrors'; see Lesser Black-backed (158)
for imm plumage differences, and actions.
Flight more graceful; carries molluscs/
crabs aloft, dropping them to break them
open. *Ad* Pale grey mantle/wings, bold
white trailing edges, white tips to black
primaries and 'mirrors' on 2 outermost;
bill yellow with orange-red spot and
whitish tip, eyes pale yellow with yellow or
orange rings, legs pink to pale flesh
(rarely yellow); in *c*Sep–Mar, whole head
streaked brown; in *c*Feb–Sep, head white,
white primary-tips smaller through wear.
Juv-3rd year Plumage sequence much as
Lesser Black-backed. VOICE As Lesser
Black-backed, but less deep. HABITAT As
Lesser Black-backed, but hardly breeding
inland. NEST Colonial; on ground, cliffs
or buildings, 2–3 eggs, end Apr–early Jul;
1 brood. FOOD As Lesser Black-backed.
RANGE Mainly sedentary, some crossing
Channel; passage/winter visitor from N
Europe, Sep–Mar (Jul–Apr).

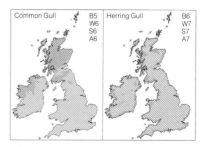

Common Gull	B5	Herring Gull	B6
	W6		W7
	S6		S7
	A6		A7

Common Gull

juv

1st winter

ad winter

ad summer

1st summer

juv

Herring Gull

ad winter

2nd winter

1st winter

juv

1st summer

2nd summer

3rd summer

juv

ad summer

yellow-legged ad winter

Lesser Black-backed Gull *Larus fuscus*
51–56 cm (*c*21 in). Barely slighter than
Herring Gull (156); *c* size of Great
Black-backed (162), with thinner bill,
smaller head, less bulky body; legs and
wings relatively longer than either, wings
narrower in flight and projecting more
beyond tail at rest. Ad has slate-grey
mantle and yellow legs, but note that N
race is as black as Great Black-backed
and some Herring Gulls have yellow legs.
Imm plumages (lasting over 3 years) are
harder to identify, but mantle colour
begins to show in 2nd winter. In general,
juv/1st year darker than Herring with
more coarsely streaked head and underparts, scalier mantle and inner wing-
coverts, blackish outer greater coverts,
almost entirely blackish outer wings, more
contrasting whitish rump and tail
emphasising blackish band near tip, and
black bill without pale base; separated
from Great Black-backed by much less
white head and chest, darker and more
scaly (not chequered) mantle, more clear-
cut tail-band, and smaller black bill

without whitish tip. Flight powerful with
leisurely beats; glides and soars; follows
boats; swims buoyantly, walks easily with
body horizontal; highly gregarious, often
standing or sitting with other large gulls
on sand-banks and shores or roosting on
water. *Ad W European race (L.f. graellsii)*
Slate-grey back and wings, bold white
trailing edges, white tips to black primaries
and 'mirrors' on 1–2 outermost; bill
yellow with red spot and whitish tip, eyes
yellow with red ring, legs creamy-yellow
or yellow; in *c*Aug–Mar, head streaked
brownish; in *c*Feb–Sep, head white, slate-
grey back becomes tinged with brown and
white primary-tips smaller through wear.
Ad N European race (L.f. fuscus) Similar,
but back blacker; head often whiter in
winter. *Juv* Head and underparts streaked
dark brown, with blackish eye/ear-patch,
and mottled blackish flanks; mantle and
inner wing-coverts dark brown scaled
paler, with blackish bar on outer greater
coverts; flight-feathers blackish; rump
and tail-base whitish, with contrasting
blackish band near tip; bill black, eyes

Lesser Black-backed Gull

brown, legs brownish-flesh. *1st year* Much as juv, but moults in Aug–Nov and Jan–Apr make head and underparts whiter, eye/ear-patch less clear, mantle less scaly; worn juv wings and tail paler brownish and more uniform. *2nd winter* After complete moult in May–Oct, head and underparts white with much dark streaking on crown, nape, breast-sides and flanks, and thicker area round eyes; mantle shows much dark grey, but inner wing-coverts still mainly pale-edged brown; outer wing-coverts and flight-feathers blackish; rump and tail mostly white with narrower blackish band near tip; bill usually pale brown or pinkish with dark patch near tip, eyes brown or greyish, legs pale creamy-flesh or tinged with yellow. *2nd summer* After moult in Jan–Apr, head/underparts whiter, mantle clearer slate-grey; wings/tail faded; eyes pale greyish, bill yellowish at base. *3rd year* After complete moult in Jun–Oct and partial in Jan–Apr, much as ad winter (streaky head) and then ad summer (white head), but some dark streaks on under-parts, variable dark mottling and barring near tail-tip, dark mark near bill-tip; also inner wings mottled brown and outer part with more black, as well as smaller white primary-tips, all fading and wearing by summer. VOICE Noisiest when nesting; loud yelping *kyow-kyow-kyow*, shrill trumpeting *kyee kyee owkyowkyow-kyowkyow*, loud angry *kee-aa*, anxious *gag-gag-gag*. HABITAT Coasts, reservoirs, rubbish tips; breeds on dunes, shingle, cliffs, buildings, moors and bogs. NEST Colonial; on ground, cliffs or buildings, 2–3 eggs, May–Jul; 1 brood. FOOD Any animal food, garbage, plant material. RANGE Mainly summer visitor, mid Feb–Oct, wintering in Iberia/ NW Africa, but many all year; passage from Iceland, and N race from Scandinavia (esp EBr), mid Feb–May, Jul–Nov.

Lesser Black-backed Gull

B6
W5
S6
A6

graellsii ad winter

graellsii 3rd winter

graellsii 2nd winter

juv

graellsii 1st winter

Iceland Gull *Larus glaucoides* 51–57 cm (*c*21 in). Near size of Herring Gull (156), but slimmer, gentler-looking and without any black on wings or tail; short thinnish bill less than half length of rounded head; legs also shorter than Glaucous and wings typically narrower and longer, projecting well beyond tail (by much more than bill-length), giving body elongated slender shape, but primaries often not fully grown in winter except in 1st year. Flight fast and buoyant. Plumages develop as Glaucous, but during *c*Apr–Aug eye-rings of ad usually red; 1st year often greyer-brown above, more neatly barred, with clearer whitish tail-end, and bill has only basal half dull grey-flesh shading into extensive black tip (may look all dark at distance); bill-pattern often still apparent in 2nd winter (but base now pale flesh), when some grey feathers may show on mantle/scapulars. VOICE As Herring but much shriller. HABITAT Much as Glaucous. FOOD Mostly fish. RANGE Scarce winter visitor from Greenland (not Iceland), Nov–Apr; rare other months.

Glaucous Gull *Larus hyperboreus* 58–69 cm (23–27 in). This and Iceland the only gulls without black on wings or tail at all ages. Size variable, from same as Great Black-backed (162) down to large Herring Gull (156); some little bigger than Iceland Gull, but still bulkier, with deeper chest, longer legs, long heavy bill over half length of fierce-looking, rather flat-crowned or angular head, and wings not projecting much beyond tail (never by more than bill-length); ad all white and pale grey with white wing-tips; 1st year rather, and 2nd year much, paler than other large gulls except Iceland, being more or less pale coffee-coloured to creamy-buff with fine barring, pale buff to whitish flight-feathers and no dark tail-band, also extensive pink on bill. Heavy flight and actions much as Great Black-backed. *Ad* White with pale grey mantle and wings, white trailing edges and tips; bill yellow with orange-red spot and whitish tip, eyes pale yellow with yellowish rings, legs pinkish; head and chest heavily streaked brownish in *c*Oct–Mar, white in *c*Feb–Sep. *1st winter* Head/

Iceland Gull

3rd year

1st winter

2nd year

ad winter

E. S. ANNEY

underparts rather uniform buff, often looking darker than wavy-barred mantle, wing-coverts and rump; flight-feathers buff with whitish tips, and pale buff tail mottled with whitish and brown; much variation all over in pattern and depth of colour, also fading in late winter; basal $\frac{2}{3}$ of bill bright pinkish to cream with well-defined black tip, eyes brown. *1st summer* After moult in Feb–Apr, more buff-white with fewer fainter markings; worn juv wings/tail faded paler; bill-base often yellow-flesh. *2nd year* With complete moult in Apr–Jan and partial in Jan–May, all pale buff-white, head/underparts variably streaked and mottled in winter, mantle/scapulars with fewer fainter bars and partly grey by summer, wings/tail faintly patterned and wearing almost uniform; bill yellow-flesh with less-defined dark end and pale tip, eyes lighten. *3rd year* Much as ad, but faint brownish mottling on underparts, mantle, rump and esp wing-coverts and tail; bill usually still marked blackish near tip and sometimes no red spot, eyes pale yellow.

VOICE Like hoarse Herring Gull. HABITAT Coasts, harbours, adjacent pastures, rubbish-tips, also inland waters. FOOD Carrion, fish, invertebrates. RANGE Winter visitor from Iceland/Arctic, Oct–Apr; occasionally other months; 1 paired with Herring Gull and bred in Shetland 1975–79. NOTE Confusion sometimes caused by pale leucistic or albinistic Herring and Great Black-backed Gulls, also moulting Herring Gulls missing outer primaries, pale imms with faded wings, and Glaucous × Herring hybrids: check bill-patterns (imms), plumage details, and shape.

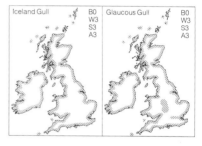

Iceland Gull   B0 W3 S3 A3   Glaucous Gull   B0 W3 S3 A3

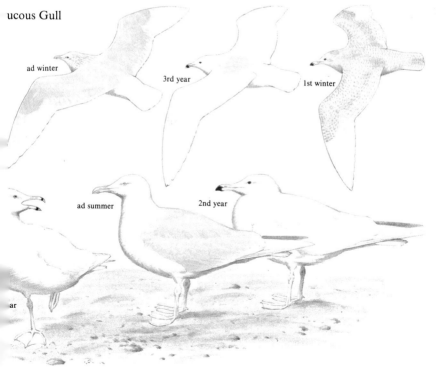

ucous Gull

ad winter

3rd year

1st winter

ad summer

2nd year

ar

Great Black-backed Gull *Larus marinus*
63–69 cm (*c*26 in). Bulky with heavy head
and stout bill, much larger than Lesser
Black-backed (158) and with relatively
shorter, broader wings and shorter legs;
ad has uniformly blackish back and wings,
otherwise mainly white, with flesh or
creamy-flesh legs; see Lesser Black-backed
for differences of juv/1st year. Actions
much as Lesser Black-backed, but flight
heavier, more ponderous; more predatory
and piratic; more often solitary. *Ad*
Blackish mantle and wings, white trailing
edges, white tips to black primaries joining
'mirrors' on 2 outermost in white patch;
underwings with dusky secondaries and
blackish tip; bill pale yellow with orange-
red spot, eyes pale yellow with red rings,
legs creamy-flesh; in *c*Sep–Mar, head
white with dark eye-mark, few streaks; in
*c*Feb–Sep, head white, black back tinged
brown, white primary-tips smaller with
wear. *Juv–3rd year* Plumage sequence
much as Lesser Black-backed; blackish on
mantle appears from 2nd/3rd year. VOICE
Stronger and deeper than Lesser Black-
backed, esp hoarse barking *yowk*,
trumpeting *ee-yowk-owk-owk*, guttural
uk-uk-uk. HABITAT Coasts, more locally
reservoirs; breeds rocky islands, headlands, locally on moors and lochs. NEST
Sometimes colonial; on ground ridges,
2–3 eggs, late Apr–Jun; 1 brood. FOOD As
Lesser Black-backed, but kills seabirds
and weak mammals. RANGE Mainly
resident, but some imms move south to
Iberia; also passage/winter visitor from
Iceland/N Europe, Aug–Apr. COMPARE
Great Black-headed Gull (282).

Kittiwake *Rissa tridactyla* 38–43 cm (*c*16
in). Near size of Common Gull (156), but
slighter, slimmer, with smaller head,
thinner pointed wings, very slightly forked
tail and short black legs; ad all grey and
white, but for black triangle of extreme
wing-tips; 1st year has blackish V on each
wing (not joining across rump in W as
Little Gull, 152), also tail-band, and often
half-collar on hindneck as juv. Flight
graceful with rapid beats, often in lines
over sea; feeds from surface in flight,
settles and dives, or plunges like tern;

coastal/pelagic; gregarious. *Ad* Darkish
grey and white, wings shading to white
trailing edges and line inside neat black
tips; bill greenish-yellow, eyes blackish
with orange-red rings, legs brown-black
to dark grey; during *c*Aug–Apr, rear head
grey as mantle, with blackish eye/ear-
marks; in *c*Feb–Oct, head all white. *Juv*
Head as ad winter, but nape only tinged
with grey, black half-collar on hindneck;
mantle and back grey as ad; wings
3-coloured with blackish outer forewings
joining diagonal carpal bar, coverts otherwise grey, and inner primaries and
secondaries whitish to white; tail white
with black tip, wider in middle and
emphasising slight fork; bill and legs
blackish. *1st winter* After moult in *c*Aug–
Oct, still as juv but back of head grey and
collar smaller or dark grey. *1st summer*
After moult in Feb–May, as 1st winter but
sometimes no ear-mark or collar; wings
and tail still juv, but blacks faded to pale
brown and partly worn away; bill
yellowish with darker tip. *2nd year* Much
as ad winter/summer after moults in Jun–
Oct and Feb–May, but sometimes traces
of imm plumage; bill often still partly
black. VOICE Noisy when nesting, esp
rhythmic nasal *kitti-week*. HABITAT Breeds
on sea-cliffs, locally on port buildings,
piers; nesting birds bathe regularly in
fresh water near shore; otherwise oceanic.
NEST Colonial; on ledges, 1–3 eggs, late
May–mid Aug; 1 brood. FOOD Fish,
marine invertebrates. RANGE At colonies
*c*Jan/Mar–Aug/Oct, otherwise ranging
across North Sea and Atlantic south to
NW Africa; also passage/weather movements from N Europe/Iceland, esp in
spring/autumn.

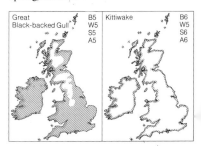

Great Black-backed Gull — B5 W5 S5 A5

Kittiwake — B6 W5 S6 A6

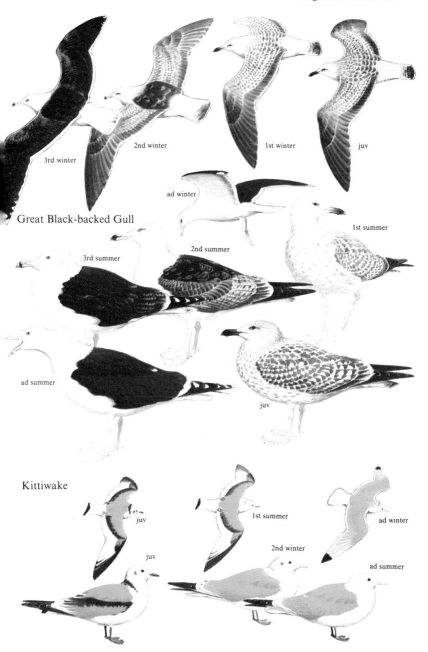

3rd winter

2nd winter

1st winter

juv

ad winter

Great Black-backed Gull

1st summer

3rd summer

2nd summer

ad summer

juv

Kittiwake

juv

1st summer

ad winter

juv

2nd winter

ad summer

TERNS (Sternidae)

Roseate Tern *Sterna dougallii* 32–40 cm
(*c*15 in). Much paler pearl-grey above
than Common or Arctic Tern (looking
whiter at distance), with shortish wings,
far longer tail. *Ad summer* Black cap; rosy
wash on breast in spring; bill black with
red base. *Ad winter* Moults Jul–Nov: head
changes as Common; bill all-black. *Juv* As
juv Common, but bill all-black, blackish
cap more complete, upperparts paler with
bolder scaling, narrow dusky inner forewing, greyish primaries, white trailing
edge to whole wings, black legs. *1st winter*
As ad winter, but wings/tail as juv.
VOICE Soft *chuik*, musical *teeo*, rasping
aaak. HABITAT Marine, nesting on islets
and beaches. NEST Colonial; in rock
hollows or under vegetation, 1–2 eggs,
Jun–Jul; 1 brood. FOOD Fish. RANGE
Summer visitor, end Apr–Sep, wintering
off W Africa.

Arctic Tern *Sterna paradisaea* 30–39 cm
(*c*15 in). Very like Common Tern, but
shorter bill, neck and legs, longer tail
(slightly longer than closed wings), no
dark wedge on primaries above, all flight-
feathers translucent from below, distinct
calls. *Ad summer* Main plumage as Common, but underparts often greyer; bill all
blood-red. *Ad winter* (unusual in Br/Ir in
moult begins in Oct) Changes as Common
but inner forewings less black. *Juv* Like
juv Common, but forehead white, crown
clear black, no buff or obvious brown on
upperparts, dusky inner forewing less
extensive, secondaries white, all flight-
feathers translucent, primaries have only
narrow black trailing edge. *1st and 2nd
year* Changes (and occurrence) as Common, but distinguished by primary pattern
of species. VOICE Resembles Common, but
less slurred shorter *kee-yah*; and *prreeo*,
piping *pee-pee-pee* and hard chattering
all distinct. HABITAT Coastal. NEST As
Common Tern, 1–3 eggs, mid May–Jul.
FOOD Fish, invertebrates. RANGE Summer
visitor, end Apr–mid Oct, wintering from
S Africa to Antarctic; also passage from
farther N/E, end Apr–Jun, and Jul–Oct.

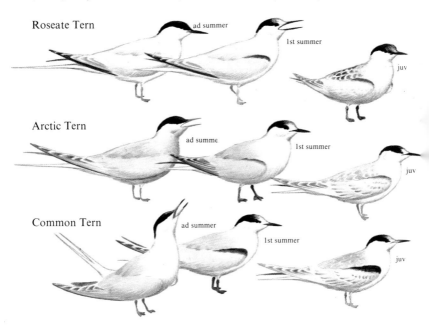

Roseate Tern — ad summer — 1st summer — juv

Arctic Tern — ad summer — 1st summer — juv

Common Tern — ad summer — 1st summer — juv

Common Tern *Sterna hirundo* 20–36 cm (*c*14 in). Slender, with deeply forked tail. (but shorter than, or at most equal to, closed wings); blue-grey above, white or grey below; outer primaries form dusky wedge on upperwings, only inner primaries translucent from below (showing as light patch behind wing-angle). Flight buoyant with deliberate beats; fishes by diving, seldom swims; waddles gawkily. *Ad summer* Black cap; bill orange-red with black tip, legs red. *Ad winter* Begins moult in Jul–Aug: forehead becomes white, front crown streaked, inner forewing blackish, bill blackish with red base, legs duller. *Juv* Like ad winter, but basal half of bill pale flesh, legs orange, crown streaked blackish, forehead and mantle with gingery wash, upperparts barred brownish, bold blackish inner forewing, dark secondaries with white trailing edge, dusky opaque primaries, short tail. *1st winter* As dull ad winter, but wings/tail as juv. *1st summer* (rare in Br/Ir) As ad winter, but variable number of dusky juv flight-feathers, short tail. *2nd summer* More like ad summer. VOICE Grating *keee-yah*, excited *kirri-kirri*, hard *kik-kik-kik*. HABITAT Coasts, lochs, rivers, gravel pits. NEST Colonial; open scrape, 2–4 eggs, May–Aug; 1 brood. FOOD Mainly fish. RANGE Summer visitor mid Apr–Oct, wintering off W Africa; also on passage from Continent, Apr–May, Jul–Oct.

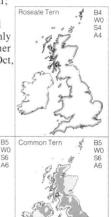

Roseate Tern | B4 / W0 / S4 / A4

Arctic Tern | B5 / W0 / S6 / A6

Common Tern | B5 / W0 / S6 / A6

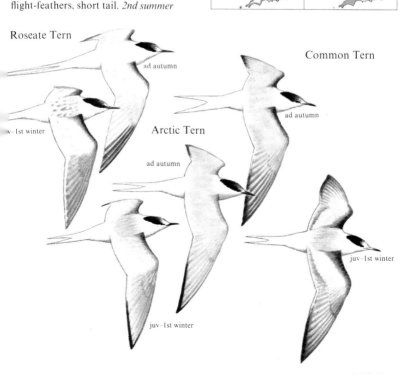

Roseate Tern

ad autumn

juv–1st winter

Arctic Tern

ad autumn

juv–1st winter

Common Tern

ad autumn

juv–1st winter

Sandwich Tern *Sterna sandvicensis* 38–43 cm (*c*16 in). Largest breeding tern; shaggy crest, long thin wings, forked tail, fine yellow tip (ad) to slender black bill, black legs; looks whiter than other terns except Roseate (164), with usually darkish wing-tips above. Flight stronger, less buoyant than smaller terns; hovers with straighter tail and plunges from greater heights. *Ad summer* Whitish-grey above, mainly white rump/tail; cap all-black to Jun. *Ad winter* With moult in Jun–Dec, forehead and then crown white, crown-sides and shaggy nape white-streaked blackish. *Juv* Cap black, heavily freckled first buff then whitish, almost no crest; wings/tail mainly greyish, rest of upperparts pale sandy-buff, wearing to white, all marked blackish with bars and clear Vs; bill all-dark. *1st year* As ad winter after moult beginning in Aug, but worn (darker) juv primaries in winter. *2nd summer* Often white forehead. VOICE Loud, shrill, grating *kier-rik*. HABITAT Sandy, shingly or rocky coasts; locally inland. NEST Colonial; scrape in open or grass, 1–2 eggs, mid May–Jul; 1 brood. FOOD Fish. RANGE Summer visitor, end Mar–Sep, wintering off W Africa; on passage mid Mar–May, Jul–mid Oct. COMPARE Gull-billed Tern (286).

Little Tern *Sterna albifrons* 23–26 cm (*c*9½ in). Tiny, squat, with narrow wings, short-forked tail, black-tipped yellow bill, orange legs; in summer, sharp white forehead, blackish outer forewings. Wing-beats much faster, more flickering than other terns; prolonged hovering before diving; less gregarious. *Ad summer* Blue-grey above; black eyestripes, crown and nape; bill-base yellow. *Ad winter* With moult from Aug, lores white, crown grey edged blackish from eyes round nape, lesser coverts dark grey, rump/central tail grey; outer primaries pale Nov–Jan; bill blackish. *Juv* Sandy-buff above, including forehead, but wearing to whitish, with black-streaked crown, brown U-bars on mantle and scapulars, but rump/tail and wings greyer, wings hoary-fringed blackish along whole leading edge; bill brown, legs brownish-yellow. *1st year* Generally much like ad winter after moult beginning in

Aug. VOICE Shrill *kitik*, harsher *kree-ik*, chattering *kirri-wirri*. HABITAT Sand or shingle coasts; scarce inland. NEST Loosely colonial; scrape on sand, shingle, mud, 2–3 eggs, mid May–Jul; 1 brood. FOOD Fish, crustaceans. RANGE Summer visitor, mid Apr–early Oct, wintering in Africa.

Black Tern *Chlidonias niger* 23–26 cm (*c*9½ in). Size of Little Tern, but bulkier; longer broader wings, barely forked tail; in summer blackish with white undertail-coverts, at other times white below with blackish patch at breast-sides, always pale grey underwings. Flight shallower than *Sterna* terns, beating to and fro, dipping to surface, not plunging in; rarely settles on water; singly or flocks. ♂ *summer* Black head, blackish underbody; bill black, legs red-brown. ♀ *summer* Greyer below, no contrast with pale wing-bend at rest. *Ad winter* With moult in Jun–Feb, black cap but white face, collar and underparts; all slaty-grey above. *Juv* Much as ad winter, but darker/browner above tipped pale; underwings whiter; bill-base and legs dark yellowish. *1st summer* Usually as ad winter. VOICE Squeaky *kik*. HABITAT Coasts, lakes; nests in flooded marshes. FOOD Insects. RANGE On variable passage from Continent, mid Apr–early Jun, Jul–Oct, wintering in Africa; nested SEBr to 19th century, irregularly since 1966, also Ir 1967, 1975. COMPARE Whiskered and White-winged Black Terns (286).

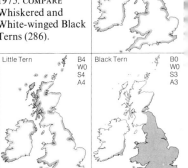

Sandwich Tern — B5 W0 S5 A5

Little Tern — B4 W0 S4 A4

Black Tern — B0 W0 S3 A3

Sandwich Tern

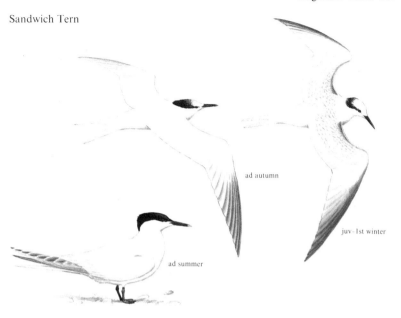

ad autumn

juv–1st winter

ad summer

Little Tern

ad summer

juv–1st winter

ad autumn

ad summer

Black Tern

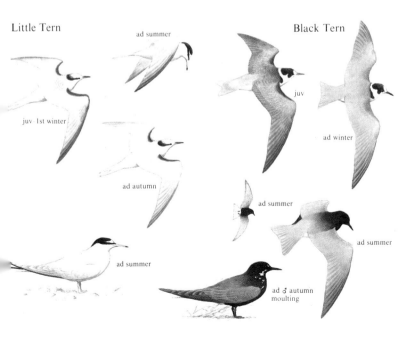

juv

ad winter

ad summer

ad summer

ad ♂ autumn
moulting

AUKS (Alcidae)

Guillemot *Uria aalge* 40–44 cm (c16½ in).
Commonest auk, slim, with slender
pointed bill, shortish rounded tail and, like
all auks, small narrow wings, short legs
set far back, and big feet; black or brown
above, white below, with white-tipped
secondaries forming wing-bar, whitish
underwing-coverts; note also 'bridled'
variety. Flight fast, direct, with whirring
beats, low over water; splashes, in breast
first; swims buoyantly, looking rather flat
with hunched neck; dives with flick of
legs and wings, and uses wings underwater; splashing take-off; at cliff-ledges,
brakes with feet out and lands with heavy
flutter; stands fairly upright, resting or
shuffling on tarsi, or waddling on feet
alone; also rests flat on rocks; highly
gregarious, parties often fly or swim in
lines. *Ad N race (U.a. aalge) summer* From
Dec–Mar onwards, black above with
deep chocolate head/neck; dark streaks
on flanks; bridled variety has white
spectacles. *Ad N race winter* With moult
in Jul–Oct, blackish crown, white throat/
cheeks divided by black line behind eyes,
sometimes whitish collar; bridled variety
still white round eyes. *Ad S race (U.a.
albionis)* As N race, but grey-brown
above, not black (many intermediate);
many fewer bridled farther south. *Juv
(both races)* As winter ad, but browner
above and scaled black, no dark streaks
on flanks; no flight- or tail-feathers till
moult in Aug–Sep. *1st winter* After moult,
hard to separate from ad winter except by
smaller bill, often whiter nape. *1st
summer* As ad summer after moult in Feb–
May, but worn juv wings pale brown,
throat often mottled white. VOICE Harsh
growls and trumpeting moans produce
enormous noise at colonies. HABITAT
Inshore and offshore waters, breeding on
cliffs. NEST Colonial; lays on bare ledges,
1 egg, May–Jul; 1 brood. FOOD Fish, also
crustaceans, molluscs, marine worms.
RANGE N race in NBr intergrades into S
race elsewhere; at colonies cJan–Aug,
many then dispersing as far as Norway/
N Iberia; others arrive from N Europe.

Guillemot

aalge
ad summer

albionis
1st summer

albionis
ad summer

aalge
ad summer
(bridled)

albionis
ad summer

aalge
ad winter
(bridled)

albionis
1st winter

albionis
ad winter

Razorbill *Alca torda* 39–43 cm (*c*16 in).
Size and pattern much as Guillemot, but
with deep, laterally flattened bill crossed
by white line when ad; heavier-headed
and thicker-necked, with longer pointed
tail; whitish line from bill to eyes, no
flank-streaks, whiter underwing-coverts;
looks blacker than browner Guillemots of
S race in mixed colonies. Actions as
Guillemot; longer tail often more cocked
when swimming; usually much less
numerous. *Ad summer* From *c*Mar, black
above, chocolate throat/cheeks, line from
bill to eyes white. *Ad winter* With moult in
Aug–Oct, white throat and lower and rear
cheeks, but brown round eyes, some
mottling behind; line from bill to eyes
faintly whitish. *Juv* Dark brown above,
scaled black; whole head also brown (*cf*
juv Guillemot) or sometimes mottled
white on throat, and smaller all-dark bill,
but still whitish line back to eyes; no flight
or tail-feathers till autumn moult. *1st
winter* As ad winter after moult in Jul–Oct,
but for smaller, more pointed, all-dark bill
and narrower white tips to secondaries.

1st summer As ad summer after early
spring moult, but worn juv wings pale
brown, throat sometimes mottled white.
VOICE Deep or shrill growls and grunts.
HABITAT As Guillemot. NEST Colonial;
lays in crevices or under boulders, sometimes on sheltered ledges, 1 egg, May–Jul;
1 brood. FOOD As Guillemot. RANGE At
colonies *c*Jan–Aug, many then dispersing
as far as Scandinavia/NW Africa; others
come into Br/Ir waters from N Europe
and France.

COMPARE Brünnich's Guillemot (286).

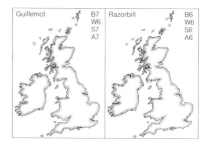

Guillemot — B7 W6 S7 A7 · Razorbill — B6 W6 S6 A6

Razorbill

1st summer

ad summer

ad summer

ad winter

juv

1st winter

Black Guillemot *Cepphus grylle* 33–35 cm (*c*13½ in). Smaller than Guillemot (168), with shorter bill, rich red legs and gape; black with white wing-patch in summer, ghostly white barred and mottled with black above in winter. Actions much as Guillemot, but walks more easily; solitary or small parties. *Ad summer* From Feb or Mar, all brown-black but for large white patch on wing-coverts, black-edged white underwings. *Ad winter* With moult in Jul–Nov, first mainly black above and mottled white below, then blackish and white above and all-white below but for blackish streaks on flanks, but still tail black, and white patch on black wings. *Juv* More uniform blackish-brown above, mottled wing-patches; mostly speckled below. *1st winter* Much as ad winter after moult in Sep–Dec, but for mottled juv wings, red-brown legs. *1st summer* Browner than ad summer, mottled juv wings; often flecked with white below. VOICE Shrill whistling or whining *speeeeee*. HABITAT Rocky coasts, staying inshore. NEST Lays in holes or under boulders, 1–2

eggs, mid May–Aug; 1 brood. FOOD Fish, crustaceans, molluscs, marine worms. RANGE Mainly sedentary; some wander S in winter, rarely even reaching Channel.

Little Auk *Alle alle* 20–22 cm (*c*8 in). Starling-sized and chubby, with tiny bill (*cf* juv Puffin) and rather long wings; black above and white below, with white-tipped secondaries forming thin wing-bar, white-streaked scapulars, white spot over eyes, dark underwings. More agile than Guillemot (168), taking off from water easily; gregarious, though often seen singly in Br/Ir. *Ad summer* Cheeks, throat and breast chocolate. *Ad winter* Cheeks, throat and breast white, variously mottled or tinged blackish. *1st winter* As ad winter, but esp wings browner, more often speckled white across back of neck. VOICE Migrants silent. HABITAT Offshore and inshore waters. FOOD Planktonic crustaceans. RANGE Winter visitor from Arctic, mid Sep–mid Mar, esp Nov–Feb; irregular except NBr, but sometimes in numbers, occasionally blown inland.

Black Guillemot

ad summer

ad winter

1st winter

1st summer

ad summer

ad winter

1st winter

juv

Puffin *Fratercula arctica* 29–31 cm (*c*12 in). Big-headed and short-tailed with unmistakable colourful triangular bill when ad; smaller and fatter than Guillemot or Razorbill (168), with short red or yellow legs; likewise black above and white below, but with greyish clown-face, no wing-bar, dark underwings. Stands upright on feet; easy, rolling walk; breeding birds carry up to 10 fish cross-wise in bill; highly gregarious. *Ad summer* From *c*Mar, cheeks grey; bill blue-grey, yellow and bright red, with frilly yellow gape-edge; legs red. *Ad winter* After moult in Aug–Sep, cheeks darker, blackish in front of eyes; bill sheds horny plates at base, becoming smaller, grey-brown, yellow and orange; legs orange fading to yellow. *Juv/1st year* Smaller, but like dull ad winter, with darker cheeks, blacker lores, browner collar, pinkish legs turning yellow; much smaller bill looks all-dark, becoming as ad in 2nd year but still smaller. VOICE Deep groan *arr-ow-er* in burrow, more growling grunt in open. HABITAT Inshore and offshore waters,

breeding on turfy slopes. NEST Colonial; lays in excavated or shearwater/rabbit burrows, or in crevices, 1 egg, May–Aug; 1 brood. FOOD As Black Guillemot, esp sand-eels when feeding young. RANGE At colonies *c*Mar–Aug, wintering mostly well out in North Sea/ Atlantic; some from Continent more in E/SBr waters.

Black Guillemot	B5
	W5
	S5
	A5

Little Auk	B0
	W3
	S3
	A4

Puffin	B7
	W5
	S7
	A7

Little Auk

ad winter

ad summer

ad winter

Puffin

ad summer

ad summer

ad winter

juv/1st year

PIGEONS, DOVES (Columbidae)

Rock Dove *Columba livia* 31–35 cm (*c*13 in). Ancestor of widespread Feral Pigeon; plump, with shortish tail; blue-grey with pale back, 2 black wing-bars, white rump/underwings/bill-base. Actions much as Woodpigeon; flight more dashing, often low; display-glides on V-wings; perches on rocks, buildings. *Ad* Blue-grey, with glossy purple-green neck, pale grey mantle/wing-coverts, white or whitish rump, white underwings. *Juv* Tinged brown, no gloss, greyer underwings. *Feral Pigeon* Some like Rock Dove but many variously blackish, white or brown. VOICE Crooning *oo-roo-coo*. HABITAT Sea-cliffs with caves, adjacent fields; Ferals much in towns, ruins, farms. NEST On ledges, 2 eggs, all year; 3–4 broods. FOOD Grain, seeds, crops, seaweed, molluscs. RANGE Mainly sedentary; any pure Rock Doves now confined to N/WBr, N/W/SIr coasts.

Stock Dove *Columba oenas* 31–35 cm (*c*13 in). Compact with shortish tail; grey-blue with blackish tips and rear edges to wings, short black bars on inner wings. Actions much as Woodpigeon, but flies with wings straighter, more flicking; usually in pairs or small parties. *Ad* Grey-blue head and rump, glossy green patch on sides of neck, purple tinge to breast. *Juv* Browner, no gloss on neck, duller breast; as ad after moult in May–Nov. VOICE Gruff repeated *coo-oh*. HABITAT Farmland, parks, wood-edges; also cliffs, ruins, dunes. NEST In holes in trees or buildings, rabbit burrows, 2 eggs, Mar–Oct; 2–3 broods. FOOD Much as Woodpigeon. RANGE Mainly sedentary, some move south; probably irregular immigrants from Continent in Oct–Apr.

Woodpigeon *Columba palumbus* 39–43 cm (*c*16 in). Small head, longish tail, deep chest; grey-brown, with white patches on dark-ended wings. Flight fast with quick beats of backswept wings, takes off with loud clatter; in display, flies up steeply, claps wings, glides down; walks with body level, head moving to and fro; perches mainly in trees; highly gregarious. *Ad* Grey-blue head and rump, green-

purple gloss and white patches on neck, purplish breast. *Juv* Dull grey head and rump, no gloss or white on neck, rusty breast; much as ad after moult in Jul–Oct. VOICE Hoarse, rhythmic *cooo-coo coo-coo cu*. HABITAT Suburbs to islands, esp farmland with woods. NEST In trees, bushes, on ground, 2 eggs, Apr–Nov; 2–3 broods. FOOD Cereals, clover, peas, nuts, roots, seeds, leaves, few invertebrates. RANGE Mainly sedentary, moving locally; some winter immigrants from Continent.

Collared Dove *Streptopelia decaocto* 29–32 cm (*c*12 in). Stockier than Turtle Dove (174), with longer tail, broader wings; pale brown and grey, breast pinkish; tail white-cornered above, widely white-ended below. Flight less tilting than Turtle Dove; sails round on spread wings, cocks tail on landing. *Ad* Black-and-white collar. *Juv* Greyer, scaled buff; no collar. VOICE Deep *coo-cooo cuk*, emphasis on 2nd syllable; harsh *kwurr* in flight. HABITAT Suburbs, villages, parks, farms. NEST Often in conifers, 2 eggs, Apr–Nov; 2–4 broods. FOOD Seeds, grain, scraps. RANGE Rapid spread after colonisation in 1955; sedentary, but surplus disperses; birds continue to arrive from Continent.

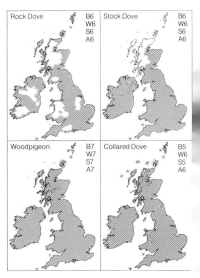

Rock Dove

Feral Pigeons

ad

ad

Stock Dove

ad

ad

Woodpigeon

ad

ad

Collared Dove

juv

ad

ad

Turtle Dove *Streptopelia turtur* 26–29 cm
(*c*10¾ in). Small, slim pigeon, with longish
graduated tail; head and outer wing-
coverts grey, back and rump grey-brown,
scapulars and most wing-coverts black-
spotted rufous, breast pink, belly white,
and tail white-edged, white-ended below.
Flight fast with clipped action of backswept wings, tilting to side; in display,
climbs steeply with spread tail, glides down
in circle; perches much on bushes, wires;
in small parties in late summer. *Ad* Grey-
blue head, black-and-white patch on
neck-sides, rufous and grey on wings,
pinkish breast. *Juv* Grey-brown head, no
neck-patches, duller rufous and less grey
on wings, buff breast. VOICE Deep purring
rroorr repeated. HABITAT Bushy areas,
copses, wood-edges, young plantations.
NEST Typically in thorn bushes, 2 eggs,
mid May–mid Sep; 2 broods. FOOD Seeds.
RANGE Summer visitor, end Apr–Sep,
wintering in Africa; some on passage from
Continent, mid Apr–May, mid Aug–mid
Oct. COMPARE Rufous Turtle Dove (288).

CUCKOOS (Cuculidae)

Cuckoo *Cuculus canorus* 32–34 cm (*c*13 in).
Familiar summer sound, much less seen,
and often confused with hawk in flight;
slender, with pointed bill and wings, long
graduated tail; usually grey above and
barred below with white-spotted tail, but
many juvs and a few ♀s rufous and heavily
barred above. Flight direct, often fairly
low, with fast shallow beats below level of
back, gliding to perch on trees, bushes,
posts; droops wings and raises tail on
landing; waddles or hops on ground;
solitary; rather shy. *Ad ♂* Grey above and
on head to upper breast; white barred
blackish below. *Ad ♀* Grey tinged brown;
browner barring on buff breast. *Juv* Either
dark grey-brown above, or rufous with
blackish bars, but always whitish fringes,
white nape-patch; buff-white below,
heavily barred blackish. *1st summer* As
ads after winter moult, but some greater
coverts and barred secondaries still juv; ♀
often has some rufous barring above and
on throat. *Hepatic ad ♀* Rare variety
resembles barred rufous juv, but rich

chestnut above, more rufous on throat/
breast. VOICE ♂ far-carrying *cuc-coo* or
cuc-cuc-coo; ♀ long bubbling chuckle;
both also hoarse *wha-wha-wha*. HABITAT
Woods, farmland, reedbeds, moors,
dunes. NEST Lays directly into nests of
other birds (esp pipits, Dunnock,
warblers, wagtails, Robin), each ♀ often
parasitising only 1 species; 6–18 eggs in
May–Jul; young Cuckoo ejects other eggs
or nestlings soon after hatching. FOOD
Mostly insects; ♀ eats 1 egg of foster
parent. RANGE Summer visitor, mid Apr–
Jul/Aug (juvs to Sep or later), wintering in
Africa. SEE Other cuckoos (290).

PARAKEETS (Psittacidae)

Ring-necked Parakeet *Psittacula krameri*
37–43 cm (*c*16 in). Very attenuated parrot
with largish head, narrow pointed wings,
and extremely long, thin, graduated tail;
mainly green with bluer-green tail. Flight
fast with shallow beats; clambers about on
branches and trunks, using bill as extra
foot; noisy, gregarious. *Ad ♂* Red bill;
black throat, thin pink collar, bluish
nape. *Ad ♀* Red bill; otherwise green. *Juv*
As ♀, but bill horn-coloured with dark tip.
VOICE Shrill screaming *keeo-keeo-keeo*.
HABITAT Open
woods, parks,
gardens, fields. NEST
In tree-holes, 2–6
eggs, Apr–Jul; 1
brood. FOOD Seeds,
nuts, fruit, berries,
scraps. RANGE Intro-
duced from Africa/
S Asia in 1960s,
now breeds ferally.

Turtle Dove · B6 W0 S6 A6

Ring-necked Parakeet · B3 W4 S3 A4

Cuckoo · B5 W0 S5 A5

Ring-necked Parakeet

juv

♂

♀

Turtle Dove

juv

ad

ad

Cuckoo

ad

♂

hepatic ♀

grey-brown juv

BARN-OWLS (Tytonidae)

Barn Owl *Tyto alba* 33–36 cm (*c*13½ in).
Nocturnal and crepuscular; smallish black
eyes set in heart-shaped white face, longish
tapering wings, short tail; orange-buff
and white, looks ghostly pale in car lights.
Flight wavering; hunts by day when
feeding young and in winter; stands
upright on longish legs; swings lowered
head to and fro when agitated; roosts in
buildings, tree holes, rocks; solitary. *Ad
W European race (T.a. alba)* Orange-buff
above, mottled grey (esp ♀); white below,
often some buff tinge and fine dark spots
(esp ♀). *Juv* As ad, but cream down
adhering to crown, back, underparts. *Ad
dark-breasted Cent/E European race (T.a.
guttata)* Darker: greyer above and more
buff and spotted below; some intermediate. VOICE Shrill drawn-out shriek in
flight, short whistled hiss, also snore,
chirrup, sharp *ke-ak*. HABITAT Farms,
ruins, church towers, parks, timbered
hedges, cliffs, quarries, in open country.
NEST In roof-spaces, hollow trees, holes in
thatch or straw, rock crevices, 4–7 eggs,
Apr–Oct. FOOD Small mammals, also
birds, insects. RANGE Largely sedentary,
imms wander; dark-breasted race vagrant,
Aug–Apr, esp Oct–Dec, most SEBr.

OWLS (Strigidae)

Snowy Owl *Nyctea scandiaca* 53–66 cm
(21–26 in), ♀ larger than ♂. Diurnal; very
big, with round head, yellow eyes, broad
rounded wings and shaggy feet; white,
more or less marked with brown. Flight
powerful, fast, often low, with long glides;
kills birds on wing; perches slanted on
rocks, hummocks and posts; solitary. *Ad
♂* All white, but for scattered brown spots
and bars. *Ad ♀* Face, throat, underwings
and legs white, sometimes also central
breast, belly and rump; rest widely barred
brown. *Juv* Downy; mainly dark grey-
brown, speckled grey-white, but face,
wings and tail white marked with brown.
1st year ♂ As small ad ♀ after moult ends
Sep–Oct, but more heavily barred on nape
and belly, mottled on wings. *1st year ♀*
Much more heavily barred and mottled.

VOICE Rather silent; barking *ergh-ergh*
(♂♀), low deep hoot *hoorh* (♂), mew and
squeal (♀), when nesting. HABITAT Moorland with rocky outcrops, also coastal
flats in winter. NEST On open ground, 4–10
eggs, May–Jul. FOOD Birds, mammals (to
size of duck, rabbit), also beetles, fish.
RANGE Bred NBr 1967–75, then only ♀s
present; otherwise irregular visitor.

Little Owl *Athene noctua* 21–23 cm (*c*8½
in). Diurnal and crepuscular; squat, flat-
headed, with fierce yellow eyes set in
frowning face, short tail; brown dappled
with white. Flight fast, low, undulating
like woodpecker; perches upright on trees,
hedges, posts, wires, and rocks; bobs
when agitated; can run; roosts in holes or
dense cover; solitary. *Ad* Dusky-brown,
spotted and streaked with white; whitish
below, broadly streaked dark brown. *Juv*
Pattern similar, but downy; browns paler,
whites more buff, streaking narrower; as
ad after moult Aug–Nov. VOICE Plaintive
mewing *keeu*; yelps, barks and chatters
when nesting; song mellow whistle, often
in duet. HABITAT Farmland with old trees,
parks, also stony wastes, cliffs, suburbs.
NEST In holes in trees, barns, haystacks,
rabbit burrows, rocks, 3–5 eggs, Apr–mid
Jul; 1 brood. FOOD
Insects, small
mammals, also
birds, worms. RANGE
Introduced Br late
19th century, largely
sedentary, some
wander; rare
vagrant Ir. COMPARE
Scops and Teng-
malm's Owls (290).

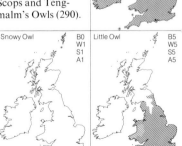

Barn Owl	B4
	W5
	S4
	A5

Snowy Owl	B0
	W1
	S1
	A1

Little Owl	B5
	W5
	S5
	A5

Snowy Owl

♀

♂

♂

Barn Owl

alba ad

guttata ad

alba ad

Little Owl

ad

Tawny Owl *Strix aluco* 36–40 cm (*c*15 in). Nocturnal, heard far more than seen; bulky, with big head, black eyes in rounded face, no ear-tufts, broad rounded wings; rufous (usually) to grey-brown, with whitish patches on scapulars. Flight slow with regular beats; may hunt by day in dark wood when feeding young, but mostly seen when disturbed from roost in hole or against trunk; often mobbed (as all owls) by chattering birds; solitary. *Ad* Red-brown, tawny or rarely greyish above, marbled and streaked; buff to whitish below with bold dark streaks. *Juv* Downy; brown to rufous above, grey-buff below, barred whitish and brown; moults from Jun–Jul, but often not as ad until Oct–Nov. VOICE Sharp *ke-wik*, juv shrill *tu-whit*; song prolonged, wavering *hoo-hoo . . . hoo . . . hoo-oo-oo-oo*. HABITAT Old woods, parks, suburbs. NEST In tree holes, chimneys, rocks, Magpie nests, rabbit holes, or on ground, 2–5 eggs, Mar–Jun; 1 brood. FOOD Small mammals, birds, also fish, frogs, insects. RANGE Sedentary.

Long-eared Owl *Asio otus* 34–37 cm (*c*14 in). Nocturnal, but also hunts by day; slender, with dark elongated cat-like face, orange eyes, V brows giving 'surprised' expression, ear-tufts (often invisible), broad longish wings, squared tail; grey-brown above, often looking uniformly darkish, and well streaked below; in flight, dark carpal patches (not obvious above), orange-buff patch on primaries, finely barred greyish secondaries and grey-buff tail (*cf* Short-eared). Flight deep jerky beats, then glide on straight, usually level wings; roosts upright by trunk, or on ground; sometimes small parties. *Ad* Grey-brown above, buff below, all dark-streaked. *Juv* Downy; brown and creamy-buff, all barred; moults from May–Jun but often not as ad until Nov. VOICE Squeals, screams, barks, also claps wings in display flight; juv mournful piping like unoiled gate; song (Jan–Apr) low, moaning, drawn-out *oo-oo-oo. . . .* HABITAT Woods, esp conifers, also moors, dunes, marshes. NEST In old nests (*eg* Magpie) or on ground, 3–6 eggs, Mar–Jun; 1 brood. FOOD Small mammals, birds, insects.

RANGE Sedentary, dispersal local; winter visitors from N Europe, Oct–mid May.

Short-eared Owl *Asio flammeus* 36–39 cm (*c*14¾ in). Diurnal; stocky, with whitish bulbous face, fiercely dark-ringed yellowish eyes, scarcely visible ear-tufts, long tapering wings and slightly wedge-shaped tail; tawny and buff above, looking blotched, and heavily streaked on throat and chest only; in flight, dark carpal patches above and below, pale buff to whitish on primaries, blotchy coverts and secondaries, pale trailing edges to wings, boldly V-barred buff tail (*cf* Long-eared). Flight more wavering than Long-eared, sometimes soaring high, and glides with wings held forward, often in shallow V; roosts in cover on ground; in parties in 'vole years' and on migration. *Ad* Blotched tawny, buff and brown; pale buff below, heavily streaked on forepart. *Juv* Downy; dark brown above, marked buff, and thinly streaked below; moults from Jun–Jul, but often not as ad until Oct. VOICE Shrill *kee-aw*, barking *kwowk*; in display flight, low *boo-boo-boo . . .*, claps wings. HABITAT Moors, marshes, dunes. NEST On ground, 4–7 eggs, end Mar–mid Jul; 1–2 broods. FOOD Small mammals, esp voles, also birds, insects.

RANGE Partial migrant, some moving SW, even to Iberia; many winter visitors from Iceland/N Europe, Sep–Jun.

COMPARE Other owls (176,290).

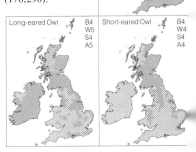

Tawny Owl	B6 W6 S6 A6
Long-eared Owl	B4 W5 S4 A5
Short-eared Owl	B4 W4 S4 A4

Tawny Owl

brown ad

grey ad

Long-eared Owl

Short-eared Owl

ad

ad

ad

ad

ad

NIGHTJARS (Caprimulgidae)

Nightjar *Caprimulgus europaeus* 25.5–28 cm (*c*10½ in). Nocturnal and crepuscular; tiny bill but huge gape, broad flat head, longish wings/tail; grey, camouflaged by brown, black, rufous and cream. Flight buoyant, erratic, with glides; by day on ground or lengthways on branch. *Ad* ♂ White on wing-tips, tail-corners. *Ad* ♀ No white. *Juv/1st winter* As ad ♀. VOICE ♂ shrill *coo-ic*, also claps wings; song loud churring, rising and falling, for up to 5 min. HABITAT Felled woods, tiny conifers, heaths, moors, dunes. NEST On bare ground, 2 eggs, end May–Aug; 2 broods. FOOD Insects, on wing. RANGE Summer visitor, May–Sep, wintering in Africa. COMPARE Common Nighthawk (290).

KINGFISHERS (Alcedinidae)

Kingfisher *Alcedo atthis* 15–16 cm (*c*6½ in). Stumpy with big head and dagger-like bill, short wings and tail; green-blue and chestnut, with brilliant blue mantle to tail,

white throat and neck-patch. Flight fast, direct, whirring, low over water; perches or hovers, then plunges; if uneasy, bobs head, flicks tail. *Ad* Crown and moustache show blue bars; ♂ bill black or red at base, ♀ often more red or orange at base. *Juv/1st year* Duller, greener, esp crown, moustache; paler below, speckled pale on breast; bill black. VOICE Shrill *chee* or *chee-kee*; song whistled trill. HABITAT Rivers, streams, lakes. NEST In excavated tunnels in banks, 5–7 eggs, Apr–Aug; 2 broods. FOOD Fish, insects. RANGE Most sedentary; some move to coasts Aug–Mar. SEE Belted Kingfisher (290).

HOOPOES (Upupidae)

Hoopoe *Upupa epops* 27–29 cm (*c*11 in). Pink,brown, with boldly pied wings and tail, curved bill, and huge fan-like crest depressed into hammer-shape at rest. Flight lazy, jerky, big oval wings closed between beats; walks unobtrusively; perches on trees, walls. *Ad* ♂ Throat/breast pinkish. *Ad* ♀ Throat/breast usually

Kingfisher

Nightjar

browner with white tips; some inseparable. *Juv* Shorter bill and crest at first, then as dull ♀; as ad after moult Aug–Oct. VOICE Song low *poo-poo-poo*, far-carrying. HABITAT Wood-edges, parks, orchards, gardens. FOOD Insects. RANGE Scarce migrant, esp Mar–May, Aug–Oct, wintering in S Spain/Africa; rarely nests SBr.

WOODPECKERS (Picidae)

Wryneck *Jynx torquilla* 15–16 cm (*c*6½ in). More like bulky chat/warbler than woodpecker relative; grey-brown, mottled and barred. Flight jerky; perches, or clings to trunk; licks insects from bark or ground, where hops with tail raised. *Ad* Grey to brown marked with rufous and black; snaky stripe on back; buff below, barred, spotted and arrowed. *Juv* Paler above, less bold marks below; as ad after moult in Aug–Sep. VOICE Shrill *kyeu-kyeu-kyeu*, like far Hobby (106). HABITAT Open woods, orchards. NEST In tree holes, 7–10 eggs, May–Jul; 1–2 broods. FOOD Ants. RANGE Summer visitor, Apr–Sep, wintering south to Africa; once widespread in S/CentBr, now colonising NBr; on passage from N Europe esp end Aug–Oct.

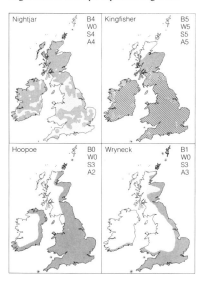

| Nightjar | B4 W0 S4 A4 | Kingfisher | B5 W5 S5 A5 |
| Hoopoe | B0 W0 S3 A2 | Wryneck | B1 W0 S3 A3 |

Hoopoe

Hoopoe

Wryneck

Green Woodpecker *Picus viridis* 30–33 cm (*c*12½ in). Robust tree-climber and wood-borer like all true woodpeckers, with strong bill, long sticky tongue, short spiky graduated tail, 2 toes forward and 2 back; dull green with red crown, black face, yellow rump, and paler grey-green below with barred yellowish underwings. Bounding flight, wings closed every 3–4 beats, sweeping up into trees; climbs or spirals up trunk with jerky hops, pressing tail (often very worn) against bark as prop, or along or under branch; hops upright on ground, alternately probing and looking round; solitary; wary. *Ad ♂* Moustache-centres red. *Ad ♀* Moustaches all black, belly often barred browner. *Juv* Greyer-green above with whitish spots and bars, and face and underparts streaked and barred with black; shorter, speckled moustaches (part red on ♂); as ads after moult Aug–Nov. VOICE Loud ringing laugh *keu-keu-keu*; rarely drums. HABITAT Farmland, orchards, copses, parks, commons, with old trees. NEST In excavated holes in trees, 5–7 eggs, end Apr–early Jul; 1 brood. FOOD Insects, esp wood-boring larvae, ants; some worms, few berries and seeds. RANGE Sedentary. COMPARE ♀ Golden Oriole (226).

Great Spotted Woodpecker *Dendrocopos major* 22–24 cm (*c*9 in). Smaller than Green Woodpecker and shorter-billed; boldly pied, with glossy black cap and back, big white or buff-tinged shoulder-patches, whitish sides of head and neck divided by black band joining moustache, whitish underparts and underwings but red under tail (*cf* Lesser Spotted). Behaviour as Green Woodpecker, but seldom on ground; wedges pine-cones in cracks to break out seeds; tamer, visits bird tables. *Ad ♂* Small red patch on nape; buff-white below with red extending to lower belly. *Ad ♀* As ♂, but no red on black nape. *Juv* Whole crown red; black moustache narrower, streaked with white; often few black streaks on shoulders and flanks; underparts paler and red area duller, less extensive; as ad after moult in Aug–Oct. VOICE Abrupt, explosive *tchick*; drums with bill on dead wood, Mar–May,

with loud hard vibration like creaking tree, lasting *c*1 sec. HABITAT Woods, copses, also gardens in winter. NEST In excavated holes in trees, 4–7 eggs, May–early Jul; 1 brood. FOOD Insects, esp wood-boring larvae; conifer seeds, nuts, berries, nestlings, eggs. RANGE Sedentary; some immigrants from Scandinavia, Sep–Apr, esp N/EBr Sep–Oct, rarely to Ir.

Lesser Spotted Woodpecker *Dendrocopos minor* 14–15.5 cm (*c*5¾ in). Sparrow-sized, with small pointed bill; crown red or whitish, no white shoulder-patches or red under tail, but wings and back barred black and white, flanks streaked blackish (*cf* Great Spotted). Actions as Green Woodpecker, but flight slower, more fluttering; mainly on high branches or twigs, rarely on ground; shy. *Ad ♂* Crown red, mottled whitish. *Ad ♀* Crown whitish to pale brown, sometimes flecked red; black of nape extends to rear crown. *Juv* Forecrown whitish, mottled black; rear part red on ♂, flecked red on ♀; flanks more spotted and streaked black; as ad after moult Jul–Oct. VOICE Shrill *pee-pee-pee-pee*, weaker, less ringing than Wryneck (180); also single *chik*, weaker than Great Spotted; drumming usually feebler, longer, *c*2 sec.

HABITAT Tall woods, parks, avenues, old orchards. NEST In excavated holes in branches, 4–6 eggs, end Apr–mid Jul; 1 brood. FOOD Wood-boring larvae. RANGE Sedentary.

Green Woodpecker B5 W5 S5 A5

Great Spotted Woodpecker B5 W6 S5 A6

Lesser Spotted Woodpecker B5 W5 S5 A5

Green Woodpecker

Great Spotted
Woodpecker

Lesser Spotted
Woodpecker

LARKS (Alaudidae)

Woodlark *Lullula arborea* 14.5–16 cm (*c*6 in). Stockier than Skylark with finer bill, more obscure crest, blunter wings; tail much shorter with brownish sides and white tips; bold whitish supercilia meet on nape, white-edged blackish mark at wing-bend; pinkish legs. Unobtrusive on ground; often lands in trees; flight undulating; usually singly or in family parties. *Ad* Streaked above and on breast; darker above and whiter below in summer through wear. *Juv* More spotted, with pale-edged, rounded feathers on upperparts and breast; as ad after moult in end Jul–Sep. VOICE Liquid *toolooeet*; outstanding song of sweet, clear notes repeated in 3–5 sec phrases (esp rich *lu-lu-lu*) and sustained from tree, ground or in circling flight. HABITAT Heaths, brecks, felled woods (esp sandy soils), with scattered trees and bushes. FOOD Insects, seeds. NEST On ground, 3–4 eggs, Mar–Aug; 2 broods. RANGE Resident, decreased; some autumn/spring dispersal.

Skylark *Alauda arvensis* 17–18.5 cm (*c*7 in). Abundant aerial songster, often invisibly high, or streaky brown flutterer over fields, with longish tail (white-sided) and wings (rather pointed, with whitish trailing edges); bill stoutish, crest often prominent, supercilia obscure. Flight strong, slightly undulating; in song, climbs vertically, hangs poised for 2–5 mins, then sinks and finally drops; usually walks or runs crouched on bent legs, rather than hopping; perches on walls, fences, bushes, seldom trees; flocks in autumn and winter. *Ad* Brown above, streaked blackish; buff-white below with streaked breast; darker above and whiter below in summer through wear. *Juv* Scaled above with pale feather-edges, breast spotted rather than streaked, no crest; as ad after moult end Jul–Sep. VOICE Rippling *chirrup*; song loud, clear, sustained warbling in high flight, sometimes on ground or on bushes. HABITAT Open fields, downs, moors, dunes, marshes, saltings. NEST On ground in grass or crops, often by tufts, 3–5 eggs,

Woodlark

Skylark

Apr–Aug; 2–3 broods. FOOD Seeds, weeds, worms, insects. RANGE Resident, but some cross Channel; many on passage/winter from N/Cent Europe, Sep–Apr.

Shore Lark *Eremophila alpestris* 16–17 cm (c6½ in). Rather uniform pink-brown above and whitish below; yellow and black of head partly obscured in winter; tail blackish with browner centre, thin white sides; bill stubby. Walks unobtrusively, runs, also hops; gregarious in winter, mixes with Snow Buntings. *Ad summer* ♂ typically bold-patterned head with black 'horns', pink-brown nape; but some like ♀, duller blackish on head, with minute 'horns', nape only tinged pink-brown. *Ad winter* Black partly concealed by yellowish edgings; ♀ generally duller, less yellow-faced, browner-naped, more streaky above. *Juv* Darker above, spotted buff-white; no black/yellow. *1st winter* As dull winter ad; inseparable unless very little black on crown or pinkish on nape and both dark-streaked. VOICE Shrill, pipit-like *tseep*, wagtail-like *tsee-seep*; song short warble from ground or in display flight. HABITAT Breeds on stony hills; winters on shingle, saltings, stubble. FOOD Seeds, insects, molluscs, crustaceans. RANGE Passage/winter visitor from Fenno-Scandia, Oct–Apr; bred NBr 1973, 1977.

COMPARE Pipits (188), vagrants (294).

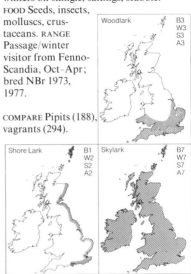

Shore Lark

winter flock

juv

♂ summer

♀/dull ♂

SWIFTS (Apodidae)

Swift *Apus apus* 16–17 cm (*c*6½ in). Scythe-like wings and short forked tail (closes to point); sooty-brown with paler under-wings and obscure whitish throat; looks all-black at distance. Flies with rapid beats of stiff wings, and long glides, tilting from side to side, often high in air; screaming parties chase round roof-tops; never perches, but will cling under eaves to roost. *Juv* Hard to separate in flight, but browner, with whitish tips on forehead and wings, and larger, whiter throat-patch. VOICE Shrill, chattering scream. HABITAT Aerial; commonest over towns and water. NEST Colonial; in hole in eaves, thatch, church towers, cliffs, 2–3 eggs, May–mid Aug; 1 brood. FOOD Insects, on wing. RANGE Summer and passage visitor, end Apr–Aug; stragglers to Oct.

SWALLOWS, MARTINS (Hirundinidae)

Sand Martin *Riparia riparia* 11.5–12.5 cm (*c*4¾ in). Slender, with barely-forked tail; brown and white with brown breast-band. Flight flitting, erratic, gliding less than Swallow, chiefly over water; perches on wires, bank vegetation; roosts gregariously in reedbeds. *Juv* As ad, but pale fringes on rump and wing-coverts, throat tinged buff. VOICE Hard, dry chirrup; song harsh twitter. HABITAT Rivers, lakes, sandpits. NEST Colonial; tunnel in sand or earth face, 4–5 eggs, May–Aug; 2 broods. FOOD Insects, on wing. RANGE Summer visitor, mid Mar–Oct; also on passage from Continent.

Swallow *Hirundo rustica* 16–22 cm (*c*7½ in). Long wings and (ad) tail-streamers; blue-black, chestnut and buff. Flight graceful, swooping, ever changing course, with regular beats and glides; perches and roosts as Sand Martin, also on and in buildings; autumn flocks common. *Ad* Metallic blue upperparts and breast-band, chestnut face, cream to buff belly, white tail-marks; longest tails on ♂, shortest on ♀, but much overlap. *Juv* Duller above; throat and smaller forehead-patch paler pink-buff; tail shorter than shortest ♀.

VOICE High *vit vit-vit-vit*; song of warbling twitters and trills. HABITAT Farms, suburbs; often over water. NEST Of mud, on ledges in sheds, porches etc., 4–6 eggs, May–Sep; 2–3 broods. FOOD Insects, on wing. RANGE Summer and passage visitor, end Mar–Oct; stragglers to Dec.

House Martin *Delichon urbica* 12–13 cm (*c*5 in). Compact, tail forked; blue-black and white with browner wings/tail, white rump. Flight slower, less swooping, often high; perches on roofs, wires; roosts in nest or trees; gregarious. *Ad* Metallic blue with white rump and underparts, buff-tinged through moult from Aug. *Juv* As ad in autumn, but bill-base yellowish, crown dull dark brown, tertials tipped white, white areas washed with brown-grey. VOICE Weak, hard *tchirrip*; infrequent twittering song. HABITAT Towns, villages, farms, bridges, cliffs; often over water. NEST Colonial; of mud, under house eaves, bridges, cliff over-hangs, 4–5 eggs, mid May–Sep, 2–3 broods. FOOD Insects, on wing. RANGE Summer and passage visitor, Apr–mid Oct; stragglers to Dec.

COMPARE Vagrant swifts, swallows (292).

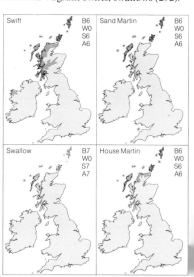

Swift

ad

juv

Sand Martin

juv

ad

juv

ad

Swallow

♂

♀

juv

House Martin

juv

ad

ad

PIPITS, WAGTAILS (Motacillidae)

Tree Pipit *Anthus trivialis* 14.5–16 cm
(*c*6 in). Very like Meadow Pipit, also with
white tail-sides, but plumper, more lightly
streaked on yellower breast; legs pinkish
with short hind-claws, bill stouter. Like all
pipits, walks, runs, wags tail; terrestrial,
but habitually also on trees; flight less
jerky than Meadow; solitary. *Ad* Olive-
brown above, streaked blackish; yellow-
buff below, streaked on breast and flanks;
in worn plumage, streaking bolder, underparts less buff. *Juv* More buff-brown
above with bolder streaks, less yellowish
below, flanks plainer; as ad after moult
in Jul–Sep. VOICE Hoarse *teez*, alarm *sip*;
song loud Chaffinch-like notes ending in
seea-seea-seea during 'parachuting' drop
after upward flight (usually from tree).
HABITAT Heaths, young plantations,
clearings, bracken slopes, scrub with
scattered trees. NEST In bank or tussock,
4–6 eggs, May–Jul; 1–2 broods. FOOD
Insects. RANGE Summer visitor, Apr–Sep;
on passage from N Europe esp Aug–Oct.

Meadow Pipit *Anthus pratensis* 14–15 cm
(*c*5¾ in). Usually more olive above and
paler below than Tree Pipit, with smaller
but denser streaks on breast and flanks;
tail-sides white; legs pink-brown with
long hind-claws. Rises and falls jerkily
in flight; mostly on ground, but also
perches on trees; gregarious in autumn/
winter. *Ad* Olive, green-brown or buff
above, streaked blackish (except rump);
whitish-grey to buff below; in worn
plumage, darker above and paler below,
with heavier streaking. *Juv* Darker above
and yellower below, with clearer streaking;
as ad after moult in Jul–Oct. VOICE Shrill
hurried *eest-eest*, alarm *tissip* (*cf* Tree
Pipit); song of accelerating calls, then
whistling trill during 'parachuting' drop
after upward flight (usually from ground).
HABITAT Moors, marshes, rough pastures,
dunes; winters in lowland marshes, fields,
coasts. NEST In tussocks, 4–5 eggs, mid
Apr–Jul; 2 broods. FOOD Insects, worms,
some seeds. RANGE Leaves uplands Nov–
Mar, some emigrating; on passage/winter
from Iceland/N Europe, mid Aug–May.

Tree Pipit

juv

ad

parachuting

buff ad

Meadow Pipit

grey ad

Rock Pipit *Anthus spinoletta* 15–16.5 cm (*c*6¼ in). Larger, longer-billed, more obscurely streaked than Meadow Pipit, with dark legs, grey tail-sides (but see Water Pipits, below). Perches on rocks; in small parties in winter. *Ad (A.s.petrosus)* Dark olive-brown above; dingy buff below streaked grey-brown. *Juv* Much as ad, but chin and throat also speckled blackish. *Scandinavian race (A.s. littoralis)* Separable only in spring, when browner above with creamy supercilia, whiter below with pinkish throat/breast and rather fewer streaks. *Water Pipit of Continental mountains (A.s. spinoletta)* Warmer brown and whiter, with white tail-sides, bold supercilia, breast streaked in winter, but plain pinkish in summer when greyer above (esp head). *American race (A.s. rubescens)* As Water Pipit, but very buff below, usually with thinner blacker streaks all year. HABITAT Rocky shores; passage/winter also on flat coasts; Water Pipit winters by lakes, watercress beds. VOICE Strong *weest*, more penetrating than Meadow; song louder, more musical, with stronger trill. NEST In rock crevices, 4–5 eggs, mid Apr–Jul; 2 broods. FOOD Insects, worms, sandhoppers, molluscs. RANGE Resident, but with some dispersal; Scandinavian race (E/SBr) and Water Pipit (SBr) passage/winter Oct–Apr; American race vagrant.

COMPARE Vagrant pipits (296).

Tree Pipit
B6
W0
S6
A6

Meadow Pipit
B7
W7
S7
A7

Rock Pipit
B5
W5
S5
A5

Rock Pipit

littoralis ad summer

rubescens ad winter

spinoletta ad winter

petrosus ad

spinoletta ad summer

Yellow Wagtail *Motacilla flava* 16-17 cm (*c*6½ in). Slim, graceful, longish-tailed, with yellow underparts, greenish back (*cf* Grey Wagtail, 192). Chiefly on ground, walking or running with wagging tail and to-and-fro motion of head, darting about and fluttering into air; perches on fences, wires, bushes and trees, often associates with cattle; flight markedly undulating; gregarious when not nesting, often roosting communally in reedbeds. Several distinctive subspecies. ♂ *summer* (*M.f. flavissima*, common race in Br) Bright yellow forecrown, supercilia and underparts; yellowish-green crown, cheeks and mantle. ♂ *winter* With moult in Aug–Sep, crown, cheeks and upperparts browner, but rump still greenish; supercilia and throat buff-yellow shading through more buff chest to yellow belly, greener flanks. ♀ *summer* Crown and upperparts browner-green than ♂; supercilia and underparts paler yellow with greener markings on upper breast. ♀ *winter* As ♂ autumn, but crown and mantle still browner, supercilia and throat whitish-

buff, upper breast buff, and belly paler yellow. *Juv* Brown above with blackish marks on sides of crown and creamy edges to all feathers of wings and tail; supercilia buff, cheeks dark brown; throat pale buff, surrounded by bib of blackish markings; breast buff, shading to yellow-buff belly. *1st winter* After moult in Jul–Sep, as ♀ autumn, though mantle still browner and belly even paler yellow; whiter edges and tips to greater wing-coverts. ♂ *summer* Blue-headed (*M.f. flava*) Crown blue-grey, cheeks similar but darker; supercilia and throat-sides white. ♂ *winter* Blue-headed Bluish-grey crown duller, partly obscured by brown tips; supercilia tinged creamy, ear-coverts brown with whitish markings (thus, head-pattern as summer but duller: same applies to autumn heads of other races described below); yellow underparts tinged buff on breast, with dark brown feathers forming obscure band. ♀ *Blue-headed* Crown and cheeks brownish-grey, supercilia whitish, throat buff-white or tinged yellow. ♂ *Grey-headed* (*M.f. thunbergi*) Crown dark grey,

Yellow Wagtail

flavissima
♀ summer

flavissima
1st winter

flavissima
juv

flavissima
♀ summer

flavissima
♂ winter

flavissima
♂ summer

cheeks blackish; no supercilia, or at most white marks over and just behind eyes; chin and throat yellow. ♂ *Black-headed (M.f. feldegg)* Black head and yellow throat; no supercilia. ♀ *Black-headed* Crown and ear-coverts blackish, thus resembling ♂ Grey-headed, but often white on throat, sometimes slightly yellow supercilia. ♂ *Ashy-headed (M.f. cinereocapilla)* As ♂ Blue-headed, but cheeks darker, supercilia ill-defined, white throat more extensive. ♂*Sykes's Wagtail (M.f. beema)* As ♂ Blue-headed, but crown much paler blue-grey, cheeks flecked white. ♂ *Eastern Blue-headed (M.f. simillima)* As ♂ Blue-headed, but crown marked with grey spots, supercilia broadening obviously behind eyes, cheeks plain blackish. ♂ *White-headed (M.f. leucocephala)* Crown, cheeks and chin all white, nape greyish. (♀s of all these races except Black-headed, described above, are usually indistinguishable from ♀ Blue-headed; ♂s showing the characters of the last four subspecies may be mutants rather than vagrants). VOICE Loud disyllabic

tswee-ip, harsh penetrating *tsee-tsreep*; irregular song short warble incorporating calls, in flight or from perch. HABITAT Water meadows, rushy pastures, gravel pits, damp heaths, boggy moorland, also arable and hayfields near water. NEST On ground, by or under tussocks, 5–6 eggs, May–Jul; 1–2 broods. FOOD Insects, small molluscs. RANGE Summer visitor, Apr–mid Oct, wintering in Africa; casual breeding by other races (Blue-headed and birds resembling Sykes's, Ashy-headed, once White-headed); also on passage end Mar–Jun, Aug–mid Oct (Yellow, some Blue-headed, few Grey-headed esp E/SBr); other races vagrants/mutants (*eg* 12 records of Black-headed, though these may be only dark variant Grey-headed). COMPARE Other wagtails (192, 296).

Yellow Wagtail
B5
W0
S5
A5

♂ SUMMER HEADS

thunbergi   *beema*   *cinereocapilla*   *feldegg*   *leucocephala*   *simillima*

flava ♂ summer

feldegg ♀ summer

flava ♂ winter

flava ♀ summer

Grey Wagtail *Motacilla cinerea* 18.5–19.5 cm (*c*7½ in). Yellow below, often confused with Yellow Wagtail (190), but flanks whitish; grey crown/back with contrasting yellow-green rump; flesh (not black) legs; white-edged black tail 2.5 cm (1 in) longer. Behaviour as Yellow Wagtail, but wagging of longer tail more obvious; seen along streams, perching on rocks and over-hanging trees; most singly or in family parties, but will roost gregariously, usually in waterside trees. ♂ *summer* Black throat, sometimes flecked whitish, separated from white-mottled grey cheeks by white stripe; supercilia also white; brightest yellow on breast and undertail-coverts. ♀ *summer* Throat white, or white mottled black and yellow; cheeks tinged green; breast paler. *Ad winter* Buff-white super-cilia and throat; ♂ buff-yellow breast shading to yellow belly, ♀ buff-white shading to yellowish. *Juv* Grey-brown above (but 2 narrow buff bars on wings, pale buff-green rump) and mainly buff below, with grey-black marks at sides of throat and breast; undertail-coverts

yellow, belly usually yellowish. *1st winter* After moult Jul–Sep, much as ♀ winter, but browner-grey above, more buff on breast. VOICE Clipped, high, metallic *tzitzi*; infrequent song louder, more trilling warble than Pied Wagtail. HABITAT Fast-flowing, rocky or gravelly streams; also lowland locks, weirs, locally lakes and slow rivers and, in winter, watercress beds. NEST On ledges or in holes of bridges, weirs, boathouses, old walls, usually over water, 4–6 eggs, Apr–Jul; 1–2 broods. FOOD Insects, also sandhoppers, molluscs. RANGE Resident, but some winter dispersal south and to lowlands; on passage Mar–Apr, Aug–Oct, inc some from Continent.

Pied Wagtail *Motacilla alba* 17–18.5 cm (*c*7 in). Black, white and grey, with long tail. Behaviour as Yellow Wagtail, but more catholic in habitat; roosts gregariously in reedbeds, bushes, trees, roofs of buildings, glasshouses, even towns. ♂ *summer* (*M.a. yarrellii*, common race in Br/Ir) Rear crown, upperparts, throat and breast solid black; forecrown,

Grey Wagtail

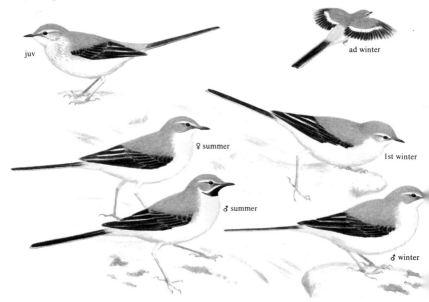

juv

ad winter

♀ summer

1st winter

♂ summer

♂ winter

sides of head, belly, tail-sides and 2 wing-bars all white. ♂ *winter* Throat white bordered with crescentic black bib, black of back (but not of rump) mixed with dark grey. ♀ *summer* As ♂ summer, but back blackish-grey to olive-grey, black of crown and breast less extensive. ♀ *winter* As ♂ winter, but black of back mixed with more grey. *Juv* Brown-grey above, grey-buff below, with buff sides of head and throat, blackish rump and 'double' breast-band. *1st winter* After moult in Aug–Oct, not always separable from ♀ winter, but usually has back dark olive-grey with no black, hindcrown black mixed with olive-grey. *1st summer* Some ♀s still show no black on olive-grey back. ♂ *summer White Wagtail* (*M.a. alba*, race of rest of Europe) Back and rump pure pale grey, usually demarcated sharply from black nape. ♀ *summer White Wagtail* As ♂, but back duller grey shading into black of crown. *Ad/1st winter White Wagtail* Forehead and crown often grey with little or no white and black (except some ad ♂s); further distinguished by greyer mantle

and grey rump from 1st winter Pied (back olive-grey, rump blackish). VOICE Shrill *tchizzik*; infrequent song simple twitter of slurred calls and warbles. HABITAT Farms, any open country, gardens, towns, often but not necessarily near water. NEST In recesses in walls, sheds, thatch, ivy, banks, rocks, or under stones, clods or plants, 5–6 eggs, Apr–Jul; 2–3 broods. FOOD Insects, some molluscs, seeds. RANGE Resident, but many move south in Oct–Mar, some emigrate; White Wagtails on passage from Iceland/N Europe, end Mar–May, Aug–Oct, seen most on W/N coasts.

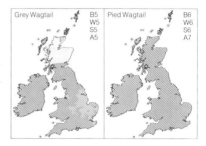

Grey Wagtail   B5 W5 S5 A5   Pied Wagtail   B6 W6 S6 A7

Pied Wagtail

yarrellii ad winter

yarrellii 1st winter

yarrellii ♂ winter

yarrellii ♀ summer

yarrellii ♂ summer

yarrellii juv

alba ♀ winter

alba ♀ summer

alba ♂ summer

WAXWINGS (Bombycillidae)

Waxwing *Bombycilla garrulus* 17–18.5 cm
(*c*7 in). Mainly pink-brown to chestnut,
with bold crest, black bib and mask, grey
rump, short yellow-ended tail, and white,
yellow and waxy red wing-marks. Flight
strong, undulating, on triangular wings
like Starling (234) but under-coverts
whitish; feeds acrobatically; gregarious,
tame. *Ad* ♂ Sharp black bib; bright yellow
and white V-tips to primaries; bold waxy
tips to secondaries; broad yellow tail-
band. *Ad* ♀ Bib smaller, fading into sooty-
grey; V-tips tend to be duller and less
complete, waxy tips smaller, tail-band
paler and narrower. *Juv* Duller, browner,
with short crest, no black bib, buff streaks
on underparts, only outer edge of
primaries tipped pale yellow. *1st winter*
After moult in Aug–Nov, more as ads, but
browner wings, primaries as juv; waxy tips
small or missing, tail-band duller and
narrower (esp ♀). VOICE Weak, high trill
zhreer. HABITAT Scattered trees, gardens,
wherever berries. FOOD Berries, hips,
buds. RANGE Scarce passage/winter visitor
from N Europe, Oct–Apr; periodically
widespread in larger numbers.

WRENS (Troglodytidae)

Wren *Troglodytes troglodytes* 9–10 cm
(*c*3¾ in). Tiny and stumpy, with short
cocked tail, slightly curved bill; rufous
and buff, barred darker, with pale supercilia. Flight whirring, usually not far;
busily seeks food in tangled cover,
crevices, leaf litter; hops crouched with
flicking tail; not gregarious, but sometimes 20 or more in roosts. *Ad/1st year*
Crown unmarked, throat faintly mottled;
undertail spotted white. *Juv* Very like ad,
but more mottled on crown and throat,
supercilia fainter; undertail not spotted.
Island races Of 4 distinct forms on St
Kilda, Outer Hebrides, Fair Isle and
Shetland, first (*T.t. hirtensis*) is esp pale,
more grey-brown, and last (*T.t.
zetlandicus*) is esp dark; these also larger,
longer-billed. VOICE Hard ticking, harsh
churring; explosive song of loud notes
with trill near end of each phrase. HABITAT

Gardens, woods, farmland, scrub, reeds,
broken cliffs. NEST Domed, in hedges, ivy,
crevices, 5–6 eggs, Apr–mid Aug; 2 broods.
FOOD Esp insects. RANGE Sedentary, some
local dispersal; migrants from Continent,
end Sep–mid Apr, esp EBr.

DIPPERS (Cinclidae)

Dipper *Cinclus cinclus* 17–18.5 cm (*c*7 in).
Plump and short-tailed, aquatic; blackish
with bold white gorget. Flight fast, mainly
low over water; runs, walks, hops on
rocks, bobbing, curtseying, jerking tail;
walks or plunges into streams, swimming
on or under water or walking on bottom;
solitary. *Ad Br race (C.c. gularis)* Blackish,
with chocolate head, white round eyes,
white gorget, chestnut belly-band. *Juv*
Slate-grey above, wings scaled whitish;
dingy white below, marked with grey. *1st
winter* As ad after moult in Jul–Sep, but
wings and belly with whitish feather-tips.
Ir race (C.c. hibernicus) Blacker above;
chestnut band duller, narrower. *N European race (C.c. cinclus)* As Br race
above; no chestnut below. VOICE Loud
zit-zit, metallic *clink*; song broken mixture
of clear, grating and warbling notes.
HABITAT Swift streams and rivers, edges of
upland lakes. NEST
Domed, on ledges or
in crevices by water,
4–6 eggs, Mar–Jun;
2 broods. FOOD
Invertebrates.
RANGE Sedentary;
also vagrants from
N Europe, Oct–
Apr, coastal EBr.

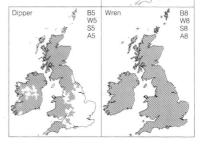

Waxwing

ad/1st winter

♂

1st winter ♀

zetlandicus ad

Wren

ad

hirtensis ad

juv

Dipper

cinclus ad
blinking

gularis ad

gularis juv
blinking

ACCENTORS (Prunellidae)

Dunnock *Prunella modularis* 14–15 cm
($c5\frac{3}{4}$ in). Unobtrusive, drab, sparrow-like,
but with dark slender bill, grey head and
breast, and streaked flanks. Flight low
and undulating, seldom far; mostly on
ground, hopping slowly or shuffling, often
flicking wings; also inside hedges, now
and then on top; special wing-waving
display in parties, but mainly solitary. *Ad*
Head and breast grey, but crown and ear-
coverts browner; mantle, wings and flanks
rufous streaked with black; eyes red-
brown. *Juv* Head browner, upperparts
less rufous, throat whitish, breast and
flanks buff with dark streaks; as ad after
moult in Aug–Oct. VOICE Shrill, piping
tseek; song high, clear, hurried warble
with broken phrases, like squeaky trolley.
HABITAT Gardens, hedges, open woods,
moorland scrub. NEST In bushes, young
conifers, tangled cover, 4–5 eggs, mid
Apr–Jul; 2–3 broods. FOOD Insects, seeds.
RANGE Sedentary; some immigrants from
N Europe, end Sep–mid May, esp coastal
EBr. COMPARE Alpine Accentor (296).

CHATS, THRUSHES (Turdidae)

Robin *Erithacus rubecula* 13.5–14.5 cm
($c5\frac{1}{2}$ in). Fat and neckless; orange-breasted
when ad, juv spotted. Flight flitting and
jerky, usually low, not far; darts from
perch to ground and back; hops crouched,
pausing upright with drooped wings, head
often on side; bobs head, flicks wings and
tail; quite tame, but skulking when in
summer moult; pugnacious, solitary. *Ad*
Face and breast red-orange, edged with
grey; upperparts olive-brown, belly white.
Juv Spotted buff; tail brown (*cf* juv Nightingale, Redstart, 198); as ad after moult in
Jun–Sep. VOICE Repeated *tic tic-tic*, thin
tseee, soft *tsip*; song of prolonged notes,
short warbles and trills, thinner and more
melancholy in autumn. HABITAT Gardens,
hedges, woods. NEST In banks or any
crevice or ledge, 5–7 eggs, mid Mar–
mid Jul; 2–3 broods. FOOD Insects, worms,
berries. RANGE Mainly sedentary, some
move SW as far as Iberia; immigrants
from Continent, end Sep–Apr, esp EBr.

Bluethroat *Luscinia svecica* 13.5–14.5 cm
($c5\frac{1}{2}$ in). Like slim dark Robin with whitish supercilia, rufous-based tail; blue
varies with age/sex, throat often whitish
above dark breast-band. Skulking; flight
Robin-like, into cover at ground-level,
spreading tail; creeps mouse-like, but
also in open with Robin-like gait and
bobbing, upright stance with tail cocked
or moved sideways and often spread. ♂
Red-spotted (L.s. svecica) Chestnut-
centred blue gorget edged below by bands
of black and chestnut; in autumn, upper
throat black, some buff and white tips.
♂ *White-spotted (L.s. cyanecula)* Smaller
spot in centre of gorget white (rarely all
blue); in autumn, this often mottled
chestnut. *Ad ♀ (both races)* Buff-white
moustaches and throat, latter edged
blackish with some blue and ill-defined
chestnut; sometimes rufous spot, rarely
blue on sides of throat in summer (even
almost as much blue as ad ♂, but not
glossy and centre of throat whitish, not
blue). *1st winter ♂* As ad ♀, but breast
and esp sides of throat often bluer; outer
greater coverts tipped with red-buff. *1st
winter ♀* Duller, no blue, little chestnut.
VOICE Sharp *tac tac*, plaintive *hweet*.
HABITAT Migrants in coastal scrub, root
crops. FOOD Insects,
some seeds, berries.
RANGE Scarce mi-
grant from N (Red-
spotted) Cent
Europe (White-),
end Aug–mid Oct,
few Mar–May;
nested NBr 1968,
2 singing ♂s 1980.

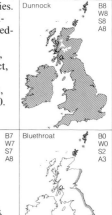

Dunnock · B8 W8 S8 A8

Robin · B7 W7 S7 A8

Bluethroat · B0 W0 S2 A3

Dunnock

ad

juv

Robin

ad

juv

Bluethroat

svecica
♂ summer

cyanecula
♂ summer

ad/1st winter

1st winter ♀

svecica
♂ winter

juv

svecica
1st winter ♂

ad ♀

Nightingale *Luscinia megarhynchos* 16–17 cm (*c*6½ in). Heard far more than seen; sturdy, with longish rounded tail; rufous and buff-white. Actions as Robin (196), but very skulking, on or near ground with tail cocked, often crown-feathers raised; solitary. *Ad* Red-brown above, all but central tail-feathers richer chestnut (more obvious when spread in flight or display); whitish around eyes; underparts buff-brown, whiter on throat and belly. *Juv* Spotted as juv Robin, but larger, with chestnut tail. *1st winter* After moult in Jul–Sep, as ad, but buff spots at tips of greater coverts and tertials. VOICE Hard *tak tak*, Chaffinch-like *hweet*, grating *kurrr*; rich song, by day or night in Apr–Jun, with repetitions of clear notes, esp slow sad *peeoo* in crescendo, fast deep *chook*, and hard trill. HABITAT Broad-leaved woods, copses, damp thickets. NEST On ground or low in tangled cover, 4–5 eggs, May–Jun; 1 brood. FOOD Insects, worms, berries. RANGE Summer/passage visitor, Apr–Sep, wintering in Africa. COMPARE Thrush Nightingale (298).

Black Redstart *Phoenicurus ochruros* 14–15 cm (*c*5¾ in). Tail as Redstart; bulkier, darker, no orange/buff below in W European stock. Actions as Redstart, but much more on ground, even running; favours cliffs, tall buildings. *Ad ♂* Mainly black with white wing-patches; after moult in Aug–Sep, black obscured by grey tips which wear off during winter. *Ad ♀/1st winter ♂♀* Dark grey-brown, no wing-patches. *Juv* Much as ♀, but browner, less grey, and speckled darker, esp on paler breast and flanks (far less spotted than juv Redstart). *1st summer ♂* Some as ♀; others with blackish throat and breast, sometimes small white patches on brown wings. VOICE Short *tsip*, stuttering *tititic*; song fast warble with scratchy 'gravelly' hiss. HABITAT Breeds in towns, power stations, cliffs; winters on cliffs, rocks, coastal ruins and dumps, stony downs. NEST In crevices or on ledges, 4–6 eggs, mid Apr–mid Jul; 2 broods. FOOD Insects, also crustaceans, berries. RANGE Breeding areas Apr–Sep; on passage from Cent Europe, Mar–May, Sep–Nov; few winter.

Nightingale

Black Redstart

♀/1st winter

ad

ad

♂ summer

♂ winter

1st summer ♂

♀/1st winter

juv

juv

Redstart *Phoenicurus phoenicurus* 13.5–14.5 cm (*c*5½ in). Slim; orange-red tail constantly shivered, not flicked; paler below than above, showing orange-buff. Flight/actions recall Robin (196), but seldom on ground, usually in trees where flits about and flutters into air; solitary. *Ad ♂* Grey upperparts, black face, white forehead, orange breast and flanks; after moult in Jul–Sep, colours obscured by brown and whitish tips which wear off during winter. *Ad ♀/1st year ♀* Brown-grey above; orange-buff breast and flanks, dulled with whitish tips in winter; pale throat and eye-rings (rarely ad ♀ much as 1st year ♂). *Juv* Spotted as juv Robin, but with red tail. *1st winter ♂* After moult in Jul–Sep, as ad ♂ but browner above, white forehead virtually hidden, black throat heavily mottled off-white. *1st summer ♂* Usually browner above than ad ♂; throat more mixed with white. VOICE Plaintive *hweet* like Chiffchaff, or *hweet tuc-tuc*; brief song clear Robin-like warble that disappointingly peters out into feeble tinny jangle. HABITAT Old woods, parks, orchards, heaths with old trees; on passage by coasts. NEST In crevices or on ledges of trees, walls or quarries, 5–7 eggs, May–mid Jul; 1–2 broods. FOOD Insects, berries. RANGE Summer visitor, Apr–Sep, wintering in Africa; on passage from Germany/Scandinavia, end Mar–mid Jun, Jul–Oct, esp E/S coasts.

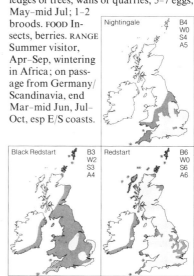

Nightingale   B4 W0 S4 A5

Black Redstart   B3 W2 S3 A4

Redstart   B6 W0 S6 A6

Redstart

♂ summer

bright ♀ summer

♀

♂ winter

1st winter ♂

juv

Whinchat *Saxicola rubetra* 12–13 cm (*c*5 in). Compact but longish-winged, with short squared tail; warm buff breast, white or whitish supercilia, white sides to tail-base (ads also white wing-mark). Perches prominently on tall plants, bushes, trees, wires or fences, bobbing and flicking wings and tail, flying low and jerkily from perch to perch; hops on ground; surprisingly active at dusk; solitary, or family parties in summer. *♂ summer* Streaky brown and blackish above, bright buff below, with bold white supercilia and line down throat-sides (showing up blackish cheeks), also white wing-band and well-defined tail-patches. *♀ summer* Duller, with less distinct buffish-white supercilia and throat-sides, brown cheeks; paler below, often with odd spots; less white on wings, less sharply defined tail-patches. *Ad winter* After moult in Jul–Sep, creamy supercilia and throat-sides, redder-brown cheeks, often with dark flecks on breast; ♂ more white on wings, clearer tail-patches. *Juv* More rufous above with pale shaft-streaks, duller buff below with dark mottling on throat/breast; supercilia ill-defined, no contrast between throat-sides and centre, no white on wings. *1st winter* As ad after moult in Jun–Sep, but usually much less white on wings. *1st summer ♂* Contrast between black inner and worn brown outer greater coverts. VOICE Scolding *tic-tic* or *tu-tic-tic*, short churring rattle; song short warble, variably like Stonechat or Redstart (198), but sweeter and more broken like Robin (196). HABITAT Commons, rough pastures, railway banks, downs, water meadows, young conifers, bracken slopes. NEST In grass tussocks, or under thicker cover, 5–6 eggs, mid May–Jul; 1–2 broods. FOOD Insects. RANGE Summer visitor, Apr–Sep, wintering in Africa; also on passage from Scandinavia, Apr–May, mid Jul–early Oct, esp E/SBr.

Stonechat *Saxicola torquata* 12–13 cm (*c*5 in). Dumpier than Whinchat, with shorter wings, perching even more upright; breast reddish, head dark with no supercilia (but see E races) or tail-patches; ♂ white on neck, wings, rump.

Whinchat

♂ winter

juv

♂ summer

♀ summer

♂ summer

1st winter

Actions as Whinchat; bobs and flicks constantly. ♂ *summer W European race (S.t. hibernans)* Black head, throat and back; bold white neck-patches and wing-marks, whitish rump streaked with black; reddish-orange breast. ♂ *winter* After moult in Aug–Sep, black upperparts streaked with rufous, white patches reduced, black throat mottled buff, breast duller reddish. *Ad* ♀ Like duller, browner winter ♂: no white on rump, less on wings; neck-patches/dark throat obscured in winter. *Juv* As ♀ but streaked pale buff as well as rufous above; grey-buff throat and rufous-buff breast speckled with black. *1st year* ♂ As ad after moult in Aug–Sep, but slight contrast between black inner and worn dark grey-brown outer greater coverts; worn juv flight-feathers pale brown by spring. *E Eurasian races (S.t. maura/stejnegeri)* Large orange or white rump; ♂ has buff (not rufous) streaks above, often bolder white patches, sandy below, blacker (not buffish) axillaries; ♀/imm plain buff throat, light wing-panel, with pale supercilia and sandy-buff colours not unlike Whinchat. VOICE Hard *tsak-tsak* (clinking stones) or *weet-tsak-tsak* (*cf* Wheatear, 202); song lively repetition of sharp and deeper notes, not unlike Dunnock (196), often in dancing flight. HABITAT Heaths, commons, moors, young conifers, coasts, esp where gorse. NEST In gorse or at end of tunnel in thick cover, 5–6 eggs, Apr–early Aug; 2–3 broods. FOOD Insects, worms, some seeds. RANGE Often resident, but many from N/uplands move south in autumn, some as far as Iberia; E races vagrant (46: Sep–May, esp Oct–Nov EBr).

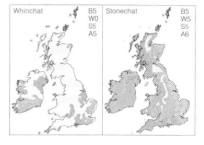

Whinchat B5 W0 S5 A5 Stonechat B5 W5 S5 A6

Stonechat

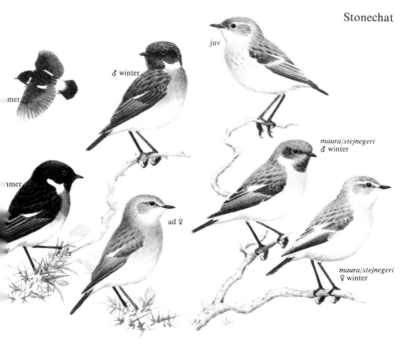

juv

♂ winter

...mer

...mer

ad ♀

maura/stejnegeri ♂ winter

maura/stejnegeri ♀ winter

Wheatear *Oenanthe oenanthe* 14–15.5 cm
(*c*5¾ in). White rear with black inverted T
on shortish tail; dapper, erect, in open
country and short grass; variously grey or
brown, and buff below, with white or pale
supercilia, more or less contrasting dark
wings. Restless, flying low, pausing on
rock or ground; bobs up and down, flicks
wings, wags and flirts tail, then moves
with long hops or flutters up to catch
insects; when nesting, often hovers;
perches on walls, fences, wires, bushes,
less on trees; solitary. ♂ *summer Eurasian
race (O.o. oenanthe)* Grey upperparts,
white supercilia, blackish mask and
wings, sandy-buff breast and white belly.
♂ *winter* With moult in Jul–Aug,
brownish-grey above and deep to creamy-
buff below (very variable), with whitish to
buff fringes on all wing-feathers, but still
blackish mask and white supercilia. *Ad* ♀
Duller, with dark brown mask, creamy
supercilia; grey-brown above and
variably buff below in summer, brown to
rufous above in winter with buff-edged
wings. *Juv* Spotted light and dark above,
and mottled brown on creamy-buff throat/
breast; much as ♀ winter after moult in
Aug–Sep. *1st summer* ♂ Much as ad ♂,
though often browner-grey above, but
worn wings clearly paler brown than
mask. *Greenland race (O.o. leucorrhoa)*
Larger, longer-winged, more erect; spring
♂ much browner-grey above, more wholly
rufous-buff below. VOICE Harsh *chak-chak*
or *weet-chak-chak* (*cf* Stonechat, 196);
song short warble mixed with harsh creaky
notes and finch-like whistles, often in
dancing flight. HABITAT Mountains, rocky
moors, upland pastures, downs, brecks,
dunes, shingle. NEST Deep in hole in rocks,
walls, rabbit burrows, or *eg* under
corrugated iron, 5–6 eggs, late Apr–Jul;
1–2 broods. FOOD Insects. RANGE Summer
visitor, Mar–Sep, wintering in Africa;
also on passage from N Europe/Iceland/
Greenland, Mar–early Jun, end Jul–Oct.
COMPARE Vagrant wheatears (298, 300).

Fieldfare *Turdus pilaris* 24–27 cm (*c*10 in).
Large thrush, with longish wings and tail;
build and white underwings like Mistle

Wheatear

leucorrhoa ♂ summer

juv

♂ summer

♀ summer

♂ summer

♂ summer

1st summer ♂

♂ winter

♀ winter/1st winter

Thrush (206), but head and rump grey, back chestnut, tail black, supercilia whitish, breast rusty-yellow streaked with black, white flanks more spotted. Flight leisurely, less undulating than Mistle Thrush; perches in open on bushes/trees, but wary; runs or hops on ground, pausing erect with wings drooping; highly gregarious in winter, congregating on berried hedges or scattered over fields, flying up into trees when disturbed (often all facing same way). *Ad ♂* Large blackish centres to crown-feathers; crown/nape and rump otherwise blue-grey tinged with brown, mantle rich chestnut, breast rufous-buff; becomes greyer and paler in summer by abrasion, with bolder markings. *Ad ♀* Smaller blackish marks on crown; otherwise browner-grey, duller chestnut, paler buff, with browner flank-marks, though head and rump rather greyer in summer. *Juv* Much duller and browner with whitish streaks above, rounder blackish spots below. *1st winter* Much as ad after moult in Aug–Sep, but often keeps juv outer greater coverts (dull brown with whitish tips or streaks) in contrast to new chestnut inners. VOICE Harsh chatter *chak-chak-chak*, soft drawn-out *seeh*; weak song of harsh and squeaky sounds mixed with flutier notes. HABITAT Breeds in wood-edges, often near water; winters in fields with berried hedges. NEST Mainly in trees, 4–6 eggs, May–Jul; 1–2 broods. FOOD Slugs, worms, insects, berries, fallen apples, grain. RANGE Mainly passage/winter visitor from Fenno-Scandia/N Russia, Sep–Apr, esp Nov–Mar; occasionally seen in summer and odd pairs have bred most years since 1967.

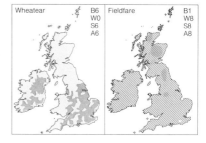

Fieldfare

Ring Ouzel *Turdus torquatus* 23–25 cm
(*c*9½ in). Near size of Blackbird, wings/
tail longer; blackish to brown with white
or more obscure crescent on breast, pale
scaling and wing-panel, yellowish bill
(yellower in summer, yellowest on ad ♂).
Actions as Blackbird, but hill-dweller,
with more dashing flight; perches on
boulders, trees, but shy, dodging behind
rocks. ♂ *summer* Sooty-brown with bold
white gorget, greyish wing-panel; sometimes traces of pale scaling, esp below. ♂
winter Blacker after moult in Jul–Sep, but
scaled greyish above (least on head) and
whitish below; gorget dulled by brown-
grey fringes. *Ad* ♀ Browner, more scaled,
with narrower gorget dulled by brown
tips and often obscure in autumn. *Juv*
Much browner, no gorget, creamier wing-
panel; whitish shaft-streaks on mantle,
scapulars, coverts; spotted and barred
creamy-buff and dark brown below, throat
buff mottled darker (*cf* more rufous juv
Blackbird). *1st winter* Much as ads after
moult in Aug–Sep, though gorget usually
duller on ♂, barely visible on ♀; juv outer

greater coverts browner with broader
whitish (♂) or creamy (♀) edges. VOICE
Loud hollow rattling scold or chatter
chaka-chaka, piping *pee-u*; far-carrying
song of 2–4 shrill piping notes *pee-pirri-
pee*, then chuckle. HABITAT Steep moorland with rocky outcrops, scrubby slopes;
on passage, lowland hedges, bushes. NEST
Usually in tufts on rock-faces or steep
banks, 4–5 eggs, mid Apr–Jul; 2 broods.
FOOD Insects, worms, snails, berries.
RANGE Summer visitor, Apr–Sep,
wintering in S Europe/N Africa; some on
passage from Scandinavia, Mar–May,
end Aug–Nov, esp EBr; rare in winter.

Blackbird *Turdus merula* 24–27 cm (*c*10
in). Stocky; black, or shades of brown
and mottled rufous, with yellow to brown
bill; white-patched and even all-white
birds not rare. Flight often low, flicking,
with glides, looking weak and undulating,
but can be high, strong, direct; raises
fanned tail and droops wings on landing;
hops or runs on ground, pausing less erect
than Song Thrush (206), head on one side,

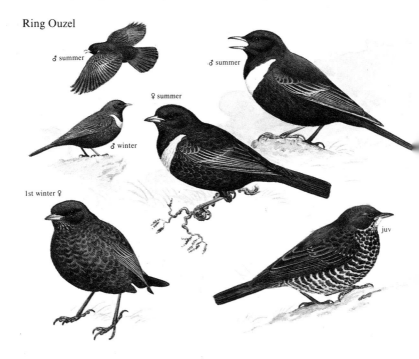

Ring Ouzel

♂ summer

♀ summer

♂ winter

1st winter ♀

♂ summer

juv

often with tail up; tends to skulk in or near cover, but readily perches high; shy or tame; gregarious only on migration or at roosts. *Ad ♂* Glossy black, with browner wings in summer; bill and eye-rings orange-yellow. *Ad ♀* Dark grey-brown to black-brown above, tinged with olive, and variable below: throat greyish with blackish to rufous streaks, breast grey-brown to rufous with dark mottling, belly pale brown to slate with pale fringes (generally browner, less rufous and more dully mottled in summer); bill dark flesh-brown to yellowish. *Juv* More rufous than ad ♀, with rufous shaft-streaks above, more extensive mottling below; ♂ darker, more blackish-brown above (esp wings/tail). *1st year ♂* After moult in Aug–Oct, brown-black above (not tinged olive as ♀) with browner wings; juv outer greater coverts paler than others, with pale tips; brown-grey to brown-black below, less uniform than ad, throat/breast sometimes as ♀; bill blackish, turning yellow in *c*Dec–Apr. *1st year ♀* As ad ♀ but for paler juv outer greater coverts. VOICE Scolding

chik-chik-chik, deeper *chook-chook-chook* (often extended into hysterical screeching alarm-chatter with repeated *chewee*), thin *tsee*; song languid clear fluty warble, ending in low squawky chuckle. HABITAT Gardens, hedges, woods, scrub, from town centres to upland brambles. NEST In hedges, trees, banks, walls, sheds or on ground under cover, 3–5 eggs, Mar–Aug; 3–5 broods. FOOD Worms, insects, snails, berries, seeds, fruit. RANGE Often sedentary, but many move south in autumn; also abundant passage/winter visitor from Continent, end Sep–May.

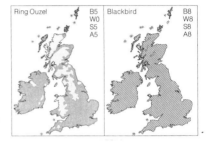

Blackbird

Song Thrush *Turdus philomelos* 22–24 cm
(*c*9 in). Compact; warm brown above, well
spotted below with yellow-buff underwings, no bold supercilia or whitish on
tail. Flight fast, direct; hops/runs, then
pauses rather upright, often with head to
one side; feeds in open or undergrowth,
smashes snails on stones; often sings
hidden; solitary except as migrant. *Ad*
Uniform above, with 2 faint wing-bars;
breast and flanks buff, throat and belly
whiter, with blackish spots/arrows.
(Hebridean race *T.p. hebridensis* darker
above, spots denser; migrants from Continent can look greyer.) *Juv* Buff streaks
above; largely buff below, spots smaller;
much as ad after moult in Jul–Sep. VOICE
Flight-call thin *tsip*; alarm loud *tchuk*
extended into chatter like Blackbird (204);
song loud, clear, with varied phrases, each
uttered 2–4 times. HABITAT Gardens, thick
hedges, woods, rough ground with cover.
NEST In hedges, trees, ivy, sheds, banks,
heather, 3–5 eggs, Mar–Aug; 2+ broods.
FOOD Worms, snails, slugs, insects,
berries. RANGE Mainly sedentary, some
winter SW to Iberia; passage/winter from
Cent/N Europe, Sep–Apr, esp E/SEBr.

Redwing *Turdus iliacus* 20–22 cm (*c*8¼ in).
Smaller, darker than Song Thrush, with
bold supercilia; streaked below, reddish
flanks/underwings. Far more gregarious
in winter; shyer. *Ad* At most, pale-edged
tips to greater coverts/tertials; streaked
and rich reddish below. *Juv* Like juv Song
(streaked above, spotted below), but for
whitish supercilia, pale chestnut-tinged
underwings. *1st winter* As ad after moult
in Aug–Sep, but triangular whitish tips to
outer greater coverts and some tertials.
VOICE Flight-call soft *tseeip*, drawn-out,
more penetrating than Song Thrush;
chattering *chittuck*, soft *chup*;
monotonous song of 3–6 fluty notes
ending in short, reedy warble; winter
flocks have babbling subsong. HABITAT
Breeds in woods, shrubberies, scrub;
winters in fields, open woods. NEST In
rhododendrons, bushes, trees, stumps,
banks, 5–6 eggs, May–Jul; 2 broods. FOOD
As Song Thrush; fewer berries. RANGE
Winter visitor from Iceland/N Europe,

Sep–Apr; few breed NBr, esp since *c*1953.

Mistle Thrush *Turdus viscivorus* 26–28 cm
(*c*10½ in). Bigger, deeper-chested than
Song Thrush, with longer wings and tail;
greyer, less uniform above with paler
rump, and whitish tail-corners; more
boldly spotted below, underwings white
(*cf* Fieldfare, 202). Distinctive flight with
marked wing-closure, often high; stands
upright with tail down, wings drooped;
not found in undergrowth; sings from
treetops; small flocks from late summer;
pugnacious, but shy. *Ad* Grey-brown
above, pale edges to back, rump, coverts;
breast and flanks light buff, throat and
belly whiter, with bold blackish spots/
wedges. *Juv* Spotted and streaked whitish
above, flecked dark; throat unmarked,
breast spots smaller; as ad after moult in
Jun–Sep, but often deeper buff below, odd
scapulars pale-streaked, greater coverts
whiter-edged. VOICE Rasping chatter like
wooden rattle, Redwing-like *seeip*, hard
tuc-tuc-tuc; song like Blackbird (204), but
less mellow, louder, faster with shorter
pauses between phrases. HABITAT Woods,
avenues, parks, orchards, conifers, upland
scrub; winters in fields, moors. NEST
Usually in trees, 3–5 eggs, Mar–Jun;
2 broods. FOOD
Berries, fruit, slugs,
worms, insects,
nestlings. RANGE
Fairly sedentary;
migrants from Con-
tinent, Sep–Apr.

COMPARE Other
thrushes (202, 204,
302, 304).

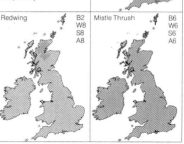

Song Thrush — B7 W7 S7 A8

Redwing — B2 W8 S8 A8

Mistle Thrush — B6 W6 S6 A6

Song Thrush

hebridensis ad

ad

juv

ad

Redwing

1st winter

ad

ad

juv

Mistle Thrush

juv

ad

ad

WARBLERS (Sylviidae)

Cetti's Warbler *Cettia cetti* 13.5–14.5 cm ($c5\frac{1}{2}$ in). Robust, with short rounded wings and longish rounded tail; dark rufous and greyish, like small Nightingale (198), but tail less chestnut than back, and short white supercilia. Skulks, emerging briefly with flicking or cocked tail (showing barred under-coverts). *Ad* Chestnut above, less on head, wings, tail; whitish below shading to grey and brown at sides. *Juv* Less rufous above, less white below; as ad after moult in Jul–Aug. VOICE Repeated *chee*; song remarkably loud and abrupt *chee cheweechoo-weechoo-weechoo-wee*. HABITAT Waterside tangles, reeds. NEST Low in thick cover, 3–5 eggs, May–Jul; 1–2 broods. FOOD Insects, snails, seeds. RANGE Resident since 1972.

Grasshopper Warbler *Locustella naevia* 12–13 cm ($c5$ in). Streaky above but only faint supercilia (*cf* Sedge Warbler); rounded tail and usually pinkish legs. Cocks tail on alighting (showing streaky under-coverts); skulks, but often sings openly; creeps or runs in undergrowth. *Ad* Olive- to yellow-brown above with dark streaks (faint on rump); buff-white below, few streaks. *Juv* Redder-brown above, darker buff below; as ad after moult in Aug–Oct. VOICE Sharp *tchick*; song (day or night) sustained churring like fishing-reel or cricket, ventriloquial with turning head. HABITAT Wet or dry: rank fens, marshes, scrub, moors, plantations. NEST Low in thick cover, 5–6 eggs, May–Jul; 1–2 broods. FOOD Insects. RANGE Summer visitor, Apr–Oct, wintering Africa.

Savi's Warbler *Locustella luscinioides* 13.5–14.5 cm ($c5\frac{1}{2}$ in). Unstreaked, like large Reed Warbler (210) but with broad, very rounded tail; redder-brown above, more rufous-buff below, with purple-brown legs. Actions as Grasshopper Warbler, inc tail-cocking, but less secretive. *Ad* Dark red-brown above; whitish below shading to red-buff at sides. *Juv* Still darker red-brown above. VOICE Sharp *tswit*; song as Grasshopper Warbler, but lower-pitched, more buzzing, often briefer. HABITAT Reed swamps with scattered bushes. NEST Low in reeds or sedges, 4–6 eggs, mid May–Jul; 1–2 broods. FOOD Insects. RANGE Summer visitor, Apr–Aug, wintering in Africa.

Sedge Warbler *Acrocephalus schoeno-baenus* 12–13 cm ($c5$ in). Bold cream supercilia, rather streaky upperparts but plain tawny rump; pointed, graduated tail. Flight jerky, usually low with tail fanned and depressed, but also short vertical song-flight; creeps in tangles, sidles up stems, but also perches in open. *Ad* Brown above with blackish streaks, thickest on crown; rump yellow-brown; white below shading to buff and tawny at sides. *Juv* Yellower above, esp rump, often ill-defined creamy crown-stripe; breast brown-speckled; some of these characters persist after moult in Jul–Sep. VOICE Sharp *tuc* extended to stutter; song fast vigorous mix of musical and harsh phrases with mimicry. HABITAT Tangled growth, mainly by water. NEST In rank cover, 5–6 eggs, May–Aug; 1–2 broods. FOOD Insects, berries. RANGE Summer visitor, mid Apr–Sep (mid Oct), wintering in Africa.

COMPARE Vagrant warblers (esp 306, 308).

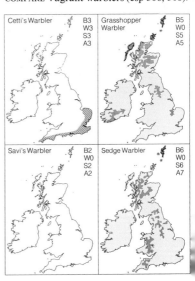

| Cetti's Warbler | B3 W3 S3 A3 | Grasshopper Warbler | B5 W0 S5 A5 |
| Savi's Warbler | B2 W0 S2 A2 | Sedge Warbler | B6 W0 S6 A7 |

Cetti's Warbler

ad

ad

Grasshopper Warbler

ad

ad

juv

Savi's Warbler

ad

ad

Sedge Warbler

ad

ad (worn plumage)

juv

Marsh Warbler *Acrocephalus palustris*
12–13 cm (*c*5 in). But for song, very like
far commoner Reed Warbler, but with
flatter crown, plumper belly and longer
wings reaching tip of tail-coverts; ad lacks
rufous tinge, more uniformly pale below;
whiter eye-rings and front of supercilia,
pinkish legs. Less skulking than Reed,
perching higher in open trees. *Ad* Olive-
brown with yellower rump, wearing to
paler/greyer with browner rump by end of
summer; white and pale yellow-buff
below. *Juv/1st winter* Rusty-tinged,
inseparable in field from Reed. VOICE Song
rich, varied, mimetic, esp Greenfinch-like
nasal *tswee* and trills. HABITAT Osiers,
bushy areas by rivers. NEST With 'basket
handles' in nettles, meadowsweet, willow-
herb, willow, 4–5 eggs, Jun–mid Jul;
1 brood. FOOD Insects, berries. RANGE
Summer visitor, end May–Aug (Oct),
wintering in E Africa.

Reed Warbler *Acrocephalus scirpaceus*
12–13 cm (*c*5 in). Longish bill, rounded
tail and wings not reaching tip of tail-
coverts; warm brown with rufous-tinged
rump, deep buff flanks; faint supercilia
and grey-brown legs. Flight jerky, low,
tail spread and depressed; skulks, sidles
up reed stems with one foot above other.
Ad Warm olive-brown with rusty rump,
wearing to greyer, less rufous, by end
summer; white and buff below, darkest on
flanks. *Juv* Rustier-brown and deeper buff;
as unworn ad after moult in Jul–Sep.
VOICE Song like Sedge Warbler (206), but
harsher, grumpier, inc *jag-jag-jag kerr-
kerr-kerr.* HABITAT Reeds, osiers. NEST
Woven round reeds, other plants, twigs,
3–5 eggs, late May–Aug; 1–2 broods.
FOOD Insects, berries. RANGE Summer
visitor, mid Apr–Sep (Oct), wintering in
Africa. COMPARE Vagrants (esp 308).

Icterine Warbler *Hippolais icterina* 13–14
cm (*c*5¼ in). Large bill, squared tail, wings
reaching tip of tail-coverts (folded
primaries $c\frac{1}{3}$ of wing); pale yellow to
whitish below, yellow supercilia, bluish
legs; wing-patches on spring ad and
autumn imm (*cf* Melodious). Flight
strong; stance rather upright; takes

berries with upward tug. *Ad* Olive-green
and lemon-yellow (few browner or greyer
above, whitish below); yellow wing-
patches lost by late summer. *Juv* Brown
and pale yellow; yellow-buff wing-
patches. *1st winter* After moult Aug–Oct,
more as ad of brown/grey type with
whitish-yellow underparts; wings as juv.
VOICE Short *teck*, churr. HABITAT Trees,
tall bushes. FOOD Insects, berries. RANGE
Scarce migrant from E/N Europe, Aug–
Oct, few Apr–Jul, wintering in E Africa.

Melodious Warbler *Hippolais polyglotta*
12–13 cm (*c*5 in). Very like Icterine, but
smaller, with plumper belly, shorter tail,
wings not reaching tip of tail-coverts
(folded primaries $c\frac{1}{4}$ of wing); yellow to
creamy below, shorter supercilia, grey
legs (seldom bluish); wing-patches rare
and in spring only. Flight more fluttery.
Ad Green-brown and rich yellow (few
grey-brown and cream). *Juv* Brown and
creamy. *1st winter* After moult in Aug–
Oct browner above than ad, pale yellow
or creamy below. VOICE Sharp *tic*, chatter
like sparrow. HABITAT/FOOD As Icterine.
RANGE Scarce migrant from SW Europe,
Aug–Oct (May–Jul), wintering W Africa.
COMPARE Garden (214), Willow etc. (216).

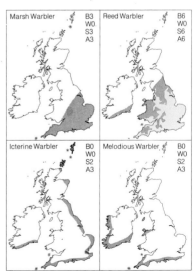

| Marsh Warbler | B3 W0 S3 A3 | Reed Warbler | B6 W0 S6 A6 |
| Icterine Warbler | B0 W0 S2 A3 | Melodious Warbler | B0 W0 S2 A3 |

Marsh Warbler

ad

Reed Warbler

ad

ad

ad Aug-Oct

Icterine Warbler

1st winter

grey ad
autumn

Melodious Warbler

ad Aug-Oct

ad

1st winter

grey ad
autumn

Dartford Warbler *Sylvia undata* 12–13.5 cm (*c*5 in). Tiny body with short wings, and often-cocked tail half total length; brown to dark grey above and more or less pinkish-brown below. Flight weak, undulating, with whirring wings and bobbing tail, usually low and brief before diving into cover; secretive, but will sit on bush-tops, esp in calm weather; flicks and fans tail; in small parties in autumn/ winter. ♂ *summer* Dark brown above with slate-grey head, rufous and greyish fringes to wing-feathers; dark brownish-pink below with small white spots on throat, white central belly. ♂ *winter* After moult in Aug–Nov, head browner, wing-feathers less clearly fringed, underparts with more whitish tips and fringes. *Ad* ♀ Not so dark brown above with browner-grey head; much paler pink–buff below. *Juv* Duller sooty-brown above than ad ♀, brownish-buff below with darker breast-sides/flanks, less rufous wing-fringes; as ads after moult in Aug–Nov. VOICE Buzzing *chirr*, hard *tik* or combined *chirr-ik-tik*; song short metallic warble mixed with mellower notes. HABITAT Heaths with gorse and rank heather. NEST In gorse or heather, 3–4 eggs, mid Apr–Jul; 2 broods. FOOD Insects, other invertebrates. RANGE Resident; some wander in autumn/winter.

Lesser Whitethroat *Sylvia curruca* 13–14 cm (5¼ in). More compact, shorter-tailed than Whitethroat; greyer above, with dark mask, no chestnut in wings, dark grey legs, very different song. Much more skulking except when young fledged; more in trees. *Ad* Grey-brown above with greyer rump, grey cap and dark grey lores/ear coverts; pinkish breast and pink-buff flanks, whitening by *c*May–Jun; some white on tail-sides. *Juv* Cap grey-brown like back, throat off-white, breast and flanks buffish, tail-sides only brownish-white. *1st winter* Much as ad after moult in Jun–Aug but for juv tail without pure white. VOICE Hard *tak tak*, hoarse *charr*; far-carrying song rapid rattle on 1 note, preceded by short fast warble audible only at close range. HABITAT Thick hedges, thorn scrub, young conifers. NEST In hedges or bushes, 4–6 eggs, May–early

Aug; 1–2 broods. FOOD Insects; berries in autumn. RANGE Summer visitor, end Apr–Sep, wintering in NE Africa/SW Asia; on passage mid Apr–Jun, mid Aug–Oct (Nov), inc few from Scandinavia.

Whitethroat *Sylvia communis* 13–15 cm (*c*5½ in). Slim, with longish white-sided tail; white throat, rufous on wings, pale brown legs. Flight undulating, jerky, usually low, diving into cover; restless, sometimes skulking, but may perch prominently; solitary or in family parties. *Ad* Brown to grey-brown above, breast/flanks tinged buff to pink; crown greyer and breast pinker in summer, when some ♂s separable by almost pure grey crown, pure white throat and tail-sides, pinkish breast, grey-tipped lesser coverts and rufous eyes (♀s may show some of these). *Juv* Brown above, buffish below, with dull white throat and belly, less rufous wing-coverts, pale brown tail-sides. *1st winter* As dull ad after moult in Jul–Sep, but no pink, still juv pale brown tail-sides. VOICE Sharp *tak tak*, harsh scolding *charr* and quieter *weet weet wit-wit-wit*; song short scratchy warble, often in brief dancing flight. HABITAT Hedges, commons, scrub wood-edges, young conifers. NEST In low cover, 4–5 eggs, May–mid Aug; 1–2 broods. FOOD Insects, berries. RANGE Summer visitor, mid Apr–Sep, wintering in Africa; passage Apr–May, Aug–Oct, inc some from Scandinavia.

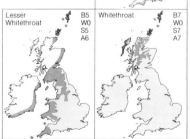

| Dartford Warbler | B3 W3 S3 A4 |

| Lesser Whitethroat | B5 W0 S5 A6 |

| Whitethroat | B7 W0 S7 A7 |

Dartford Warbler

♂ summer

♀

♂

♂ winter

juv

Lesser Whitethroat

ad

ad (worn plumage)

juv

Whitethroat

♂ song-flight

♂ summer

1st winter

♀/dull ♂

juv

Barred Warbler *Sylvia nisoria* 14.5–16 cm (*c*6 in). Robust warbler with stout bill and legs, steep forehead, and longish, squared tail; grey, whitish and barred (ad) or grey-brown and buff (imm), with narrow white tail-sides and whitish tips to flight-feathers and wing-coverts. Flight heavy, undulating; restless, skulking; often raises crown, flicks tail. *Ad summer* Grey/grey-brown above with white/whitish tips on wings; white below, barred with grey crescents except on mid breast and belly; fierce yellow eyes (♂s often – but not reliably – greyer, more barred, with whiter tail-sides, brighter eyes). *Ad winter* After moult in Jul–Aug, browner above, only sides of breast and flanks barred. *1st winter* Brown to grey-brown above with broad whitish to pale buff tips on wings; buffish below with little barring (often only on undertail-coverts); eyes grey-brown, rarely yellowish by mid Sep. VOICE Harsh chatter, tacking, churring. HABITAT Migrants in coastal trees, bushes, crops. FOOD Insects, berries. RANGE Migrant from E Europe (most 1st winter), Aug–mid Oct, wintering in Africa; very rare in spring. COMPARE Imm with imm Orphean (310).

Garden Warbler *Sylvia borin* 13.5–14.5 cm (*c*5½ in). Plump, with stubby bill, rounded head, shortish tail; brown and buff, rather featureless but for obscure line over eyes and grey-tinged neck, yet shape and soft shades distinctive. Actions as Blackcap; more skulking. *Ad* Brown and buff, with buff-white throat and belly; in worn plumage, greyer-brown above and paler below, with whiter throat, olive-grey flanks; after moult in Jul–Sep, more olive-brown above, flanks olive-buff. *Juv* Tinged rusty above, darker buff below; as ad in fresh plumage after moult in Jul–Sep. VOICE *Tac tac* and grating churr, much as Blackcap; song mellow warble, usually faster, quieter, more even and prolonged than Blackcap. HABITAT As Blackcap, but also scrub, young plantations. NEST Low in brambles, nettles, small conifers, 4–5 eggs, May–mid Jul; 1–2 broods. FOOD As Blackcap. RANGE Summer visitor, mid Apr–mid Sep, wintering in Africa; on passage from Continent, mid Apr–mid Jun, end Jul–Oct (Nov), esp E/SBr. COMPARE Brown Icterine and Melodious Warblers (210).

Blackcap *Sylvia atricapilla* 13.5–14.5 cm (*c*5½ in). Slim, with thinnish bill, longish tail; brown and grey, with distinctive black or rufous cap to eye-level. Flight jerky, undulating, tree to tree; restless, often skulking; in parties on migration. *Ad ♂* Cap glossy black; grey-brown above, greyer in worn plumage; nape, cheeks, throat and breast grey. *Ad ♀* Cap red-brown; olive-brown above, browner and paler when worn; cheeks, throat, breast and flanks grey-brown. *Juv* Cap black-brown (♂) or yellow-brown (♀); otherwise as ad ♀, but tinged rusty above, breast and flanks darker and duller. *1st winter ♂* As ad ♂ after moult in Jul–Sep, but black cap mixed with brown; old juv greater coverts edged with brown in contrast to other new grey-edged coverts. VOICE Hard *tacc tacc* and churr; song short, rich and varied warble with clear phrasing, but subdued versions very like Garden Warbler. HABITAT Broadleaved/mixed woods with undergrowth, to gardens. NEST In hedges, evergreens, ivy, brambles, 4–5 eggs, May–Jul; 1–2 broods. FOOD Insects, berries in autumn. RANGE Summer visitor Apr–Sep, wintering in Africa, W/S Europe; on passage end Mar–mid Jun, mid Aug–Oct, esp E/SBr; some winter. COMPARE Orphean, Sardinian Warblers (310).

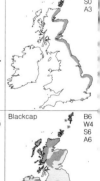

Barred Warbler
B0
W0
S0
A3

Garden Warbler
B6
W0
S6
A6

Blackcap
B6
W4
S6
A6

Barred Warbler

1st winter

ad

Garden Warbler

ad

juv

Blackcap

♂

1st winter ♂

♀

juv ♀

Wood Warbler *Phylloscopus sibilatrix*
12–13 cm (*c*5 in). Larger than Willow
Warbler, with longer wings, shorter tail;
yellow-green above, yellow supercilia,
throat and chest, contrasting white belly.
Less restlessly active; droops rather than
flicks wings; more arboreal. *Ad* Bright
yellow-green and yellow, wearing greyer-
green and dull yellow by *c*Jun; after body
moult in Jul–Sep, brownish-green and
paler yellow, with worn brown flight-
feathers and tail. *Juv/1st winter* As ad
autumn, but duller greyer-green, new
flight-feathers/tail with yellow-green
fringes. VOICE Plaintive piping *piur*; song
accelerating *stip-stip* . . . ending in
shivering trill *shrreeee*, also repeated
mournful *pwee*. HABITAT Woods, upland
scrub, with sparse undergrowth. NEST
Domed, on ground in thin cover, 5–7 eggs,
mid May–Jul; 1–2 broods. FOOD Insects.
RANGE Summer visitor, mid Apr–Aug,
wintering in Africa; scarce on passage
from Continent, Apr–Jun, Aug–Sep.

Chiffchaff *Phylloscopus collybita* 10.5–
11.5 cm (*c*4¼ in). Dumpier than Willow,
rounder head, shorter wing-point of
folded primaries; typically dingier above,
less yellow below, clearer eye-rings, dark
grey-brown legs (sometimes pale).
Constantly flicks wings, wags tail. *Ad W
race (P.c. collybita)* Olive-brown and
buff, wearing to browner and whiter by
*c*Jun till moult in Jul–Sep. *Juv* Browner
also below; as ad after moult Aug–Sep.
N Eurasian races (P.c. abietinus/tristis)
Increasingly grey and whitish towards E,
sometimes pale wing-bar. VOICE Emphatic
hweet (N races *tseep/tseeoo*); song
staccato mix of *tip, tap* and *titti* (= *chiffchaff*), interspersed with low *chrr-chrr*.
HABITAT Open woods with undergrowth;
on passage in scrub, gardens, reeds. NEST
Domed, off ground in tangle, 6 eggs, May–
Jul; 1–2 broods. FOOD Insects. RANGE
Summer visitor, mid Mar–Oct, wintering
in Mediterranean/Africa; also on passage
from Continent, inc N races, and some
winter. COMPARE Greenish Warbler (312).

Willow Warbler *Phylloscopus trochilus*
10.5–11.5 cm (*c*4¼ in). Far the commonest

leaf-warbler; small, neat, green-brown
above, yellow below, pale supercilia, pale
brown legs (sometimes dark). Flits restlessly, flicking wings and tail; flycatches,
hovers. *Ad W race (P.t. trochilus)* Olive-
green/brown, streaky yellowish below,
wearing to browner and whiter by *c*Jun
till moult in Jul–Aug. *Juv* Brown above,
buff below (*cf* Chiffchaff); much as ad
after moult in Jul–Aug, but more evenly
yellow below. *E European race (P.t.
acredula)* Sometimes grey-brown and
whitish (*cf* Chiffchaff). VOICE Plaintive
disyllabic *hoo-eet*; short rippling song
starts quietly, grows louder, falls away in
terminal flourish *swee-sweetew*. HABITAT
Copses, bushes, scrub. NEST Domed, on or
near ground in cover, 6–7 eggs, May–Jul;
1–2 broods. FOOD Insects. RANGE Summer
visitor, Apr–Sep, wintering in Africa; also
passage end Mar–Nov, inc E race.

Yellow-browed Warbler *Phylloscopus
inornatus* 9.5–10.5 cm (*c*4 in). Tiny; green
and whitish with 2 creamy wing-bars, bold
supercilia (few also faint crown-stripe).
Ad = 1st winter. VOICE Shrill sharp *swee*
or *sweeoo*. HABITAT Trees, scrub. FOOD
Insects. RANGE From Asia, Sep–Oct (end
Aug–Dec). COMPARE Pallas's (312).

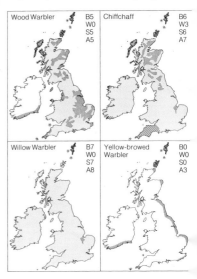

Wood Warbler

ad Apr–May

juv/1st winter

Chiffchaff

ad Apr–May   ad Jun–Jul

juv

N Eurasian ad/1st winter

Willow Warbler

1st winter

ad Jun–Jul

E European ad/1st winter

ad Apr–May

juv

Yellow-browed Warbler

W Asian
ad/1st winter

E Asian
ad/1st winter

FLYCATCHERS (Muscicapidae)

Spotted Flycatcher *Muscicapa striata*
13.5–14.5 cm (c5¼ in). Like all flycatchers,·
has flat broad-based bill, large dark eyes,
longish wings, squared tail and short legs;
grey-brown and whitish, looking rather
featureless but for dark streaks on head
and breast; told by stance and behaviour.
Perches upright on bare twigs or fences
and sallies after insects, twisting, turning,
often low over ground, then back to same
or nearby perch; usually seen well below
tree canopy, c1–5 m up, flicking or
drooping wings, wagging tail; solitary. *Ad*
Brown to grey-brown above, with crown
streaked blackish, coverts and tertials
edged buff to whitish; whitish below but
for brown breast-streaks. *Juv* Scaled above
by dark edges to pale buff spots; breast
spotted with brown rather than streaked.
1st winter As ad after moult in Jul–Sep,
but new plumage browner; broader pale
edges to tertials; still buffish spots at tips
of greater coverts. VOICE Thin scratchy
tzee (*cf* Robin, 196), extended into *tzee-
tzucc* of alarm; song c6 faint squeaky
notes, well separated. HABITAT Wood-
edges, parks to suburban gardens,
avenues, quarries. NEST On ledges or in
open cavities of trees, ivy, creepers, walls
rocks, 4–5 eggs, end May–mid Aug; 1–2
broods. FOOD Insects. RANGE Summer
visitor, end Apr–Sep, wintering in Africa;
on passage from Continent, end Apr–early
Jun, Aug–mid Oct, esp EBr.

Red-breasted Flycatcher *Ficedula parva*
11–12 cm (c4½ in). Small; grey-brown and
buff with bold white patches at base of
blackish tail (only ad ♂ has red throat).
Secretive, restless, keeping to cover
and often feeding more like warbler;
frequently cocks tail. *Ad ♂* Grey to grey-
brown head, pale eye-rings, orange-red
throat; brighter in spring than autumn.
Ad ♀ Head browner, still with pale eye-
rings; whole underparts creamy-buff. *1st
winter* As ad ♀, but buffish spots on tips of
coverts/tertials; ♂ rarely tinged orange
on throat (usually not until 1st summer
or even 2nd autumn). VOICE Low rattle,
chic, sad *hwee*. HABITAT Migrants in

coastal trees, scrub. FOOD Insects. RANGE
Scarce migrant from E Europe, mid Aug–
Nov, rare Apr–Jul, wintering in SE Asia.

Pied Flycatcher *Ficedula hypoleuca* 12–13
cm (c5 in). Smaller and plumper than
Spotted Flycatcher; boldly pied, or brown
and whitish, with white wing-patches.
Changes perch frequently, often dropping
to ground, also takes prey from bark and
leaves by clinging briefly to trunk or
hovering; flicks wings and tail often. ♂
summer Jet-black above, with white forehead, wing-patches, tail-sides, underparts;
rarely grey-brown instead of black, but
still with white forehead, blacker tail. *Ad*
♀ Olive-brown and whitish, no white on
forehead; less white on wings and more
buff below in autumn. ♂ *winter* Inseparable
from ♀ after moult in Jul–Aug, unless
some white on forehead or blackish on
coverts, rump or tail. *Juv* Scaled/spotted
as juv Spotted Flycatcher, but white in
wings and tail. *1st winter* As ad after moult,
but few median coverts often still have
pale spots. VOICE Sharp *whit*, short *tic*,
often combined; song deliberate repeated
zee-chi, then liquid jangle. HABITAT Old
open woods, parks. NEST In holes in trees,
walls, boxes, 5–8 eggs, May–Jul; 1 brood.
FOOD Insects. RANGE
Summer visitor,
mid Apr–Aug,
wintering in Africa;
on passage from
N/E Europe, mid
Aug–mid Oct, fewer
Apr–mid Jun, esp
EBr. COMPARE Col-
lared Flycatcher
(312).

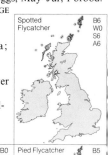

Spotted Flycatcher

ad

1st winter

juv

♀/1st winter

♂

1st summer ♂

Red-breasted Flycatcher

1st winter

♀

♀

Pied Flycatcher

♂ summer

well-marked ♂ winter

juv

♀

KINGLETS (Sylviidae)

Goldcrest *Regulus regulus* 8.5–9 cm (c3½ in). This and next are smallest European birds, small-billed, short-tailed, with black-edged yellow/orange crowns, 2 white bars and dark band on wings; Goldcrest otherwise dull green and whitish, with 'surprised' pale area around large-looking eyes. Flits restlessly from tree to tree; usually in canopy with flicking wings; winter flocks mix with tits; unobtrusive but not shy. *Ad ♂* Crown yellow and orange. *Ad ♀* Crown yellow. *Juv* Browner above, no yellow crown, but black mottling at edges; as ad after moult in Jul–Sep. VOICE Persistent high *zi-zi-zi*; song repeated *zeeda* ending in flourish *zeeda-zeeda-zeeda-sissi-peeso*. HABITAT Woods, gardens, esp in conifers; locally in bushes. NEST Esp in conifer or ivy, 7–8 eggs, mid Apr–Aug; 2 broods. FOOD Spiders, insects. RANGE Mainly sedentary, but some move south; on passage/wintering from Continent, end Sep–Apr, esp E/SBr.

Firecrest *Regulus ignicapillus* 8.5–9 cm (c3½ in). Brighter green and whiter than Goldcrest, with white supercilia and black eye-stripes, bronzy by shoulders. Actions similar; often in low cover. *Ad ♂* Crown yellow and orange. *Ad ♀* Crown yellow. *Juv* As juv Goldcrest, but whitish supercilia, dark eye-stripes. VOICE Lower stronger *zit-zit-zit*; song crescendo extension of calls, often with terminal flourish. HABITAT Esp mixed woods; also bushes, scrub in winter. NEST Usually in conifers, 7–11 eggs, mid May–mid Aug; 1–2 broods. FOOD As Goldcrest. RANGE Scarce breeder since c1961; on passage/wintering from Continent, mid Sep–Apr.

REEDLINGS (Timaliidae)

Bearded Tit *Panurus biarmicus* 16–17 cm (c6½ in). Tit-like reed-bird with long tail; tawny, marked with black and whitish. Flight weak, whirring, with 'loose' twisting tail, usually low over reeds; gregarious. *Ad ♂* Grey head, black moustaches, pink-grey breast, black under tail; bill orange. *Ad ♀* Tawny head, greyer breast; bill brown and yellow. *Juv* As ♀ but black on mid-back and tail-sides; ♂ black lores and yellow bill, ♀ usually blackish bill; as ads from moult in Jul–Oct. VOICE Twanging *ping ping*; ticks, churrs. HABITAT Big reedbeds. NEST Low in reeds, 5–7 eggs, Apr–Aug; 2–3 broods. FOOD Insects, reed seeds. RANGE Sedentary, but spreads in cJul–Apr, inc Dutch birds.

LONG-TAILED TITS (Aegithalidae)

Long-tailed Tit *Aegithalos caudatus* 13.5–14.5 cm (c5½ in). Tiny bill and body, very long narrow tail; blackish and dull white, pink scapulars, rump and belly. Flight weak, undulating; restless, acrobatic; gregarious. *Ad Br/Ir race (A.c. rosaceus)* Dark head-bands, whitish wing-patches, much pink. *Juv* Tail shorter; browner, with dark cheeks, whitish scapulars, little pink; as ad after moult in Aug–Sep. *Ad N/E European race (A.c. caudatus)* White head, whiter wing-patch, less pink. VOICE Low *tupp*, persistent *zee-zee-zee*, rippling *tsirrp*. HABITAT Wood-edges, thick hedges, bushy places. NEST Oval ball esp in thorny bushes or high tree-forks, 7–12 eggs, Apr–Jun; 1 brood. FOOD Insects, seeds. RANGE Mainly sedentary; N/E race rare vagrant.

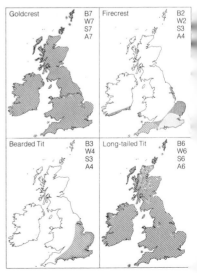

Goldcrest	B7 W7 S7 A7
Firecrest	B2 W2 S3 A4
Bearded Tit	B3 W4 S3 A4
Long-tailed Tit	B6 W6 S6 A6

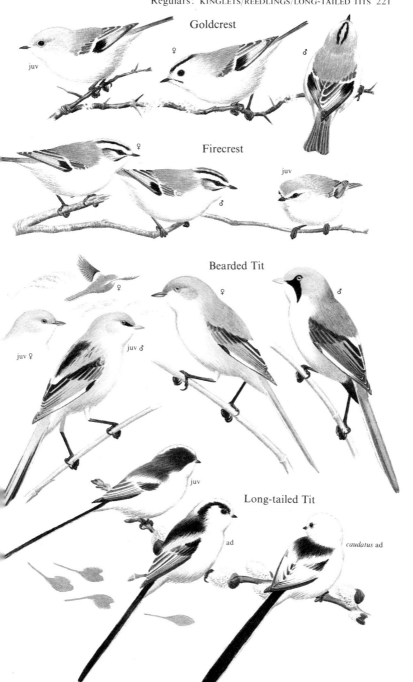

Goldcrest

juv

♀

♂

Firecrest

♀

♂

juv

Bearded Tit

♀

♀

♂

juv ♀

juv ♂

Long-tailed Tit

juv

ad

caudatus ad

TITS (Paridae)

Marsh Tit *Parus palustris* 11–12 cm ($c4\frac{1}{2}$ in). Like all tits, stubby-billed, thick-necked, acrobatic, social; looks sleek, round-headed; brown and buff-white with glossy black cap, whitish cheeks, neat bib, pale flanks, no wing-panel (*cf* Willow Tit). Actions as Blue Tit (224); less in canopy or parties. Cap glossy, bib flecked with white, warm brown above, uniformly buffish below; abrasion by summer makes brown darker, bib blacker. *Juv* Cap dull sooty, bib browner, greyer-brown above, paler below, like juv Willow Tit; as ad after moult in Aug–Sep. VOICE Loud *pitcheu*, often with short nasal *tchay-tchay* . . . ; scolding *chika-ke-ke-ke*, thin *zee-zee-zee*; song clear *chip* *c*7 times or extension of *pitcheu* note. HABITAT Dry or damp scrubby broadleaved woods, copses (not marshes). NEST In holes in trees, stumps, walls or ground, 6–8 eggs, Apr–Jun; 1 brood. FOOD Insects, seeds, berries. RANGE Sedentary.

Willow Tit *Parus montanus* 11–12 cm ($c4\frac{1}{2}$ in). Very like Marsh Tit, but bigger longer head, more bull-neck, dull sooty-black cap, larger whitish cheeks, more diffuse black bib, darker flanks and pale panel on wings. *Ad Br race (P.m. klein-schmidti)* Pale wing-panels and deep buff flanks most obvious after moult in Aug–Sep, less so by summer through abrasion. *Juv* Inseparable from juv Marsh Tit. *Ad N European race (P.m. borealis)* Larger, cheeks whiter, upperparts greyer, wing-panels grey-white. VOICE Buzzing *erz-erz-erz*; high thin *zi-zi-zi* or *chi-chi*, often followed by loud, long, harsh *tchay tchay* . . . (*cf* Marsh Tit); song clear sad *piu piu piu*, not unlike Wood Warbler (216), or short warbling trill. HABITAT Overlaps Marsh Tit, but esp in elder and damp birch/alder woods, also conifers; in winter, also hedges, scrub. NEST Excavates holes in rotten stumps, 6–9 eggs, Apr–Jun; 1 brood. FOOD As Marsh Tit. RANGE Sedentary; N European race rare vagrant.

Coal Tit *Parus ater* 10.5–11.5 cm ($c4\frac{1}{2}$ in). Smallest tit, with big head and stumpy

tail; olive-grey and buff, with crown and extensive bib black, cheeks and large nape-patch white or yellowish, 2 white wing-bars. Actions as Blue Tit (224); on trunks rather like Treecreeper (226); unobtrusive. *Ad Br race (P.a. britannicus)* Cheeks and nape white; after moult in Aug–Sep, crown glossy, bib flecked white, upperparts olive-grey, flanks buff; by summer, abrasion makes crown duller, bib blacker, upperparts greyer, wing-bars thinner, flanks paler. *Ad Ir race (P.a. hibernicus)* Cheeks and nape yellower, esp in winter; upperparts olive-buff, flanks yellower-buff. *Juv (both races)* Browner above, yellower below; crown and small bib sooty-brown; cheeks, nape, wing-bars yellowish. *Continental race (P.a. ater)* Cheeks and nape purer white, upperparts slate-grey. *1st winter (all races)* As ads after moult in Jul–Sep, but buff-edged greyish juv outer greater coverts contrast with other new grey-edged blackish coverts. VOICE Piping *tseu*; thin *zee-zee-zee* call and *titsissi-sissi-sissi-sissiwee* song resemble Goldcrest (220), but usual song sweet piping *weecho-weecho-weecho* (*cf* Great Tit, 226). HABITAT Woods, gardens, esp conifers, highland scrub. NEST In holes in ground, tree-roots, low stumps, rocks, walls, 7–11 eggs, Apr–early Jul; 1–2 broods. FOOD Insects, seeds, nuts, fat. RANGE Sedentary; immigration from Continent as Blue Tit, but much more irregular and usually few.

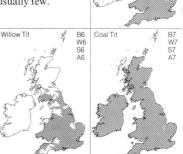

Marsh Tit	B6
	W6
	S6
	A6

Willow Tit	B6
	W6
	S6
	A6

Coal Tit	B7
	W7
	S7
	A7

Marsh Tit

ad

juv

Willow Tit

ad Sep–Mar

borealis ad

ad Apr–Aug

Coal Tit

britannicus ad

hibernicus
ad winter

juv

Crested Tit *Parus cristatus* 11–12 cm (*c*4½ in). Brown and whitish, with pointed crest speckled with black and white; otherwise dingy white head but for black bib, thin collar and curve behind eyes. Actions as Blue Tit; fluttering display flight round tree-tops; moves rather like Treecreeper (224) on trunks. *Ad* Crest up to 2 cm long from moult in Aug–Oct, but dull white fringes gradually abraded, so shorter and blacker by summer; throat and collar black. *Juv* Crest shorter, more rounded, duller; bib browner and flecked white, no collar; as ad after moult in Aug–Sep. VOICE Deep purring trill, repeated loudly as song *chirr chirr chirr-r-r*; thin *zee-zee-zee* as other tits. HABITAT Old pine forest with stumps and heather, or pines mixed with birch/alder. NEST Excavates holes in rotten wood, 5–7 eggs, mid Apr–mid Jun; 1 brood. FOOD Insects, pine seeds, berries. RANGE Sedentary.

Blue Tit *Parus caeruleus* 11–12 cm (*c*4½ in). Blue and yellow, with green back, white cheeks and wing-bar; but juv more green and yellow. Flight looks weak, fluttery, often tree to tree, but higher and undulating across fields; in display slow, moth-like and floating; hops on ground or branches, hangs acrobatically from twigs; uses foot to hold down food that needs breaking; winter parties mix with other tits; common at bird-tables. *Ad* Blue crown, wings and tail, also black bib, brighter in summer (esp ♂); white crown-border and cheeks contrast with black eye-stripes and dark blue collar and nape with whitish spot; otherwise green above, yellow below with dark belly-mark. *Juv* Much duller, esp head with greenish-brown crown and hindneck, whites replaced by yellow, no clear bib; back more olive, wings and tail greener-blue. *1st winter* As ad after moult in Aug–Sep, but dull blue-green juv primary-coverts contrast other new bright blue coverts. VOICE Varied, esp quick *tsee-tsee-tsee-tsit*, scolding churr; song 2–3 *tsee* notes, then fast trill. HABITAT Woods, orchards, gardens, parks, hedges; even reeds in winter. NEST In holes , *eg* in trees or walls, 7–16 eggs, mid Apr–Jul; 1 brood.

FOOD Insects, also seeds, nuts, fruit. RANGE Sedentary, or moving locally; variable immigration from Continent, end Sep–Apr, esp SEBr.

Great Tit *Parus major* 13.5–14.5 cm (*c*5½ in). Larger than other tits; black head with white cheeks and yellowish spot on nape, black band on yellow underparts, green and blue-grey upperparts with white wing-bar, white-sided tail; but juv more brown and yellow. Actions as Blue Tit, but flight heavier, more undulating. *Ad* ♂ Band on underparts black, broad, widest on belly; crown and throat shiny blue-black, duller in summer; wings blue-grey. *Ad* ♀ Band sooty, usually narrower or even may be broken, mixed with white on belly; throat dull blackish; most wing-fringes greener-grey. *Juv* Much duller, esp head; blacks all sooty-brown, cheeks yellowish, upperparts browner, underparts duller. *1st winter* As ads after moult in Jul–Sep, but on ♂ dull green-grey juv primary-coverts contrast with other new blue-grey coverts. VOICE Very varied inc Chaffinch-like *zink zink*, hard scolding; song loud, ringing or rasping *teecha-teecha-teecha* and variations. HABITAT Much as Blue Tit; less ubiquitous in winter. NEST As Blue Tit, but larger holes, less in walls, 5–12 eggs, mid Apr–Jul; usually 1 brood. FOOD Insects, also slugs, snails, worms, seeds, fruit. RANGE Sedentary, or moving locally; immigration as Blue Tit, but irregular.

Crested Tit B4 W4 S4 A4

Blue Tit B7 W8 S7 A8

Great Tit B7 W7 S7 A7

Crested Tit

ad Sep–Mar

ad Apr–Aug

juv

Blue Tit

ad Sep–Mar

ad Apr–Aug

juv

Great Tit

♀

♂

juv

NUTHATCHES (Sittidae)

Nuthatch *Sitta europaea* 13.5–14.5 cm
(*c*5½ in). Sleek, short-tailed, with sharp
bill and woodpecker-like actions; blue-
grey and buff, with black mask, white
throat, whitish tail-corners. Flight
undulating, mainly from tree to tree;
moves in jerks up, down and sideways on
trunk, not using tail as prop; breaks open
wedged nuts by heavy blows (loud tapping
noise); hops on ground; wary, restless;
often in pairs, joins tit flocks. *Ad ♂* Flanks
chestnut, demarcated from buff breast/
belly. *Ad ♀* Flanks paler rufous-buff,
shading into breast/belly. *Juv* Upperparts
tinged with brown, mask brown-black,
flanks duller than ♀; as ad after moult in
Jul–Aug. VOICE Ringing *chwit chwit*; song
shriller, rapid *twee-twee-twee . . .* or fast
trill. HABITAT Woods, parks, gardens,
with old trees. NEST In holes in trees or
walls, reduces entrance size with mud,
6–9 eggs, Apr–Jun; 1 brood. FOOD Nuts,
large seeds, insects. RANGE Sedentary;
some wander, mainly locally.

TREECREEPERS (Certhiidae)

Treecreeper *Certhia familiaris* 12–13 cm
(*c*5 in). Mouse-like trunk-climber with
thin curved bill and stiff pointed tail;
streaky brown (blending with bark), with
whitish supercilia, dark-edged buff wing-
bar, white underparts. Climbs jerkily in
spirals round trunk or along underside of
branch, with feet apart, tail pressed on
bark, then drops with tit-like flight to foot
of next tree; solitary, or in families, but
joins tit flocks. *Ad Br/Ir race (C.f.
britannica)* Brown streaked buff and dark,
with rufous rump; underparts white
(often dirty from rubbing on trees), but
flanks pale buff. *Juv* Colder brown above
and spotted buff, rump paler red-brown;
dull white to buff below, flecked brown on
breast and flanks; as ad after moult in
Aug–Oct. *Ad N race (C.f. familiaris)*
Paler above, flanks nearly white. VOICE
Shrill *tseu*, softer *tsit*; song thin, high *tsee-
tsee-tsee-tissi-sissi-tsee* (*cf* Goldcrest,
220). HABITAT Woods, parks, gardens.
NEST Behind bark or ivy, or in cracks,

Treecreeper

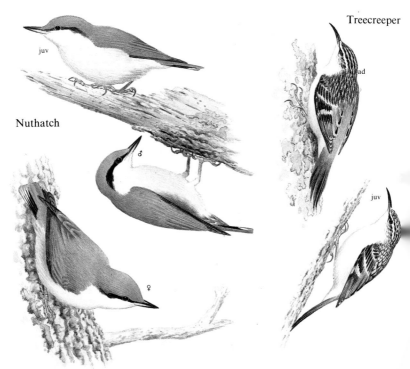

Nuthatch

5–6 eggs, mid Apr–Jun; 1–2 broods. FOOD Insects. RANGE Mainly sedentary; N race vagrant, EBr. COMPARE Short-toed (314).

ORIOLES (Oriolidae)

Golden Oriole *Oriolus oriolus* 23–25 cm (*c*9½ in). Usually heard more than seen; yellow and black, or yellow-green/grey/brown, with pink-red bill (ad). Flies in long undulations, ending in upward sweep into tree; secretive, arboreal, rarely on ground; solitary, or in family parties. *Ad ♂* Rich yellow but for black lores, mainly black wings and tail. *Ad ♀* Yellow-green and greyish, streaked dark brown below, with browner wings and tail (old ♀s very like ♂, but greyish lores). *Juv* As ad ♀, but speckled yellow above, less streaked below; bill brown. *1st year* As ad ♀, but ♂ often yellower, with blacker tail, weaker streaking; ♀ duller green, with greener tail, stronger streaking; 1st autumn ♂♀ also have brown bills, usually yellow-tipped median coverts. VOICE Harsh Jay-like notes, but song unmistakable: loud, melodious, fluty whistle *weela-whee-oh*. HABITAT Broadleaved/mixed woods, parks. NEST In tree-forks, 3–5 eggs, end May–Jul; 1 brood. FOOD Insects, berries, fruit. RANGE Rare summer/passage visitor, Apr–Jul (few Aug–Nov), wintering in Africa. COMPARE ♀ with Green Woodpecker (182).

Nuthatch	B5
	W5
	S5
	A5

Treecreeper	B6
	W6
	S6
	A6

Golden Oriole	B2
	W0
	S2
	A1

Golden Oriole

♀

♂

juv

1st year ♂

old ♀

♀

SHRIKES (Laniidae)

Red-backed Shrike *Lanius collurio* 16–18 cm (*c*6¾ in). Slim, with hook-tipped bill, longish tail, pointed wings; chestnut or red-brown back, no white on scapulars, wings or rump. Flight strong, undulating, with glides, often low from bush to bush ending in upward sweep; also hovers but mostly darts down on prey from lookout perch; often fans and waves tail; carries prey in bill or feet, may impale it on thorns in 'larder'; solitary. *Ad ♂* Grey crown and rump, chestnut wings and back, black mask, white-sided black tail; pink-white below. *Ad ♀* Rufous above, with browner crown/rump, rufous ear-coverts, whitish supercilia and lores, white-sided brown tail, and whitish below barred with dark crescents (crown rarely grey with blackish mask/tail, so resembling ♂, but still some barring below). *Juv* Rufous above and creamy below, all barred with blackish. *1st winter* As ♀ after moult in Jul–Sep, but crown and rump redder, upperparts still barred with blackish. VOICE Harsh *chack* or *chee-uk*; song prolonged warble mixed with mimicry and harsh calls. HABITAT Bushy heaths with gorse. NEST In thorny bushes or tangles, 3–6 eggs, mid May–Jul; 1 brood. FOOD Big insects, small birds. RANGE Scarce summer-visitor, May–Sep, wintering in E Africa; much decreased, but now colonising NBr; passage from Continent, May–Jun, Aug–Oct. COMPARE Isabelline and Woodchat Shrikes (314).

Great Grey Shrike *Lanius excubitor* 23–25 cm (*c*9½ in). Large with longish bill and tail, but short rounded wings; grey/black/white with grey forehead, and white supercilia and scapulars. Actions as Red-backed but perches more on tree-tops, telegraph wires. *Ad* Grey above and white below, with white line over black mask, white on scapulars, white bar on black wings, white sides to black tail; some ♀s show faint brown crescents on breast. *Juv* Brown-grey above and brownish-white below with much faint barring; supercilia very small, mask and wings browner. *1st winter* After moult in Jul–Dec, as ♀ with faint wavy bars on breast, but greater

coverts dull black-brown tipped with whitish. VOICE Harsh *shek shek*. HABITAT Winters among scattered trees/bushes. FOOD Small birds, voles, big insects. RANGE Winter visitor from N Europe, Oct–Apr. COMPARE Lesser Grey (314).

CROWS (Corvidae)

Jay *Garrulus glandarius* 33–36 cm (*c*13½ in). Thickset, with stout bill and rounded wings; brownish-pink with streaked erectile crown, black moustache, white throat, blue and white on wings, white rump usually seen contrasting with black tail when flying among trees. Flight laboured, with quick jerky beats; hops clumsily both on branches and ground, jerking tail; like all crows, buries excess food, esp acorns in autumn; usually in pairs or noisy groups; very wary. *Ad* Whitish crown streaked with black; body soft brownish-pink. *Juv* Crown streaks smaller, body redder-brown above and red-buff below; as ad after autumn moult. VOICE Harsh *kaaa*, barking *kah*, drawn-out mew; sub-song mixture of weak gurgling and harsh notes. HABITAT Woods, plantations, parks; visits hedges, orchards, gardens. NEST In trees, tall bushes, 5–6 eggs, end Apr–mid Jul; 1 brood. FOOD Acorns, nuts, fruit, berries, peas, eggs, nestlings, voles, snails, worms, insects. RANGE Sedentary; irregular migrants from Continent, Oct–Apr, E/SBr.

Red-backed Shrike	B2
	W0
	S3
	A4

Great Grey Shrike	B0
	W2
	S2
	A3

Jay	B6
	W6
	S6
	A6

Red-backed Shrike

Great Grey Shrike

Jay

Magpie *Pica pica* 42-50 cm (*c*18 in). Long wedge-shaped tail; pied plumage with contrasted white scapulars, flanks, belly and, in flight, broken panels near tips of rounded wings. Flight looks weak with fast beats, long glides; walks with tail up or moves with sidling hops; perches in open in trees or tall hedges; wary; often in pairs or parties, at times larger flocks, esp at roosts. *Ad* Tail half total length; black parts show metallic sheens at close range (head, breast and back blue-purple, wings blue and green, tail bronze-green to red-purple); whites pure white, but rump varies from whitish to black-brown. *Juv* Tail much shorter at first; blacks of body dull sooty, rump dark, wings/tail less glossed, whites tinged buff; as ad from moult in Aug-Sep, but tail averages 2-3 cm shorter (much overlap). VOICE Rapid, harsh, rattling *chaka-chaka-chaka*; more musical chattering and piping in spring. HABITAT Grassland with tall hedges, wood-edges, parks, moorland fringes, coastal scrub. NEST Domed, in trees or thorn bushes, 5-7 eggs, Apr-Jun; 1 brood. FOOD Insects, slugs, worms, nestlings, eggs, rodents, carrion, grain, berries, fruit. RANGE Sedentary; some winter dispersal.

Chough *Pyrrhocorax pyrrhocorax* 36-41 cm (*c*15½ in). Glossy black, with curved red bill, red legs; in flight, broad wings with tips usually well spread/upcurved, and squared tail. Flight strong, buoyant, acrobatic, but splayed wings give ragged look; soars, glides, dives with wings almost closed; walks, runs, hops; perches on rocks and cliffs, but rarely in trees; wary; in pairs, parties or flocks, mixing with Jackdaws. *Ad* Glossy blue-black, with greener wings and tail. *Juv* Duller, tinged with brown, hardly glossy on body; bill pinkish-yellow, turning redder. *1st year* As ad from moult Aug-Sep, but wings and tail less glossy, wearing brown by 1st summer. VOICE Drawn-out explosive *kee-ah*, higher pitched and clearer than Jackdaw; also softer *chuff*, deeper gull-like *kaa* and *kwuk-uk-uk*. HABITAT Coastal cliffs, inland crags and quarries, adjacent pastures and rough grazing. NEST In cliff crevices, sea caves or old mineshafts, 3-5

eggs, Apr-Jun; 1 brood. FOOD Insects, worms, slugs, grain. RANGE Sedentary.

Jackdaw *Corvus monedula* 32-34 cm (*c*13 in). Small, compact, short-billed; dark with grey nape, contrasting glossy black cap and throat; in flight, rather narrow wings with tips little spread, rounded tail. Flight hurried, pigeon-like, with faster beats than larger crows (230); glides and dives; walks jauntily; perches on trees, buildings, cliffs; bold, inquisitive; gregarious, also mixes with Rooks. *Ad Br/ Ir/W European race (C.m. spermologus)* Back and wings glossy black, nape ash-grey, underparts tinged with grey; eyes pearl-grey. *Juv* Browner, less glossy, with black-brown crown and back, brown nape, paler brown underparts; eyes brown. *1st year* As ad from moult in Aug-Sep, but wings and tail browner, less glossy, wearing browner still by 1st summer; eyes dull whitish. *Ad Scandinavian race (C.m. monedula)* Nape often paler silver-grey, and whitish at base of neck, but many inseparable. VOICE Shrill *kya* or *keeaw*; short, high *chak*, often repeated. HABITAT Farmland, old woods, parks, towns, ruins, quarries, cliffs. NEST In cavity in trees, buildings or rocks, 4-6 eggs, mid Apr-Jun; 1 brood. FOOD Insects, slugs, worms, nestlings, eggs, mice, frogs, grain, berries, fruit. RANGE Largely sedentary; immigrants from Continent (inc Scandinavia), Oct-Apr.

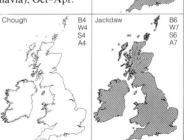

Magpie B6 W6 S6 A6

Chough B4 W4 S4 A4

Jackdaw B6 W7 S6 A7

Magpie

ad

juv

ad

Chough

ad

juv

ad

Jackdaw

monedula ad

ad

ad

juv

Rook *Corvus frugilegus* 44–47 cm (*c*18 in). Glossy black, with rather slender pointed bill; ad has bare whitish face, often swollen with pouched food; peaked head, loose thigh feathers ('baggy trousers') and, in flight, long 'hands' backswept as Raven but rounded tail (*cf* Carrion Crow). Flies with rapid, rather flexible beats; also glides, and autumn flocks tumble, roll and dive; waddles on ground, and hops; not shy; gregarious, mixing with Jackdaws. *Ad* Black, glossed purple (esp head) and green; nostrils/chin/lores bare. *Juv* Duller and browner, esp above; head fully feathered. *1st year* As ad from moult in Jul–Aug, but wings and tail increasingly dull brown; chin and lores bare from Jan–Feb, nostrils from Apr–May. VOICE Very varied: esp cawing *kaah* or drawn-out *kaa-aah*, higher and less raucous than Carrion Crow, not in series but often in chorus. HABITAT Mainly lowland arable and pasture with trees, also parks, open downs. NEST Colonial; in tree-tops, 4–6 eggs, mid Mar–mid Jun; 1 brood. FOOD Corn, roots, potatoes, berries, worms, insects, molluscs. RANGE Largely sedentary; immigrants from Continent, end Sep–Apr, mainly EBr.

Carrion/Hooded Crow *Corvus corone* 45–49 cm (*c*18½ in). All-black (Carrion) or black and grey (Hooded), intermediate where ranges meet; Carrion separated from imm Rook by stouter, more rounded bill, rounder cap, neater thighs and, in flight, shorter head, shorter straighter 'hands' and squarer tail (*cf* also Raven). Flight slower, more deliberate than Rook, not normally soaring like Raven; drops hard-shelled prey from height to break it open; sedate walk, sidling hops; perches anywhere; wary; often solitary, but also in parties/flocks. *Ad Carrion (C.c. corone)* Black, glossed green (esp on head) and purple. *Juv* Browner, hardly glossed (very like juv Rook). *Ad Hooded (C.c. cornix)* Back, breast, belly and also lesser/median underwing-coverts grey with fine streaks. *Juv* Browner-grey with dark speckles above, browner wings/tail. *1st year (both races)* As ads after moult in Jul–Aug, but wings/tail duller, browner. *Intermediate Carrion*

x *Hooded* Very variable: usually at least some grey, esp below. VOICE Loud, harsh, croaking *kraa*, repeated 3–4 times; also higher *keerk*, plaintive *honk* like old motor-horn. HABITAT Farmland, woods, town parks, lakes, moors, hills, cliffs, open shores. NEST In trees, hillside bushes, or on rock ledges, buildings, telegraph poles, 4–6 eggs, Apr–Jun; 1 brood. FOOD Carrion, small mammals, birds, eggs, frogs, crabs, molluscs, insects, worms, grain, fruit. RANGE Largely sedentary; immigrants (both races) from Continent, Oct–Apr, esp EBr.

Raven *Corvus corax* 60–67 cm (*c*25 in). Largest crow; black, with heavy bill, shaggy throat and, in flight, well projecting head, long thin 'hands' backswept, wedge-shaped tail (*cf* Carrion Crow). Flight powerful, with slow beats, often high up; glides, soars, tumbles, dives with wings closed; gait as Carrion Crow; often in pairs; flocks at food/roosts. *Ad* Black, glossed green or purple. *Juv* Browner, far less glossy. *1st year* As ad, but wings and tail increasingly dull brown. VOICE Deep *prruk prruk*; other croaks, grunts. HABITAT Coast and inlands crags, woody glens. NEST On rock-ledges or in trees, 4–6 eggs, mid Feb–May; 1 brood. FOOD Carrion, sheep placentae, dead fish, injured mammals and birds, eggs, frogs, snails, beetles, some grain. RANGE Mainly sedentary, but some winter dispersal.

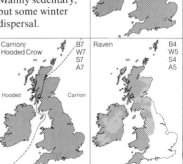

Rook | B7 W7 S7 A7

Carrion/Hooded Crow | B7 W7 S7 A7

Hooded Carrion

Raven | B4 W5 S4 A5

Rook

1st winter

ad

ad

juv

Carrion/Hooded Crow

corone × *cornix* ad

corone ad

cornix ad

corone ad

Raven

ad

ad

juv

STARLINGS (Sturnidae)

Starling *Sturnus vulgaris* 20.5–22.5 cm
(c8½ in). Abundant and familiar, with
longish pointed bill, flat forehead, short
tail, triangular wings in flight; mainly
blackish, glossed green/purple, variously
pale-spotted, with buff-edged wings (but
see juv). Flight direct with rapid beats,
glides; hawks insects; singing ♂ droops
and flutters wings; bustles jerkily or runs
on ground, probing by opening bill;
boisterous, noisy, quarrelsome; highly
gregarious; huge winter roosts in reeds,
conifers, cities. ♂ *summer* No spots; bill
yellow with bluish-grey base, eyes dark
brown. ♂ *winter* After moult in Jun–Sep,
finely spotted buff above and white below;
bill mainly brown. ♀ *summer* Some spots;
bill yellow with pinkish base, eyes usually
brown with thin whitish circle. ♀ *winter* As
♂ winter, but larger, rounder spots; eyes
as ♀ summer. *Juv* Grey-brown, with dark
lores, whitish throat and belly-streaks,
buff fringes on brown wings/tail; bill
brown. *1st winter* Much as ad ♀ after
moult in Jul–Oct (when strikingly patchy);
♂♀ eyes differ as ads. VOICE Grating
tcheerr, whistled *tsoo-ee*, clicking, harsh
scream; all but last in rambling gurgling
song with much mimicry (*eg* Curlew,
telephone). HABITAT Urban areas, farmland, cliffs; also breeds in woods. NEST In
any holes, or in ivy, 4–7 eggs, Apr–mid
Jul; 1–2 broods. FOOD Insects, worms,
seeds, berries, fruit, cereals. RANGE Mainly
sedentary; abundant passage/winter
visitor from N/NE Europe, Oct–Apr.
COMPARE Rose-coloured Starling (316).

SPARROWS (Passeridae)

House Sparrow *Passer domesticus* 14–15.5
cm (c5¾ in). Brown and buff-white with
black-streaked mantle, ♂ also has grey
crown and blackish throat; often dingier
in towns. Flight direct or undulating,
with hurried beats; hops with flicking tail
or stands erect; cheeky, but wary;
gregarious. *Ad* ♂ Chestnut and whitish,
with grey crown and rump, black throat/
chest, short white wing-bar; black bill in

Starling

♂ summer

juv

♀ winter

♂ winter

juv moulting

summer, brown and yellowish in winter (when upperparts duller, bib mixed with whitish). *Ad* ♀ Buff streak behind eyes, 2 faint buff wing-bars; bill as ♂ winter. *Juv* As ♀, but crown and rump mottled dark, mantle and wings paler, throat whiter (if dusky central patch, usually ♂), bill yellow with blackish base; as ads after moult in Jun–Oct. VOICE Chirps and twitters, esp *chee-ip* and *chreek* in flocks; chirruping song. HABITAT Houses, farms. NEST Colonial; in holes, or in foliage, 3–6 eggs, Apr–Aug; 1–4 broods. FOOD Seeds, scraps, insects. RANGE Most sedentary. COMPARE Spanish Sparrow (316).

Tree Sparrow *Passer montanus* 13.5–14.5 cm (*c*5½ in). ♂♀ alike with chestnut crown, neat bib and cheek-spot, partial white collar, yellow-brown rump, 2 thin wing-bars. Shy; mixes in winter with House Sparrows and finches. *Ad* Bib/cheek-spot black, wing-bars white; bill black in summer, base yellowish in winter. *Juv* Crown duller, bib/cheek-spot dark grey, wing-bars buff, bill as ad winter; as ad

after moult in Aug–Oct. VOICE In flight *tek tek*; chirps higher-pitched than House Sparrow, esp fast *chip chip chip*. HABITAT Pollard willows, old trees, ruins, cliffs. NEST Colonial; mostly in holes, 4–6 eggs, mid Apr–Jul; 2–3 broods. FOOD Seeds, insects. RANGE Mainly sedentary; immigrants from N Europe, Sep–Apr.

Starling	B8
	W8
	S8
	A8

House Sparrow	B7
	W8
	S7
	A8

Tree Sparrow	B6
	W6
	S6
	A6

House Sparrow

♂ summer

♂ winter

♀

juv ♂

Tree Sparrow

ad

juv

FINCHES (Fringillidae)

Chaffinch *Fringilla coelebs* 14.5–16 cm (*c*6 in). Commonest finch, with thick pointed bill, slightly peaked head, shallow-forked tail; white shoulder-patch and wing-bar, white tail-sides, yellow-green rump. Flight undulating, as all finches, closing wings every few beats; hops jerkily or walks with short steps; gregarious in autumn/winter. ♂ *summer* Abrasion makes forehead black, crown/nape grey-blue, mantle chestnut, cheeks and breast pinkish; bill blue-grey. ♂ *winter* After moult in Aug–Sep, crown/nape grey-blue washed rufous-buff, mantle, cheeks and breast duller; bill whitish-brown with dark tip. *Ad* ♀ Yellow-brown above with greyer central crown/nape (esp summer) and brown-grey cheeks and underparts, often tinged pink on breast; bill brown. *Juv* As ♀ winter, but white nape-spot, paler buff face and breast, smaller brownish-green rump, ♂ mantle chestnut-tinged; moults in Jul–Sep. VOICE Loud metallic *pink-pink*, low *chip* in flight; spring ♂ clear *wheet*, rattling song *chip-chip-chip-chwee-chwee-tissi-chooeeo* ('cricketer running to wicket, bowling'). HABITAT Woods, hedges, orchards, gardens; winters in farmland. NEST In bushes, trees, 4–5 eggs, mid Apr–Jul; 1 brood. FOOD Seeds, fruit, insects. RANGE Resident; passage/winter visitor from esp N Europe, end Sep–Apr.

Brambling *Fringilla montifringilla* 14–15 cm (*c*5¾ in). Shape as Chaffinch, but tail slightly shorter and more forked; less white in wings and tail, orange-buff shoulders and breast, narrow white rump (*cf* Bullfinch), yellow on axillaries. Flight more erratic than Chaffinch. ♂ *summer* Abrasion makes head/mantle black, breast and shoulders pale orange; bill blue-black. ♂ *winter* After moult in Aug–Sep, head and mantle mottled buff, nape and neck-sides greyish, breast and shoulders rich orange-buff; bill yellow with black tip. *Ad* ♀ Browner-black head and mantle mottled buff, greyer nape and cheeks, duller breast and esp shoulders; bill varies as ♂. *Juv* As ♀, but rump and belly tinged with yellow. *1st winter* ♂ As ad after moult

in Aug–Sep, but primary coverts and outer greaters paler grey-brown (not black), lesser coverts pale rufous (not orange) and often spotted black. VOICE Hoarse *tsweek*, hard Chaffinch-like *chik* in flight; spring ♂ prolonged *dzwee* like Greenfinch (238). HABITAT Winters in beech woods, farmland; breeds in birch/conifer woods. FOOD Beechmast, seeds, berries. RANGE Passage/winter visitor from N Europe, end Sep–May; has nested NBr, may colonise.

Bullfinch *Pyrrhula pyrrhula* 14–15 cm (*c*5¾ in). Portly and neckless, with short deep bill joining curve of large head, shortish rounded wings, and squared tail; black cap, wings and tail, whitish wing-patch, bold white rump. Flight slow and bouncing; secretive; in pairs or families. *Ad* ♂ *Br/Ir race (P.p. pileata)* Blue-grey above, pink-red below. *Ad* ♀ Dark grey-buff above with greyer hindneck, paler below, tinged with pink. *Juv* Head and back brown, rump tinged buff, underparts yellow-buff; much as ads after moult in Aug–Oct. *N Eurasian race (P.p. pyrrhula)* Larger; ♂ paler grey, brighter pink; ♀ much greyer above. VOICE Low *deeu*; sub-song broken creaky warble. HABITAT Woods, bushes, orchards. NEST In bushes or brambles, 4–6 eggs, May–Aug; 2 broods. FOOD Seeds, berries, buds, also insects. RANGE Largely sedentary; N race scarce migrant, end Mar–early May, esp end Oct–Nov, mainly NBr.

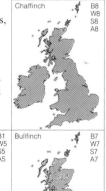

Chaffinch

♂ winter

♀

♂ summer

juv

Brambling

♂ winter

juv

♂ summer

♀

♀

Bullfinch

pyrrhula ♂

pyrrhula ♀

♀

♂

♀

juv

Greenfinch *Carduelis chloris* 14–15 cm (*c*5¾ in). Thickset, with stout pale bill and short well-forked tail; green to streaky brown, rump yellow-green (not juv), yellow patches on primaries and sides of tail-base. Actions much as Chaffinch (236); ♂ makes butterfly-like display-flights round tree-tops in spring. *♂ summer* By abrasion, olive-green above and bright yellow-green below, with greyish greater coverts/inner secondaries. *♂ winter* After moult *c*Jun–Aug, grey-brown above with greyer cheeks/flanks, all tinged green; still yellow-green below but tinged grey. *Ad ♀* Grey-brown above with faint streaks, greyer below tinged yellow, whiter belly, all slightly more green-yellow in summer; less yellow on wings and tail than ♂. *Juv* Dark-streaked brown above, inc rump, and yellow-grey below streaked brown; ♂♀ wings/tail differ as ads; as ads after moult in Jul–Sep if no brown juv greater coverts. VOICE Trill in flight, *chup* or *teu* repeated, uneasy *tsooeet*; in spring ♂ drawn-out nasal *tsweee*, mixed with twittering song. HABITAT Gardens, parks, hedges, wood-edges; winters in farmland. NEST In bushes, trees, 4–6 eggs, mid Apr–Aug; 2–3 broods. FOOD Seeds, berries, buds, also insects. RANGE Mainly resident, but some go as far as Iberia; winter visitor from Continent, Oct–Apr.

Goldfinch *Carduelis carduelis* 11.5–12.5 cm (*c*4¾ in). Dainty, with pointed whitish bill, well-forked tail; red, white and black (not juv), yellow wing-band, white tips on black wings/tail. Flight dancing; perches high or flits about on thistles, often hanging head down; flocks seldom mix with other finches. *Ad* Head coloured; tawny above and buff breast in winter, greyer-brown and whitish with whiter nape-spot and less white on wing/tail-tips in summer; ♂ red extends farther back above and below eyes, ♀ lesser coverts have much broader greyer tips. *Juv* Mostly grey-buff, paler below, with faint dark spots and streaks; much as ads after moult in Aug–Sep. VOICE Liquid twittering *tswitt-witt-witt*, clear high whistled *pee-u*; song fast twittering trill. HABITAT Gardens, parks, wood-edges;

feeds on weedy ground. NEST In trees, tall bushes, 5–6 eggs, May–Aug; 2–3 broods. FOOD Seeds, insects. RANGE Many go south to Iberia/NW Africa, Sep–Apr.

Siskin *Carduelis spinus* 11.5–12.5 cm (*c*4¾ in). Dumpy with sharply pointed bill and short well-forked tail; yellow-green to green-grey above and yellowish to white below, all variably streaked, with yellow wing-bars and sides to tail-base. Flight fast, undulating; mainly in trees, flits restlessly, hangs acrobatically; gregarious with Redpolls; ♂ makes butterfly-like display-flights in spring. *Ad ♂* Yellow-green above, faintly streaked except on yellower rump, and grey-yellow below, streaked black on whiter flanks; crown and bib black, mottled with grey in winter. *Ad ♀* Greyer above, whiter below, more heavily streaked (also rump); no black on head. *Juv* More streaked than ♀ and browner above, rump greyish; as ads from *c*Aug, but ♂ more streaked above and ♀ browner. VOICE Shrill clear *tsu*, wheezier *tsu-eet* and hard twitter, often combined; song warbling twitter ending in discordant bleating note. HABITAT Breeds in coniferous/mixed woods; winters in birch/alder thickets. NEST High in conifers, 4–5 eggs, end Apr–mid Jul; 2 broods. FOOD Tree seeds. RANGE Mainly sedentary, some dispersal south; passage/winter visitor from N/E Europe, mid Sep–mid May. COMPARE Serin (316).

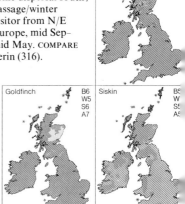

Greenfinch

♂ summer

♂ winter

♀

♀

juv ♂

Goldfinch

ad

juv

ad

Siskin

♀

♀

juv

♂

Linnet *Carduelis cannabina* 13–14 cm (*c*5¼ in). Small finch with pointed bill, long wings and longish forked tail; streaky brown with streaked buff throat, white in wings and tail, dark bill in winter; ♂ also shows grey, chestnut, and red or pink. Flight undulating and flitting; hops on ground; perches on low bushes and fences; gregarious. ♂ *summer* Abrasion makes head greyer, mantle plain chestnut, throat whiter, forehead and breast red. ♂ *winter* After moult in Aug–Oct, dark streaks and buff fringes obscure colours. *Ad* ♀ Duller, no pink/red, less chestnut, more heavily streaked. *Juv* As ♀, but narrower streaks, throat nearly plain buffish; juv ♂ more chestnut-buff above; as ads with moult in Jul–Sep. VOICE Flight-note rapid *chichichichit*, call *tsooeet*; song musical twitter of fluty and twangy notes. HABITAT Commons with gorse, thorn bushes, young plantations, hedges, dunes; winters in stubble, fallow marshes. NEST In bushes or in cover on ground, 4–6 eggs, mid Apr–mid Sep; 2–3 broods. FOOD Seeds, also insects. RANGE Partial migrant, some going to S France/Spain, others coming from N Europe, Sep–Apr.

Twite *Carduelis flavirostris* 13–14 cm (*c*5¼ in). Suggests small ♀ Linnet and looks longer-tailed; darker, tawnier above, with plain warm buff throat, less white in wings and tail, yellow bill in winter; ♂ pink rump. *Ad* ♂ Streaked blackish above and dark rufous on breast/flanks; in summer, stronger streaking, pink rump, greyish hindneck, buff throat, yellow-grey bill; in winter, paler above, buff-pink rump, rufous-buff throat, less streaked below, yellow bill. *Ad* ♀ As ♂, but rump streaky, usually no pink. *Juv* Slightly greyer head, rustier mantle, no pink rump, dirty buff throat, paler and more streaked below, with bill cream-yellow; as ads after moult in Jul–Sep. VOICE Flight-note and song Linnet-like, but harder, more metallic; *chweek* call nasal, twanging. HABITAT Moors, upland pastures, rocky ground near sea; winters on shores, saltmarshes, coastal fields. NEST In heather, banks, walls, bushes, on ground, 5–6 eggs, May mid Aug; 1–2 broods. FOOD Seeds, also

insects. RANGE Some resident, but others move south on coasts, even cross Channel; few come from Norway, Oct–Apr.

Redpoll *Carduelis flammea* 11.5–13 cm (*c*4¾–5 in). Dumpy finch with short tail; red forehead, black chin, yellowish bill, pale rump, 2 buff wing-bars; streaked tawny, buff or greyish upperparts/flanks; ♂ rump and breast pink. Actions as Siskin (238); similar circling song-flight, acrobatic feeding. *Ad* ♂ *Br/Ir race (C.f. cabaret)* Tawny above, with variably pink rump, cheeks, throat, breast and upper flanks, all much brighter in summer. ♀/*1st year* ♂ Little or no pink, streakier below. *Juv* No red on crown, less black on chin, much streakier; moults in Jul–Sep. *N race = Mealy Redpoll (C.f. flammea)* Larger, paler, greyer above with whiter wing-bars and rump (may be almost plain pink in ♂). Greenland race *(C.f. rostrata)* More as Br/Ir race, but bulkier, bill heavier, 'striped' flanks. VOICE Metallic flight-note used as song with rolling trill *rrrr*, *chee-chee-chee*; call plaintive *tsooeet*. HABITAT Birches, alders, willows, conifers, in woods, parks, gardens; rocky ground on passage. NEST In bushes or trees, 4–6 eggs, May–mid Aug; 1–2 broods. FOOD Seeds, also insects. RANGE Partial migrant, many wintering in Low Countries/Germany; immigrants from N Europe/Greenland, Oct–May. COMPARE Arctic Redpoll (316).

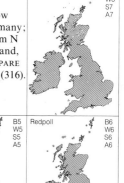

Linnet
B7
W6
S7
A7

Twite
B5
W5
S5
A5

Redpoll
B6
W6
S6
A6

Redpoll

cabaret
♂ winter

cabaret
♀

♀

cabaret
♂ summer

flammea
♂ winter

juv

Linnet

♂ summer

♂ winter

♀ summer

rostrata
♂ winter

juv ♂

♀ winter

♀

Twite

♂ summer

juv

♀

♂ winter

♀ summer

♀ winter

Crossbill *Loxia curvirostra* 16–17 cm
(*c*6½ in). Thickset, big-headed finch with
long wings, short forked tail and elongated
mandibles crossed at tip (lower turned to
left or right); crimson, orange, yellow-
green or streaky greenish-grey according
to sex/age, all with dark wings and tail.
Flight fast, undulating, usually at tree-top
level; clambers or sidles on branches like
parrot, even using bill as support; hangs
down to wrench off conifer cones, holds
them with foot while extracting seeds with
tongue (dropped cones have characteristically split scales); except for drinking,
seldom on ground, hopping awkwardly,
but migrants will hang from thistles;
gregarious; tame. *Ad ♂* Crimson of
varying richness, often mixed with orange:
brightest on crown, rump and underparts;
more vivid in summer. *Ad ♀* Generally
yellow-green with grey tinge, but some
more golden or even with few orange-red
feathers; throat greyer, breast and flanks
mottled brown. *Juv* Green-grey heavily
streaked blackish; mandibles not crossed
for 1–2 weeks after fledging. *1st year ♂*

With moult in May–Nov, greenish-gold
to orange, mixed with red and yellow-
green: some like ad ♂ but for green-
fringed juv wings and tail, others have
orange only on crown and rump like bright
♀. *1st year ♀* As ad ♀, but wing-coverts
buff-tipped. VOICE Metallic *jip jip*, more
explosive than Greenfinch (238); song
5–10 calls trilled together, then series of
high clearer *jee* or *terjee*, ending with
warble like Redstart (198). HABITAT
Conifers, esp woods or clumps, but also
in parks/gardens after invasions. NEST
High in conifers, 3–4 eggs, Feb–Jun; 1–2
broods. FOOD Conifer seeds, also berries,
thistles, insects. RANGE Fluctuating, and
boosted by periodical invasions from
Continent, end Jun–Sep; has bred in
most counties. COMPARE Other Crossbills,
Pine Grosbeak (318).

Scottish Crossbill *Loxia scotica* 16–17.5
cm (*c*6⅝ in). Differs from Crossbill only in
deeper, blunter-tipped bill; plumages and
habits similar. VOICE Similar; also stronger
joop. HABITAT Caledonian pine forest.

Crossbill

FOOD Pine seeds. RANGE Endemic resident.

Hawfinch *Coccothraustes coccothraustes* 16–17 cm (*c*6½ in). Stout, bull-necked, with long wings, short squarish tail, and huge bill on big head; rich brown mantle, grey hindneck, white wing-patches, black bib; identified in flight by call, shape, transparent band on primaries and white-tipped tail. Flight fast, undulating, high; perches in tree-tops; rather upright on ground, with strong hops or gawky waddle; solitary or parties; very shy. *Ad ♂* Hindcrown and rump rufous, underparts mainly pink-brown, much black round bill-base, flight-feathers predominantly glossy black; bill blue in summer, yellowish in winter. *Ad ♀* Head, rump and underparts greyer-brown, less black on face, flight-feathers predominantly grey, bill alters as ♂. *Juv* Brown above, buff below, all mottled/barred blackish, with green-brown head, yellowish throat, horn-yellow bill; ♂♀ wings differ as ads, juv ♂ also black line round bill-base and ♀ whiter underparts; as ads after moult in

Aug–Sep. VOICE Explosive clicking *pzik* or *pzik-ik*, thin whistling *tzeeip*; song halting *teek teek tur-whee-whee*. HABITAT Broadleaved woods, orchards, parks. NEST In trees, 3–6 eggs, end Apr–Jun; 1 brood. FOOD Kernels, seeds, berries; insects in summer. RANGE Resident, but wanders (? also from Continent), Oct–Jun.

Crossbill	B4
	W4
	S4
	A5

Scottish Crossbill	B3
	W4
	S3
	A4

Hawfinch	B5
	W5
	S5
	A5

Scottish Crossbill

♂

♂

juv ♂

Hawfinch

♂ winter

♂ summer

♀ summer

BUNTINGS (Emberizidae)

Lapland Bunting *Calcarius lapponicus*
14–16 cm (*c*6 in). Bulkier, longer-winged,
shorter-tailed than similar Reed Bunting
(248); in autumn/winter has yellowish bill,
pale crown-stripe, black-cornered ear-
coverts, thin moustaches, obscurely
marked breast, chestnut greater coverts
between thin whitish bars (instead of
rufous shoulders), less white tail-sides and
often at least hint of rufous nape; ♂ has
black, white and chestnut head in summer.
Flight fast, undulating, often high; much
on ground, creeps or runs crouched, also
hops; shy; gregarious in winter with other
buntings, finches, larks. ♂ *summer* Black
head and throat, chestnut nape; upper-
parts/flanks streaked black and chestnut.
♂ *winter* After moult in Aug, black and
chestnut largely hidden by brown and
buff-white tips, head-sides sandy-buff
with black ear-corners and faint
moustaches, upperparts/flanks duller.
♀ *summer* Browner crown, buff supercilia
reaching bill, blackish face/cheeks/throat
mixed with whitish and pale brown, pale
chestnut nape streaked black, flank-
streaks narrower and more chestnut. ♀
winter As ♂ winter, but nape streaked
black/buff so chestnut barely visible, ear-
corners and chest-marks browner-black,
less black on crown and flanks. *Juv*
Mainly buff, paler below, streaked
blackish; chestnut on wings as ads. *1st
winter* ♂ As ♂ winter after moult in Aug–
Sep, but obscure chestnut nape spotted
black. *1st winter* ♀ As ♀ winter, but ear-
corners and moustaches browner, chest-
marks streakier. VOICE Dry rippled *trrrr*,
soft *chew*. HABITAT Coastal fields, saltmarshes; nests on hummocky moors. FOOD
Seeds; insects in summer. RANGE Passage/
winter visitor from Greenland/?N Europe,
end Aug–May; has nested since 1977.
COMPARE Rustic and Little Buntings (326).

Snow Bunting *Plectrophenax nivalis* 16–17
cm (*c*6½ in). Largish and stocky, with long
wings reaching well down tail; whitish
below, white in wings, white tail-sides,
variously tawny on head and breast, but

Lapland Bunting

♀ winter

♂ winter

♂ summer

summer ♂ black and white. Flight fast, undulating, flock dropping like flickering snowflakes, then skimming ground; much on ground, runs, also hops; perches on rocks, also posts, wires; gregarious in winter. *♂ summer* White head (often with rufous speckles), rump (sometimes black streaks), secondaries, most wing-coverts; black bill, back, primaries, central tail. *♂ winter* After moult in Aug–Sep, tawny-buff crown, cheeks, breast-sides (or even across chest); black mantle obscured by tawny to whitish-buff; brownish-yellow bill. *♀ summer* Rufous and greyish head, grey-black mantle/rump streaked brown and whitish; much less white on browner wings with dark marks on secondaries, usually blackish-based coverts; bill as ♂. *♀ winter* As ♂ winter, but dull buff above, crown/nape and rump speckled black, wings as ♀ summer. *Juv* Grey-buff above streaked black, throat grey, breast/flanks buff marked darker; wings only little white on secondaries, covert-tips. *1st winter ♂* As ♂ winter after moult in Aug–Sep, but darker tawny above, speckled

black on nape, wings as juv but median coverts white; as ad by summer but for black flecks on nape, mainly black rump. *1st winter ♀* As ♀ winter but wings less white, often black-speckled breast-band. VOICE Rippled *tirrirri-ripp*; loud *peeu* as Little Ringed Plover; song high musical *titti-turee-turee*. HABITAT Breeds on bare mountains; winters on coasts, adjacent pastures, also moors. NEST In crevices, 4–6 eggs, end May–early Aug; 1–2 broods. FOOD Seeds, moss, invertebrates. RANGE Passage/winter visitor from Greenland/Scandinavia, mid Sep–mid Apr; few nest.

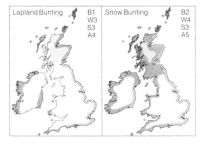

| Lapland Bunting | B1 W3 S3 A4 | Snow Bunting | B2 W4 S3 A5 |

Snow Bunting

♀ winter

♂ winter

1st winter ♂

♀ summer

♂ summer

♂ winter

juv

Yellowhammer *Emberiza citrinella* 16–17 cm (*c*6½ in). Slim, with longish wings, longish cleft tail; yellow on head/under-parts, streaky chestnut upperparts, plain chestnut rump, white on tail-sides. Flight undulating or direct; much on ground, mainly hops; perches prominently, often flicking tail; gregarious in winter with other buntings and finches. ♂ *summer* Mainly yellow head and underparts, variably streaked with olive on sides of head and with blackish on chestnut flanks (some much brighter, with more yellow than others); usually chestnut moustache; often pale chestnut band across breast. ♂ *winter* After moult in Aug–Oct, head and throat more streaked brownish-green (but still much yellow), chest greener, breast-sides and flanks duller chestnut and more streaked, wings with yellowish fringes. *Ad* ♀ Duller than ♂ winter, much less yellow and more dark grey-brown on crown and throat, more rufous breast and flanks with heavier streaking, paler yellow belly; rather brighter and more clearly streaked in summer. *Juv* Much duller than ad ♀: heavily streaked head, browner and streakier rump, bolder and blacker streaks on browner breast and flanks; ♂ shows dull yellowish on central crown, throat and belly, ♀ more greyish. *1st winter* ♂ After moult in Jul–Oct, much as ad ♀, but yellows brighter, breast and flanks more chestnut. *1st winter* ♀ Crown/nape yellow-brown with blackish streaks, throat/breast more buff, belly paler. VOICE Sharp *twik* or *twitik*, hoarse *chiff*; song tinkling series of high notes, ending usually with prolonged wheezy *chwee* ('little-bit-of-bread-and-no-cheese'). HABITAT Arable with hedges, bushy areas, young conifers, scrub, bracken slopes; often stubble and stackyards in winter. NEST On or near ground in banks, hedge-bases, brambles, 3–5 eggs, mid Apr–Aug; 2–3 broods. FOOD Seeds, grain, shoots, berries; insects in summer. RANGE Largely sedentary; apparently some immigrants from N Europe, Sep–May.

COMPARE ♀/imm Yellow and Cirl with vagrant buntings showing yellow (326, 328).

Yellowhammer

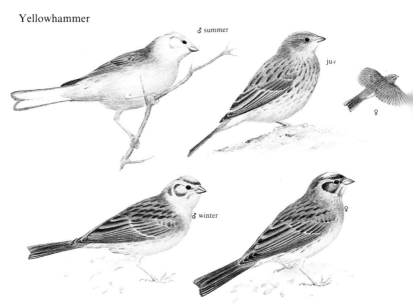

♂ summer

juv

♀

♂ winter

♀

Cirl Bunting *Emberiza cirlus* 15.5–16.5 cm
(*c*6¼ in). Slightly smaller and more compact than Yellowhammer, with shorter,
more rounded wings; most plumages
rather similar except for olive-grey to
grey-brown (not chestnut) rump, but ♂
has black, olive and yellow head-pattern.
Flight weaker than Yellowhammer, more
undulating; less gregarious. ♂ *summer*
Black throat and eyestripes bordered with
yellow bands; olive-grey crown streaked
black; grey-green chest-band with
chestnut at sides; chestnut mantle/
scapulars, olive-grey rump and shoulders.
♂ *winter* After moult in Aug–Oct, black
and chestnut partly obscured by buffish
tips, chest-band greyer. *Ad* ♀ Much duller
than ♂: less chestnut above, crown and
rump browner, supercilia and dark-
speckled throat yellow-buff, chest and
flanks buff and well-streaked, only
chestnut tinge at breast-sides, belly pale
yellow; in summer, yellow-buff and
chestnut brighter, less marked below, and
greyer crown, rump and breast. *Juv* Buff
above, yellow-grey below, all streaked

blackish, with vague supercilia, buff-
tipped blackish (not grey-green) lesser
coverts; as winter ads with moult in Aug-
Oct. VOICE Thin *sip* or *sissi-sissi-sip* in
flight, churring alarm; rattling song like
fast Lesser Whitethroat (212). HABITAT
Bushy chalk/limestone slopes, pastures
with timbered hedgerows, scrubby coastal
cliff-tops, parkland and gardens near sea,
esp with elms. NEST In hawthorn, gorse,
brambles, yew, or in banks, 3–4 eggs, mid
May–Aug; 2–3 broods. FOOD Much as
Yellowhammer. RANGE Largely sedentary,
much decreased in numbers and range.

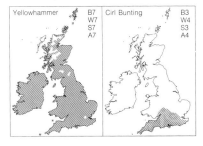

| Yellowhammer | B7 W7 S7 A7 | Cirl Bunting | B3 W4 S3 A4 |

Cirl Bunting

♂ summer

♀

♀/juv

juv

Ortolan Bunting *Emberiza hortulana* 15.5–16.5 cm (*c*6¼ in). Slim, long-winged; ads greenish head, yellowish throat, chestnut-buff underparts and yellow-brown rump; juvs streaked; always reddish bill/legs, pale eye-rings, white on tail-sides. Actions as Yellowhammer (246); shyer. *♂ summer* Head and chest grey-olive but for yellow throat, cheek-stripe. *♂ winter* After moult in Jul–Aug, yellow more buffish, crown streaked, chest mottled dark (even spotted, then inseparable from ♀ unless olive band clear). *Ad ♀* Very like *♂* winter, but head browner, chest grey-buff (not olive) with dark marks. *Juv* Streaked black and buffish; paler throat and cheeks. *1st winter* More as ad ♀ after moult in Aug–Oct, but crown browner, throat paler, chest greyer-buff with heavier streaks. VOICE Soft *tlip*, harder *twik*, whistled *cheu*. HABITAT Migrants in coastal scrub, fields. FOOD Seeds, insects. RANGE Scarce migrant from Continent, Aug–Nov (esp Sep), rare end Apr–Jun, wintering in Mediterranean/E Africa. COMPARE Cretzschmar's Bunting (326).

Reed Bunting *Emberiza schoeniclus* 14–16 cm (*c*6 in). Rather rounded wings, longish tail; buff to rufous with blackish streaks and moustaches, buff supercilia, brownish cheeks, grey-brown rump, rufous shoulders, white on tail-sides; summer *♂* has black and white head. Flight jerky, often low; hops, creeps or runs on ground; perches on reeds or bushes, flicks wings, opens tail; mixes with other buntings, finches, pipits. *♂ summer* Black head, white collar and cheek-stripe; white below, flanks streaked. *♂ winter* After moult in Aug–Nov, head-pattern obscured by rufous-buff tips, whitish collar and blackish throat just visible. *Ad ♀* No white collar (greyish when very worn in summer); buff below (whiter in summer), streaked also on breast. *Juv* As ♀, but paler, less rufous, with bolder streaks, yellower-buff below. *1st winter ♂* More as *♂* winter after moult in Aug–Sep, but black throat largely obscured, less collar, supercilia often buff. VOICE Shrill *tsee-u*, metallic *chink*; dreary song 2–5 wheezy notes then *zizzizik*. HABITAT Marshes, young conifers, gorse, hedges, coastal bushes; often winters in farmland. NEST On or near ground in tussocks, bushes, 4–5 eggs, end Apr–mid Aug; 2–3 broods. FOOD Seeds, insects. RANGE Sedentary but leaves uplands in winter; also passage/winter visitor from Continent, end Sep–May. COMPARE Little and Pallas's Reed Buntings (326, 328).

Corn Bunting *Miliaria calandra* 17–18.5 cm (*c*7 in). Big, thickset, with heavy head and shortish tail; streaky brown, yellowish bill, no white on tail. Flight sparrow-like; perches on wires, bushes; singing *♂* often flutters off with legs dangling; hops on ground; gregarious in winter. *Ad summer* Grey-brown above, streaked blackish; whitish-buff below finely streaked from throat-sides to flanks, variably across breast. *Ad winter* After moult in Sep–Nov, more buff; more streaked below. *Juv* Paler buff with bolder streaks above, wings fringed pale buff (not rufous), throat-sides/flanks less streaked; as ad after moult Sep–Oct. VOICE Harsh *chip*, scolding *zeep*; sharp *kwit* or *kwit-it* in flocks; stuttering song speeds into harsh trill like jangling keys. HABITAT Downs, extensive arable with low hedges, coastal scrub. NEST On ground in cover, 3–5 eggs, end May–Aug; 1–3 broods. FOOD Seeds, berries, insects. RANGE Sedentary; apparently some immigrants from Continent, Sep–May.

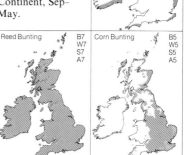

Ortolan Bunting — B0 W0 S2 A3

Reed Bunting — B7 W7 S7 A7

Corn Bunting — B5 W5 S5 A5

Ortolan Bunting

♂ summer

♀ summer

1st winter

1st winter

juv

Reed Bunting

♀

juv

♂ summer

♂ winter

♀ winter

♀ summer (worn plumage)

Corn Bunting

ad

juv

ad

DIVERS (Gaviidae)

White-billed Diver *Gavia adamsii* 75–90 cm (*c*32 in). Very like Great Northern Diver (42), separated by colour/shape of bill, angular outline of uptilted head, pattern of upperparts, and white-shafted primaries. *Ad summer* Bill whitish-yellow with straight culmen and up-angled lower mandible; fewer/wider streaks on collars than Great Northern, larger checks on upperparts. *Ad winter* Bill often darkish towards base, but outer culmen pale; face-sides lighter than Great Northern, and whitish round eyes like Red-throated (42). *Juv* Bill much as Great Northern, but paler (esp outer culmen); head and neck paler, upperparts greyer-brown with clearer scaling than juv Great Northern. RANGE 74: Oct–Jun, mainly coastal N/EBr, 2 Ir. (Arctic Russia, Asia, NW America.)

GREBES (Podicipedidae)

Pied-billed Grebe *Podilymbus podiceps* 31–38 cm (*c*13½ in). Shape like large Little Grebe (46), but stout chicken-like bill, larger head, longer neck. *Ad summer* Black-banded white bill, white eye-rings, black forehead and throat. *Ad winter* Bill yellow-brown, foreneck grey-brown, throat whitish; white stern conspicuous. *Juv* Bill darker yellow-brown than ad winter, with pinker lower mandible; head stripy, no eye-ring; lower foreneck rufous, breast and flanks greyer than ad winter; white stern as ad. *1st winter* After moult by Dec, much as ad winter, but eye-rings dull green, bill greyish. VOICE Spring 'song' loud, slurred, gulping *cow-cow-cow* speeding up and rising in pitch before ending in wail. HABITAT Shallow waters with emergent cover. FOOD Invertebrates, fish. RANGE 7: all months (some for long periods), most E/SBr. (N/S America.)

ALBATROSSES (Diomedeidae)

Black-browed Albatross *Diomedea melanophris* 75–90 cm (*c*33 in), wingspan 215–245 cm (*c*7½ ft). Huge, stout-bodied, with heavy bill, short tail, long narrow

Pied-billed Grebe

White-billed Diver

ad summer

ad winter

juv

juv

ad winter

ad summer

wings; 1 of several species in Atlantic, so important to note bill colour/shape, whether grey on head, form of any eye-patches, back colour, underwing pattern, and build. *Ad* Bill yellow with black basal line, head white with frowning eye-patches; back blackish; broad, ill-defined blackish margins to white underwings, wider in front. Gliding flight, heavy head, thick neck and humped shape similar to outsize Fulmar (48). *Juv/imm* As ad, but bill grey-black, later yellow with dark tip; top of head and neck grey at first, then only lower neck; underwings show little white, then increasing central stripe. VOICE Silent at sea. HABITAT Oceanic. FOOD Squids, jellyfish, offal. RANGE 23 (also 17 not identified to species): Feb–Dec, esp Mar–Oct, mostly coastal SW/NWIr, E/SBr, but 2 inland; single summering ads on Bass Rock (1967–79) and Hermaness, Shetland (since 1974). (S Oceans.)

FRIGATEBIRDS (Fregatidae)

Magnificent Frigatebird *Fregata magnifi-*

cens 95–110 cm (*c*40 in), wingspan 215–245 cm (*c*7½ ft). Black or pied, rakishly elongated with hook-tipped bill, narrow pointed wings and forked tail; 4 frigate-bird species in Atlantic often inseparable, but points to note include bill and leg colour, shape of any white areas, whether white tinged rusty (juvs), colour of throat (♀s), and any paler collar, wing-band or breast-patch on the black. All soar and sail, sometimes flap with deep beats; never settle on sea. *Ad ♂* Glossy black with red throat-pouch (barely visible unless inflated in display); bill grey to dark horn, legs black. *Ad ♀* Blackish with white anvil-shape below and narrow collar, pale band on wings; bill blue-grey, legs red. *Juv/imm* As ♀, but head and underbody white (at first with broken brownish breast-band), then becoming mottled. VOICE Silent at sea. HABITAT Aerial, oceanic. FOOD Fish, squids, offal, snatched from surface or other birds. RANGE 1: Jul, Argyll; 2 others in Aug (Aberdeen, Cork) not identified to species. (Tropical Atlantic, E Pacific.)

Black-browed Albatross

ad

imm

Magnificent Frigatebird

♂

imm

♀

PETRELS, SHEARWATERS (Procellariidae)

Bulwer's Petrel *Bulweria bulwerii* 25–28 cm (*c*10½ in). Rather small, all-dark petrel with stubby bill, long narrow backswept wings, and long tail actually wedge-shaped but looking round-ended at distance or from side; lacks white rump of still smaller storm-petrels (52, and below), and shape and flight different from them and from also mainly dark, but larger, longer-billed and shorter-tailed Sooty and Balearic Shearwaters (50, 52). Flight fast with swooping careening action and erratic twisting glides, and beats slower and deeper than shearwaters. *Ad/juv* Sooty-brown, duller below, but for paler band on upperwings, grey chin; legs pinkish. VOICE Silent at sea. HABITAT Oceanic. FOOD Plankton. RANGE 4: Feb, May, Aug, Yorks/Cork. (Cent Atlantic, Pacific.)

Little Shearwater *Puffinus assimilis* 25–30 cm (*c*11 in). Small, compact shearwater, ⅓ smaller than normal-sized Manx Shearwater (52) (but Manx runts may be hardly any bigger); similarly black above and white below, but shorter wings, smaller bill, whitish round eyes. Flight distinct from other shearwaters (50, 52), with far more flapping and, even when banking/gliding (mainly in stronger winds), frequently interspersed with rapid beats; fluttering action and short wings recall Puffin (170) (at distance); feeds while swimming and by plunging, as Manx. *Ad/juv Madeira/Canaries race (P.a. baroli)* Black above and mainly white below, with more restricted black cap than Manx (cheeks in front of/around eyes mottled grey, like sides of neck and breast, and looking whitish at distance); undertail-coverts white, extending almost to end of tail; legs blue (not pinkish as Manx). *Cape Verdes race (P.a. boydi)* Browner above; less whitish in front of eyes; undertail-coverts largely brown, so tail looks dark. VOICE Silent at sea. HABITAT Oceanic. FOOD Fish, cephalopods. RANGE 58: Apr–Oct (esp Aug–Oct), most SW/NWIr, also W/EBr; only Madeira/Canaries race certainly identified (Cent Atlantic, S oceans.)

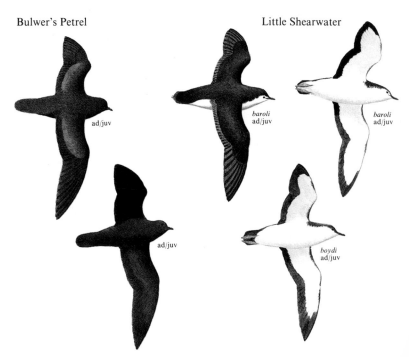

Bulwer's Petrel

ad/juv

ad/juv

Little Shearwater

baroli
ad/juv

baroli
ad/juv

boydi
ad/juv

STORM-PETRELS (Hydrobatidae)

Wilson's Petrel *Oceanites oceanicus* 17–18 cm (*c*7 in). Small, black with white rump, very like Storm Petrel (52), but with long spindly legs usually projecting well beyond short square tail, broader and more rounded wings uniformly dark underneath. Flight less bat-like than Storm Petrel with stronger fluttering, longer glides, more rolling from side to side; similarly patters on sea, but also regularly 'hops', with wings level or slightly raised and tail fanned, stretching legs forward to dip toes and then pushing back with them as it rises; even 'stands' on water, facing into wind with rigid wings and webbed feet acting as anchors; flight sometimes rather more wader-like, with flicking action and feet retracted, or martin-like, darting around and up into air; follows ships, sometimes settles on sea. *Ad/juv* Sooty-black, but for white rump curving down to lower flanks and, in new plumage, whitish line on upperwings; yellow on webs of feet rarely visible. VOICE Silent at sea. HABITAT Oceanic. FOOD Fish offal, plankton. RANGE 8: Aug–Oct, esp SWBr/ Ir. (S oceans, migrating to N Atlantic.)

Madeiran Petrel *Oceanodroma castro* 18–20 cm (*c*7½ in). Very like Leach's Petrel (52), but bolder and laterally more extensive white rump, less marked band on upperwings, larger bill, much less forked tail (often looking square). Flight intermediate between rapid and erratic bounding of Leach's and fluttering of Storm: typically steady with fast shallow beats, and glides on bowed (not angled) wings; at least sometimes also proceeds in regular horizontal zigzags, beating to left and then right. *Ad/juv* Black-brown with all-white rump more evenly curved than Leach's above tail and more clearly extending to lower flanks; wing-band slightly browner and less distinct (but whiter and bolder on juv in new plumage). VOICE Silent at sea. HABITAT Oceanic. FOOD Plankton, tiny fish, offal scraps. RANGE 2: Oct–Nov, Hants/Mayo (E/Cent Atlantic, Pacific.)

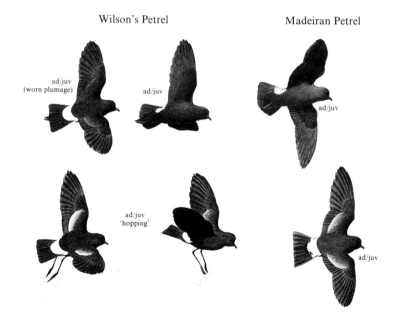

Wilson's Petrel

ad/juv (worn plumage)

ad/juv

ad/juv 'hopping'

Madeiran Petrel

ad/juv

ad/juv

ad/juv

BITTERNS, HERONS (Ardeidae)

American Bittern *Botaurus lentiginosus* 60–70 cm (*c*26 in). Smaller, browner than Bittern (56) (*cf* also imm Night Heron), with much less bold markings above, warm brown crown, creamy supercilia, blackish flight-feathers, usually black stripe on sides of neck. Faster beats of narrower, less rounded wings; feeds more in open. *Ad* Clear black neck-stripe (longer on ♂). *Juv* No neck-stripe until moult in Aug–Nov. VOICE Throaty *ok-ok-ok-ok*. HABITAT Marshes, meadows. FOOD Frogs, fish, insects. RANGE 55: Sep–Mar (esp Oct–Nov), most Ir, S/WBr. (N America.)

Little Bittern *Ixobrychus minutus* 33–38 cm (*c*14 in). Tiny; black and buff, or streaky, with pale wing-panel. Flight rapid, with shallow beats, dropping into cover with glide, bank and pitch; walks crouched, climbs reeds, very skulking; camouflage posture as Bittern (56). *Ad* ♂ Black and pale buff, hardly streaked, with large rounded patch on inner wings. *Ad* ♀ Pattern as ♂, but duller, variously tinged rufous: upperparts much browner with narrow buff streaks, underparts striped brown; wing-patches brown-buff with rusty carpal. *Juv* More boldly streaked buff above and brown below; crown also streaky and wing-patches mottled brown; some redder above. *1st year* As ads after moult in Nov–Jan, but wing-patches darker, more spotted; ♂ also browner flight-feathers and more streaked below. VOICE Flight-call *kwer* or *ker-ack*; ♂ in spring muffled croaking bark at 2 sec intervals. HABITAT Reeds in swamps, lakes, rivers. FOOD Fish, frogs, insects. RANGE 280 + : most Apr–Jun, also Jul–Sep, esp S/EBr, few Ir/NBr. (Eurasia, Africa, Australia.)

Night Heron *Nycticorax nycticorax* 58–65 cm (*c*24 in). Stocky, with stout bill, shortish legs; ad black, grey and white, but juv not unlike Bittern (56). Crepuscular; flight rapid on short rounded wings, only toes projecting beyond tail; clambers bittern-like in reeds. *Ad* Black above, grey wings/tail; white nape-plumes, forehead, and below; legs briefly red in spring. *Juv* Dark brown above, boldly spotted whitish-buff; grey-buff below, streaked dark brown. *Imm* From *c*Jan, becomes dark brown above, spotted only on worn wings until *c*May, and whiter below with brown streaks; more as ad from 2nd autumn, but greys/blacks tinged brown, no plumes till 2nd summer. VOICE Raven-like croak. HABITAT Roosts by day in trees; feeds in shallows. FOOD Frogs, fish, insects. RANGE 278: all months (esp Apr–Jun), most S/EBr. (S Eurasia, Africa, N/S America.)

Squacco Heron *Ardeola ralloides* 43–48 cm (*c*18 in). Small, thick-necked, with striped mane; brown or buff at rest, but on take-off white wings, rump and tail alter whole appearance. Flight faster, more fluttery than other small herons; rather skulking. *Ad summer* Mostly yellow-buff and pink-buff with black and cream mane; long scapulars cover white areas at rest; bill with black tip, green or blue base. *Ad winter* Browner above, shorter mane blackish and buff; breast streaked grey-brown; bill-base yellower. *Juv* As ad winter, but darker, more streaked; wings mottled brown, exposed by short scapulars. *1st winter* More as ad winter after moult in Jul–Dec, but tinged rusty above; still mottled juv wings. VOICE Harsh *karr*. HABITAT Rank marshes. FOOD Insects, frogs, fish. RANGE 116: most May–Oct, esp SBr. (S Europe, SW Asia, Africa.)

Cattle Egret *Bubulcus ibis* 48–53 cm (*c*20 in). Short-necked, with heavy jowl; mainly white, with pale bill. Wing-beats faster, shallower than other small herons; walks less gracefully with swaying motion, neck hunched or straight; often with cattle; not shy. *Ad summer* Long feathers of crown, breast and mantle pink-buff; bill and legs briefly red. *Ad winter* Crown paler; only ♂ has mantle and chest feathers slightly elongated, tinged cream-buff; bill yellow, legs dark green and yellowish. *Juv* Crown white, then just tinged buff, legs blackish-green; as ♀ winter after moult in Sep–Dec. VOICE Usually silent. HABITAT Grassland, drier marshes. FOOD Mainly insects. RANGE 26: Mar–May, Jul–Jan, esp S/W/EBr, 3 Ir. (Cosmopolitan, inc S Europe.)

American Bittern

ad

ad

juv

Little Bittern

juv

♀

♂

Night Heron

juv

1st year Feb–May

ad

Squacco Heron

ad

ad spring

juv/1st winter

Cattle Egret

ad summer

ad winter

juv

Little Egret *Egretta garzetta* 53–58 cm (*c*22 in). White, with thin neck; long bill and legs black, but feet yellow. Leisurely flight on rounded wings; darts about in shallows. *Ad summer* 2 long head-plumes; elongated aigrettes on mantle and scapulars. *Ad winter* No head-plumes; fewer, shorter aigrettes. *Juv* No aigrettes or long breast-feathers; these appear rudimentarily during moult in Aug–Nov. VOICE Usually silent. HABITAT Lakes, marshes, estuaries. FOOD Largely fish, insects, frogs. RANGE 260: all months, esp Apr–Jul, most coastal S/SEBr, SIr, few NBr. (S Eurasia, Africa, Australia.)

Great White Egret *Egretta alba* 85–100 cm (*c*37 in). Slim, white, with long, angular, sinuous neck, at least partly yellow bill and long blackish legs variously yellow at tops; note possibility of albino Grey Heron (56). Flight more buoyant than Grey Heron, slower than Little Egret; walks sedately. *Ad summer* Elongated scapular aigrettes, loose feathering on chest; bill black with yellow base, lower legs black. *Ad winter* No aigrettes; bill yellow, lower legs blackish-green. *Juv* As ad winter, but no loose chest-feathering until moult in Aug–Nov; lower legs browner. VOICE Usually silent. HABITAT/ FOOD As Little Egret. RANGE 21: Apr–Oct (esp May–Jun), most coastal S/EBr. (Cosmopolitan, inc SE Europe.)

Purple Heron *Ardea purpurea* 75–85 cm (*c*31 in). Slighter, much darker than Grey Heron (56), with thin head, snaky neck. Flight less ponderous, body lifting on downstroke, with drooping neck-bulge, narrower wings, larger feet; skulks. *Ad* Red-buff, chestnut, dark grey and black; ♂ purple gloss on mantle, chestnut (♀ buff) tips to long scapulars. *Juv* Browner above, buffish below, brown streaking; crown mainly chestnut. *Imm* Some longer scapulars and breast-feathers appear in Nov–Apr; more like ad from 2nd autumn, but duller, some chestnut on crown, less black on belly. VOICE Higher *frarnk* than Grey Heron. HABITAT Wetlands with dense reeds. FOOD As Little Egret. RANGE 378: Feb–Nov, esp S/SEBr. (S Eurasia, Africa.)

STORKS (Ciconiidae)

Black Stork *Ciconia nigra* 90–100 cm (*c*38 in). Form as White Stork, but mainly dark. Wing-beats faster; shy. *Ad* Glossy black with white lower underparts; bill and legs scarlet in summer, dark red in winter. *Juv* Browner, less glossy; head to breast dark grey-brown, specked paler; bill and legs grey-green; moults in Feb–Oct. VOICE Silent. HABITAT Marshes with cover. FOOD Fish, frogs, insects. RANGE 46: May–Aug (Mar–Nov), most E/SBr, few NBr. (SW/E Europe, Asia, S Africa.)

White Stork *Ciconia ciconia* 95–105 cm (*c*40 in). Large with long neck, red bill and legs; white with black flight-feathers. Flies with neck extended, slow beats; glides, soars; neck stretched in walking, hunched at rest. *Ad* Black areas glossy; bill and legs bright red. *Juv* Blacks browner, less glossy; bill brown-red with blackish tip, legs dull red; moult in Dec–Aug. VOICE Silent. HABITAT Open grassland, marshes. FOOD Insects, frogs, small mammals. RANGE 269: all months, esp Apr–Jun, well scattered but most E/SBr. (Cent/S Europe, SW Asia, NW Africa.)

IBISES, SPOONBILLS (Threskiornithidae)

Glossy Ibis *Plegadis falcinellus* 50–65 cm (*c*22 in). All-dark, with decurved bill, long neck and legs. Flies with fast beats, glides, looking elongated, flattened; walks sedately with neck in extended curve. *Ad summer* May appear black, but mainly deep chestnut (inc shoulders); purple gloss on upperparts, green on wings. *Ad winter* Head and neck blackish streaked with white, mantle blacker, underparts browner. *Juv* Duller, mainly brown, little gloss; face and foreneck variously white, spotted white, or brown. *Imm* After moult in Aug–Oct, head and neck streaked as ad winter; no chestnut shoulders before 2nd winter. VOICE Harsh croak; usually silent. HABITAT Marshes, mud-flats. FOOD Mainly insects, leeches, molluscs. RANGE Many in past, but only 23 since 1958: all months, esp Aug–Dec, May, widely scattered; some probably escapes, inc 2 in Kent for several years. (Cosmopolitan, inc SE Europe.)

Little Egret

ad summer

juv

Great White Egret

ad summer

juv

Purple Heron

ad

juv

ad

Black Stork

ad

ad

juv

White Stork

ad

juv

ad

Glossy Ibis

ad

juv

ad winter

SWANS, GEESE, DUCKS (Anatidae)

Lesser White-fronted Goose *Anser erythropus* 53–66 cm (21–26 in). Some overlap in size with White-fronted (62), but daintier, neater, with small rounded head and shorter neck, longer folded wings projecting well beyond tail, small bright pink bill, swollen yellow eye-rings; darker above, white on face up to fore-crown over eyes and usually less black barring below (ad). Actions as Greylag (60); flight even more agile than White-fronted; walks/feeds noticeably faster; seen with White-fronted or Bean Geese. *Ad* Extensive white round base of bill on to forecrown; dusky brown above with dull pale bars, paler below with usually few black blotches on belly; bill bright pink with white nail, eye-rings and legs orange-yellow. *Juv/1st winter* Forehead blackish with no white, no black bars below, back almost uniform; bill, eye-rings and legs duller; as ad with moult in Nov–Mar. VOICE As White-fronted, but higher, squeakier. HABITAT Wet grassland.

FOOD Grass. RANGE 107: esp Dec–Mar, most Glos, EBr, SW Scot. (N Eurasia.)

Red-breasted Goose *Branta ruficollis* 51–58 cm (20–23 in). Thick-necked with tiny bill; mainly black with bold white flanks and face-spot, russet cheeks and foreneck outlined in white. Flight agile and walks/feeds fast and daintily; mainly with White-fronted. *Ad* Blacks, whites and russets clearly defined. *Juv/1st winter* Blacks browner, whites less well defined, russets dingier, and browner cheek-patch smaller or even missing; as ad in course of winter moult. VOICE Shrill staccato screech *kee-kwa*. HABITAT Wet grassland. FOOD Grass. RANGE 25: Oct–Mar, esp SBr; some may be escapes. (W Siberia.)

Ruddy Shelduck *Tadorna ferruginea* 61–67 cm (*c*25 in). Thickset, goose-like duck with small blackish bill, dark legs (*cf* Egyptian Goose, 66); orange-brown with paler head, black wing-tips and tail; in flight, striking white forewings, green speculum. Actions as Shelduck (66), but flight

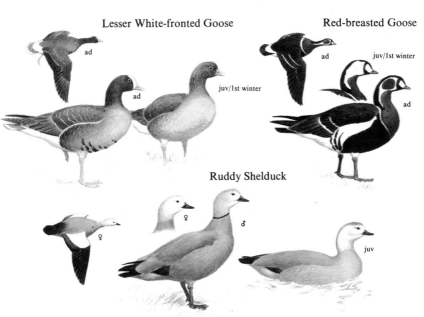

Lesser White-fronted Goose

Red-breasted Goose

ad

juv/1st winter

ad

ad

juv/1st winter

ad

Ruddy Shelduck

♀

♂

juv

heavier; swims stern-high; walks easily, grazing like goose. *Ad ♂* Head yellow-buff, face creamier; black collar (reduced or lost during moult in *c*Jul–Oct); body orange-brown, wing-coverts white or tinged pink/cream. *Ad ♀* Head whiter, no collar. *Juv* As ad ♀, but head pale grey, crown browner (juv ♀ often whiter face); upperparts duller and browner; as ads after moult in Jul–Nov, but ♂ lacks collar until *c*Feb, greater coverts grey till 2nd winter. VOICE Loud nasal honking. HABITAT Lagoons, wet pastures. FOOD Grass, water-plants, invertebrates. RANGE Many: most/?all in last 50 years probably escapes. (NW Africa, S Eurasia.)

American Wigeon *Anas americana* 44–50 cm (*c*18½ in). Shape and actions as Wigeon (70), only ♂ distinctive; head greyish, paler than rufous body (reverse of Wigeon ♂, but not always of ♀); white (not grey) axillaries hard to see; ♀ tertials may be more contrasted. *Ad ♂* White crown, speckled grey head, green patches; body pink-brown, forewings white. *Ad ♀* Greyish head, spotted sepia, reddish body, some whitish on forewings. *Juv* Head more streaked than ♀; as ads by *c*Nov–Mar, but ♂ wings not white till 2nd winter. VOICE ♂ 2–3 soft whistles *whee-whee-whee*. HABITAT/FOOD As Wigeon. RANGE 110: Oct–Apr, widely scattered. (N America.)

Black Duck *Anas rubripes* 53–61 cm (*c*22 in). Shape and actions as Mallard (72); ♂♀ both resemble very dark sooty-brown ♀ Mallard, but with contrasting pale head and white underwings; no white on tail or at front of purple-blue speculum (and less at rear). *Ad ♂* Body sooty-black, and head mainly pale buff finely streaked sepia; bill yellow to olive-yellow, legs orange-red. *Ad ♀* Body almost as dark, but head greyer and more coarsely streaked; bill dull olive-green, legs orange-brown. *Juv* As ad ♀, but browner below, streaked with buff; bill and legs of juv ♀ dusky-olive; as ads by *c*Dec. VOICE/HABITAT/FOOD As Mallard. RANGE 11: all months, esp Oct–Mar, most SBr/SEIr; ♀ hybridised with ♂Mallard, Scilly, 1977–80. (N America.)

American Wigeon

Black Duck

Baikal Teal *Anas formosa* 39–43 cm (*c*16 in). Larger and bulkier than other teals, with high forehead, slender bill. *Ad ♂* Black stripe down cream cheeks, white stripes at front and rear of body. *Ad ♀* Brighter than other ♀ teals, esp contrasted nead with dark-ringed white spot by base of bill, broken supercilia, dark vertical line below eyes sometimes extended into 'bridle' at side of throat; rufous band in front of speculum. *Juv* Much as ad ♀, but line below eye more smudged, wing-band almost white; as ads by late winter. VOICE ♂ deep chuckling *wot-wot* or *proop*; ♀ quacks. HABITAT Lakes, marshes, sometimes on sea. FOOD Seeds, invertebrates. RANGE 3: Sep–Apr, NBr/Ir (others considered to be escapes). (Cent/E Siberia).

Blue-winged Teal *Anas discors* 36–40 cm (*c*15 in). Shape and actions as Garganey (74); forewings pale blue. *Ad ♂* Grey head glossed with magenta, white face-crescent and pied stern; bright blue forewings, white band, green speculum. *Ad ♀* Dark crown/eye-stripes, pale supercilia and

patch by base of bill (*cf* Baikal Teal); whitish under tail; forewings nearly as bright as ♂, but band and speculum much duller. *Juv* Much as ad ♀, but ♂♀ wings differ as ads; as ad by *c*Dec–Mar. VOICE Usually silent: ♂ faint *peep*, ♀ soft quack. HABITAT Marshes, lakes, pools. FOOD Plants, invertebrates. RANGE 95: all months, esp Apr–May, Sep–Oct, widescattered. (N America.)

Ring-necked Duck *Aythya collaris* 40–46 cm (*c*17 in). Like Tufted Duck (80) but flatter forehead, peaked rear crown, no crest, grey (not white) wing-band. *Ad ♂* 2 white bands on grey bill, grey flanks with white peak at front. *Ad ♀* Pale band near bill-tip, white spectacles, variably whitish by bill-base. Swims higher than Tufted; often in shallows, dabbling or up-ending. *Juv* Duller brown above than ad ♀, with ill-defined head/bill markings, and more mottled below; ♂ chest blackish by *c*Sep–Oct, as ad by *c*Apr. VOICE Usually silent; ♀ soft growl in flight. HABITAT Marsh pools, shallow-edged lakes. FOOD Much as

Baikal Teal

Blue-winged Teal

Ring-necked Duck

Tufted. RANGE 128: all months, esp Nov–May, wide-scattered. (N America.)

King Eider *Somateria spectabilis* 53–59 cm (*c*22 in). On average, smaller than Eider (82) and shorter-billed, rounder-headed and neater; ♀/imms distinguished by pointed extension of frontal feathering to above nostrils and well beyond lores. Mixes with Eiders; flight lighter with slightly faster beats. *Ad* ♂ Black back; looks white from front with orange bill/shield and pale mauve-grey crown/nape, and black from rear but for white patches at stern and on forewings in flight. *Eclipse* ♂ Dull black with paler chest; shield smaller, duller. *Ad* ♀ Paler than Eider, more rusty-buff; bolder-spotted scapulars, paler throat, more crescentic flank-marks; sometimes pale round eyes and at corner of bill; expression 'self-satisfied'. *Juv* More like juv Eider, with heavily streaked head, less rusty colour, more barred below, but head/underparts paler; 2 years to ad plumages, with much variation as Eider, but ♂s show grey on crown and black on scapulars in 1st summer, bill much as ad in 2nd winter. VOICE Mostly silent. HABITAT/FOOD Much as Eider. RANGE 159: all months, esp Oct–Jun, most NBr. (Circumpolar Arctic.)

Steller's Eider *Polysticta stelleri* 43–48 cm (*c*18 in). Much smaller than Eider (82), more like dabbling-duck; squarer head, long triangular bill, longish tail; white underwings, speculum much like Mallard, (72). Flight lighter than other eiders, narrower wings making singing noise like weak Goldeneye (88). *Ad* ♂ Mainly white head and orange-buff underparts. *Ad* ♀ Rich dark red-brown with paler cheeks, chest and esp eye-rings. *Eclipse* ♂ Like ad ♀ but hint of ♂ pattern on foreparts; white forewing. *Juv* Like ad ♀, but greyer above fringed buff, paler below; speculum with less white, little blue in ♂ and none in ♀; 2 years to ad plumages. VOICE Vagrants usually silent. HABITAT/FOOD Much as Eider. RANGE 13: all months because of long stays, most NBr. (Arctic Russia east to NW Canada.)

King Eider

Steller's Eider

Harlequin *Histrionicus histrionicus* 41–45 cm (*c*17 in). Small dark sea-duck with short bluish bill, high forehead, pointed tail; plain-winged ♀/imm confusable with imm Long-tailed Duck (84), though more uniformly dark with usually 3 light head-patches, but even harlequin-patterned ♂ mainly blackish at distance. Flight fast, swinging from side to side; swims buoy-antly with jerking head, tail often cocked (or slowly raised and lowered); dives in rough water, also plunges in from wing; rarely with other ducks. *Ad* ♂ Dark grey-blue with bizarre black-edged white marks on head, breast, scapulars, wings and stern, and rufous crown-bands, chestnut flanks. *Ad* ♀ Dark slate to sooty-brown with white circle behind eyes, 2 patches in front (latter mottled brown when new, merge as whitish face/throat when worn); belly only mottled whitish. *Juv* As ♀, but paler, more olive-brown above; colours variably like ads on head and later upper-parts/ flanks during Sep–May, but ♂ still duller in 1st summer with smaller white patches, mottled belly, plain juv wings.

VOICE Usually silent; ♂ piping whistle, ♀ harsh *ek-ek-ek*. HABITAT Surf off rocks. FOOD Molluscs, crustaceans. RANGE 9: esp Dec–Feb (1 pair Jan–May), NBr. (Iceland, Greenland, N America, NE Asia.)

Surf Scoter *Melanitta perspicillata* 51–56 cm (*c*21 in). Resembles Velvet Scoter (86), but Eider-like profile with deeper, less knobbed bill (♂'s multicoloured), more white/whitish on flatter head, frontal feathers to near nostrils; no white in wings, underwings dark. *Ad* ♂ Dull black but for red-orange and white bill with large black patch near base, white tri-angles on forehead and nape (latter lost during eclipse). *Ad* ♀ Sooty-brown with 2 whitish patches on head-sides (as ♀ Velvet Scoter), clearer in worn plumage and mottled brown after moult in *c*Aug–Nov; also variably distinct whitish nape-patch. *Juv* As ♀, but greyer-brown, with less clear buffish patches on head-sides, no white on nape, mottled whitish or almost white belly; variably as ads, but still mottled belly, after moult in *c*Nov–May; ♂ then

Harlequin

Surf Scoter

white on nape but not forehead, bill as ad from cMar. HABITAT/FOOD As Velvet Scoter. RANGE 166: all months (esp Sep–Apr), most NBr, few Ir/SEBr. (N America.)

Bufflehead *Bucephala albeola* 33–38 cm (c14 in). Like tiny Teal-sized Goldeneye (88) with small bill, puffy head, dark eyes; ♂ has large white bonnet on glossy head, ♀/imm white oblong on rear cheeks and only small white wing-patch in flight. Restless; springs easily from water; no wing-noise in flight. *Ad* ♂ Black and much white, as ♂ Goldeneye, but head glossed green, purple and bronze, with wide white wedge from below eyes over hindcrown; outer scapulars more evenly white, stern mostly grey. *Ad* ♀ Darker above but whiter chest than ♀ Goldeneye; white patch on slaty head. *Juv* Much as ♀; ♂ pale greyish uppertail-coverts from Aug–Sep, white mottling on scapulars/flanks from Oct–Nov and some ad plumage in Mar–Jun, rarely full but for juv wings. HABITAT/FOOD As Goldeneye. RANGE 6: Jan–Mar (Jun), NW/SW/EBr. (N America.)

Hooded Merganser *Mergus cucullatus* 42–48 cm (c17½ in). Smaller, shorter-bodied than Red-breasted Merganser (90), with shorter thin bill and larger head, ♂ mainly black and white with erectile fan crest, ♀/imm darker than Red-breasted (esp bill, head, neck, upperparts) with bushy crest; both much less white (mainly striped) on inner wings. Flight faster, more agile; walks more easily, with body horizontal; secretive; rarely with other ducks. *Ad* ♂ Head and back black with huge white patch behind eyes (forming black-edged rounded cockade when oblong crest raised); breast white with 2 black sidebands, vermiculated flanks buff shading to rufous; bill black. *Ad* ♀ Head dark grey-brown with tawny crest, whitish throat; blackish above, greyish and buff below with white belly; bill black, edged orange. *Juv* As ♀ but browner above, crest shorter, still less white on wings, bill grey with pinkish edges; partial ad plumage in 1st year. HABITAT Shallow wooded lakes, marsh pools. FOOD Fish, invertebrates. RANGE 5: Dec–Jan, most Ir. (N America.)

Bufflehead

Hooded Merganser

KITES, HARRIERS, ETC (Accipitridae)

Black Kite *Milvus migrans* 53–59 cm (*c*22 in). More compact than Red Kite (94) with shorter, less forked tail (often straight-ended when spread) and relatively broader wings similarly bowed forward; darker, browner, with dark-streaked greyish head, duller pale panel on upper wing-coverts, less contrasting underwing-patches (clearer on juv) and brown tail. Flight as Red Kite, but less graceful; likewise glides on slightly arched wings (*cf* dark Marsh Harrier, 94). *Ad* Grey-brown to rufous below, with indistinct paler area at base of primaries. *Juv* Head paler, with darker ear-coverts; upperwing panel more obvious; brighter and cream-streaked below, with paler belly and tail-base (latter can look reddish against light like dull Red Kite), clearer whitish area at base of primaries; as ad after 1st summer moult. HABITAT Open country, by water. FOOD Carrion, rodents, insects, frogs, birds. RANGE 43: esp Apr–Jun, also Jul–Nov, most SE/NEBr. (Eurasia, Africa.)

White-tailed Eagle *Haliaeetus albicilla* 69–91 cm (27–36 in). Bulky with huge bill (*cf* Golden, 102); in flight, head and short wedge-shaped tail protrude equally from long, broad, rectangular wings, giving 'flying door' appearance; ad pale head and white tail, juv mainly dark. Flight rather clumsy with shallow beats, but soars effortlessly with wings almost flat; often hunts low over ground or water; snatches prey from surface or plunges in; perches on rocks, trees or hunched motionless on ground. *Ad* Brown, scaled paler, with yellow bill, buffish head, dark flight-feathers, white tail; wing-coverts/body wear lighter. *Juv* Dark brown, mottled rufous, with grey-black bill, rustier breast and patch on mid wings above, whitish marks on 'armpits' and greater coverts below, variably whitish-centred tail-feathers; mottled whitish above and below from 1st summer/2nd winter; all brown with yellow bill and mottled tail from *c*4th year (not full ad until *c*8th). HABITAT Rocky coasts, estuaries. FOOD Fish, birds, mammals, carrion.

RANGE Bred to *c*1916 (esp NBr, Ir); then vagrant, most Oct–Apr E/SBr; attempted reintroductions Fair Isle (1968), Rhum (since 1975). (N Eurasia to Greenland.)

Pallid Harrier *Circus macrourus* 41–48 cm (16–19 in), ♂ smaller than ♀. Shape as Montagu's (96), but ♂ slimmer, much paler, wing-tips black-wedged; ♀/juv separated from Montagu's by head-pattern. ♂ flight more buoyant, almost tern-like. *Ad ♂* Pale grey above, white below; narrow black wedge on primaries. *Ad ♀/juv* Very like Montagu's (juv likewise plain below), but clear black eye-stripes, whitish collar behind dark crescent on ear-coverts, emphasised on juv by dark neck-patches. HABITAT Grasslands. FOOD Voles, birds. RANGE 3: Apr–May, Oct, NE/SBr. (E Europe, SW Asia.)

FALCONS (Falconidae)

Gyrfalcon *Falco rusticolus* 50–62 cm (20–24 in). Larger/stouter than Peregrine (106) with longer broader tail, broader-based and blunter wings; varies from dark grey-brown heavily spotted/barred or streaked below, through range of dark/light grey and whitish intermediates with heavy pale scaling above and variable dark markings below, to largely white. Flight slower than Peregrine with shallower beats; glides and soars on level or slightly bowed wings; hunts low over ground, also stoops like Peregrine. *Darkest ad* Dark grey-brown above, with dark-streaked creamy forehead and often nape, obscure moustaches; below, densely spotted and barred body/wing-coverts contrast with lightly marked flight-feathers/tail, pale area at base of dark-tipped primaries. *Whitest ad* All white but for dark wing-tips and scattered blackish Vs, spots or bars above, sometimes also on flanks. *Juvs* As ads, but marks mainly streaks, cere/legs blue-grey to greenish (not yellow); darkest are heavily streaked below, clearer moustaches; whitest with brownish streaks, sparser below. HABITAT Rocky coasts, fells, open country. FOOD Birds, mammals. RANGE Many (61 since 1958): Sep–May, scattered, esp N/SWBr (most white). (Circumpolar Arctic.)

Black Kite

juv

ad

ad

White-tailed Eagle

ad

juv

Pallid Harrier

♂

♀

Gyrfalcon

dark ad

grey ad

white ad

Lesser Kestrel *Falco naumanni* 29–32 cm (*c*12 in). Very like Kestrel (104), but slimmer with narrower wings, thinner and often wedge-tipped tail; ♂ bluer head and tail, also wing-coverts, whiter below, no moustaches, unspotted back, but ♀ much as ♀ Kestrel; claws pale brown to whitish (not black). Flight looser, shallower, more winnowing; hovers much less, hawks insects far more. *Ad* ♂ Crown/hindneck and tail grey-blue, mantle/wing-coverts plain chestnut but outer coverts grey-blue; cream to pink-buff below, plain or lightly spotted, but underwings white, sometimes spotted, with darker tips and trailing edges. *Ad* ♀ As ♀ Kestrel, but narrower bars above, obscurer moustaches, paler and less spotted below. *Juv* As ad ♀; less yellow on bill. *1st year* ♂ As ad ♂ with moult in Oct–May, but still worn juv flight-feathers and odd spots/bars above. HABITAT Open country. FOOD Insects. RANGE 18: Feb–May, Jul–Nov, most S/EBr. (S Europe, Asia, NW Africa.)

American Kestrel *Falco sparverius* 23–28 cm (9–11 in). Smaller than Merlin (104), with relatively longer tail, shorter thinner wings; 3 black strips on white and buff sides of slate-capped head with rufous central crown; otherwise rufous above barred black, but ♂ plain tail with black band, grey-blue wings. Flight fast, graceful; habitually hovers, soars (showing translucent spots along tips of flight-feathers); perches on trees, wires, buildings, often jerking tail. *Ad* ♂ Narrowly barred above, tail with black band, white tip and barred white edges; wing-coverts grey-blue, spotted black; breast/flanks pink-buff, lightly spotted. *Ad* ♀ Head duller, whole upperparts browner-rufous and more barred; underparts buff, streaked rufous. *Juvs* Much as ads, but far paler yellowish legs/cere; ♂ browner crown-patch, more barred tail, streaked breast; moults Sep–Oct, but worn juv tail until 1st summer. HABITAT Open country. FOOD Insects, mice, birds. RANGE 2: May–Jun, Shetland/Cornwall. (N/S America.)

Red-footed Falcon *Falco vespertinus* 28–31 cm (*c*11½ in). Shape as small Hobby (106),

with broader-based wings, longer tail; ♂ dark grey with chestnut 'trousers', red legs; ♀ grey and barred above, with rufous-buff crown/underparts. Flight as Hobby, but faster beats; glides, soars, hawks insects, hovers; perches on trees, wires, bushes, ground; often crepuscular. *Ad* ♂ Dark grey, with paler flight-feathers and underbody, chestnut thighs/undertail-coverts; legs/cere/eye-rings red. *Ad* ♀ Grey above, barred blackish, inc tail, but head/ underparts rufous-buff with cream throat, blackish eye-patches/moustaches; flight-feathers dark above, barred below; legs/ cere/eye-rings orange. *Juv* Browner than ♀ above with rufous fringes, streaked crown, whitish half-collar, stronger moustaches; below, creamier and more streaked, broad dark trailing edge to wings; legs/cere/eye-rings yellow. *1st summer* ♂ Grey above with rufous nape, worn brown juv flight-feathers and barred tail-sides; variably rufous to grey below; flight-feathers pied in moult in 2nd autumn. HABITAT Open country, trees. FOOD Insects. RANGE 327: mainly Apr–Oct (esp May–Jun), mostly S/EBr. (E Europe, Asia.)

Eleonora's Falcon *Falco eleonorae* 35–41 cm (*c*15 in). Slim, like large Hobby (106) with even longer narrower wings, longer tail (both less clear on juv); all blackish-grey (*cf* ♂ Red-footed), or rufous-buff below with heavy streaks whitish throat (*cf* Hobby), always underwing-coverts darker than flight-feathers. Flight fast, agile, or with flatter, slower beats; soars, stoops as Peregrine (106), hawks insects as Hobby; perches on rocks, trees. *Dark ad* Blackish-slate above (♀ browner), dark grey-brown below with paler-based flight-feathers/tail; cere bluish-yellow (♂) or blue (♀), legs yellow. *Pale ad* Differs mainly in rufous underbody streaked blackish, with cream throat/lower cheeks, black moustaches. *Juvs* Browner than ads, scaled cream/rufous above, tail barred, cere blue, legs greenish; dark form also barred flanks/undertail-coverts; pale form brownish below with broader streaks, white tail-coverts. HABITAT Usually sea-cliffs. FOOD Insects, birds. RANGE 1: Aug, Merseyside. (Mediterranean, NW Africa.)

Lesser Kestrel

American Kestrel

♀

♂

♀

♂

Red-footed Falcon

♂

♀

juv

Eleonora's Falcon

light ad

dark ad

juv

RAILS, CRAKES, GALLINULES (Rallidae)

Sora *Porzana carolina* 20–23 cm (*c*8½ in). Resembles Spotted Crake (116), but has longer neck, shorter wings, yellow bill (no red) with long nostrils; black centre to plain tawny crown, more uniform chest and wing-coverts, whiter long undertail-coverts; ad also has black face/throat, white speck behind eyes; juv black lores, plain buff supercilia and whitish throat. More erect than Spotted Crake; feeds more in open. ♂ *summer* Bold black face/throat; usually only greater coverts speckled. ♂ *winter* After moult in Jul–Sep, black throat mottled grey, grey chest with white fringes (not spots). *Ad* ♀ Usually black more restricted and grey supercilia extending across forehead, wing-coverts more speckled. *Juv* Buff supercilia and underparts, whitish throat and belly, flanks less strongly barred; as ad winter after variable moult in *c*Aug–Feb, but black throat narrower and more mottled (esp ♀), less grey below, bill greener as juv. VOICE Sharp *keek*. HABITAT/FOOD As Spotted Crake, but winters more in salt-marshes. RANGE 6: Sep–Nov, Apr; only 1 since 1920 (Scilly 1973). (N America.)

Little Crake *Porzana parva* 18–20 cm (*c*7½ in). Slender, with longer neck, wings, tail and legs than Baillon's; olive-brown above with indistinct whitish streaks and mostly uniform wing-coverts, grey or buff below with boldly barred undertail but only faint narrow flank-bars, red-based bill, usually green legs. *Ad* ♂ Face and underparts slate-grey, faint white bars on lower flanks; bill pale green with red base. *Ad* ♀ Face pale grey, throat whitish, underparts creamy-buff, faint white bars on greyish flanks; bill as ♂. *Juv* Face creamy-white, underparts creamy-buff, variably barred grey and buff on chest (or chest-sides) and flanks; scapulars and wing-coverts more marked white than ad; bill olive with pinkish gape; much as ads after variable moult in *c*Sep–Jan, but ♂ browner on flanks/belly, ♀ paler buff on belly. VOICE Sharp explosive squawks; ♂ song repeated barking *kwek* dropping into

Sora

Little Crake

juv

juv

ad

♀ winter

♂ summer

guttural ending, ♀ shriller and accelerating into trill. HABITAT/FOOD Much as Spotted Crake (116). RANGE 94: all months, esp Mar–May, Aug–Nov, most E/SBr, also SWIr, NBr. (Cent/E Europe, W Asia.)

Baillon's Crake *Porzana pusilla* 17–18.5 cm (*c*7 in). Rounded, with short neck, wings, tail and legs; ♂♀ resemble ♂ Little Crake, but more rufous above with many small white spots/streaks outlined in black (also on wing-coverts), flanks boldly barred as undertail, bill plain green, legs usually brownish to green-grey. Flight weaker, more fluttering than other crakes. *Ad* Face and underparts slate-blue, black and white bars on lower flanks/belly, bill dark green; ♀ throat often paler grey in summer and whitish in winter (when ♂ paler grey), sometimes brown streak behind eyes. *Juv* Face rufous-buff; chest and upper flanks barred brown and whitish-buff, lower flanks blackish and white; bill olive-brown; much as ads after variable moult in *c*Sep–Jan. VOICE Resembles Little Crake, but song repeated rasping or creaking *trrrrr-trrrrr*. HABITAT/FOOD As Little Crake. RANGE Many before 1900, even nested; only 5 Br since 1958: Feb, May–Jun. (Eurasia, Africa, Australasia.)

American Purple Gallinule *Porphyrula martinica* 31–35 cm (*c*13 in). Size/actions as Moorhen (118), but deeper bill, longer neck and legs; ad purple-blue and green, juv sandier below than juv Moorhen; no dark centre to white undertail, or white/buff line on flanks. *Ad* Head/underparts purple-blue, mantle/wings bronze-green, with some light blue on hindneck and wings; bill red with yellow tip, shield blue-white, legs yellow. *Juv* Olive-brown above but green-tinged mantle/wings, and pale buff to cream below; bill greenish with red-brown base, shield grey-brown, legs green-brown to yellowish; as ad after variable moult in *c*Sep–Mar. HABITAT/FOOD Much as Moorhen. RANGE 1: Nov, Scilly. (Americas north to S Carolina.) NOTE Old World **Purple Gallinule** *Porphyrio porphyrio* sometimes escapes, but far larger with heavy red bill and legs.

Baillon's Crake

American Purple Gallinule

juv

♂ summer

juv–1st winter

ad

CRANES (Gruidae)

Crane *Grus grus* 106–118 cm (*c*44 in). Tall,
stately, with shortish bill, long neck and
legs, long tertials drooping over tail; grey
(browner-grey with wear) but for black and
white head with obscure bare red patch,
blackish flight-feathers and 'tail' (imm all
brownish). Flight strong, with slow beats
of rectangular wings, neck/legs extended;
soars like eagle; flocks fly in Vs or lines;
sedate walk with long strides, body level,
neck curved; often stands more upright;
shy. *Ad* Head/upper neck black with white
curve, red crown-patch. *Juv/1st winter*
Brown to rufous head and mottling on
darker body; shorter 'tail'. VOICE Short
rolling *krroo*; juvs pipe. HABITAT Marshes,
fields. FOOD Esp plant material. RANGE
775 + since 1958 (500 + in 1963, SBr), all
months, esp Mar–Jun, Aug–Nov, widely
scattered; bred Br/?Ir until *c*1600.
(N/Cent Eurasia.) NOTE **Sandhill Crane**
G. canadensis has occurred (1905, 1981);
other species escape, esp Sarus *G. anti-
gone* and Demoiselle *Anthropoides virgo*.

BUSTARDS (Otididae)

Little Bustard *Tetrax tetrax* 41–45 cm
(*c*17 in). Compact, duck-sized, with
shortish neck; sandy-brown above, finely
marked with black; in flight, rounded
wings mainly white with black tips and
primary-coverts (like giant Snow Bunting). Flight fast, often high, with shallow
beats of bowed wings, also gliding grouse-
like with occasional flicks; ♂'s wings
whistle; walks, runs, crouches in cover
with neck extended; rises sharply with
wing-rattle; shy/skulking. ♂ *summer*
Slate-blue cheeks/throat; black neck with
2 white bands. ♂ *winter* Fine wavy black
bars above; head/neck buff, streaked and
barred black; breast/belly white, few black
spots on flanks. *Ad* ♀ As ♂ winter, but
coarse bars above, inc secondaries; more
buff and barred on breast/flanks. *Juv/1st
winter* As ♀, but black of wings mottled
buff, more black marks on secondaries;
after moult in Mar–Apr, 1st summer ♂
much as winter ♂. VOICE Grunt when
flushed. HABITAT Grassland, crops. FOOD

Crane   Little Bustard

ad

juv/1st winter

ad

♀

♂ summe

♀

Plants, invertebrates. RANGE *c*100 (only 10 since 1958): all months, esp Oct–Jan, esp E/SBr. (S Europe, W Asia, NW Africa.)

Houbara Bustard *Chlamydotis undulata* 51–56 cm (*c*25 in). Goose-sized; longish neck, long tail, long rather narrow and pointed wings with little white (like huge Stone-curlew); sandy-buff, above, finely marked with black; grey foreneck, long black and white tufts on neck-sides. Flight low; slow, rather flicked wing-beats; walks sedately, or runs with short steps and body horizontal. *Ad ♂* Black-tipped white crest, whitish nape, fine buff and black tips on grey throat. *Ad ♀* Shorter mainly black crest, buff nape, stronger tips on throat. *1st winter* Much as ad ♀, but imm ♀ has tail barred brown (not slate), no crest; both ♂♀ tend to show brown on white tail-tips, rufous tinge at base of black on outer primaries, white mottling at tips. HABITAT Deserts, steppes; vagrants in fields. FOOD Seeds, plants, invertebrates. RANGE 5: Oct–Dec, EBr (last Suffolk 1962). (Asia, N Africa.)

Great Bustard *Otis tarda* ♂ 95–105 cm (*c*40 in), ♀ 75–85 cm (*c*31½ in). Swan- to goose-sized, turkey-shaped, stout, deep-chested, with long thick neck, longish tail, and very long white and black spread-tipped wings, but ♀ slighter; rufous above boldly marked with black, white below, head grey. Flight powerful with slow, shallow beats of bowed wings; very shy. *♂ summer* Head grey, throat and long side-whiskers white, chest rufous marked with black. *♂ winter* Head and throat grey, short side-whiskers whitish, only sides of chest rufous and black. *♀ summer* Head grey, very short side-whiskers, foreneck tinged buff; more dark marks on white of wings than ♂. *♀ winter* Rufous and black bars on crown, no side-whiskers, foreneck grey. *1st year* Much as small winter ♀, but narrow pointed outer primaries with buff tips, mottling on secondaries and greater coverts. HABITAT Grassland, crops. FOOD Plants, insects, voles. RANGE 10 since 1958: Jan–May, Aug, esp EBr; bred Br to 19th century; recent attempt at reintroduction (Wilts). (Cent/S Eurasia.)

Houbara Bustard   Great Bustard

STILTS, AVOCETS (Recurvirostridae)

Black-winged Stilt *Himantopus himantopus*
36–40 cm (*c*15 in). Slender, long-necked,
with needle-bill, thin triangular wings,
extraordinarily long pink legs; white,
with dark back and wings. Flight direct,
usually low, with neck normally drawn in,
legs trailing; often glides, esp before
alighting when legs dangle as rudders or
brakes; walks delicately with long strides,
neck hunched or extended, and wades
deeply; bends legs to pick up food and
even more to spring into air; bobs head to
and fro when suspicious; often rests on
one leg. *Ad* ♂ Mantle glossy black; crown/
nape black or mainly white in summer,
grey-brown in winter. *Ad* ♀ Mantle dark
brown against glossy black wings; crown/
nape usually mottled dusky. *Juv* All upperparts marked with buff, flight-feathers
mostly white-tipped; legs pink-grey. *1st
winter* After moult in Jul–Feb, as ad ♀,
but flight-feathers white-tipped (sometimes also 1st summer), wing-coverts buff-
fringed. VOICE Shrill *kyik-kyik-kyik*.
HABITAT Wet marshes, lagoons. FOOD
Insects. RANGE 163: Apr–Feb, esp Apr–
Jun, Aug–Sep, most SBr; 2 pairs bred
in Notts in 1945. (S Eurasia, Africa,
Australiasia, N/S America.)

COURSERS, PRATINCOLES (Glareolidae)

Cream-coloured Courser *Cursorius cursor*
22–24 cm (*c*9 in). Slim, plover-like, with
short decurved dark bill, long creamy legs,
short tail, surprisingly large wings; mainly
sandy, but white supercilia and black eye-
stripes meeting on nape, black underwings and outer upperwings, white-tipped
secondaries and tail. Flight direct, fast;
runs fast with pauses, crouches to hide.
Ad Uniform sandy above, breast greyer;
head-marks white and black, grey on rear
crown. *Juv* More buff, barred brown above,
spotted on breast; head-marks cream and
brownish; legs greyer. *1st winter* More as
ad after moult in May–Nov, but still juv
buff-tipped primaries, usually some juv
coverts. VOICE Harsh *praak-praak*.
HABITAT Deserts; vagrants in dunes, fields.
FOOD Insects. RANGE 32: Sep–Dec, esp
Oct, widely scattered. (SW Asia, Africa.)

Collared Pratincole *Glareola pratincola*
24–27 cm (*c*10 in). Rather tern-like wader
with long pointed wings, deep-forked tail,
short legs, stubby bill and red gape-patch;
brown above, with white rump, white-
tipped secondaries, chestnut underwings
(not easy to see). Flight buoyant, erratic,
tern-like, hawking insects; walks or runs
like plover; often crepuscular. *Ad summer*
Uniform brown above, black line round
creamy throat; ♂ lores black, ♀ olive-
brown. *Ad winter* Streaked head with ill-
defined border of streaks round throat.
Juv Mottled buff and blackish above,
heavily streaked head and throat-border,
shorter tail; much as ad after moult in
Aug–Nov, but buff-tipped inner secondaries. VOICE Tern-like *kik* or *kirrikik
kit-ik*. HABITAT Dry mud, grass, esp near
water. FOOD Insects. RANGE 61 + of 88
pratincoles: most May–Jul (Feb–Nov),
scattered. (S Europe, SW Asia, Africa.)

Black-winged Pratincole *Glareola nord-
manni* 24–27 cm (*c*10 in). As Collared, but
darker above (little contrast between
coverts and flight-feathers), secondaries
not white-tipped, underwings black, less
red on gape. Plumage sequence similar;
black lores in spring, far more on ♂.
RANGE 16 + (see above): Aug–Sep (May–
Sep), esp SBr. (S Russia, W Asia.)

TYPICAL WADERS (Scolopacidae)

Wilson's Phalarope *Phalaropus tricolor*
22–26 cm (*c*9½ in), ♂ smaller than ♀.
Larger than other phalaropes (146), with
longer needle-bill, longer black (summer)
or yellowish legs; very pale in winter, no
wing-bar but white rump; dark and chestnut down neck-sides on to back in summer.
Often runs; swims less. ♂ *summer* Brown
or grey-brown above; dark brown eye-
stripes and dull cinnamon on neck and
back. ♀ *summer* Blue-grey above; black
eye-stripes extend into chestnut on back.
Ad winter Pale grey above. *1st winter* By
end Aug/Sep, grey above with many buff
fringes; later, as ad winter (sometimes
through 1st summer). VOICE Low croak.
HABITAT Marsh, mud. FOOD Invertebrates.
RANGE 134: May–Nov (esp Aug–Oct), all
since 1954, widely scattered. (N America.)

Black-winged Stilt

♂ summer

juv

ad

Cream-coloured Courser

ad

ad

1st winter

Wilson's Phalarope

1st winter

♂ summer

♀ summer

1st winter

Black-winged Pratincole

ad

juv

♂ summer

Collared Pratincole

ad

♂ summer

PLOVERS (Charadriidae)

Semipalmated Plover *Charadrius semi-palmatus* 17–19 cm (*c*7 in). Very like Ringed Plover (122), but neater, slimmer, with stubbier bill, smaller rounded head; webbing both sides of middle toes (not just outer); breast-band and white collar narrower, wing-bar shorter and less distinct (esp at base), head-markings less clear, secondaries darker, legs duller; call distinct. Differs also as follows. *Ad* Less white behind eyes (sometimes almost missing in summer), bill-base with less orange; in winter, mask/breast-band always largely brown. *Juv/1st winter* Supercilia more obscure, buff edges to wing-coverts clearer, bill blackish with little yellow-pink at base, legs duller greenish to yellowish-flesh. VOICE Plaintive *chur-wit*, piping *chip*. RANGE 1: Oct–Nov, Scilly. (N America.)

Killdeer *Charadrius vociferus* 23–25 cm (*c*9½ in). Much larger than Ringed Plover (122) with longer black bill, smaller head, long wedge-tail, longer legs; 2 black chest-bands, orange rump, black on tail, bold white wing-bar. *1st winter* Till *c*Jan some scapulars/inner medians fringed pale (ad rufous). VOICE Loud repeated *killdea*. HABITAT Grass or ploughed fields, gravel pits, reservoirs, coasts. FOOD Insects, crustaceans. RANGE 33: Nov–Mar, widely scattered. (N/S America.)

Greater Sand Plover *Charadrius leschenaultii* 22–24 cm (*c*9 in). Thickset, hunched, with heavy bill, biggish head, longish (usually grey) legs; brown and white, with white wing-bar and tail-sides, brownish patches at breast-sides in winter, no white collar. *Ad summer* Black forecrown/mask, rufous nape and breast-band; ♀ often duller. *Ad winter* Grey-brown above, pale forehead and supercilia; brown breast-patches, often joined by thin line. *1st winter* As ad, but inner medians fringed buff; breast-patches warmer buff. VOICE Short trilling *chirrirrip*. HABITAT Mud/sand by fresh or salt water. FOOD Invertebrates. RANGE 3: Nov–Feb, Jun, Sussex/Avon/Orkney. (S Asia.)

Lesser Golden Plover *Pluvialis dominica* 23–25 cm (*c*9½ in). Smaller, slighter than Golden Plover (124), with longer bill and legs, narrower wings extending beyond tail; underwings buff-grey. *Ad summer* Black below to flanks/undertail, ♀ with some white speckling. *Ad winter* American race (*P.d. dominica*) greyer and Asiatic race (*P.d. fulva*) more buff, both lightly mottled on breast, with blackish crown and clearer supercilia (*cf* winter Dotterel, 126). *Juv/1st winter* As ad, but brown-speckled belly/flanks to at least Dec, more marked on American race; Asiatic race much yellower on head and body. VOICE Flight-call soft *quee*, whistled *queedel-oo*. HABITAT Fields, marshes, mud. RANGE 66: Apr–Feb (esp Sep–Oct), scattered, most SIr, SW/EBr. (N America, NE Asia.)

Sociable Plover *Chettusia gregaria* 28–31 cm (*c*11½ in). Size of Lapwing (126), but longer black bill and legs, less rounded narrower wings; grey-brown, with dark cap, pale supercilia meeting on nape, white tail with black patch near tip, white secondaries, black primaries. *Ad summer* Black crown, white supercilia; ♂ belly black and chestnut, ♀'s often greyer and speckled white. *Ad winter* With moult in Jun–Nov, crown brown, supercilia buff, breast mottled, belly white. *Juv/1st winter* Buff fringes above (many kept to spring) and breast distinctly streaked till *c*Nov. VOICE Short whistle, harsh *etch-etch-etch*. HABITAT Grassy/sandy areas, near water. FOOD Insects. RANGE 24: Jul–May, esp Oct, E/SBr. (SE Russia, W/Cent Asia.)

White-tailed Plover *Chettusia leucura* 26–28 cm (*c*10¾ in). Slimmer than Sociable, longer legs yellow; grey-brown above, pale face; white belly, tail and black-edged band from secondaries to base of primaries. Elegant, stretches neck when alert; stoops on long legs. *Ad* Breast rufous and grey; mantle/coverts tinged mauve, belly pinkish. *Juv* Blotched black and buff above; breast browner. *1st winter* As ad from *c*Oct, but inner medians buff-fringed. VOICE Loud *kee-wik*. HABITAT Marshy shallows. FOOD Insects. RANGE 2: Jul, Warwicks/Dorset. (SW/Cent Asia.)

Semipalmated
Plover

juv/1st winter

♂ summer

Killdeer

ad

Greater Sand Plover

1st winter

♂ summer

Lesser Golden Plover

dominica
juv

dominica
ad summer-winter

dominica
♂ summer

Sociable Plover

juv/1st winter

juv

White-tailed Plover

ad

♂ summer

TYPICAL WADERS (Scolopacidae)

Broad-billed Sandpiper *Limicola falcinellus* 16–17 cm (*c*6½ in). Smaller than Dunlin (132), with long broad kink-tipped bill, abrupt forehead, shorter legs looking set far back; summer/juv very dark above with double supercilia; in winter, blackish shoulders (*cf* Sanderling, 128), at least traces of head-pattern, often green tinge to dark legs and paler-based bill. Very sluggish. *Ad summer* By May, blackish above with bold buff/whitish fringes, much blacker with wear; white below with heavy streaks on throat/chest, arrows on flanks. *Ad winter* With moult in Aug–Jan, grey-brown above, coverts fringed white, lessers blackish; double supercilia often still clear; breast thinly streaked grey-brown. *Juv* As ad summer above, but coverts edged pale buff, cheeks/breast buffish with faint brown streaks; as ad winter after moult in *c*Sep–Dec, but buff-fringed inner medians. VOICE Dry trilled *tirrreek*. HABITAT Saltmarshes, creeks, pools. RANGE 65: May–Sep, also Oct–Nov, scattered, esp E/SBr. (N Eurasia.)

Semipalmated Sandpiper *Calidris pusilla* 14–15.5 cm (*c*5¾ in). Very like Little Stint (128), but slightly bulkier, with blunter-tipped and stouter-based bill, and partly webbed toes; much overlap in pattern and only juv reliably separable by colour (rather drab above with less chestnut, no whitish V lines). Plumage sequence similar. VOICE Low husky *chirrp*. RANGE 27: Jul–Dec, esp SWIr/SWBr. (N America.)

Western Sandpiper *Calidris mauri* 15.5–17 cm (*c*6½ in). Larger than Little Stint (128), with character more of small Dunlin (132), including usually longer, more droop-tipped and stouter-based bill, longer-looking legs; much like Semi-palmated, even to partly webbed toes, but summer/juv more rufous above (often partly retained into winter on head/scapulars) and stronger-streaked below, with broader supercilia. Plumage sequence similar. Wades much more than stints. VOICE High thin *cheet*. RANGE 6: most Jul–Oct, SIr/SBr. (N America, NE Asia.)

Least Sandpiper *Calidris minutilla* 13.5–14.5 cm (*c*5½ in). Smaller than Little Stint (128) with thinner bill, smaller squarer head, shorter wings, shorter and usually greenish or yellowish legs (*cf* Temminck's, 128); clearer breast-band of brown streaks, summer/juv much darker. HABITAT Grassy marshes, pools, less on open mud. VOICE High grating *kreeet*. RANGE 23: most Aug–Oct, esp Ir, WBr. (N America.)

White-rumped Sandpiper *Calidris fusci-collis* 16–18 cm (*c*6¾ in). Slim with short straight bill, long wings projecting beyond tail, short legs, horizontal stance; white above tail, very faint wing-bar (*cf* Curlew Sandpiper, 132). *Ad summer* Black-brown above streaked with chestnut, buff, grey and whitish; white below with brown-streaked breast/flanks. *Ad winter* After moult in *c*Aug–Oct, grey-brown above and on streaked breast, coverts still fringed whitish. *Juv* As ad summer, but bolder-marked above with more whitish fringes; coverts broadly fringed buff and whitish; streaked breast/flanks tinged grey-buff; much as ad winter with moult in Sep–Jan, but mantle more mixed with brown, inner medians fringed buff. VOICE Thin squeaky *jeet*. HABITAT Mud-flats, beaches, lagoons, marshy pools. RANGE 199: most months, esp Aug–Nov, widely scattered, most SIr, SW/EBr. (N America.)

Baird's Sandpiper *Calidris bairdii* 17–19 cm (*c*7 in). Shape and stance as White-rumped Sandpiper (only similar wader with wings projecting well beyond tail; distinctively buffish head/breast, bold supercilia, blotched or scaled mantle, dark rump/uppertail, short thin wing-bar. *Ad summer* Blackish and buff blotches on mantle; coverts grey-brown fringed pale buff. *Ad winter* With moult in *c*Aug–Oct, mottled grey-brown and buff above; coverts fringed whitish. *Juv* Blackish mantle scaled whitish; coverts fringed tawny; breast brighter buff, less streaks; as ad winter by *c*Nov, but inner medians still fringed tawny. VOICE Trilled *krreep*. HABITAT Stony and grassy pools. RANGE 88: Aug–Oct (May–Nov), scattered, most SIr, SW/EBr. (N America, NE Asia.)

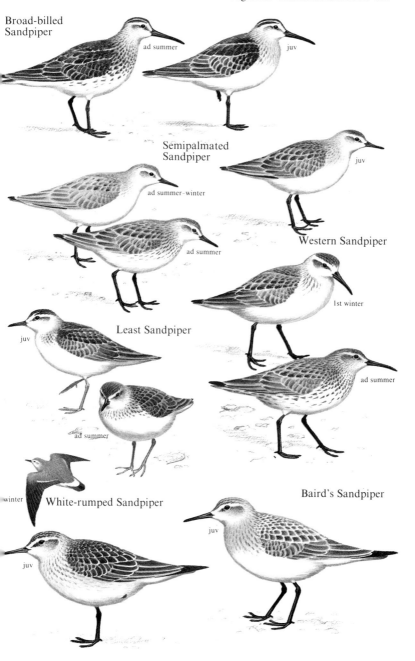

Broad-billed Sandpiper

ad summer

juv

Semipalmated Sandpiper

ad summer-winter

ad summer

Western Sandpiper

1st winter

ad summer

Least Sandpiper

juv

ad summer

winter

White-rumped Sandpiper

juv

Baird's Sandpiper

juv

Sharp-tailed Sandpiper *Calidris acuminata* 17–21 cm (*c*7 in). Like Pectoral (130), inc tail-pattern, but rather portlier with slightly shorter straighter bill, flatter crown; whiter supercilia wider behind eyes, cap more rufous than mantle, no clear-cut gorget, streaked under tail. *Ad summer* Dark brown above, fringed tawny and grey-buff; scalloped/V-marked on buff breast/white flanks. *Ad winter* Grey-brown coverts whitish-edged; breast grey-buff, lightly marked, merging into white belly. *Juv* Bolder cap/supercilia, whitish face; blackish above, fringed rufous and cream; orange-buff breast, streaked necklace; as ad by *c*Nov, but buff-edged brown inner medians. VOICE Soft *weep* or *trrt*. RANGE 15: Aug–Oct (Jan, Apr), most E/Cent/SBr. (NE Siberia.)

Buff-breasted Sandpiper *Tryngites subruficollis* 19–21 cm (*c*8 in). Short bill, small head, longish neck; scaly above, all buff below; pale eye-rings (bare-faced look), plain rump, no wing-bar, white on underwings, yellow legs (*cf* juv Ruff). Flight low, twisting; erect stance, high steps; tame. *Ad* Blackish above, scaled buff; dark spots at chest-sides. *Juv* Browner above, scaled creamy; spots paler; as ad after moult in Oct–Dec, but worn coverts with dark subterminal band. VOICE Trilled *pr-r-r-reet*, sharp *tik*. HABITAT Short grass. FOOD Insects. RANGE 388: Sep–Oct (Apr–Nov), esp Ir, SWBr. (NW America.)

Stilt Sandpiper *Micropalama himantopus* 20–22 cm (*c*8¼ in). Slender with longish droop-tipped bill, long spindly greenish or green legs; bold supercilia, white rump, plain wings with darker flight-feathers. Actions recall Curlew Sandpiper (132). *Ad summer* Blackish above with pale fringes, chestnut cheeks/nape; barred black-brown below. *Ad winter* Brown-grey with white fringes; white below. *Juv* Dark brown with grey-brown coverts, fringed pale buff; whitish below with buff throat/chest, few dark streaks. *1st winter* As ad winter, but some dark juv feathers remain. VOICE Low husky *chu*. HABITAT Marshes, mudflats. FOOD Invertebrates. RANGE 13: Jul–Oct (Apr), SE/N/WBr, SIr. (N America.)

Great Snipe *Gallinago media* 27–29 cm (*c*11 in). Bulkier than Snipe (136), shorter stouter bill, bigger head, broader wings; less striped above, largely barred below, with mealy head, white-edged dark central wing-panel and obscure pale rear edge. Flight slower, straighter, usually brief, with bill more level, like small Woodcock (136). *Ad* Coverts broadly tipped white; tail-corners white. *Juv* Thin covert-tips, tail more as Snipe; as ad by *c*Dec. VOICE Silent, or gruff croak. HABITAT/FOOD As Snipe; more in dry grass/heather. RANGE 226: Aug–May, most EBr. (N Eurasia.)

Long-billed Dowitcher *Limnodromus scolopaceus* 27–31.5 cm (*c*11½ in). Chunky, with Snipe-like bill (5½–8 cm), shortish legs; whitish supercilia, tips to secondaries, wedge on back; tail-bars blackish, wider than white between. Feeds with sewing-machine action. *Ad summer* Blackish above, fringed pink-buff, but many coverts greyish; all brick-red below, well marked, chest-sides barred. *Ad winter* After moult in Aug–Sep, grey-brown, fringed white on inner medians; grey neck/chest finely streaked, white below. *Juv* Dark brown, fringed red-buff; tertials plain; crown and neck/breast greyish, obscurely speckled, belly buff; as ad after moult in Sep–Dec, but worn juv wings/tail, buff-tipped inner medians. VOICE High *keek*, 1–3 times; other mono/polysyllabic calls. HABITAT More by fresh water. FOOD Invertebrates. RANGE 71 + (? nearly all) of 185 dowitchers: all months (esp Sep–Nov), scattered Br/Ir. (N America, NE Asia.)

Short-billed Dowitcher *Limnodromus griseus* 26–30 cm (*c*11 in). *Very* like Long-billed, overlapping bill-length (5–7 cm); tail-bars browner, usually narrower than white between; summer/juv distinct. *Ad summer* Paler orange-red below, less marked, chest-sides spotted, belly whitish moult in Jul–Aug. *Juv* Fringes above wider/paler buff; tertials tiger-striped; crown brown, neck/breast buff, more spotted; moult in *c*Oct. VOICE Soft rattled *tu-tu-tut*; other mono/polysyllabic calls. HABITAT More on coastal flats. RANGE 2 + (see above): Oct–Nov, SEBr. (N America.

Sharp-tailed Sandpiper

juv

ad summer

Buff-breasted Sandpiper

Stilt Sandpiper

1 winter

1st winter

ad

ad summer

Great Snipe

ad

Long-billed Dowitcher

ad winter

ad

ad summer

Short-billed Dowitcher

ad winter

ad summer

juv

juv

Upland Sandpiper *Bartramia longicauda*
25–28 cm (c 10½ in). Short thin bill, small
head, long thin neck, long wings, longish
wedge-tail; head/body pattern like tiny
Whimbrel (140), but rump and tail-centre
dark, whitish underwings boldly barred,
legs yellow. Flight low, flicking like
Common Sandpiper (144), or high with
strong beats, head withdrawn; runs
plover-like; readily perches on posts; shy.
Ad Scapulars/coverts barred blackish.
Juv/1st winter Scapulars darker/unbarred,
coverts paler/scaled brown. VOICE Mournful whistle. HABITAT Grass, stubble. FOOD
Insects. RANGE 33: Sep–Dec, scattered,
esp SWBr/SIr. (N America.)

Marsh Sandpiper *Tringa stagnatilis* 22–24
cm (c9 in). Like small, slender Greenshank (142), with needle-bill, long spindly
green legs. Active, graceful. *Ad summer*
Boldly spotted blackish. *Ad winter* Paler,
more uniform, coverts scaled white; white
face and underparts. *Juv* Mantle/coverts
dark brown heavily marked buff; usually
as ad by Oct, but many brown coverts.
VOICE Weak *teu*, sharp *chik*. HABITAT
Marshes. FOOD Invertebrates. RANGE 33:
Apr–Oct, esp E/SBr. (SE Europe, Asia.)

Greater Yellowlegs *Tringa melanoleuca*
30–33 cm (c12½ in). Shape as Greenshank
(142); paler above, more barred tail,
square whitish rump, bright yellow legs
projecting beyond tail. Actions similar.
Plumage sequences as smaller slighter
Lesser Yellowlegs, but ad more boldly
marked below in summer, head more
streaked in winter, juv darker above.
VOICE Greenshank-like *teu* 3–5 times.
HABITAT/FOOD As Lesser Yellowlegs, but
more by salt water. RANGE 24: esp Jul–
Oct, mainly Ir, S/WBr. (N America.)

Lesser Yellowlegs *Tringa flavipes* 24–27
cm (c10 in). Smaller, slimmer than Redshank (142), with thin black bill, long
spindly yellow legs projecting well beyond
tail; pale-spotted above, squared whitish
rump, barred tail. Actions like Wood
Sandpiper (144), but flight slower. *Ad
summer* Black-brown above, spotted
whitish; breast/flanks streaked and

barred. *Ad winter* Grey-brown above with
fewer spots, tertials barred; thin breast-
streaks. *Juv* Browner with pale spots, inc
tertials; breast greyer, streaked. *1si
winter* As ad with moult in Aug–Jan, but
scapulars and tertials brown with buff
notches. VOICE Flat *tu* 1–2 times. HABITAT
Marshes. FOOD Invertebrates. RANGE 151:
all months, esp Ir, S/NEBr. (N America.)

Solitary Sandpiper *Tringa solitaria* 19–21
cm (c7¾ in). Like small Green Sandpiper (144), also with dark underwings,
but paler olive-brown above, obvious
white eye-rings, dark rump, barred tail-
sides whiter; wings extend beyond tail.
Actions/plumage sequences similar; juv
chest more buff. VOICE Thin *pzik*, piping
pit-weet-weet. HABITAT Muddy streams,
marshes, pools. FOOD Insects. RANGE 20:
Jul–Oct, esp SIr, SBr. (N America.)

Terek Sandpiper *Xenus cinereus* 22–24 cm
(c9 in). Like large Common Sandpiper
(144), but long tapering upcurved bill,
short orange-yellow legs; greyer-brown
above, dark 'shoulders', white trailing
edge to wings. Similar bobbing; rushes
around, seems to trip on to bill as it
picks food. *Ad summer* Blackish bands on
scapulars; bill dark. *Ad winter* Uniform
above; bill orange-based. *Juv* Scapulars
streaked blackish, coverts fringed buff; as
ad with moult in Sep–Jan. VOICE Sharp
whistled *wit-e-wit*. HABITAT Mud-flats.
FOOD Invertebrates. RANGE 18: May–Sep,
esp E/SBr. (NE Europe, Siberia.)

Spotted Sandpiper *Actitis macularia* 18–20
cm (c7½ in). Shape as Common Sandpiper
(144), but shorter tail; in autumn/winter,
greyer above, shoulders more barred,
wing-bar shorter, tail-sides less white,
usually yellowish bill-base and legs.
Ad summer Spotted below; bill-base/legs
flesh-pink. *Ad winter* Brown-grey above,
indistinct blackish bars on wing-coverts
(*cf* juv). *Juv* More uniform greyish above,
tertials plain with thin buff tips and
coverts boldly barred blackish and buff;
as ad with moult in Sep–Jan. VOICE Sharp
peet-weet. RANGE 53: all months, most
SW/SBr; nested NBr 1975. (N America.)

Upland Sandpiper

juv/1st winter

Marsh Sandpiper

ad summer

ad winter

Lesser Yellowlegs

ad summer

Greater Yellowlegs

1st winter

1st winter

Solitary Sandpiper

ad/juv

juv

Spotted Sandpiper

ad summer

juv

Terek Sandpiper

ad summer

GULLS (Laridae)

Laughing Gull *Larus atricilla* 37–41 cm
($c15\frac{1}{2}$ in). Just smaller than Common Gull
(156), longer droop-tipped bill, thinner
wings, longer legs; ad back/wings slate-
grey, almost plain black wing-tips, black
hood in summer; 1st year has much dark
grey on head and underparts, brown and
blackish wings, white rump, grey tail with
broad black band. Flight light, graceful.
Ad Neat black wing-ends, small white tips
to inner primaries; in *c*Feb–Oct, head
black (white eye-crescents at all ages),
bill/legs dull red; in *c*Aug–Mar, hindhead
grey with blackish eye/ear-marks, bill
legs blackish. *1st year* Head, breast and
flanks with much dark grey, but whitish
face and belly (head variably hooded in
summer); outer wings/secondaries mainly
blackish, coverts brown; bill/legs black.
2nd year More as ad, but wing-tips black
almost to carpal joint, traces of tail-band
and bar on secondaries, summer hood
often incomplete. HABITAT Coasts. FOOD
Fish, aquatic invertebrates. RANGE 28:
Feb–Dec, widely scattered. (N America.)

Franklin's Gull *Larus pipixcan* 33–36 cm
(*c*13 in). Smaller, rounder-winged than
Black-headed (154); dark grey Laughing,
but smaller, dumpier, with shortish
wings, tail and legs, shorter bill, ad
differing in pied wing-tips and grey-
centred tail, winter/imms in half-hood,
thicker white eye-crescents and white-
tipped primaries, 1st winter also in whiter
underparts/underwings, grey inner
primaries, narrower tail-band not reaching
corners. Flies buoyantly, hawks insects,
picks from surface, follows plough. *Ad*
Black on wing-tips surrounded by white;
in *c*Apr–Sep, head black, rosy tinge
below; in *c*Aug–May, half-hood, bill/legs
blackish or still red. *1st winter* Blackish
half-hood, white underparts tinged grey at
breast-sides, brown wing-coverts, blackish
flight-feathers and tail-band, white-tipped
primaries; bill/legs blackish. *1st summer*
Full or partial hood, dark grey wings with
blackish ends like 2nd year Laughing but
for white-tipped primaries; sometimes
faint tail-band and bar on secondaries;

bill/legs blackish or bill red-based. *2nd
winter* As ad, but more black on wing-tips,
no whitish line on inside edge. HABITAT
Coasts, lakes, fields. FOOD Insects. RANGE 6:
Oct–May, Jul, most S/EBr. (N America.)

Bonaparte's Gull *Larus philadelphia* 30–33
cm (*c*$12\frac{1}{2}$ in). Like small Black-headed
(154); similar pattern on less pointed
wings, but white below on primaries, and
always largely black bill; whole ad head
grey-black with bold white eye-crescents
in *c*Mar–Oct, more orange-red legs;
winter plumages with blacker ear-spot,
grey nape; 1st year also has darker brown
carpal bar, inner primaries with neater
black border and white tips. Plumage
sequence as Black-headed. Flight more
tern-like, with quicker beats, dipping to
surface to feed. HABITAT As Black-headed.
FOOD Invertebrates. RANGE 34: Jun–Apr,
scattered, most S/EBr. (N America.)

Slender-billed Gull *Larus genei* 41–45 cm
(*c*17 in). Larger than Black-headed (154)
with longer bill, flat forehead, long neck;
wings similar, but more white on outer
primaries at all ages, paler carpal bar
on 1st year; head all white (except juv),
obscure eye/ear-marks in winter; ad pink-
tinged in summer, bill/legs dark red/
orange-red (bill looking black), eyes pale,
1st year bill/legs paler. Plumage sequence
(except head) as Black-headed. Head/neck
droop in low flight, tilted forward on
water. HABITAT Coasts. FOOD Fish,
invertebrates. RANGE 4: Apr, Jun–Sep,
SBr. (N Africa, S Europe, S/Cent Asia.)

Ring-billed Gull *Larus delawarensis* 43–47
cm (*c*$17\frac{1}{2}$ in). Like large Common (156),
bulkier with stouter bill, flatter head; ad
paler grey with faint eyebrows, fiercer
expression (like Herring), less white on
folded tertials, clear black band on yellow
bill, pale eyes; 1st year more spotted on
nape and flanks, blacker outerwings and
secondaries, grey greater coverts, less
distinct tail-band, bill dark-tipped but
band appearing in 1st summer, eyes dark
until 2nd winter. Plumage sequence and
HABITAT/FOOD As Common. RANGE 37:
Nov–Sep, esp SWBr, WIr. (N America.)

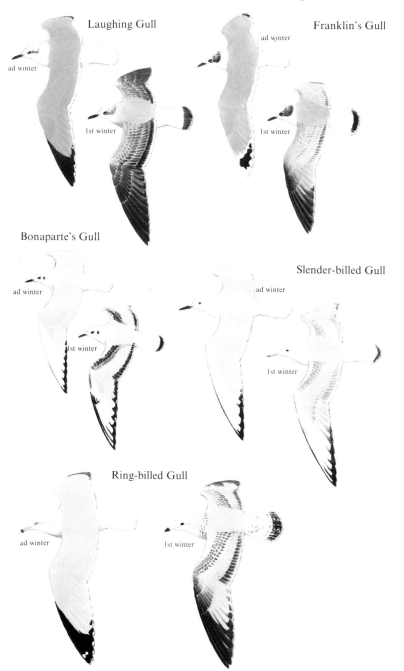

Laughing Gull

ad winter

1st winter

Franklin's Gull

ad winter

1st winter

Bonaparte's Gull

ad winter

1st winter

Slender-billed Gull

ad winter

1st winter

Ring-billed Gull

ad winter

1st winter

Great Black-headed Gull *Larus ichthyaetus*
60–67 cm (*c*25 in). Near size of Great
Black-backed (162), but slighter, with flat
forehead, peaked hindcrown, longer wings,
tertials often humped; ad pale grey back,
much white on outer wings, black summer
hood, dark winter mask, in 1st year wide
clear tail-band and wings of imm Common
Gull type, with grey mantle and white
underparts like small gulls. *Ad* Jagged
black band near wing-tips; in *c*Jan–Sep,
head black (white eye-crescents at all
ages), bill yellow with black band and
red tip, legs yellow; in *c*Aug–Feb, head
white with dark mask behind eyes, bill/
legs duller. *1st year* Head/body much as
ad winter, but nape/breast-sides mottled
blackish; wings banded brown/grey-
brown/blackish; legs and black-tipped bill
grey-flesh. *2nd year* More as ad (mainly
pale grey wings, variable hood in summer),
but largely black outer primaries, narrow
tail-band. *3rd year* Blacker wing-ends
than ad, often faint tail-band. HABITAT
Coasts, lakes. FOOD Fish. RANGE 6: Aug–
May, esp SBr. (S Russia, W/Cent Asia.)

Ross's Gull *Rhodostethia rosea* 30–33 cm
(*c*12½ in). Size much as Little Gull (152);
tiny bill, dove-like head, short legs,
long pointed wings, wedge-tail; ad pinkish below, grey underwings; 1st year dark
tail-band, W on wings/rump (*cf* Little
Gull, Kittiwake). Flight buoyant, shear-
ing, or pigeon-like with deep beats;
hovers to pick from water; walks with
short steps, nodding head. *Ad* Thin black
leading edge to outer wings, secondaries
white; in *c*Feb–Oct, thin neck-ring, rich
pink below, orange-red legs; in *c*Aug–
Apr, eye/ear-marks, greyish hindneck,
duller legs. *1st year* Dusky W on wings/
rump, black tail-band, both brownish by
summer, when neck-ring and pink often
develop; more white on hindwing than
Little Gull. HABITAT Coasts. FOOD
Invertebrates, fish. RANGE 25: all months,
esp Nov–Jan, Apr–May, most N/EBr, but
even SIr. (NE Siberia, arctic America.)

Ivory Gull *Pagophila eburnea* 42–47 cm
(*c*17 in). Plump, pigeon-like, with short
neck, short blackish legs, pointed wings;

all white, with dark marks in 1st year.
Flight strong, tern-like; rolling walk. *Ad*
Bill greyish tipped yellow-orange, eye-
rings red. *1st year* Blackish face and
spotting on wings/upperbody, all less or
lost by summer; black-tipped primaries,
broken tail-band; bill duller, eye-rings
black. HABITAT Coasts. FOOD Invertebrates, fish, carrion. RANGE 98: Aug–Jun,
esp Oct–Feb, esp N/EBr. (High Arctic.)

TERNS (Sternidae)

Caspian Tern *Sterna caspia* 48–56 cm
(*c*20½ in). Near size of Herring Gull (156),
with huge orange-red bill, shallow tail-
fork, longish legs; primaries blackish
below. Flight gull-like. *Ad* Black cap in
*c*Feb–Sep, closely streaked crown and
blackish eye-patch in *c*Aug–Feb; bill
orange-red. *Juv* Crown more buff than ad
winter; upperbody mottled dark brown;
wings as ad but dusky lesser coverts, tail
with dusky end; bill orange with dark tip.
1st summer As ad winter. VOICE Harsh
kraaa. HABITAT Coasts. FOOD Fish. RANGE
147: Apr–Nov, esp S/EBr. (Most world.)

Royal Tern *Sterna maxima* 45–51 cm (*c*19
in). Near size of Caspian; less stout bill
orange to orange-yellow, longer deeper-
forked tail, shorter legs; head more
crested, winter crown much whiter, forehead white in Jun–Feb, upperparts paler;
primaries less dark below. *Juv* Wings
more contrasted than Caspian (primaries
darker than ad, lesser coverts dark,
median whitish, greater dusky), tail-tip
dusky; bill duller than ad or pinkish. *1st
summer*. More like ad winter. VOICE High
chirrip. HABITAT Coasts. FOOD Fish, crabs.
RANGE 4: most Jul–Sep, S/WBr (Mar, dead,
EIr). (N America, W Indies, W Africa.)

Forster's Tern *Sterna forsteri* 34–37 cm
(*c*14 in). Like Common (162), but longer
tail/legs, heavier bill; silvery panel on
outer wings (esp ad), white sides to grey
tail; ad winter/imm head white with black
mask-patches, grey nape; ad summer bill-
base more orange; 1st winter much fainter
carpal bar. Shallower wing-beats. VOICE
Soft low *krurr*. HABITAT/FOOD As Common.
RANGE 1: Jan–Mar, Cornwall. (N America.)

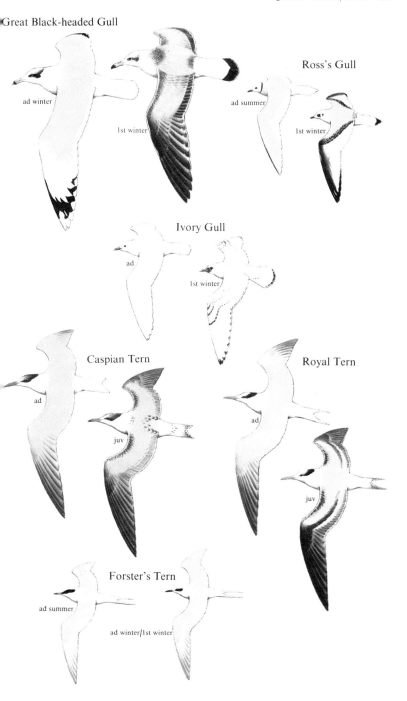

Great Black-headed Gull

ad winter

1st winter

Ross's Gull

ad summer

1st winter

Ivory Gull

ad

1st winter

Caspian Tern

ad

juv

Royal Tern

ad

juv

Forster's Tern

ad summer

ad winter/1st winter

Gull-billed Tern *Gelochelidon nilotica* 35–39 cm (*c*14½ in). Stockier than Sandwich Tern (166); shorter stouter all-black bill, shorter broader wings, less forked tail and longer legs; wing-tips paler, tail grey, head largely white in winter. Flight heavier, seldom plunges, dips down to water or ground. *Ad summer* Black cap, black legs. *Ad winter* With moult in Jul–Oct, head white but for blackish round eyes, greyish crown/nape. *Juv* As ad winter, but above tinged buff and mottled brown; also darker primaries, brown-tipped tail, red-brown legs. *1st winter and summer* With moult in Sep–Feb, as ad winter but outer primaries dark. VOICE Throaty *ka-huk*. HABITAT Coasts, marshes, lakes. FOOD Insects, voles. RANGE 206: Mar–Oct, esp May–Sep, most S/EBr. (Cosmopolitan.)

Aleutian Tern *Sterna aleutica* 33–36 cm (*c*13½ in). Like Bridled Tern but slate-grey above, white forehead to over eyes, rump/tail white, dark secondaries below; juv brown-grey above, tail greyish. VOICE Soft, 4–5 note, wader-like whistle. HABITAT Oceanic. RANGE 1: May, NEBr. (N Pacific.)

Bridled Tern *Sterna anaethetus* 34–37 cm (*c*14 in). Dark grey-brown above, white forehead to behind eyes, pale collar, palish-tipped underwings. Deep stiff beats of broadish wings; settles on water, perches. *Ad summer* Grey-brown above; black crown, white-sided tail. *Ad winter* Mantle tipped whitish; black on head browner, streaked white. *Juv* Dark brown above with creamy tips, crown streaked black and white; tail shorter, no white on sides. *1st winter.* As ad, but worn juv wings/tail. VOICE Harsh calls. HABITAT Oceanic. FOOD Fish, invertebrates. RANGE 7: Apr, Aug–Nov, widely scattered. (Tropics.)

Sooty Tern *Sterna fuscata* 39–43 cm (*c*16 in). Larger than Bridled. Slow fluid beats of narrowish wings; rarely settles, snatching food from surface. *Ad* Black above (fringed white in winter) with white forehead to eyes, tail-sides; white below with blackish wing-tips and trailing edges. *Juv/1st winter* All sooty-brown, greyer

below, with buff or, in 1st winter, white flecks above; whitish-grey vent and underwings. As ad by 3–5 years old. VOICE Nasal *waaki-waak*. HABITAT Oceanic. FOOD Fish. RANGE 25: Apr–Oct, esp E/SBr. (Tropics.)

Whiskered Tern *Chlidonias hybridus* 26–29 cm (*c*10¾ in). More like Common (164) than Black Tern (166), with more forked tail than Black; in summer white cheeks, dusky underparts; in autumn silvery grey and white without contrasting collar, rump or dark breast-patches (but variegated saddle on juv). Actions as Black Tern. *Ad summer* Black cap, white cheeks; dark grey shading to blackish below; bill/legs dark red. *Ad winter* With moult in Jul–Dec, grey above and white below but for black-streaked white crown, blackish U from eyes round nape; bill blackish. *Juv* As ad winter, but for mottled brown/buff/greyish mantle, slaty shoulders; as ad winter with moult in Jul–Oct. RANGE 71: Apr–Sep, esp May–Jun, most SBr. (S Eurasia, Africa, Australia.)

White-winged Black Tern *Chlidonias leucopterus* 22–24 cm (*c*9 in). Stockier than Black Tern (166), with stubbier bill and broader-based wings. Actions as Black Tern; slower, shallower wing-beats. *Ad summer* Glossy black but for white shoulders, rump and tail (last greyer on ♀); bill red-black, legs red. *Ad winter* With moult in *c*Jul–Nov, as Black Tern, also with white collar, but isolated black ear-coverts, white-flecked crown/nape, no dark breast-patches, paler grey rump, white underwing; bill black. *Juv* As ad winter, but blackish saddle, white rump; bill blackish, legs red-brown; as ad winter with moult in Aug–Feb. *1st summer* Usually as ad winter. RANGE 436: Mar–Nov, most SEBr. (E Europe, Asia.)

AUKS (Alcidae)

Brünnich's Guillemot *Uria lomvia* 40–44 cm (*c*16½ in). As Guillemot (168), but almost black above; shorter stouter bill, pale line at base; in winter black of crown down over ear-coverts (*cf* juv Razorbill, 168); imm not separable until Nov. RANGE 14: Jul–Apr, NBr/EIr. (Arctic.)

Gull-billed Tern

ad summer

juv

ad summer

1st summer

Aleutian Tern

Sooty Tern

1st autumn

Bridled Tern

ad summer

ad

ad summer

1st autumn

Whiskered Tern

juv

ad summer

ad winter

White-winged Black Tern

Brünnich's Guillemot

ad summer

juv

ad summer

ad summer

ad winter

ad winter

ad winter

SANDGROUSE (Pteroclididae)

Pallas's Sandgrouse *Syrrhaptes paradoxus* 33–41 cm (13–16 in). Plump, pigeon-like, but with very long and thin pointed tail, long curved wings, and short legs; sandy-buff, spotted/barred black above, with orange head, grey breast and primaries, black belly-patch. Flight fast with flicked beats, rising awkwardly with pigeon-like clatter; otherwise always on ground, waddling with tiny steps; gregarious, but recent vagrants singly; shy. *Ad/1st year ♂* Head orange-buff with greyish crown/ nape and curve behind eyes to grey breast with band of black crescents; wing-coverts almost plain sandy-buff; wings and tail needle-pointed. *Ad/1st year ♀* Head paler with black band on throat (but none on breast); crown, neck and wing-coverts spotted; wings and tail less pointed. VOICE Repeated *cu-reru*. HABITAT Vagrants on dunes, stubble, dry marshes. FOOD Seeds, grain. RANGE Several invasions 1859–1909 (some nested), only 6 birds since: May, Sep, Dec, EBr. (W/Cent Asia.)

PIGEONS, DOVES (Columbidae)

Rufous Turtle Dove *Streptopelia orientalis* 32–34 cm (*c*13 in). Patterned like Turtle Dove (174), but larger, bulkier, darker; heavier black marks on mantle/coverts and less grey on outer coverts, back/rump bluer, breast darker pink-brown and belly hardly paler; grey (not white) on undertail-coverts, tail-border and neck-patches. Flight/gait heavier than Turtle Dove. *Ad* Strongly rufous above, with black and blue-grey neck-patches, slate-blue back and rump, and pink-brown below. *Juv* Paler, browner: rufous-buff above, no neck-patches, browner back/rump, and dull grey below tinged pink-buff; as ad after moult in Sep–Jan. VOICE Dull sleepy *croo croo-croo crooo*. HABITAT Woods, fields, scrub. FOOD Seeds, grain. RANGE 8: Oct–Nov, May (Jan), E/SWBr. (Asia.)

CUCKOOS (Cuculidae)

Great Spotted Cuckoo *Clamator glandarius* 38–41 cm (*c*15½ in). Larger than Cuckoo (174), crested, with graduated tail half total length; dark brown above with greyer cap, orange eye-rings, boldly spotted wings, white-edged tail, and creamy below with yellower throat. Flight slightly dipping. *Ad* Cap blue-grey with crest; large white spots on scapulars/wing-coverts, long white tail-tips; primaries brown. *Juv* Cap black, less crested; smaller creamier spots above and short white tail-tips; primaries largely rufous. *1st summer* Intermediate after moult in Jan–Mar: cap blackish-grey; smallish white spots above; primaries mixed rufous and brown. VOICE Harsh *keeow* and repeated chattering *kittera*. HABITAT Wood-edges, bushy areas with scattered trees. FOOD Insects. RANGE 24: Mar–May, Aug–Oct, esp SWBr spring, EBr autumn. (S Europe, SW Asia, Africa.)

Black-billed Cuckoo *Coccyzus erythroph-thalmus* 27–29 cm (*c*11 in). As Yellow-billed, but little or no rufous on wings, no black and much less white on tail; black bill, red or yellow eye-rings. *Ad* Glossy brown above with narrow white tips on graduated tail; eye-rings red. *Juv/1st winter* Speckled whitish above till Sep–Oct moult; tail faintly tipped buff-white, rufous fringes on wings; eye-rings yellow. VOICE/HABITAT/FOOD As Yellow-billed. RANGE 7: Sep–Nov, scattered but most SW/NEBr, 1 Ir. (N America.)

Yellow-billed Cuckoo *Coccyzus americanus* 27–29 cm (*c*11 in). Smaller, slimmer, more dove-like than Cuckoo (174), with curved bill, shorter wings, longer graduated tail; brown above, whitish below, with much black and white in tail, rufous primaries, yellow bill-patch, grey or yellow eye-rings. Actions as Cuckoo, but flight weaker; secretive, usually in cover, often low. *Ad* Slightly glossy brown above; boldly white-tipped blackish edges and underside of tail; eye-rings greyish. *Juv/1st winter* Duller; tail browner with less clear white tips; more rufous on wing-coverts and primaries; eye-rings yellow. VOICE Vagrants silent. HABITAT Wood-edges, bushy areas, scrub. FOOD Insects; berries in autumn. RANGE 38: Oct–Nov (end Sep–Dec), well scattered but most S/W/NBr, Ir. (N America.)

Pallas's Sandgrouse

♂

♀

♂

Rufous Turtle Dove

juv

ad

Great Spotted Cuckoo

juv

ad

juv

ad

1st summer

Black-billed Cuckoo

Yellow-billed Cuckoo

ad

ad

juv/1st winter

juv/1st winter

ad

ad

OWLS (Strigidae)

Scops Owl *Otus scops* 18–20 cm (*c*7½ in). Strictly nocturnal; smaller, slimmer and longer-winged than Little Owl (176), with ear-tufts forming concave top to thinner head; brown-grey to rufous, delicately marked. Flight wavering; roosts by day against trunk or in cover. *Ad = 1st year*. VOICE Monotonous whistled *pew*. HABITAT Woods, parks, avenues. RANGE 77: esp Apr–Jun, also Jul–Nov, most SBr, also Ir/NBr. (S Europe, W Asia, NW Africa.)

Hawk Owl *Surnia ulula* 35–41 cm (*c*15 in). Diurnal; big head, shortish pointed wings, long tail; brown and white, barred below, with black face-edge. Flight low, dashing, hawk-like; perches in open, leaning forwards, jerking tail. *Ad = 1st year*. VOICE Chattering *kikikiki*. HABITAT Conifers, birches. FOOD Mammals, birds. RANGE 10: Aug–Mar, most SW/NBr, inc 3 of American race. (N Eurasia, N America.)

Tengmalm's Owl *Aegolius funereus* 24–27 cm (*c*10 in). Mainly nocturnal; longer-tailed than Little Owl (176), with large rounded head and 'surprised' look, shorter shaggy legs; chocolate and white, mottled below, with black face-edge. Flight wavering. *Ad = 1st year*. VOICE Soft liquid *poo-poo-poq*.... HABITAT Conifers. FOOD Mammals, birds. RANGE 53, but only 4 since 1950: Oct–Jan, May, all Orkney. (E Europe, N Asia, N America.)

BEE-EATERS (Meropidae)

Blue-cheeked Bee-eater *Merops superciliosus* 28–31 cm (*c*11½ in). Shape and actions as Bee-eater but with longer tail-points; mainly green, with blue surrounding black mask, and coppery throat and underwings. *Ad* Bright green, blue across forecrown; ♂ longer tail-points. *Juv* Duller green, no blue across forecrown, throat paler, no tail-points; as ad after moult in Dec–Mar. VOICE Throaty *pruuk*. RANGE 2: Jun–Jul, Scilly. (SW Asia, N Africa.)

Bee-eater *Merops apiaster* 27–29 cm (*c*11 in). Long curved bill, triangular wings, projecting tail-points; chestnut and turquoise, with gold V above, yellow

throat, pale chestnut underwings. Flight graceful, mixing quick beats with gliding, wheeling, not unlike large House Martin; perches in open. *Ad summer* Chestnut and gold above, with greenish tail; blue-green below, with black-edged yellow throat; ♀ tinged greenish on back and wings, with tail-points shorter. *Ad winter* After moult in Aug–Sep, more green (esp ♀) or blue-green above, almost no black throat-band. *Juv/1st winter* As ad winter, but still less chestnut; greyer scapulars, paler throat, tail-points hardly projecting. VOICE Liquid *pruup*. HABITAT Open country, scattered trees. FOOD Insects, on wing. RANGE 266: Apr–Nov, esp S/EBr; nested 1920, 1955. (S Europe, SW Asia, NW Africa.)

ROLLERS (Coraciidae)

Roller *Coracias garrulus* 29–32 cm (*c*12 in). Rather Jay-like, but heavier bill, longer pointed wings; turquoise and chestnut with blackish flight-feathers, but juv much duller. Flight Jackdaw-like but more floppy; 'rolls' in display; waits on trees, wires, swooping on to prey; hops heavily. *Ad summer* Turquoise and chestnut. *Ad winter* With moult in Jul–Nov, crown and breast dull brownish-green, mantle duller brown. *Juv* Still duller and paler till moult during Nov–Dec; wings and tail tipped with brown, latter without pointed black corners. VOICE Loud harsh *krrak-ak*. HABITAT Open country, scattered trees. FOOD Large insects. RANGE 199: Apr–Nov (esp May–Jul), scattered, most S/EBr. (S/Cent Europe, W Asia, NW Africa.)

KINGFISHERS (Alcedinidae)

Belted Kingfisher *Ceryle alcyon* 30–34 cm (*c*12½ in). Jackdaw-sized, with long thick bill, large head, double crest, rounded wings, longish tail; mainly blue-grey and white. Actions as Kingfisher (180), but wing-beats deeper, less regular, floppier; often hovers; very noisy. *Ad* ♂ Blue-grey chest-band. *Ad* ♀ Also rusty breast-band. *Juv/1st winter* Chest-band tipped rufous, only flanks rusty (both more on ♀); crest darker; more white tips on wings, central tail spotted as ad ♀. VOICE Harsh rattle. HABITAT Fresh water. FOOD Fish. RANGE 3: Nov–Aug, Cornwall/Mayo. (N America.)

Scops Owl

1st year/ad

Hawk Owl

1st year/ad

1st year/ad

Tengmalm's Owl

1st year/ad

Blue-cheeked Bee-eater

ad

juv

ad

♂ summer

Bee-eater

ad

juv

♂ summer

Roller

ad summer

juv

ad summer

Belted Kingfisher

ad

♀

♂

NIGHTJARS (Caprimulgidae)

Common Nighthawk *Chordeiles minor*
21–25 cm (*c*9 in). Smaller, darker and
greyer than Nightjar (180) with long,
pointed, white-banded wings and notched
tail. Crepuscular, but also hunts by day;
flight buoyant, tern-like. *Ad ♂* White
throat and band across tail. *Ad ♀* Throat-
patch smaller, more buff; no tail-band.
Juv As ♀, but mottled greyer, throat
obscured by barring. VOICE Nasal *peent*.
HABITAT Pinewoods, fields, moors, towns.
FOOD Insects, on wing. RANGE 8: Sep–Oct,
most Scilly, also Cent/NEBr. (N America.)

SWIFTS (Apodidae)

Needle-tailed Swift *Hirundapus caudacutus*
19–21 cm (*c*7¾ in). Body size of Alpine
Swift but stouter, wings broader-based;
tail very short, squarish ('needle' points
usually invisible); dark brown with green
gloss (purple or mat when abraded), esp
on wings; white throat and U under tail,
grey-brown triangle on back (fading to
whitish). Flight slower, more fluttery

than Swift (186). *Juv/1st winter* As ad,
but white undertail-coverts dark-tipped.
VOICE Vagrants silent. HABITAT Aerial.
FOOD Insects, on wing. RANGE 3: Jun–Jul,
Essex/Hants/Cork. (E Asia.)

Pallid Swift *Apus pallidus* 16–17 cm (*c*6½
in). *Very* like Swift (186), but wings
broader-based, blunter; paler, scalier,
with rather larger whitish face and throat
(emphasising dark eye-mark); light inner
wings contrast with darker back, breast
and outer primaries. Flight more deliberate, more gliding. RANGE 1: May, Kent.
(S Europe, SW Asia, N Africa.)

Alpine Swift *Apus melba* 20–22 cm (*c*8¼
in), wingspan 50–55 cm (*c*21 in). Much
larger and paler than Swift (186), with
white throat and belly, brown breast-
band. *Juv* White edgings to wing-feathers
(but ad has thin fringes in fresh plumage).
VOICE Vagrants silent. HABITAT Aerial,
often near coast. FOOD Insects, on wing.
RANGE 302: mid Apr–Oct (Mar–Nov),
scattered, esp S/EBr. (S Eurasia, Africa.)

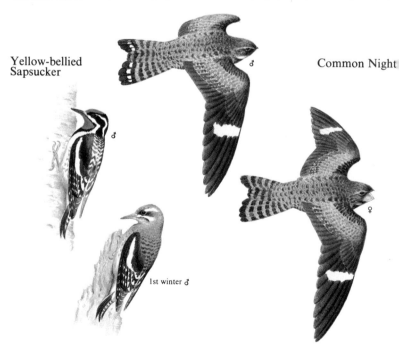

Yellow-bellied
Sapsucker

♂

Common Night

♂

♀

1st winter ♂

Little Swift *Apus affinis* 12–13 cm ($c5\frac{1}{2}$ in). Smaller, more compact than Swift (186) with shorter, broader-based wings, square-ended tail and square white rump. *Juv/1st winter* Whitish edgings to wing-feathers. VOICE Vagrants silent. HABITAT Aerial. FOOD Insects, on wing. RANGE 2: Jun, Nov, Cork/Gwynedd. (S Asia, Africa.)

WOODPECKERS (Picidae)

Yellow-bellied Sapsucker *Sphyrapicus varius* 19–23 cm ($c8\frac{1}{4}$ in). Smallish woodpecker with mottled/barred back, white rump, wing-patches, and bands behind and below eyes on black head-sides. *Ad ♂* Black-bordered red forecrown and throat. *Ad ♀* Less red on forecrown (or all-black), throat white. *Juv* Brown and buff; whitish traces of ad pattern on head, whitish throat. *1st winter ♂* assumes some red and black in Aug–Sep, ♀ not before Oct. VOICE Nasal mew; migrants usually silent. HABITAT Woods, orchards; vagrants in coastal areas with few trees. FOOD Drills rows of holes in trees, returns to feed on

sap, insects. RANGE 1: Sep–Oct, Scilly. (N America.)

SWALLOWS, MARTINS (Hirundinidae)

Red-rumped Swallow *Hirundo daurica* 17–18.5 cm ($c7$ in). Longer-bodied than Swallow (186), with thicker incurved tail-streamers, broader wings; chestnut supercilia and nape, chestnut to buff (often 2-tone) rump, black undertail-coverts; no breast-band or tail-spots. Flight slower, more deliberate, more as House Martin. *Ad* Glossy blue-black above, faintly streaked below. *Juv* Tail shorter; faint buff fringes above, little gloss; collar and rump paler; no streaks below. *1st winter* More as ad after moult in Jul–Sep, but still duller above, and still unstreaked below. VOICE Drawn-out soft *chirrup*, longer and softer than Swallow. HABITAT Open country. FOOD Insects, on wing. RANGE 74: Mar–Jun (esp Apr–May), also end Aug–early Nov, most S/EBr, with some north to Yorks., few Ir/NBr. (S Eurasia, Africa.)

Pallid Swift

Needle-tailed Swift

Alpine Swift

Little Swift

Red-rumped Swallow

LARKS (Alaudidae)

Calandra Lark *Melanocorypha calandra*
18–20 cm (*c*7½ in). Stout with pale bill,
heavy head, bulky body, short tail, no
crest; whitish underparts contrast with
bold black neck-patches (look narrow
when hunched) and dark upperparts; tail-
sides white; broad triangular wings look
black from below in flight, and dark above
with paler coverts, narrow white trailing
edges. Does not crouch flat like Skylark
(184). *Juv* Scaled above with buff feather-
edges, tail-sides tinged buff; black spots
on breast and ear-coverts; neck-patches
partly obscured; as ad after moult end
Jul–Sep. VOICE Nasal rippling *chrrreet*.
HABITAT Open wastes, farmlands. FOOD
Seeds, insects. RANGE 2: Apr, Dorset/
Shetland. (Mediterranean east to Iran.)

Bimaculated Lark *Melanocorypha bimacu-
lata* 16.5–17.5 cm (*c*6¾ in). Like small
Calandra, but more rufous with whiter
supercilia, narrower and less clear neck-
patches, and buff sides but white tips to
tail; wings lack white trailing edges in
flight. HABITAT Mountain fields, deserts in
winter. FOOD As Calandra. RANGE 3:
May–Jun, Oct, Devon/Scilly/Shetland.
(SW Asia north to Kirghiz Steppes.)

White-winged Lark *Melanocorypha
leucoptera* 17–18.5 cm (*c*7 in). Shape as
Calandra, but more rufous above, white
on wings, no neck-patches; in flight wings
narrower with wide white trailing edges
divided from chestnut forewings by black
stripe. *Ad ♂* Cap, lesser and median
coverts, and sides of breast all chestnut,
clearer in summer when also fainter chest-
spots. *Ad ♀* Crown as mantle, only tinged
chestnut; wing-coverts paler than ♂; sides
of breast more streaked, less chestnut.
Juv Crown and wing-coverts brown;
upperparts scaled with buff fringes, breast
and cheeks spotted blackish; tail-sides
and less extensive white in wings all tinged
buff; as ads after moult end Jul–Sep.
HABITAT Dry grassland. FOOD Seeds,
insects. RANGE 6: Aug–Nov, SBr. (SE
Russia to Cent Asia.)

Calandra Lark

Bimaculated Lark

White-winged Lark

Short-toed Lark *Calandrella brachy-dactyla* 13.5–14.5 cm (*c*5½ in). Small, pale, sandy above and whitish below; dark bar on median coverts, but patch at sides of neck often obscure; short yellowish bill, rather flat head; white-sided dark tail in flight. *Ad S races* Sandy-buff to pale grey-brown above, often reddish cap (esp summer); unstreaked below, but sides of throat finely spotted above neck-patch, sandy wash on chest. *Ad E races* Paler and greyer above; no rufous cap. *Juv* Rather spotted above; irregular narrow band of obscure blotches across chest, rarely on upper flanks; as ad after moult in late Jul–Sep, but chest-marks may sometimes remain into 1st winter. VOICE Short hard *chichirrp*. HABITAT Sandy wastes, fields. FOOD Seeds, insects. RANGE 227: Apr–Dec, esp May (S races) and Sep–Oct (mainly E races), wide-scattered but majority Shetland/Scilly. (S Eurasia, Africa.)

Lesser Short-toed Lark *Calandrella rufescens* 13.5–14.5 cm (*c*5½ in). Like grey Short-toed (see 1st winter), but regular streaks on breast, throat-sides, usually flanks (all much less on juv); no covert-bar or neck-patches; rounder head. VOICE Distinctive *prrt*. HABITAT Dry marsh to desert. RANGE 4 records of 42 birds: Jan–May, all Kerry/Wexford/Mayo. (Spain and N Africa east to Manchuria.)

Crested Lark *Galerida cristata* 16.5–17.5 cm (*c*6¾ in). Sometimes confused with Skylark (184), but plumper, with pointed crest, longer bill and much shorter buff-sided tail; diffusely streaked breast and, in flight, buff undersides to broader wings. *Juv* Crest less pointed; upperparts more spotted and scaly, 2 thin whitish wing-bars (tips of greater and median coverts); less heavily marked below; as ad after moult end Jul–Sep. VOICE Liquid whistle *whee-wheeoo*. HABITAT Farmland, waste ground, roadsides. FOOD Seeds, insects. RANGE 20: Mar–Jun, Sep–Jan, most SBr but also north to Shetland. (Temperate Eurasia, Africa.) NOTE Thekla Lark *G. theklae*, of Mediterranean area, is very similar, has bold breast-streaks, grey underwings.

Short-toed Lark

Lesser Short-toed Lark

E races juv–1st winter

E races ad

S races ad

ad

Crested Lark

juv

ad

PIPITS, WAGTAILS (Motacillidae)

Richard's Pipit *Anthus novaeseelandiae* 17–18.5 cm (*c*7 in). Largest pipit, with stout bill, white-sided tail, long stout legs, large feet, upright stance; brown above, heavily streaked, and boldly marked on breast; whitish supercilia, black moustaches. *Juv* Blacker above, scaled with buff; whiter below, but well-streaked; moults in Aug–Dec, still many pale-edged juv feathers. VOICE Explosive *schreep*. HABITAT Wet grassland. FOOD Insects, worms, seeds. RANGE 1064: Aug–May, esp Sep–Nov, most coastal E/S/ WBr, rare Ir. (Asia, Africa, Australasia). NOTE Blyth's Pipit *A. godlewskii* (Sussex, Oct 1882) is very like Richard's, but in autumn more intermediate between it and imm Tawny, with some orange-buff below.

Tawny Pipit *Anthus campestris* 16–17 cm (*c*6½ in). Large, slim, wagtail-like, with slender bill, longish tail. *Ad* Sandy above, creamy below, almost unstreaked; creamy supercilia, line of dark spots on median

coverts. *Juv* Streaked above and boldly spotted on breast, like Richard's Pipit, but greyer, slimmer, less erect, with thinner bill and legs; moults in Aug–Nov, still streaked to Sep–Oct. VOICE Wagtail-like *tseep*, more metallic *tseuk*. HABITAT Sandy ground, farmland. FOOD Insects. RANGE 583: mainly end Jul–early Nov (esp Sep–Oct), also Apr–mid Jun, most coastal S/ SEBr; rare NBr, Ir. (Eurasia, N Africa.)

Olive-backed Pipit *Anthus hodgsoni* 14.5–16 cm (*c*6 in). Size of Tree Pipit (188); olive and whitish with bold breast-spots; black-edged buff and white supercilia; white patch and black mark at rear cheeks. Skulks; pumps tail. VOICE Hoarse *tseep*. HABITAT Typically trees. FOOD Insects. RANGE 18: Sep–Nov, Apr–May, mainly S/E/NEBr. (NE Russia, Asia.)

Pechora Pipit *Anthus gustavi* 14–15 cm (*c*5¾ in). Like Tree Pipit (188) but shorter tail; whiter wing-bar/underparts, 2 whitish lines on back, buffish tail-sides, boldly streaked rump. Very skulking. VOICE Loud

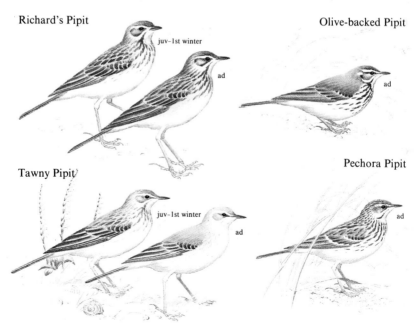

Richard's Pipit

juv–1st winter

ad

Olive-backed Pipit

ad

Tawny Pipit

juv–1st winter

ad

Pechora Pipit

ad

hard *pwit*. HABITAT Swamps; migrants in crops. FOOD Insects. RANGE 24: end Aug–Nov (Apr), N/EBr. (NE Russia, Asia.)

Red-throated Pipit *Anthus cervinus* 14–15 cm (*c*5$\frac{3}{4}$ in). Darker, browner than Meadow Pipit (186); heavier streaking extends to rump. *Ad summer* Pink to brick-red throat, usually supercilia, sometimes breast/forehead (♂ often redder but sexing unsure); streaks below mainly on flanks. *Ad winter* May show pinkish throat; breast boldly streaked. *Juv* Throat streaked, yellower below; as ad after moult in Aug. VOICE High drawn-out *psssss*, more hissing than Tree Pipit. HABITAT Marshes, wet fields. FOOD Insects, also molluscs, worms, seeds. RANGE 144: mid Apr–mid Jun, mid Aug–Nov, mainly coastal E/SBr, also SIr. (N Eurasia.)

Citrine Wagtail *Motacilla citreola* 16–17 cm (*c*6$\frac{1}{2}$ in). Like Yellow Wagtail (190) from front, White Wagtail (192) from rear; grey back and 2 white wing-bars at all ages. ♂ *summer* Yellow head and under-

parts, black half-collar. ♂ *winter*/♀ Crown and nape grey; forehead, supercilia and underparts dull yellow. *Juv* Forehead buff, crown and ear-coverts grey, supercilia white or yellowish, throat white, breast buff (often indistinctly spotted gorget), underparts brownish-white; as ad winter by end of moult in Sep–Oct. VOICE Hard *tsreep*. HABITAT/FOOD As Yellow Wagtail. RANGE 26: most imms, Sep–Nov, NE/EBr; 2 ♂s, May/Jul, EBr. (E Russia, Asia.)

ACCENTORS (Prunellidae)

Alpine Accentor *Prunella collaris* 17–18.5 cm (*c*7 in). Larger than Dunnock (196); dark patch between 2 whitish wing-bars, buff tips to tail. *Ad* Throat white with black spots, flanks streaked chestnut. *Juv* Duller with plain buff-grey throat, dark-streaked flanks and underparts; as ad after moult in Jul–Oct. VOICE Lark-like *chirrirrip*. HABITAT Mountains; vagrants on rocky ground. FOOD Insects, seeds, berries. RANGE 35: Mar–Jun, Aug–Jan, most SBr. (Cent/S Eurasia, NW Africa.)

Red-throated Pipit

ad winter

ad summer

Alpine Accentor

juv–1st winter

Citrine Wagtail

♂ summer

ad

♀

juv–1st winter

THRASHERS (Mimidae)

Brown Thrasher *Toxostoma rufum* 26.5–29.5 cm (*c*11 in). Rather thrush-like, but slimmer, with long tail, slightly curved bill; bright rufous above with greyish cheeks, 2 pale wing-bars; whitish below with heavy brown streaks. Flight slow, heavy, low; much on ground in or near cover; walks, runs, hops; cocks and thrashes tail about; hammers seeds; unobtrusive. *Ad* Greater and median coverts tipped whitish; eyes yellow. *1st winter* As ad if no buff-tipped juv coverts left; eyes may still be grey as juv. VOICE Explosive *chak*, huskier *chaaak*. HABITAT Wood-edges, thickets. FOOD Insects, acorns, berries. RANGE 1: Nov–Feb, Dorset 1966/67. (N America.)

CHATS, THRUSHES (Turdidae)

Rufous Bush Robin *Cercotrichas galactotes* 14.5–16 cm (*c*6 in). Near size of Nightingale (198), but slimmer, with longer bill, longer graduated tail tipped with white and black; more or less rufous above, with creamy supercilia. Perches in open, hops on ground, cocking and fanning tail. *W race (C.g. galactotes)* Wholly rufous above; creamy below. *E races (C.g. syriacus/familiaris)* Head/back grey-brown; tinged greyish below. *Ad = 1st winter*. VOICE Hard *tek tek*. HABITAT Scrub, bushy areas. FOOD Insects. RANGE 10: end Aug–Oct (Apr), most SBr, SIr. (Iberia, N Africa, S Asia.)

Thrush Nightingale *Luscinia luscinia* 16–17 cm (*c*6½ in). Very like Nightingale (198), but dark olive-brown above, tail darker rufous, breast mottled grey-brown. Actions and plumage sequence similar; much louder song lacks crescendo. RANGE 41: most May–Jun, also end Jul–Oct, esp E/NBr. (E Europe, W Asia.)

Siberian Rubythroat *Luscinia calliope* 15–16.5 cm (*c*6¼ in). Near size of Nightingale (198), but character more like Robin or Bluethroat (196); rufous wing-panel and rump, brown back/tail, with whitish

Brown Thrasher

Rufous Bush Robin

syriacus ad

galactotes ad

ad

1st winter ♂

♀

ad

♂

Thrush Nightingale

Siberian Rubythroat

supercilia, eye-rings, moustaches and belly, red or white throat. *Ad ♂* Throat ruby-red, edged black; breast greyish; supercilia/moustaches white. *Ad ♀* Throat whitish (rarely little red), edged grey-brown; breast buff; supercilia/moustaches whitish. *1st winter* As ad ♀, but greater coverts tipped buff; ♂ obscure red traces on white throat. VOICE Plaintive *chee-wee*, churr. HABITAT/FOOD Much as Bluethroat. RANGE 2: Oct, Shetland/Lincs. (Asia.)

Red-flanked Bluetail *Tarsiger cyanurus* 13.5–14.5 cm (*c*5½ in). Build of Robin (196); rump and tail (at least) blue or grey-blue (but tail often simply looks dark), flanks orange-rufous. Jerks (not shivers) tail; often on ground. *Ad ♂* Grey-blue above with bluer supercilia, bright blue shoulders, rump and tail-coverts; creamy-white below; blue partly obscured by grey-brown tips in autumn/winter. *Ad ♀/1st year* Olive-grey above but for dull blue rump/tail; pale eye-rings; centre of throat whitish, surrounded by defined brown-grey. VOICE Short *tik tik*.

HABITAT Trees with undergrowth. FOOD Insects, berries. RANGE 8: most Oct (Sep/May-Jun), EBr. (NE Europe, Asia.)

Isabelline Wheatear *Oenanthe isabellina* 16–17 cm (*c*6½ in). Larger than Wheatear (202), with longer heavier bill, bigger rounder head, shorter-looking tail; pale sandy above, creamy-buff below, thin dark eye-line, usually more blackish on tail (forming square with projection towards white rump, rather than inverted T), whitish underwings in flight (not mottled black and white); in autumn/winter, creamy-edged primary coverts isolate black-brown alula over dark primaries. Upright stance, bounding gait; often tame. Sexes indistinguishable but for extremes: ♂ black lores, clear whitish supercilia, black-ended tail; ♀ grey-speckled lores, obscure creamy supercilia, brown-ended tail. *Ad = 1st winter.* VOICE Quiet *cheep*, whistled *weet-wit.* HABITAT Open sandy areas, short grass. FOOD Insects. RANGE 4: Sep-Nov, May, most EBr. (SE Europe, Cent/S Asia.)

Red-flanked Bluetail

♂ summer

♀/1st summer ♂

1st winter

Isabelline Wheatear

♂ summer

♀ summer

ad/1st winter

Pied Wheatear *Oenanthe pleschanka*
14–15.5 cm (*c*5¾ in). Smaller, slimmer, and
less upright than Wheatear (202); longer
tail has similar pattern, but more black
at sides, and tip often broken by white;
♂ has dark mantle, wings and (usually)
throat, and whitish crown/shawl, variably
obscured by brown-buff in autumn; ♀ very
like some other ♀ wheatears, esp E race of
Black-eared, though darker above, with
distinct pale fringes in autumn, and more
defined tawny chest-band. Perches on
bushes and trees, dropping to ground and
flying up again. ♂ *summer* Mantle, wings
and throat black, crown/nape whitish.
♂ *winter* After moult in Jun–Sep, looks
generally darkish above, with crown/nape
mainly grey-brown mottled buff, and
black areas broken by brown and creamy
fringes. ♀ *summer* Grey-brown above and
brownish-white below; throat often
mottled darker, chest tawny. ♀ *winter* Bold
pale fringes above, throat brownish-white.
1st year ♂ As ad, but mantle/wings much
browner; in autumn, fringes buffer and
wider, dark throat also obscured. VOICE
Harsh *zack-zack*. HABITAT Sandy/stony
areas, open or with thin scrub. FOOD
Insects. RANGE 8: Sep–Nov (May), most
E/SBr, 1 SWIr. (SE Europe, S Cent Asia.)

Black-eared Wheatear *Oenanthe hispanica*
14–15.5 cm (*c*5¾ in). Shape, actions and
tail-pattern like Pied Wheatear; ♂ buff,
pale grey-brown or white above, with
black wings, scapulars and either mask or
whole throat; ♀ has darker cheeks and
scapulars than ♀ Wheatear (202), wings
more fringed buff in summer than Pied,
but mantle lacks Pied's pale fringes in
autumn. ♂ *W race (O.h. hispanica)* Crown
and mantle buff (paler with wear); mask
hardly extends above bill; after moult
in Jul–Aug, wings more fringed buff.
Ad ♀ Pale sandy-buff above, throat
whitish-buff or mottled grey-brown; ear-
coverts brown, wings brown with buff
fringes. ♂ *E race (O.h. melanoleuca)* As
W race, but crown/mantle pale grey-brown
(white with wear); mask crosses forehead;
if present, black throat extends farther
down. *Ad* ♀ As W race, but darker grey-
buff above, looking more like ♀ Pied. *1st*

year ♂ *(both races)* As ad ♂s, but wings
much browner, and more obscured by buff
fringes in autumn (as is throat of black-
throated birds); mask of E race may not
cross forehead. VOICE Grating *zerrk*,
plaintive whistle. HABITAT/FOOD As Pied.
RANGE 34: Mar–Nov, most Apr–Jun/Sep
in E/SBr. (S Europe, SW Asia, NW Africa.)

Desert Wheatear *Oenanthe deserti* 14–15.5
cm (*c*5¾ in). Shape and actions much as
Pied Wheatear, but rump buff-white, most
of tail black (white only at basal corners);
♂ otherwise much as black-throated
Black-eared Wheatear, but with sandy
(not black) scapulars and much white on
inner wing-coverts; ♀ like dull ♂ with
whitish throat (sometimes blackish in
summer), but usually more buff rump,
more pale fringes on wings. *Ad* ♂ Ear-
coverts, throat and wings black; throat
tipped with white and wings fringed
whitish after moult in Jul–Aug. *Ad* ♀ Ear-
coverts and wings browner; throat buff-
white, mottled with or even largely blackish through wear by summer. *1st year* ♂
As ad ♂, but wings much browner, with
broad buff fringes as ♀; throat obscured
more by whitish in autumn/winter. VOICE
Mournful grating whistle. HABITAT/FOOD
Much as Pied. RANGE 20: Aug–Apr (Jun),
all E/SBr. (SW/Cent Asia, N Africa.)

Black Wheatear *Oenanthe leucura* 17–19
cm (*c*7 in). Larger, more thrush-like; all
blackish but for white rump, undertail-
coverts and tail with black inverted T at
end (tip rather narrow). *Ad* ♂ Glossy black.
Ad ♀ Sooty-blackish, barely glossed;
tinged rufous below after moult in Jul–
Oct, duller brown by summer. *1st year*
Much as ads (♂s tinged brown), but flight-
feathers/outer coverts browner, contrasting with blackish inner/smaller coverts.
VOICE Slurred *chak*, piping *pee-pee*.
HABITAT Usually cliffs, mountains. FOOD
Insects. RANGE 5: Jun, Aug–Oct, NE/SE/
WBr, WIr. (SW Europe, N Africa.)

NOTE But for summer ♂s, wheatears can
be hard to identify. Look at colours of
mantle/rump/underparts, exact pattern of
tail and markings of head/throat/wings.

Pied Wheatear

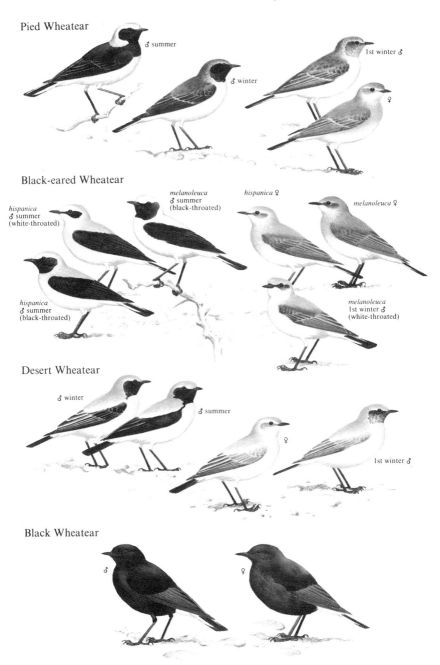

♂ summer

♂ winter

1st winter ♂

♀

Black-eared Wheatear

hispanica
♂ summer
(white-throated)

melanoleuca
♂ summer
(black-throated)

hispanica ♀

melanoleuca ♀

hispanica
♂ summer
(black-throated)

melanoleuca
1st winter ♂
(white-throated)

Desert Wheatear

♂ winter

♂ summer

♀

1st winter ♂

Black Wheatear

♂

♀

Rock Thrush *Monticola saxatilis* 18–20 cm ($c7\frac{1}{2}$ in). About size of fat Song Thrush, with much shorter, mainly orange tail and more wheatear-like stance; summer ♂ grey-blue and orange with variably white back, but other plumages mottled above and crescent-marked below. Flight low, usually from rock to rock, often tending to dive round corners; also perches on trees, wires, buildings; hops on ground, either erect or crouching, and jerks and flirts tail; shy. ♂ *summer* Grey-blue head, at least some white on back, blackish wings, orange below. ♂ *winter* After moult in Jul–Sep, buff-speckled blackish-brown above (blue and white largely hidden); wing-feathers edged buff-white; central throat whitish to pale blue, otherwise orange below, all with whitish tips and dark crescents. *Ad/1st winter* ♀ As ♂ winter, but paler brown above and pale buff to orange-buff below (more orange in summer); little bluish, no pure white. *1st winter* ♂ As ♂ winter, but not so dark above, paler orange below; almost no blue, but clearly distinct from ♀ if traces of pure white on back. VOICE Soft *chak chak*. HABITAT Rocks, grassland. FOOD Insects, also snails, worms, berries. RANGE 13: most May–Jun (also Oct–Nov), scattered S/E/NBr. (Cent/S Eurasia, NW Africa.)

Hermit Thrush *Catharus guttatus* 17–19 cm ($c7$ in). Much smaller than Song Thrush (206); pattern not dissimilar, but thin buff-white eye-rings, rusty rump/tail. Shy, skulking; habitually slowly raises and lowers tail. *Ad* Olive-brown above, but for rufous rump/tail; whitish below, tinged buff on breast, with blackish spots strongest on chest and throat-sides. *1st year* As ad but for buff-tipped greater coverts. VOICE Low *chuk*. HABITAT Damp woods, thickets. FOOD Insects, berries. RANGE 1: Jun, Shetland. (N America.)

Swainson's Thrush *Catharus ustulatus* 17.5–19.5 cm ($c7\frac{1}{4}$ in). Hardly larger than Hermit Thrush, without rufous; very much like Grey-cheeked, but creamy-buff throat and breast, usually bold eye-rings. Skulks in ground cover, also high in trees.

Rock Thrush

ad/1st winter ♀

♂ winter

♂ summer

White's Thrush

ad

ad

Hermit Thrush

1st winter

ad winter

Ad Brownish-olive above with more or less grey tinge; eye-rings and line in front yellow-buff, throat/breast similar and spotted blackish, rest of underparts whitish. *1st year* As ad but for buff-tipped greater coverts. VOICE High *whit*. HABITAT/FOOD As Hermit Thrush. RANGE 8: most Oct (May), W/SIr, S/NEBr. (N America.)

Grey-cheeked Thrush *Catharus minimus* 17.5–19.5 cm (*c*7¼ in). Very like Swainson's Thrush, but greyer cheeks and breast, obscure eye-rings. Usually in ground cover. *Ad* Greyish-olive above; cheeks greyish, faint eye-ring whitish; whitish throat and greyer breast spotted blackish. *1st year* As ad but for buff-tipped greater coverts. VOICE High nasal *kwee-a*. HABITAT/FOOD. As Hermit. RANGE 14: Oct–Nov, esp W/NBr. (N America, NE Asia.)

Veery *Catharus fuscescens* 17–19 cm (*c*7 in). Warm brown (not really rufous) above, no eye-rings, only ill-defined smudges on breast. Usually in ground cover; often stands still, rather upright.

Ad Warm brown to rich tawny above; buff and whitish below, with indistinct grey-brown spots. *1st year* As ad but for buff-tipped greater coverts. VOICE Low *phew*. HABITAT/FOOD As Hermit Thrush. RANGE 1: Oct, Cornwall. (N America.)

White's Thrush *Zoothera dauma* 25–28 cm (*c*10½ in). Size of Mistle Thrush (206), but bill longer; yellow-brown and whitish, with bold black crescents all over head/body, white and black bands on under-wings. Flight undulating; mostly skulks in undergrowth with crouched stance; shy. *Ad* Yellow-brown above, tinged olive in winter but greyer in summer, and yellowish-white below, all boldly scaled black; brown and yellow-olive pattern on upperwings; central tail-feathers brown, rest blackish with white tips. *1st winter* As ad but for yellow-buff tips to central tail. VOICE Monotonous and tuneless whistle. HABITAT Woods with dense undergrowth. FOOD Insects, berries. RANGE 38: most Oct–Feb (also May, Sep), widely scattered but most E/SBr. (Cent/E Asia, Australia.)

Swainson's Thrush

Grey-cheeked Thrush

Veery

1st winter

ad winter

1st winter

ad winter

1st winter

ad winter

Siberian Thrush *Zoothera sibirica* 22–24 cm (*c*9 in). Slightly smaller, flatter-headed than Blackbird (204); black with white supercilia, or brown with buff eyebrows and crescent-marked underparts; white tail-corners, bands on underwings (*cf* White's Thrush, 302). Actions as Blackbird, but shy, skulking. *Ad ♂* Slate-black but for supercilia, tail-corners, grey or whitish belly. *Ad ♀* Olive-brown above, with buffish supercilia, pale-speckled cheeks, whitish throat, extensive brown crescent-marks below. *1st winter ♂* Duller: throat buff, less uniform below; retained juv wings and tail olive-brown. VOICE Soft *zit*. HABITAT Woods, thickets, esp near water. FOOD Insects, worms. RANGE 3: Oct–Dec, scattered E/SBr. (Cent/E Asia.)

Eye-browed Thrush *Turdus obscurus* 20–22 cm (*c*8¼ in). Size, actions and (whiter) supercilia as Redwing (206), but longer bill, plain orange-buff chest/flanks, white belly, pale grey underwings. *Ad ♂* Head (and variably lower throat) greyish; white under eyes and on upper throat; chest/flanks orange-rufous. *Ad ♀* Head grey-brown to olive-brown, no patch under eyes, dark streaks on throat; chest/flanks duller orange-buff. *1st winter* Duller than ads, with buff-tipped greater coverts; chest/flanks often only warm buff, little or no grey about head. VOICE Thin *tlip-tlip*, loud *keuk*. HABITAT Woods, fields. FOOD Insects, worms, berries. RANGE 4: Oct–Dec, scattered W/CentBr. (Cent/E Asia.)

Dusky Thrush *Turdus naumanni* 22–24 cm (*c*9 in). Size of Song Thrush (206), but with heavy bill; dark above, variously marked chestnut, with broad whitish supercilia, blackish ear-coverts, breast-patches and flanks. Actions recall Fieldfare (204), esp erect stance with bill up; not skulking. *Ad ♂* Black-brown above, with variable chestnut on back, rump, tail-base, scapulars, and esp coverts/secondaries; cheeks/throat creamy and underparts white with blackish on breast and flanks (more uniform in summer, scaled white in winter). *Ad ♀* Usually, browner above with less and paler chestnut, breast-patches

Siberian Thrush

Eye-browed Thrush

Dusky Thrush

browner, flanks rustier. *1st winter* Imm ♂ intermediate between ads, ♀ duller than ad ♀ with buff on wings and rusty-brown on breast/flanks; paler edges and shaft-streaks on some coverts. VOICE Blackbird-like clucking, wheezy flight-call. HABITAT Wood-edges, grassland. FOOD Insects, worms, berries. RANGE 6: Sep–Mar, N/CentBr. (Cent/E Asia.)

Black-throated Thrush *Turdus ruficollis* 23–25 cm (*c*9½ in). Just larger than Song Thrush (206); black or densely spotted throat/chest, orange-buff axillaries, yellow-based bill. Actions as Blackbird (204). *Ad* ♂ Brown-grey above with blackish streaks on crown/nape; black supercilia and throat/chest, thinly scaled whitish in winter; dull white below with greyer flanks. *Ad* ♀ Olive-brown above; faint supercilia grey-buff, throat white with blackish streaks, chest blackish with broad grey-buff fringes; more grey-brown below. *1st winter* As ad ♀, but ♂ face to chest more as ad ♂ winter; grey-white tips to any unmoulted outer greater coverts.

VOICE Blackbird-like chuckle, thin *tseep*. HABITAT Open woods, fields. FOOD Insects, worms, berries. RANGE 10: Oct–Apr, most NE/EBr. (Cent Asia.)

American Robin *Turdus migratorius* 24–27 cm (*c*10 in). Typical thrush, size and shape of Blackbird (204) with mainly yellow bill, brick-red breast; grey to blackish above, with white eye-crescents, throat (streaked black), tail-corners and lower belly. Actions much as Blackbird; restlessly flicks wings and tail. *Ad* ♂ Dark grey above, head and tail blacker; breast rich orange-red, with whitish feather-fringes in winter. *Ad* ♀ Browner-grey above, head/tail less contrasting; breast paler, often fringed whitish all year. *1st winter* As ads, but browner above, with buff-tipped outer greater coverts, and duller rufous below. VOICE Anxious *tcheep* and *tut-tut-tut*, often combined; flight-note very like Blackbird. HABITAT Woods, fields. FOOD Insects, worms, snails, berries. RANGE 23: Sep–May (esp Oct–Feb), most Ir, SBr, also NBr. (N America.)

Black-throated Thrush

American Robin

WARBLERS (Sylviidae)

Fan-tailed Warbler *Cisticola juncidis* 9–11 cm (*c*4 in). Tiny, with longish bill but short rounded wings and tail; tawny-buff above with bold dark streaks (more blotched in summer), whitish below with warm buff breast/flanks; beady eyes in pale face, rufous rump, black and whitish tips to all but central tail (esp underside). Flight weak, jerky, but high in undulating display; skulking, but also perches in open and often cocks thin or fanned tail, looking like minute Sedge Warbler (208) or scruffy Wren (194). *Ad = 1st winter.* VOICE Short *zip*, explosive *tew*; song sharp penetrating *zeep . . . zeep . . . zeep . . .* in time with dips in display-flight or from perch. HABITAT. Rushy marshes, rank grassland, cornfields. FOOD Insects. RANGE 3: Apr–Sep, Cork/Dorset/Norfolk; is spreading north in Europe, may colonise. (W/S Europe, S Asia, Africa, Australia.)

Pallas's Grasshopper Warbler *Locustella certhiola* 13–14 cm (*c*5¼ in). Shape/actions as Grasshopper Warbler (208), but larger, more striated above and whiter below, with thin creamy supercilia and rufous rump (*cf* Sedge Warbler, 208), contrasting dark tail shading to blackish near end with grey-white tips on all but central feathers (esp underside). *Ad* White throat and belly, plain warm buff breast and flanks; wings worn in autumn. *1st winter* Creamy below, chest dark-spotted; wings fresh. VOICE Double *chirr* or *cherk*. HABITAT/FOOD As Lanceolated. RANGE 5: Sep–Oct, NE/EBr, EIr. (Cent/E Asia.)

Lanceolated Warbler *Locustella lanceolata* 11–12 cm (*c*4½ in). Shape/actions as Grasshopper Warbler (208), but smaller, darker, heavier-streaked; faint buff-white supercilia, necklace of bold short streaks, usually also longer streaks on flanks, sometimes spots on throat. *1st winter* As ad, but wings fresh. VOICE Chuckled churr. HABITAT Reeds, swamps, thick cover. FOOD Insects. RANGE 28: Sep–early Nov (May), most NE/EBr (esp Shetland). (E Russia, Asia.)

Fan-tailed Warbler

Pallas's Grasshopper Warbler

song-flight

ad

ad

juv–1st winter

ad (worn plumage)

Lanceolated Warbler

juv–1st winter

ad (worn plumage)

River Warbler *Locustella fluviatilis* 13.5–14.5 cm (*c*5½ in). Shape/actions as Grasshopper Warbler, but larger, longer-winged, with unstreaked upperparts (*cf* Savi's, 208); faint off-white supercilia, blurred grey-brown streaks on whitish throat/chest, broad whitish tips to brown undertail-coverts. *Ad* Dark olive-brown above but for slightly warmer tail, much whitish below; wings worn. *1st winter* Slightly tinged rufous above (esp scapulars, wing/tail-coverts), more creamy-buff below; wings fresh. VOICE Low harsh churr. HABITAT Damp tangles, thickets. FOOD Insects. RANGE 3: Sep, NE/WBr. (E Europe, W Asia.)

Moustached Warbler *Acrocephalus melanopogon* 12–13 cm (*c*5 in). Very like Sedge Warbler (208), but shorter wings, more rounded tail, pure white supercilia broader behind eyes and square-ended; crown blacker (esp in summer), cheeks duskier, upperparts/flanks more rufous, mantle bolder-streaked, underparts whiter. *Ad* Wings/tail worn until moult in Aug–Oct. *1st winter* Wings/tail fresh. VOICE Calls as Sedge, but harsher *chuk*. HABITAT Reeds. FOOD Insects. RANGE Pair bred Cambs 1946; 5 others; Apr–Aug, all SEBr. (S Europe, SW Asia, NW Africa.)

Aquatic Warbler *Acrocephalus paludicola* 12–13 cm (*c*5 in). Like spiky-tailed Sedge Warbler (208), but head striped with creamy crown-band and long supercilia, blackish crown-sides (but *cf* ill-defined crown-stripe of juv Sedge); bolder black streaks above extend thinly on to rump. Skulking, often on or near ground. *Ad* Ground-colour above greyish in summer, then tawnier with moult in *c*Aug–Oct but worn wings/tail faded grey-brown; creamy below, thinly streaked (esp in summer). *Juv/1st winter* Ground-colour above bright sandy-buff with tawny-buff fringes on fresh wings/tail; more buff below, usually unstreaked. VOICE Calls resemble Sedge Warbler. HABITAT Sedgy marshes; reeds on passage. FOOD Insects. RANGE 569: Apr–Nov, most Aug–early Oct, esp SBr, few EBr and SIr. (Cent/E Europe.)

River Warbler   Moustached Warbler

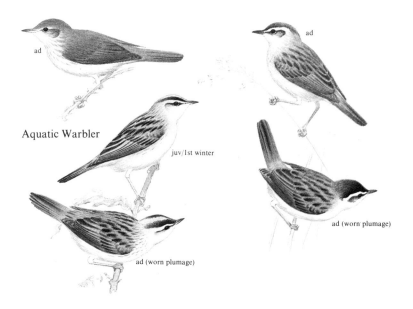

Aquatic Warbler

Paddyfield Warbler *Acrocephalus agricola* 12–13 cm (*c*5 in). Looks smaller than Reed Warbler (210), with shortest bill, shortest roundest wings, and longest tail of any unstreaked *Acrocephalus*; often brighter rufous above (esp rump) and sandy-buff below, with creamy supercilia broadest behind eyes, legs pale brown to flesh. Flight more whirring than Reed; cocks tail on landing, often flicks tail and raises crest. *Ad* Usually rufous above, but sometimes greyer (except rump); wings/tail worn in autumn. *1st winter* Sandier-brown above; wings/tail fresh with rufous fringes. VOICE Hard *chik*. HABITAT Reeds, waterside cover. FOOD Insects. RANGE 5: Sep–Oct, NE/SWBr. (SE Europe, Asia.)

Blyth's Reed Warbler *Acrocephalus dumetorum* 12–13 cm (*c* 5 in). Very like Marsh Warbler (210), but more peaked crown, shorter rounder wings, longer-looking tail; brown or grey-brown above, with 'spectacled' appearance and supercilia indistinct at rear, legs grey-brown. Flight like Paddyfield; rather deliberate creeping movements; flicks tail. *Ad* Greyish olive-brown above, wearing to grey-brown or brown; wings/tail worn in autumn. *1st winter* Warmer brown, tinged rufous on rump; wings/tail fresh with rufous fringes. VOICE Harsh *tak* and trill, soft *tup tup*. HABITAT Trees, tangles, swamps. FOOD Insects. RANGE 11: Aug–Oct, most N/EBr. (NE Europe, Asia.)

Great Reed Warbler *Acrocephalus arundinaceus* 18–20 cm (*c*7½ in). Much as Reed Warbler (210), but far larger, twice as bulky, much stouter longer bill, angular head, bold supercilia, dusky lores (*cf* Thick-billed). Flight heavy with rounded tail often fanned, crashing into reeds; actions more lumbering. *Ad* Warm olive-brown above and orange-buff below, wearing greyer and whiter by autumn; faint streaks on throat. *1st winter* More rusty-buff above, esp rump and fresh wings; orange-buff below, no streaks. VOICE Harsh *chak*, churring croak; song loud raucous creaking *karra-karra-karra-gurk-gurk-gurk*. HABITAT Reeds, osiers. FOOD Insects. RANGE 123: May–Nov, esp May–Jun (sometimes in song), most S/EBr. (Cent/S Europe, Asia, NW Africa.)

Thick-billed Warbler *Acrocephalus aedon* 18.5–20.5 cm (*c*7¾ in). Size of Great Reed; shorter thicker bill (clearly curved on top), much shorter rounded wings, longer and more graduated tail; plumage similar, but no supercilia or throat-streaks, lores whitish, rump redder, legs blue-grey. Flight looks weak; raises crest, moves tail like shrike; hops in cover rather than creeping and sidling. *Ad* Olive-brown above; wings/tail worn in autumn. *1st winter* More rufous above, richer buff below; wings/tail fresh. VOICE Loud *chook-chook* and *tak-tak*. HABITAT Trees, scrub, not always near water. FOOD Insects. RANGE 2: Sep–Oct, Shetland. (Asia.)

Olivaceous Warbler *Hippolais pallida* 12–14 cm (*c*5¼ in). Like non-yellow form of Icterine (210), but flatter crown, shorter wings (as Melodious, 210), fatter belly, more rounded tail, W race also longer bill; olive-grey to brown above, buffish-white below, with thin whitish supercilia, eye-rings (often obvious) and tail-sides, bluish to brownish-flesh legs (*cf* Garden Warbler, 214). Flight fluttery, as Melodious. *Ad W race (H.p. opaca)* Larger, with longer tail and esp bill; olive-grey above. *Ad E race (H.p. elaeica)* Smaller, more grey-brown, with shorter bill and tail (*cf* Booted Warbler). *1st winter* As ad, but wings fresh in autumn. VOICE Calls as Melodious. HABITAT Trees, scrub. FOOD Insects. RANGE 12: Aug–Oct, most SBr. (SW Europe/ NW Africa, SE Europe/SW Asia.)

Booted Warbler *Hippolais caligata* 11–12 cm (*c*4½ in). Smaller than Olivaceous (not unlike *Phylloscopus*), with shorter finer bill, rounder head, squarer tail, short wings; brown, greyish, even sandy above, creamy below, with longer supercilia and faint dusky eye-stripes (otherwise similar eye-rings, tail-sides, legs). Flight fluttery. *Ad winter* Warm brownish-olive above; wings worn or moulting in autumn. *1st winter* Greyer or sandier, and whiter; wings fresh. VOICE Sharp *tic*, quiet *chuk*. HABITAT/FOOD As Olivaceous. RANGE 12: Aug–Oct, N/E/SBr. (E Europe, Asia.)

Paddyfield Warbler

ad

1st winter

Great Reed
Warbler

Blyth's Reed Warbler

ad

1st winter

ad

Thick-billed Warbler

1st winter

ad (worn plumage)

ad (worn plumage)

Olivaceous Warbler

Booted Warbler

opaca
1st winter

1st winter

elaeica
1st winter

ad

Spectacled Warbler *Sylvia conspicillata*
11.5–12.5 cm (c4¾ in). Like tiny slim
Whitethroat (212) with shorter rufous
wings; whitish spectacles often inconspicuous, legs pale red-brown to yellowish.
Very lively; shy. *Ad ♂* Head slate-grey
with darker lores/ear-coverts, browner
nape; bold white throat shades down into
grey; breast pink, flanks brownish-pink.
Ad ♀ Head browner, often with greyish
lores/ear-coverts; throat tinged buff;
breast dull pink, flanks pink-buff. *1st
winter ♂♀* As dull ad ♀, no greyish. VOICE
Sharp *tek tek*, rattling alarm call.
HABITAT Low scrub. FOOD Insects. RANGE
3: Oct/Jun, SW/NEBr. (SW Europe,
Middle East, NW Africa.)

Subalpine Warbler *Sylvia cantillans*
11.5–12.5 cm (c4¾ in). Shape as tiny Lesser
Whitethroat (212) with longish tail; ♂
grey and pinkish with white moustaches;
♀ smaller, slimmer, paler, buffer than ♀
Sardinian, with more white on tail-sides,
sometimes rusty-buff (not bright rufous)
fringes on wings (*cf* Spectacled), legs pale
ochre. Cocks tail. *Ad ♂* Blue-grey above
with pale-fringed brown wings, pink to
orange-brown below with bold moustaches; eye-rings red. *Ad ♀* Brown above,
greyer on head; pink-buff (variably
showing moustaches) to pale buff below;
eye-rings red or yellowish, often whitish
circle outside. *1st winter* As ads, but wings
browner (less grey), tail-sides brownish-
white, eye-rings yellowish; ♀ creamier
below. VOICE Sharp *tek tek*, chatter.
HABITAT Scrub, trees. FOOD Insects. RANGE
90: Apr–Nov (esp May–Jun), most NE/
E/SBr. (S Europe, Turkey, NW Africa.)

Sardinian Warbler *Sylvia melanocephala*
12.5–14 cm (c5¼ in). Shape as smallish
Whitethroat (212) but short wings, rounded tail; darkish above with dark hood,
white cornered tail, whitish underparts,
dark flanks, brown legs, often red eye-
rings (*cf* Subalpine, Orphean, Rüppell's).
Cocks and fans tail; skulking. *Ad ♂* Hood
black, mantle dark grey, flanks grey; eye-
rings red. *Ad ♀* Hood dark grey-brown,
mantle brown, flanks dull brown; eye-
rings reddish to brown. *1st winter* As ads,

but ♂ browner above (esp nape and
wings), ♀ hood brown; tail-corners
brownish-white, eye-rings brownish.
VOICE Harsh stutter. HABITAT Scrub, trees.
FOOD Insects, seeds, berries. RANGE 8:
Apr–May, Aug–Oct, most SBr (2 NEBr).
(S Europe, Middle East, N Africa.)

Rüppell's Warbler *Sylvia rueppelli* 13.5–
14.5 cm (c5½ in). Larger than Sardinian
with longer wings; paler above (not tail),
black or creamy throat, whitish moustaches, red-brown eye-rings and legs.
Ad ♂ Crown, face and throat black,
moustaches white; blue-grey above, pink-
white below with greyer flanks. *Ad/1st
winter ♀* Crown grey-brown, throat
creamy (both often mottled black on ad),
moustaches whitish; brown above, buff
below with browner flanks. *1st winter ♂*
Browner above; white fringes on throat.
VOICE Harsh chatter, *tak tak*. HABITAT
Scrub, trees. FOOD Insects. RANGE 2: Jun–
Sep, Shetland/Devon. (E Mediterranean.)

Desert Warbler *Sylvia nana* 11–12 cm (c4½
in). Tiny, wings/tail longish; sandy with
white-edged brown tail, yellowish eyes,
bill and legs. Often on ground by scrub.
Asian race (S.n. nana) Greyish sandy-
brown above, with warm buff rump;
creamy to greyish below with buff flanks.
N African race (S.n. deserti) Pale sandy
and whitish with rufous rump. VOICE
Sharp *wee-churr*. HABITAT Low scrub.
FOOD Insects. RANGE 3: Oct–Jan, S/EBr
(all Asian). (Cent Asia, N Africa.)

Orphean Warbler *Sylvia hortensis* 14.5–16
cm (c6 in). Larger than Lesser Whitethroat
(212), with heavy bill, squared tail; dark
hood (crown browner, cheeks blacker)
merging into grey-brown or brown mantle,
white-sided tail, greyish legs, usually
yellow-white eyes (*cf* Sardinian). Mainly
arboreal. *Ad ♂* Crown brown-black
(spring) to dark brown-grey (autumn);
breast/flanks pink-white. *Ad ♀* Crown
duller grey-brown; breast/flanks buff-
white. *1st winter ♂♀* As ad ♀, but crown
brown as mantle (*cf* Barred, 212). VOICE
Hard rattle, *tak tak*. HABITAT Trees, tall
scrub. FOOD Insects, berries. RANGE 3:
Jul–Oct, SW/EBr. (S Eurasia, N Africa.)

Spectacled Warbler

1st winter

♂

Subalpine Warbler

1st winter ♀

♀ summer

♂

Sardinian Warbler

♂

1st winter ♀

♀

Rüppell's Warbler

♂ summer

♀

1st winter ♂

Desert Warbler

nana
1st winter

deserti
1st winter

Orphean Warbler

♂ winter

♀

1st winter (dark-eyed)

Greenish Warbler *Phylloscopus trochiloides* 10–11 cm (*c*4¼ in). Size/shape of Chiffchaff (216); greyish-olive and whitish, with clear creamy supercilia, usually 1 short whitish wing-bar (but *cf* E Chiffchaff); bill-base pinkish, legs brown-grey. *Ad summer/1st winter* Brighter, greener; wing-bar clear on greater coverts, sometimes trace of 2nd on medians. *Ad winter* Greyer; wings/tail worn; wing-bar faint or missing. VOICE Penetrating *chee-wee*; song short high shrill phrase ('full of saliva') or Wren-like trill. HABITAT Trees, bushes. FOOD Insects. RANGE 133: Aug–Jan, May–Jul (sometimes in song), esp E/SBr, SIr. (E Europe, Asia.)

Arctic Warbler *Phylloscopus borealis* 11.5–12.5 cm (*c*4¾ in). Robust, larger than Greenish, with heavier bill, flatter forehead; olive and whitish, with long upturned creamy supercilia, 1–2 thin whitish wing-bars; bill-base orange-yellow or yellow-brown as legs. *Ad winter* Wings/tail faded brown; often median wing-bar missing, rarely both; whitish below. *1st winter* Wings/tail dark brown; median wing-bar present till *c*Sep; darker greenish above, yellower-white below. VOICE Husky *tssik*, hoarse *tswee-ip*. HABITAT/FOOD As Greenish. RANGE 105: Aug–Oct (Jul), esp EBr. (N Eurasia, Alaska.)

Pallas's Warbler *Phylloscopus proregulus* 8.5–9.5 cm (*c*3½ in). Tiny, like Goldcrest (236); bright green and whitish, with long yellow supercilia, crown-stripe, 2 wing-bars, rump. Hovers among leaves. *Ad = 1st winter*. VOICE Shrill *sweep* and *choo-ee*. HABITAT Trees. FOOD Insects. RANGE 146: Oct–Nov, esp E/SBr. (Cent/E Asia.)

Radde's Warbler *Phylloscopus schwarzi* 12–13 cm (*c*5 in). Larger, bulkier than Chiffchaff (216), with longer thicker bill, longer tail, stout legs, similar shortish rounded wings; brownish- to greenish-olive and buff-white, with browner head, long broad upturned creamy supercilia edged with black, rusty vent; bill-base pink to orange, legs pinkish-yellow. Skulks; much on ground. *1st winter* More

Greenish Warbler

1st winter/ad summer

1st winter

Arctic Warbler

ad winter

ad winter

Pallas's Warbler

Radde's Warbler

1st winter

1st winter/ad

ad winter

buff throat(?). VOICE Soft *tchwit*, harder *tchwik* and *chirp trok-trok*. HABITAT Wood-edges, scrub. FOOD Insects. RANGE 28: end Sep–Oct, esp E/SBr. (Cent/E Asia.)

Dusky Warbler *Phylloscopus fuscatus* 11.5–12.5 cm (*c*4¾ in). Slighter than Radde's with finer bill, shorter tail; brown and creamy-grey, with longish rusty-white supercilia, rusty cheeks and flanks; bill-base and legs yellow-brown. Skulks; much on ground; cocks tail and flicks wings. *Ad winter* Brown above, no yellow below. *1st winter* Olive-brown above, some yellow on belly. VOICE Loud *tak*, *chik*, chattering *tsek-tsek*. HABITAT Scrub, reeds. FOOD Insects. RANGE 29: Aug–Nov (May), esp E/SBr. (Cent/E Asia.)

Bonelli's Warbler *Phylloscopus bonelli* 11–12 cm (*c*4½ in). Just larger, bigger-headed than Chiffchaff (216), wings less rounded; grey-brown above with greyer head, yellowish wing-panel, rump, and tail-fringes, white below; bill-base pinkish, legs dark pink-brown. *Ad* Rump yellow-green; wings/tail faded by autumn. *1st winter* Mantle greyer, rump pale olive-brown; wings/tail fresh, bright-edged. VOICE Loud *hoo-eet*; song short even trill. HABITAT Trees, bushes. FOOD Insects. RANGE 68: Aug–early Nov, also Apr–Jun (sometimes in song), esp S/E/WBr, SIr. (Cent/S Europe, NW Africa, SW Asia.)

FLYCATCHERS (Muscicapidae)

Collared Flycatcher *Ficedula albicollis* 12–13 cm (*c*5 in). Like long-winged Pied (218); differs as follows. ♂ *summer* White collar, whitish rump, more white on fore-head and base of primaries, little or none on tail-sides. *Ad* ♀ Greyer above, usually white patch on primaries, often hint of pale collar and rump. ♂ *winter* As ♀ from *c*Aug–Sep but for black flight-feathers, outer wing-coverts and central tail. *1st winter* As ad ♀ unless pale spots on some or all median coverts. VOICE Drawn-out *whee*. HABITAT Trees, scrub. FOOD Insects. RANGE 10: May–Jun (Sep), most N/EBr. (Cent/SE Europe, W Asia.)

Bonelli's Warbler

ad (worn plumage)

1st winter

Collared Flycatcher

♂ winter

♂ summer

Dusky Warbler

1st winter

1st winter

ad winter

♀

WALLCREEPERS (Tichodromadidae)

Wallcreeper *Tichodroma muraria* 16–17 cm (*c*6½ in). Long curved bill, long broad rounded wings narrowing at base; largely grey with crimson patches and white spots on blackish wings, white-edged dark tail. Flits jerkily like butterfly; climbs rock faces with small hops, leisurely flicking wings, and probes into crevices. ♂ *summer* Throat to breast black *c*Apr–Aug. ♀ *summer* Throat whitish with small black patch, or no black (probably 1st year), and breast grey. *Ad winter* Throat whitish. *Juv* Bill straighter at first, all underparts brown-grey; as ad winter after moult in Aug–Nov. VOICE Thin high piping. HABITAT Cliffs, ruins. FOOD Insects. RANGE 10: Sep–Jun, most SBr; wintered Nov–Apr in 3 years 1969–78. (S/Cent Eurasia.)

TREECREEPERS (Certhiidae)

Short-toed Treecreeper *Certhia brachydactyla* 12–13 cm (*c*5 in). *Very* like Treecreeper (226): tends to be duller/greyer above with less rusty rump, shorter/less distinct supercilia, and less white below with rufous-tinged flanks; on average, bill longer/more curved, hind-claws shorter, but much overlap. Calls similar, but include loud *chink*, Dunnock-like *zeet*. RANGE 7: Sep–Oct, Apr–May, SE/EBr. (W/Cent/S Europe, Turkey, NW Africa.)

PENDULINE TITS (Remizidae)

Penduline Tit *Remiz pendulinus* 10.5–11 cm (*c*4¼ in). Tiny with prominent tail; grey head, black mask, rusty back, white-edged blackish flight-feathers and tail, and buff underparts tinged pinkish on breast and flanks. Flight more fluttery than Blue Tit (224); flicks tail. *Ad ♂* Mask black, crown to upper mantle grey, lower mantle chestnut, back rufous. *Ad ♀* Mask smaller and not solid black, crown to nape grey-brown, mantle pale chestnut. *Juv* Duller, browner, no mask; as ad after moult in Aug–Sep. VOICE Thin plaintive *tsee*, rather Robin-like. HABITAT Waterside thickets; vagrants in coastal bushes. FOOD Insects, seeds. RANGE 3: Oct/May, Humberside/Scilly/Kent. (S/Cent Eurasia.)

SHRIKES (Laniidae)

Isabelline Shrike *Lanius isabellinus* 16–18 cm (*c*6¾ in). Shape as Red-backed Shrike (228), but grey-buff above, with rusty rump and tail, white bar on base of primaries (S/E races sandier above, browner mask, often no wing-bar). *Ad ♂* Grey-buff above in summer, paler in winter; narrow black mask; white below with pink-buff flanks. *Ad ♀* Even paler above; mask not pure black on lores; greyish crescent bars on breast-sides. *1st winter* Duller, barred additionally on wing-coverts and flanks. VOICE/HABITAT/FOOD Much as Red-backed. RANGE 15: Aug–Oct (Mar–May), most E/SBr (1 SWIr). (S/Cent Asia.)

Lesser Grey Shrike *Lanius minor* 19–21 cm (*c*8 in). Like small Great Grey (228), with stubbier bill, longer wings, shorter tail; mask over forehead, no white supercilia, less white on scapulars, bolder wing-bar. Flight straighter; perches more upright. *Ad ♂* Deep mask black; pink tinge below. *Ad ♀* Narrower mask blackish, mottled grey on forehead; creamier below. *Juv–1st winter* Brown-grey above, with varying dark bars, greyish forehead, brown-black wings and tail; traces of faint bars on flanks. VOICE/HABITAT As Great Grey. FOOD Esp insects. RANGE 112: May–Nov, esp EBr, only 2 Ir. (S Europe, SW Asia.)

Woodchat Shrike *Lanius senator* 16–18 cm (*c*6¾ in). Size of Red-backed Shrike (228), but larger head, broader wings, shorter tail; pied, with chestnut crown/nape, white scapulars, wing-bar and rump, bold white underparts. Perches more unobtrusively. *Ad ♂* Mask black, mantle blackish, wings/tail black. *Ad ♀* Narrower mask mixed with brown and whitish, mantle brown, wings/tail brown, some crescents on breast/flanks. *Juv–1st winter* Greyish to rufous above, and paler and more scaly than imm Red-backed, with pale scapulars, rump and wing-bar; creamy below, barred with black crescents. VOICE Hard chatter. HABITAT Trees, scrub. FOOD Birds, insects. RANGE 402: Apr–Oct, esp SW/EBr, SIr. (Cent/S Europe, SW Asia, NW Africa.)

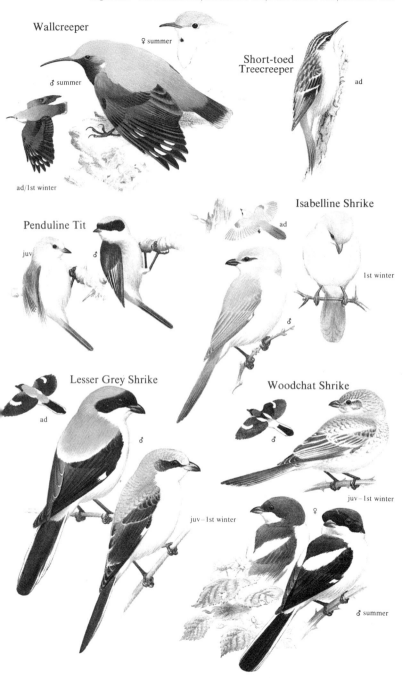

Wallcreeper

♀ summer

♂ summer

ad/1st winter

Short-toed Treecreeper

ad

Penduline Tit

juv

♂

Isabelline Shrike

ad

1st winter

♂

Lesser Grey Shrike

ad

♂

juv–1st winter

Woodchat Shrike

♂

juv–1st winter

♀

♂ summer

CROWS (Corvidae)

Nutcracker *Nucifraga caryocatactes* 30–33 cm (c21½ in). Shape closest to small Jay (228), but longer pointed bill, short tail; chocolate speckled with white, but plain cap, blacker wings/tail, bold white on undertail-coverts, white tail-end (obvious from below). Actions much as Jay, with rather slow jerky flight; perches more in open (often on tree-tops); hops clumsily. *1st winter* Tends to be browner than ad, less glossy wings with more spots on coverts. VOICE Harsh high *kraak*. HABITAT Conifers; vagrants in any woods, fields. FOOD Conifer seeds, hazel nuts, berries. RANGE 399 (315 in 1968): most Aug–Jan, esp SEBr. (Eurasia.)

STARLINGS (Sturnidae)

Rose-coloured Starling *Sturnus roseus* 20.5–22.5 cm (c8½ in). Shape/actions as Starling (234), but bill more thrush-like; ad pink and black with crest; juv sandy. *Summer* Ad ♂ brighter pink, glossier black, crest fuller; ♀/1st summer ♂ duller, pink variably obscured by grey-brown. *Winter* After moult in Aug–Oct, pattern variably obscured by grey-buff tips, esp on pink upperparts and more so on ♀/1st winter ♂, while 1st winter ♀ brown, dull, short-crested, almost no pink above. *Juv* Sandy-fawn with paler throat/rump, dark wings/tail, dark-tipped yellowish bill; moults in cAug–Nov. VOICE Starling-like but higher, harsher. HABITAT Fields, open country. FOOD Insects, fruit. RANGE 267: all months, esp Jun–Oct, wide-scattered, esp NE/SBr. (SE Europe, SW Asia.)

SPARROWS (Passeridae)

Spanish Sparrow *Passer hispaniolensis* 14–15.5 cm (c5¾ in). As House Sparrow (234), but ♂ has chestnut crown, whiter cheek-patches, more black on breast, heavily streaked shoulders/flanks; other plumages show traces of this pattern in paler cheeks, more striped and contrasted back, faint flank-streaks. VOICE Similar, but richer, less harsh. HABITAT Scrub, trees, woods. FOOD Seeds. RANGE 3: Jun, Oct, Devon/Scilly. (Mediterranean, SW Asia.)

FINCHES (Fringillidae)

Serin *Serinus serinus* 11–12 cm (c4½ in). Tiny, with stubby bill, longish wings, short notched tail; streaky, yellowish, with yellow rump (not juv), no yellow in tail. Flight fast, undulating; often in trees, but feeds much by hopping on ground. ♂ *summer* Forecrown, hindneck, throat/breast unstreaked yellow. ♂ *winter* After moult in Aug–Sep, yellow of forecrown, supercilia and hindneck more or less obscured, throat/breast greener-yellow, flanks less clearly streaked. *Ad* ♀ Crown/hindneck yellow-green, heavily streaked; supercilia and throat/breast yellow-white streaked dark. *Juv* Brown-buff above, rump barely paler, all streaked dark; yellow-buff below streaked brown; as ads after moult in Aug–Sep. VOICE Flight-call liquid twittering trill; other calls include weak *chip-chip*, sharp tit-like *chirr*, anxious *tsooeet*; song rapid hissing jangle like miniature Corn Bunting (248). HABITAT Gardens, parks, wood-edges, esp near weedy ground. NEST In trees, tall bushes, 3–5 eggs, end Apr–Jul; 2 broods. FOOD Seeds of weeds, alder, birch. RANGE 397: all months, esp Feb–Jun, Oct–Nov, mainly SBr; nested 1967, 1969, 1978. (Europe, Asia Minor, NW Africa.)

Arctic Redpoll *Carduelis hornemanni* 12–13.5 cm (c5 in). Like Mealy race of Redpoll (240), not always separable; typically shows clear white rump and paler head with contrasting grey back, bolder wing-bars, whiter underparts with few thin streaks on breast-sides/flanks, but rather variable (*eg* rump and flanks may be tinged buff). *Ad* ♂ Variably tinged pink on cheeks, breast, esp rump. ♀/*1st year* ♂ No pink (except red crown), but some 1st year ♂s slightly pink on rump. *Greenland (C.h. hornemanni) and N Eurasian (C.h. exilipes) races* Many inseparable, but Greenland ♂ typically bigger, whiter, less streaked, often with 'hoar-frosted' face. VOICE Flight-note slower, sharper than Redpoll. HABITAT/FOOD Much as Redpoll, but less linked with trees. RANGE 89: Jul–Apr, most Oct–Feb, esp N/EBr. (Circumpolar Arctic.)

Nutcracker

1st winter/ad

1st winter/ad

Rose-coloured Starling

juv

1st summer

♂ winter

♂ summer

Spanish Sparrow

♀

♂ winter

♂ summer

Serin

♂

♂ summer

juv

♀

Arctic Redpoll

♂ summer

♂ winter

♀

♀

Two-barred Crossbill *Loxia leucoptera*
14–15 cm (*c*5¾ in). Like small Crossbill
(242), but rather brighter, with 2 white
wing-bars, white-tipped inner secondaries.
Habits as Crossbill. *Ad* ♂ Red areas
uniform bright scarlet-carmine. *Ad* ♀
Yellower-green than Crossbill with
yellower rump; streaks on crown and
mantle stand out more. *1st year* ♂ Colours
mixed as Crossbill, but paler, brighter;
white wing-marks smaller than ad. VOICE
Less emphatic Crossbill-like *jip jip*,
drier *jif jif* not unlike Redpoll (240).
HABITAT Conifers, esp larches. FOOD
Conifer seeds. RANGE 63: most Jul–Feb,
scattered, esp EBr. (N Eurasia, America.)

Parrot Crossbill *Loxia pytyopsittacus*
16.5–17.5 cm (*c*6¾ in). Differs from Crossbill and Scottish Crossbill (242) in larger,
deeper, stouter bill giving top-heavy look;
plumages and habits similar. VOICE
Deeper, stronger *jop jop*. HABITAT
Conifers, esp pines. FOOD Pine seeds.
RANGE Over 70: mostly Sep–Mar, esp
1962/63, mainly EBr. (N Europe.)

Trumpeter Finch *Bucanetes githagineus*
12–13 cm (*c*5 in). Linnet-sized (240), but
dumpier, shorter-tailed, with big head and
stout, round-tipped, red or yellowish bill,
often pinkish legs; sandy-brown with
darker wings/tail, more or less tinged
pink. Inconspicuous ground-feeder, often
crouched, upright when alert; suddenly
flies off high. ♂ *summer* Bill orange-red
like blob of sealing wax; much pink, esp
on face, rump, wing-edges and underparts; head grey. ♂ *winter* Bill orange-
brown; body duller, pink obscured by
buff. *Ad* ♀ Bill pink-orange to yellowish;
body much less bright, but usually faint
pink wash in summer. *Juv/1st winter* Bill
yellow-brown; yellow-buff cheeks; pink
first on rump. VOICE Flight-call nasal
buzzing note, far-carrying. HABITAT
Desert, stony uplands; vagrants in dunes,
fields. FOOD Seeds. RANGE 2: May–Jun,
Suffolk/Sutherland. (N Africa, SW Asia.)

Scarlet Rosefinch *Carpodacus erythrinus*
14–15 cm (*c*5¾ in). Dumpy, with stout
conical bill, rounded head, beady black

Two-barred Crossbill

♂ ♀

♀

1st year ♂

Parrot Crossbill

♂

Trumpeter Finch

juv–1st winter

♂ summer

♀

eyes; carmine-pink, or brown and streaky; 2 faint bars on darker wings. Settles on bushes or ground. *Ad ♂* Head, rump and breast carmine-pink, brighter in summer; otherwise brown with whitish belly, variably tinged pink. *♀/1st year ♂* Olive-brown to grey-brown above and whitish-buff below, streaked esp on breast. VOICE Soft *teu-ik*. HABITAT Marshy woods, scrub; migrants in fields. FOOD Seeds. RANGE 750 + : most Aug–Oct, few May–Jun, esp N/EBr. (E Europe, Asia.)

Pine Grosbeak *Pinicola enucleator* 20–22 cm (*c*8 in). Starling-sized finch with heavy bill, flat crown, stout body, longish tail; mainly rose-pink or greenish-gold with 2 white bars on brown wings. Flight strong, undulating; clambers in trees like Crossbill (242), much on ground; tame. *Ad ♂* Rose-pink to scarlet, with greyish back, scapulars and belly, dark brown wings and tail with pink-white edges and wing-bars. *Ad ♀* Greenish-gold where ♂ pink, esp on head and breast, wearing to duller yellow-green in summer. *1st year ♂* As ad ♀, but

often pinker-yellow on head/breast. VOICE Low whistling *tee-tee-tew*. HABITAT Coniferous/mixed woods, scrub. FOOD Berries, seeds, buds. RANGE 9: Apr–May, Oct–Nov, EBr. (N Eurasia, N America.)

Evening Grosbeak *Hesperiphona vespertina* 20–22 cm (*c*8 in). Shape of big Hawfinch (242) with huge bill, short tail; mainly yellow or greyish, with much black on wings/tail, and white inner secondaries. On trees or ground; tame. *Ad ♂* Primarily yellow with bold U back from forehead showing against olive-brown head and forebody; tail all black; white on secondaries tinged yellow in winter, whitish-horn bill turns green in spring. *Ad ♀* Greyish, tinged yellow on nape and flanks, with whitish throat, dirty white on secondaries, other white marks on wings and tail. *1st winter* As ads, but white inner secondaries edged buff. VOICE Harsh penetrating chirp. HABITAT Conifer forests; seeding trees in winter. FOOD Seeds (esp maple), berries, buds, insects. RANGE 2: Mar, St Kilda/Highland. (N America.)

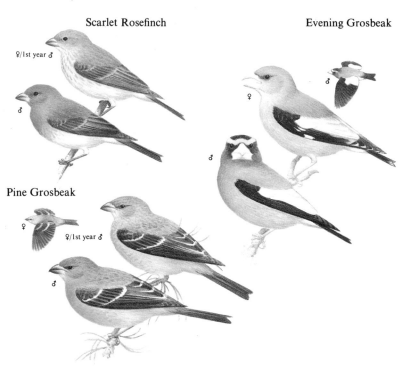

Scarlet Rosefinch

Evening Grosbeak

♀/1st year ♂

♂

♀

♂

Pine Grosbeak

♀

♀/1st year ♂

♂

AMERICAN WARBLERS (Parulidae)

Black-and-white Warbler *Mniotilta varia*
13–14 cm (*c*5¼ in). Striped black and
white; white crown-stripe and supercilia.
Creeps up and down trunks and branches;
moves slowly, often hops from side to
side; catches flies. *Ad* ♂ Cheeks black;
throat black in summer, streaked black in
winter. *Ad* ♀ Cheeks whitish, throat white,
flanks less streaked; blacks browner, esp
in winter when flanks washed buff. *1st
winter* ♂ Cheeks and throat as ad ♀, but
body blacker and whiter, clearer flank-
streaks. *1st winter* ♀ Browner still than ad
♀ with dull white stripes, very obscure
flank-streaks. VOICE Weak *chip*, louder
chink, buzzing notes. HABITAT Woods,
trees. FOOD Insects. RANGE 6: Sep–Oct
(1 Mar), SW/NEBr, SWIr. (N America.)

Tennessee Warbler *Vermivora peregrina*
12–13 cm (*c*5 in). Winter plumages like
stocky Willow Warbler (216), but bright
green above, 0–2 pale wing-bars, white
undertail-coverts, grey legs. ♂ *summer*
Grey crown, white supercilia, black eye-
stripes, green above with no wing-bars,
whitish below. ♀ *summer* Crown washed
green; yellowish below. *Ad/1st winter*
Bright olive-green above, yellow below
but for white at rear; yellowish supercilia/
eye-rings, 1–2 pale wing-bars. VOICE
Firecrest-like *zit-zit*. HABITAT Tree-tops;
migrants in bushes. FOOD Insects. RANGE
2: Sep, Shetland. (N America.)

Parula Warbler *Parula americana* 11–12
cm (*c*4¾ in). Bluish and yellow with white
broken eye-rings, wing-bars, belly. Clings
to trunks, hangs from twigs like tit. *Ad* ♂
Blue above with green patch, breast-band
blackish/chestnut; in winter, blue tinged
green, less breast-band. *Ad* ♀ Duller; little
or no breast-band. *1st winter* As ads, but
greener above, duller below; ♂ traces of
breast-band. VOICE Soft *weet*, buzzy trill.
HABITAT Trees, bushes. FOOD Insects.
RANGE 3: Oct–Nov, SWBr. (N America.)

Yellow Warbler *Dendroica petechia* 12–13
cm (*c*5 in). Mainly yellow; 2 yellow wing-
bars, yellow-edged wing/tail-feathers, bold
black eyes. *Ad* ♂ Very yellow, but greener

above, with chestnut-tinged crown,
chestnut streaks below; duller, less
streaked in winter. *Ad* ♀ Duller, head less
yellow; few streaks below, none in winter.
1st winter Pale greenish above, dull yellow
below; ♂ lightly streaked. VOICE Sharp
chip, thin *tsee*. HABITAT Trees, bushes, esp
by water. FOOD Insects. RANGE 1: Aug,
Gwynedd. (N America.)

Cape May Warbler *Dendroica tigrina*
12–13 cm (*c*5 in). Mainly greenish above,
with yellowish rump and neck-sides, 2
white wing-bars, white near tips of outer
tail; yellow or whitish below with dark
streaks. *Ad* ♂ Blackish crown, chestnut
cheeks, white shoulder-patches, and much
yellow, boldly streaked above and below;
in winter, much duller (no chestnut),
obscured by grey and whitish edgings, but
crown still blackish, back streaked. *Ad* ♀
More uniform above, but for wing-bars
and rump, with yellowish supercilia and
neck-sides, yellowish throat/breast
streaked blackish-grey; duller in winter.
1st winter ♂ As ♀ winter, and scarcely
streaked above, but yellower below with
heavier streaks. *1st winter* ♀ Duller,
browner above; dull whitish below with
smudgy grey streaks. VOICE Song of high
thin *seet* notes. HABITAT Spruce forests;
trees, bushes. FOOD Insects. RANGE 1: ♂
singing, Jun, Strathclyde. (N America.)

Yellow-rumped Warbler *Dendroica
coronata* 13.5–14.5 cm (*c*5½ in). Yellow
patches on rump, breast-sides and crown,
2 white wing-bars, white in outer tail.
Clings to trunks, often feeds on ground.
Ad ♂ Blue-grey, streaked black, with
whitish supercilia, black cheeks; whitish
below, with black on breast/flanks; in
winter, browner above, no black on
cheeks, less heavily marked below. *Ad* ♀
Duller, browner, less yellow, less boldly
marked below. *1st winter* Duller brown
and less streaked above with obscure
crown- and breast-patches (esp ♀); dull
white below, buff throat and flanks,
faintly streaked. VOICE Loud *chek*.
HABITAT Conifers; trees, bushes. FOOD
Insects; berries, seeds. RANGE 7: Oct–Feb
(1 May), most SWBr/SIr. (N America.)

Black-and-white Warbler

♀

♂ winter

st winter ♀

Tennessee Warbler

ad/1st winter

♂ summer

Parula Warbler

1st winter ♂

♀

♂ summer

Yellow Warbler

1st winter ♀

♀

♂ summer

Cape May Warbler

1st winter ♀

♀

♂ summer

Yellow-rumped Warbler

♀

♂ summer

1st winter

Blackpoll Warbler *Dendroica striata*
13–14 cm (c5¼ in). Streaky grey-green and yellowish (but summer ♂ black, grey and white), with 2 wing-bars, white vent and undertail-patches, and legs brownish or yellowish with yellow feet. ♂ *summer* Black cap/moustaches, white cheeks/ underparts, black streaks on flanks and greyish mantle. ♀ *summer* Grey-green above, whitish below, streaked blackish on mantle/flanks. *Ad winter* After moult in Jul–Aug, greener and yellow-white, with thinner streaks. *1st winter* Yellower below, all streaking obscurer; tertials edged whiter. VOICE High *zit*, louder *chik*. HABITAT Trees, scrub. FOOD Insects. RANGE 15: Sep–Nov, all SW/WBr. (N America.)

American Redstart *Setophaga ruticilla*
12–13 cm (c5 in). Butterfly-like warbler; black with white belly, or olive-brown and white, with orange or yellow patches on breast-sides, wings and tail. Flits, fly-catches, droops wings, fans tail. *Ad ♂* Black and orange; buff fringes in autumn. *Ad ♀* Olive-brown, white and yellow with grey head, white eye-rings. *Imm ♂* As ♀, but greener and duller white, with grey-buff throat, orangy breast-sides; little black by 1st summer, all by 2nd winter when wing/tail-patches sometimes still yellow. *1st winter ♀* Browner above, less yellow on wings and breast-sides. VOICE Clear *tseet*, short *chip*. HABITAT Trees, bushes. FOOD Insects. RANGE 2: Oct, Cork/ Cornwall. (N America.)

Ovenbird *Seiurus aurocapillus* 14.5–16 cm (c6 in). Portly, terrestrial warbler ('oven-like' nest on ground); olive-green above with black-edged orange crown, white eye-rings, creamy below with stripes of black spots, pink legs. Walks and runs like pipit or tiny thrush, quivers and cocks tail. *Ad* Crown pale orange; mainly white below. *1st winter* Crown greenish-orange; creamier below with more buff flanks. VOICE Sharp *chik*. HABITAT Undergrowth. FOOD Insects, berries. RANGE 2: Oct/Dec, Shetland/Mayo. (N. America.)

Northern Waterthrush *Seiurus noveboracensis* 14.5–16 cm (c6 in). Plump, pipit-like warbler with short tail; olive-brown above with bold yellowish to buff supercilia, yellowish below with lines of brown streaks, spotted throat, dirty pink legs. Walks and runs with constant teetering and tail-wagging. *Ad* White inner tips to outer 2–4 tail-feathers. *1st winter* No white tips. VOICE Sharp *spink*, *pweet*. HABITAT Low cover by water. FOOD Insects. RANGE 2: Sep–Oct, Scilly. (N America.)

Yellowthroat *Geothlypis trichas* 12–13 cm (c5 in). Olive-brown above, yellow throat, whitish belly; ♂ has black mask. Dodges Wren-like in and out of cover; cocks tail; often on ground. *Ad ♂* Grey band above mask; yellow below, white belly, brown flanks. *Ad ♀* Throat yellow, breast/flanks buff, belly whitish. *1st winter ♂* Variable grey-black traces of mask on cheeks, throat paler yellow. *1st winter ♀* Browner above, throat buff. VOICE Hoarse *chep*. HABITAT Thickets by water. FOOD Insects. RANGE 1: Nov, Devon. (N America.)

Hooded Warbler *Wilsonia citrina* 13–14 cm (c5¼ in). Plain olive and yellow with yellow face, ♂ black 'hood'; longish tail often flicked or fanned, showing white on outer 3 feathers. *Ad ♂* Black head, yellow mask. *Ad ♀* Yellow face/under-parts; often traces of (sometimes much) black on crown/neck-sides. *1st winter ♂* Yellow fringes on black of head, esp throat. *1st winter ♀* As ad ♀, but greenish cheeks below yellow supercilia, no black, browner wings/tail. VOICE Metallic *chink*. HABITAT Damp thickets. FOOD Insects. RANGE 1: Sep, Scilly. (N America.)

VIREOS (Vireonidae)

Red-eyed Vireo *Vireo olivaceus* 14.5–16 cm (c6 in). Like largish thickset warbler with stout bill, short tail, thick grey legs; olive-green and whitish, with blue-grey crown, bold white supercilia edged with black (*cf ♂* Tennessee Warbler, 320). Movements deliberate. *Ad* Eyes red. *1st autumn*. Eyes brown. VOICE Whining nasal *chway*. HABITAT Woods, tall cover. FOOD Insects, berries. RANGE 11: Oct, all SWBr, SIr. (N America.)

Blackpoll Warbler

♂ summer

♀ summer

1st winter

American Redstart

♂ summer

♀

1st winter ♂

Ovenbird

ad

Northern Waterthrush

1st winter/ad

Yellowthroat

♂ summer

1st winter ♂

♀

Hooded Warbler

♀

1st winter ♀

♂ summer

Red-eyed Vireo

1st winter

ad

TANAGERS (Thraupidae)

Summer Tanager *Piranga rubra* 17.5–19.5 cm (*c*7¼ in). Like big finch with heavy pale bill; red, or olive and orange-yellow with yellow underwings, no black. Flight fast, also flycatches; arboreal, actions rather deliberate, shy. *Ad ♂* All rose-red, bill whitish. *Ad ♀* Brownish-olive and dull gold, bill yellowish; old ♀s have some red feathers. *1st winter* As ad ♀, but ♂ all tinged orange, ♀ yellower. *1st summer ♂* Red or mottled, but wings still greenish. VOICE Low rattling *piki-tuki-tuk*. HABITAT Trees. FOOD Insects (*eg* bees), berries. RANGE 1: Sep, Gwynedd. (N America.)

Scarlet Tanager *Piranga olivacea* 17–19 cm (*c*7 in). Shape/actions as Summer Tanager, smaller bill often darker; red, or green and yellow with whitish underwings, black or grey-brown wings/tail. *♂ summer* Scarlet and black, bill whitish. *♂ winter* Blotched during moult in Jul–Sep, then yellow-green above, yellow below, wings/tail still black. *Ad ♀* As winter ♂, but olive-green above with dark grey-brown wings/tail fringed greenish, duskier shoulders; bill pink-grey. *1st winter ♂* As ad ♀, but variably black wing-coverts. *1st winter ♀* Duller, less yellow, no black. *1st summer ♂* Scarlet or orange with black coverts/tail, brown flight-feathers. VOICE Low *chik-kurr*. HABITAT/FOOD As Summer Tanager. RANGE 2: Oct, Scilly. (N America.)

BUNTINGS, AMERICAN SPARROWS (Emberizidae)

Rufous-sided Towhee *Pipilo erythrophthalmus* 19–21.5 cm (*c*8 in). Big 'sparrow' with long rounded tail; dark head/upperparts, white wing-patches/tail-corners/belly, rufous flanks, usually red eyes. Flight jerky, with pumping tail; much on ground, rummages in dead leaves, cocks/fans tail. *Ad ♂* Dark parts black. *Ad ♀* Rich brown instead. *1st year* As ads, but ♂ primary-coverts brownish; eyes brown at first. VOICE Loud *cheweek*. HABITAT Thick scrub. FOOD Seeds, berries, insects, snails. RANGE 1: Jun, Devon. (N/Cent America.)

Summer Tanager

Scarlet Tanager

♂

♂ summer

♀

1st winter ♂

♀

1st winter

Rufous-sided Towhee

♀

♂

Fox Sparrow *Zonotrichia iliaca* 17–19 cm (*c*7 in). Size of Corn Bunting; grey-buff above, white below, all heavily streaked chestnut; 2 buff bars on rufous wings, plain foxy-red rump/tail, often breast-smudge. Rummages about like Towhee; skulks. *Ad/1st year* Very chestnut above in autumn, greyer by summer. VOICE Loud *chek*, thin *tseep*. HABITAT Woods, thickets. RANGE 1: Jun, Co Down. (N America.)

Song Sparrow *Zonotrichia melodia* 15–16.5 cm (*c*6¼ in). Dunnock-like, but with bunting bill, and longish rounded tail; dark-streaked grey-brown to chestnut above with striped head, and whitish below with heavy rufous-black streaks, breast-smudge. Pumps tail in flight and perched; skulks. *Ad = 1st year*. VOICE Nasal *chip*, high *tseet*. HABITAT Thickets. RANGE 5: Apr–Jun, N/WBr. (N America.)

White-crowned Sparrow *Zonotrichia leucophrys* 16–18 cm (*c*6¾ in). Larger, bulkier than Yellowhammer, with high puffy crown; bold-striped head, 2 wing-bars, greyish above with dark streaks, grey below with whitish chin, yellow-pink bill (*cf* White-throated). Perches erect; much on ground in open. *Ad* Cap white with black stripes meeting at front. *1st winter* Head-stripes buff and chestnut, body more buff-grey; as ad after moult in Mar–May. VOICE Metallic *chink* and *peet*. HABITAT Open scrub areas. RANGE 2: May, Shetland/Humberside. (N America.)

White-throated Sparrow *Zonotrichia albicollis* 16–18 cm (*c*6¾ in). More compact/Dunnock-like than White-crowned; more chestnut above, black-edged white throat, yellow front to supercilia, dark bill. Flicks wings, skulks. *Ad* Head-stripes either white and black in summer (white usually tinged buff in *c*Aug–Apr) or much as 1st winter all year. *1st winter* Stripes tawny and black-brown (crown sometimes grey or white); throat duller, browner-grey below with variable thin streaking. VOICE Hard *pink*, high *tseet*. HABITAT Forest undergrowth, thickets. RANGE 12: Apr–Jun, Oct–Nov, scattered. (N America.)

Fox Sparrow

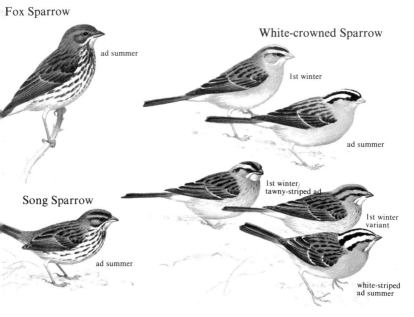

White-crowned Sparrow

ad summer

1st winter

ad summer

Song Sparrow

1st winter/tawny-striped ad

1st winter variant

ad summer

white-striped ad summer

White-throated Sparrow

Slate-coloured Junco *Junco hyemalis*
15–16.5 cm (*c*6¼ in). Neat bunting; slate
or brown with bold white belly/tail-sides,
pink-white bill. Much on ground, flicking
tail; not shy. *Ad ♂* Slate-grey, darkest on
head, with grey-edged blackish wings;
brown fringes after moult in Aug–Sep.
Ad ♀ Paler browner-grey. *1st year* As ads,
but broader brown fringes on ♂ (esp
mantle, flanks), browner worn juv flight-
feathers (tertials with faded tawny fringes)
and tail (2 rather than 3 white outer
feathers), bill often duller flesh. VOICE
Twittering *tit-it-it*, abrupt *chet*, smacking
tack. HABITAT Scrub, untended fields.
FOOD Seeds, insects. RANGE 9: Apr–May
(Jan), N/E/WBr, WIr. (N America.)

Pine Bunting *Emberiza leucocephalos* 16–
17 cm (*c*6½ in). Like Yellowhammer (246)
in many ways, inc rump/tail, but white
instead of yellow, lesser coverts brown.
Ad ♂ White, chestnut and black on head,
chestnut streaks on white breast/flanks;
all partly obscured by grey-buff after
moult in Aug–Sep. *Ad ♀* Dark-streaked

brown-grey head, buff-white to white
below with blackish streaks on breast/
flanks. *1st winter ♂* As ad, but black
streaks on crown. VOICE Calls softer in
tone. RANGE 7: esp Oct–Nov (Jan, Apr,
Aug), most NBr. (NE Russia, N Asia.)

Rock Bunting *Emberiza cia* 15–16.5 cm
(*c*6¼ in). Black-striped grey head, grey
throat/chest, orange-buff below, chestnut
rump, white-edged tail. Much on ground,
but also in bushes, trees; wary. *Ad ♂* Head
cold grey (tinged buff after moult in Aug–
Oct), all stripes black; flanks unmarked.
Ad ♀ Head browner-grey, lores blackish-
brown; flanks often thinly streaked. *1st
winter* Much as ♀, but eyes brown (ad red-
brown), no white on 3rd tail-feathers;
imm ♀ has more buff head, more streaked
chest/flanks. VOICE Thrush-like *zit*, thin
tsee. HABITAT Rocks, scrub. FOOD Seeds,
insects. RANGE 5: Feb–Oct, S/W/EBr.
(S Eurasia, NW Africa.)

Cretzschmar's Bunting *Emberiza caesia*
15–16.5 cm (*c*6¼ in). Like Ortolan (248),

Slate-coloured Junco

Pine Bu~~

Rock Bunting

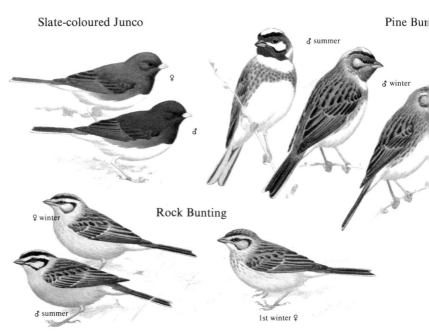

♂ summer

♂ winter

♀

♂

♀ winter

♂ summer

1st winter ♀

but smaller, dumpier, shorter-winged, with grey head/chest, orange-buff throat, rufous rump, whitish underwings. *Ad ♂* Blue-grey crown (may be faintly streaked) and chest. *Ad ♀* Crown/chest duller grey, finely streaked blackish. *1st year* Much as ad ♀, but more buff and streaked (more chestnut-buff upperparts and orange-buff throat, less clear eye-rings and wing-bars than imm Ortolan). VOICE Hard *tsyip*. HABITAT/FOOD As Rock Bunting. RANGE 2: Jun, Shetland. (Balkans, Middle East.)

Rustic Bunting *Emberiza rustica* 14–15 cm (*c*5¾ in). Shorter-tailed than Reed Bunting (248); white throat, stripe behind eyes, and belly, and more or less chestnut nape, scapulars, rump and blotches on chest/flanks. Often raises crown-feathers. ♂ *summer* Crown/cheeks jet-black; stripe behind eyes, throat and belly silky white; chestnut areas nearly uniform. ♀ *summer* Crown/cheeks brown, generally streaked black; clear broken moustaches, often some dark brown streaks on chest; whites and chestnuts variably tinged buff. *Ad/1st*

winter Much as dull ♀ summer; some ad/imm ♂s have jet-black rear cheek-patch and crown-marks. VOICE High sharp *tsip*, *tsip*. HABITAT Swampy thickets, wood-edges, fields. FOOD Seeds, insects. RANGE 142: Sep–Nov, May–Jun (few Mar–Apr), most NE/E/SWBr. (NE Europe, N Asia.)

Little Bunting *Emberiza pusilla* 13–14 cm (*c*5¼ in). Like small compact ♀ Reed Bunting (248) with short tail, straight (not convex) culmen; uniform chestnut cheeks with black lower edge not reaching bill, brown (not rufous) lesser coverts, whiter below with neater black streaks, usually bold creamy eye-rings, pinker legs. Jerks closed tail. *Ad summer ♂♀* alike except bright ♂s (face and broadly black-edged crown rich chestnut), dull ♀s (cheeks and brown-edged dark-streaked crown pale). *Ad/1st winter* Crown obscured by buff; ad head usually more rufous (esp lores), imm whiter throat. VOICE Hard sharp *zik*. HABITAT Scrub, fields. FOOD Seeds, insects. RANGE 268: Sep–Oct (few Nov–May), most NE/E/SWBr. (NE Europe, N Asia.)

Cretzschmar's Bunting

♂ summer

♀ summer

Rustic Bunting

1st winter/♀/♂ winter

♂ summer

Little Bunting

ad

1st winter

Yellow-breasted Bunting *Emberiza aureola*
13.5–14.5 cm (*c*5½ in). Clearly smaller
than Yellowhammer (246); yellow below,
buff under tail, streaked flanks. 2 wing-
bars, some white on tail-sides; ♀/imm
striped head. *Ad ♂* Chestnut and yellow;
chest-band, black face, white shoulders;
all partly obscured by buff after moult in
Aug–Oct. *Ad ♀* Dark-streaked tawny
above, tinged grey to chestnut; striped
crown; pale buff-yellow below. *1st winter*
As ♀, but fresh wings/tail. *1st summer ♂*
Dark-streaked brown, tinged chestnut
(esp rump, crown), and pale yellow; chest-
band thin, face blackish, wings as ♀. VOICE
Robin-like *tik*, nasal *tsit*. HABITAT Scrub,
marshes. FOOD Seeds, insects. RANGE 94:
most Aug–Oct, esp NEBr. (N Eurasia.)

Pallas's Reed Bunting *Emberiza pallasi*
13–14 cm (*c*5¼ in). Like small Reed (248),
but lesser coverts greyish (not rufous),
rump paler, almost unstreaked below (*cf*
Little, 326). *Ad ♂* As ♂ Reed, but striped
black and grey above, whitish rump, nape
yellow in spring; much obscured by buff

in winter, no bib or white nape, thin
supercilia. *Ad/imm ♀* More buff above,
whiter below than ♀ Reed with clear pale
'braces', almost no dark edges to cheeks,
thin moustaches ending in hook or blob;
in summer greyish collar/rump. VOICE
Sparrow-like *chireep*, shrill *peeseeoo*.
HABITAT Scrub, reeds. FOOD Seeds, insects.
RANGE 1: Sep–Oct, Shetland. (Asia.)

Black-headed Bunting *Emberiza melano-*
cephala 16–17 cm (*c*6½ in). Bulkier than
Yellowhammer (246); all unstreaked
yellow or pale buff below, yellow undertail-coverts, no pure white on tail. *Ad ♂*
Plain chestnut and yellow, black hood; all
partly obscured by grey-buff after moult
in Jul–Aug but face/cheeks still blackish.
Ad ♀ Dark-streaked grey-brown, tinged
rufous, and pale or dingy yellow, more
buff on breast; sometimes blackish crown,
wings/tail worn by autumn. *1st winter*
All more buff (yellow under tail as ads);
wings/tail fresh. VOICE Loud *zit*, soft *chup*.
HABITAT Fields, scrub. RANGE 58: Apr–
Oct, esp NE/SBr. (SE Europe, SW Asia.)

Yellow-breasted Bunting

Pallas's Reed Bunting

Black-headed Bunting

Rose-breasted Grosbeak *Pheucticus ludo-vicianus* 19–21 cm (*c*7¾ in). Size of small fat thrush with big head, huge pale bill; black, white and rosy, or streaked with striped head, 2 wing-bars. Flight undulating; often furtive. *Ad ♂* Black head/upperparts, white on wings, rump, tail-corners; white below, breast and under-wings rose-red; body (not wings/tail) variably browner in winter, often much as ♀ but rosy throat/breast. *Ad ♀* Brown and whitish, all streaked, with white-striped head, eye-crescents, wing-bars, plain tail, yellow underwings. *1st winter* Markings/underbody more buff; ♂ less pinkish, rump buff, wings and plain tail browner. VOICE Sharp *keek*. HABITAT Trees, thickets. FOOD Seeds, berries, insects. RANGE 9: Oct–Jan, most Ir/SWBr. (N America.)

AMERICAN ORIOLES (Icteridae)

Bobolink *Dolichonyx oryzivorus* 17–19 cm (*c*7 in). Conical bill, flat forehead, long body, pointed tail-feathers; yellowish, streaked above, with striped head; summer ♂ all black below. Flight direct, fans tail.

♂ summer Black face/underparts, yellowish nape, whitish scapulars/rump. *♂ winter* As ♀ after moult in Jul–Aug, but odd black feathers on throat/breast. *♀/imm* Yellow-buff with blackish stripes on head, streaks on back/flanks. VOICE Soft *cheek*, clear *pink*. HABITAT Fields, marshes. FOOD Seeds, insects. RANGE 7: Sep–Oct, most SWBr. (N America.)

Northern Oriole *Icterus galbula* 18–20 cm (*c*7½ in). Starling-shaped head; black and orange, or olive and yellow, with bluish bill, bold wing-marks, coloured rump/tail-sides. Flight direct; secretive, in high cover. *Ad ♂* Orange with black head, back, tail-centre and white-edged wings. *Ad ♀* Olive-grey and orange-yellow, 2 wing-bars; often traces of black on head/throat. *1st winter* Much as ad ♀, but no black; ♂ browner above, more orange below; as ads after spring moult, but worn brown juv flight-feathers. VOICE Low whistled *kew-li*. HABITAT Esp trees. FOOD Insects, nectar, seeds, berries. RANGE 12: Sep–Oct, May, S/W/NEBr. (N America.)

Rose-breasted Grosbeak

♂ summer · 1st winter ♂ · ♀

Bobolink

Northern Oriole

♂ summer

bright ♀

dull ♀/1st winter

♂ winter

♂

♀/1st winter

Bibliography

Many of the following books which have been used for reference in the preparation of this guide make valuable further reading. In addition to these are countless notes and papers in *British Birds*, which also publishes annual reports on rare birds. These have enabled the totals and patterns of vagrants to be given in this book.

Bent, A. C. *Life Histories of North American Birds*. Dover Pubns., Washington 1919–68 (23 vols).

Campbell, B., and Ferguson-Lees, I. J. *A Field Guide to Birds' Nests*. Constable, London 1972.

Cramp, S., Simmons, K. E. L., and others. *The Birds of the Western Palearctic*. Oxford, London 1977 onwards (1st 2 vols).

Dementiev, G. P., and Gladkov, N. A. *Birds of the Soviet Union*. Moscow 1951–54 (Israel translation: Jerusalem 1966–68).

Grant, P. J. *Gulls: A Guide to Identification*. Poyser, Calton (Staffs) 1982.

Hollom, P. A. D. *The Popular Handbook of Rarer British Birds*. Witherby, London 1980 (revised edition).

King, B., Woodcock, M., Dickinson, E. C. *A Field Guide to the Birds of South-East Asia*. Collins, London 1975.

Peterson, R. T. *A Field Guide to the Birds of Eastern and Central North America*. Houghton Mifflin, Boston 1980.

Peterson, R., Mountfort, G., and Hollom, P. A. D. *A Field Guide to the Birds of Britain and Europe*. Collins, London 1974 (revised edition in collaboration with I. J. Ferguson-Lees and D. I. M. Wallace).

Porter, R. F., Willis, I., Christensen, S., and Nielsen, B. P. *Flight Identification of European Raptors*. Poyser, Berkhamsted 1980 (3rd revised edition).

Prater, A. J., Marchant, J. H., and Vuorinen, J. *Guide to the Identification and Ageing of Holarctic Waders*. British Trust for Ornithology, Tring 1977.

Records Committee of British Ornithologists' Union. *The Status of Birds in Britain and Ireland*. Oxford, London and Edinburgh 1971.

Robbins, C. S., Bruun, B., and Zim, H. S. *A Guide to Field Identification: Birds of North America*. Golden Press, New York 1966.

Sharrock, J. T. R. *The Atlas of Breeding Birds in Britain and Ireland*. Poyser, Tring and Berkhamsted 1976.

Sharrock, J. T. R. and E. M. *Rare Birds in Britain and Ireland*. Poyser, Berkhamsted 1976.

Svensson, L. *Identification Guide to European Passerines*. Naturhistoriska Riksmuseet, Stockholm 1975 (revised edition).

Tuck, G., Heinzel, H., *A Field Guide to the Seabirds of Britain and the World*. Collins, London 1978.

Williamson, K. *Identification for Ringers: 1–3* (warblers). British Trust for Ornithology, Tring 1967–68 (revised editions).

Witherby, H. F., Jourdain, F. C. R., Ticehurst, N. F., and Tucker, B. W. *The Handbook of British Birds*. Witherby, London 1938–41 (5 vols).

This book covers all the species recorded wild or breeding ferally in Britain and Ireland in the 50 years 1931–80 (except for Yellow-browed Bunting *Emberiza chrysophrys* which occurred in 1980 but was accepted too late for inclusion). Thus, it excludes a few vagrants which have been found here for the first time since 1980, and also the following 14 from before our period:

Capped Petrel *Pterodroma hasitata*; White-faced Petrel *Pelagodroma marina*; Green Heron *Butorides striatus*; Egyptian Vulture *Neophron percnopterus*; Griffon Vulture *Gyps fulvus*; Spotted Eagle *Aquila clanga*; Allen's Gallinule *Porphyrula alleni*; Sandhill Crane *Grus canadensis* (also recorded 1981); Caspian Plover *Charadrius asiaticus*; Eskimo Curlew *Numenius borealis*; Eagle Owl *Bubo bubo*; Red-necked Nightjar *Caprimulgus ruficollis*; Egyptian Nightjar *Caprimulgus aegyptius*; Citril Finch *Serinus citrinella*.

Index